Aleister Crowley

THE WORKS

OF

ALEISTER CROWLEY

WITH PORTRAITS

VOLUME II

ISBN: 979-8-89096-153-2

Printed: June 2023

Published and Distributed By:
Lushena Books
607 Country Club Drive, Unit E
Bensenville, IL 60106
www.lushenabks.com

ISBN: 979-8-89096-153-2

CONTENTS OF VOLUME II

CONTENTS

ORACLES

THE AUTOBIOGRAPHY OF AN ART *

1905

THE DEATH OF THE DRUNKARD.[1]

I.

TERROR, and darkness, and horrid despair !
Agony painted upon the once fair
Brow of the man who refused to give up
The love of the wine-filled, the o'erflowing
cup.
" Wine is a mocker, strong drink is raging."
No wine in death is his torment assuaging.

II.

.   .   .   .   .

.   .   .   .   .

Just what the parson had told me when
young :
Just what the people in chapel have sung :
" Wine is a mocker, strong drink is raging."

.   .   .   .   .

Desunt cetera.

A PEEP BEHIND THE SCENES.

In the hospital bed she lay,
  Rotting away !
Cursing by night and cursing by day,
  Rotting away !

[1] This, the earliest poem ever written by me,
has perished save the above fragment. Its
date is 1886.—A. C.
It should be noted that this fragment is of a
wildly revolutionary tendency. It made him
the Ibsen of a school where a parson and a
chapel were considered with the rest of the
non-Plymouth-Brethren world as so many
devils let loose from hell.

The lupus is over her face and head,
Filthy and foul and horrid and dread,
And her shrieks they would almost wake the
  dead ;
    Rotting away !

In her horrible grave she lay,
    Rotting away !
Rotting by night, and rotting by day,
    Rotting away !
In the place of her face is a gory hole,
And the worms are gnawing the tissues foul,
And the devil is gloating over her soul,
    Rotting away !

LINES ON BEING INVITED TO MEET THE PREMIER IN WALES, SEPTEMBER 1892.

I WILL not shake thy hand, old man,
  I will not shake thy hand ;
You bear a traitor's brand, old man,
  You bear a liar's brand.
Thy talents are profound and wide,
  Apparent power to win ;
It is not everyone has lied
  A nation into sin.

And look thou not so black, my friend,
  Nor seam that hoary brow ;
Thy deeds are seamier, my friend,
  Thy record blacker now.

* This volume consists of unpublished poems dating from 1886–1903. Concerning the title
Crowley writes, " The sense is of dead leaves drifting in the dusty cave of my mind." He
does not seem to have been aware that Coleridge gave the title " Sibylline Leaves " to a similar
collection.

Your age and sex forbid, old man,
  I need not tell you how,
Or else I'd knock you down, old man,
  Like that extremist cow.[1]

You've gained your every seat, my friend,
  By perjuring your soul ;
You've climbed to Downing Street, my friend,
  A very greasy poll.
You bear a traitor's brand, old man,
  You bear a liar's brand ;
I will *not* shake thy hand, old man,
  I will *not* shake thy hand.

            [*And I didn't.*

THE BALLOON.

*Written (at the age of fifteen, and still unsur-
passed) while in bed with measles at Ton-
bridge in Kent.*

FLOATING in the summer air,
  What is that for men to see ?
Anywhere and everywhere,
  Now a bullet, now a tree—
Till we all begin to swear :
  What the devil can it be ?

See its disproportioned head,
  Tiny trunk and limbs lopped bare,
Hydrocephalus the dread
  With a surgeon chopping there ;
Chopping legs and arms all red
  With the sticky lumps of hair.

Like a man in this complaint
  Floats this creature in the sky,
Till the gaping rustics faint
  And the smirking milkmaids cry,
As the cord and silk and paint,
  Wood and iron drifteth by.

Floating in the summer sky
  Like a model of the moon :—
How supreme to be so high
  In a treacherous balloon,
Like the Kings of Destiny,
  All the earth for their spittoon.

  [1] Mr. Gladstone was attacked by a cow in
Hawarden Park in 1891.

Toads are gnawing at my feet.
  Take them off me quick, I pray !
Worms my juicy liver eat.
  Take the awful beasts away !
Vipers make my bowels their meat.
  Fetch a cunning knife and slay !

Kill the tadpoles in my lung,
  And the woodlice in my spine,
And the beast that gnaws my tongue,
  And the weasel at my chine,
And the horde of adders young
  That around mine entrails twine !

Come, dissect me ! Rip the skin !
  Tear the bleeding flesh apart !
See ye all my hellish grin
  While the straining vitals smart.
Never mind ! Go in and win,
  Till you reach my gory heart !

While my heart's soft pulse did go,
  Devils had it in their bands.
Doctors keep it in a row,
  Now, on varnished wooden stands :
And I really do not know
  If it is in different hands.

      .   .   .   .

SPOLIA OPIMA.

MY home is set between two ivory towers,
Fresh with the fragrance of a thousand flowers.
And the twin portals of a ruby door,
Portcullissed with the pearls of India's shore,
Loosed with a smile and opened with a kiss,
Bid me a joyous welcome there, I wis.
My home is on the brink of heaven's delight,
But for that endless day a lovelier night
Is in my home, that sunset's arms enfold,
Lit with the mellowness of autumn gold.

      .   .   .   .

Pillowed on linen of the purest white,
Half-hidden by her locks' luxurious night,
Maddened by those soft eyes of melting glow,
Enamoured of that breast of breathing snow,
Caught in the meshes of her fine-spun hair,
Rocked by the beating of her bosom fair,

Held by her lips too tempting and too warm,
Bewitched by every beauty of her form,
The blush upon her cheek is deeper red,
Half glad, and half repenting what she said.
A moment's struggle, as her form I press :—
One soft sad sigh. Love conquers. I possess.

A WELCOME TO JABEZ.[1]

Reprinted from the " Eastbourne Chronicle."

GREAT Liberator, come again,
    Thy country needs thee sadly ;
In Scotland Yard they all complain
    They "want" thee, oh ! so badly.

Thou canst not tell the sighs and sobs
    That for thy presence yearn ;
And the great heart of England throbs
    With joy at thy return.

For many a year prolong thy stay
    By Portland's shady harbour ;
And all expenses we will pay—
    Especially the barber.

A change of work is rest, they say,
    So honest toil shall rest thee ;
No fears that thou must go away
    Need haunt thee and molest thee.

We pray a level-headed set
    Of fellow men, who know thee,
In some small measure grateful yet,
    May pay thee what is owed thee.

The joys of single blessedness,
    And undisturbed seclusion,
We envy for thee, we confess,
    Until thy final fusion.

ELVINA.

Written at Eastbourne.

Tune—" German Evening Hymn."

WAS thy fault to be too tender ?
    Was thine error to be weak ?
Was my kiss the chief offender
    Pressed upon thy blushing cheek ?

[1] Jabez Balfour, author of the " Liberator " frauds.

Was it sin to press and press thee
    Till thy burning lips at last
Madly kissed me ? How I bless thee,
    Now, for that superb repast !

All-consuming, all-devouring,
    All-absorbing, burnt the flame ;
Burnt unchecked till, hotly showering,
    Passion disregarded Shame !

Was it sin—that moonlight madness ?
    Was our passion so accurst ?
Sweetness damned to mother Sadness ?
    Satisfaction to bring Thirst ?

Was our love to bring division ?
    Nay ! ten thousand devils ! nay !
And a devil in a vision
    Hisses as I slumber, " Yea !

" Heaven of your accurst creation
    Shall become a hell of fire ;
Death for kisses, and damnation
    For your love shall God require."

ADAPTATION OF "ONWARD, CHRISTIAN SOLDIERS" TO THE NEEDS OF BRETHREN.[1]

PREFACE.

IN response to many suggestions from dear Brethren, I have adapted a hymn to the wants of the Church. In view of the grossly unscriptural nature of the original hymn (so-called) many changes have been rendered necessary, but I hope and trust that this has been effected without losing the grandeur of the original.[2] To this effort of mine certain "false brethren unawares brought in " have objected, saying, " Touch not the accursed thing." I pass over the blasphemy of their thus adapting verses of Scripture to their own vile ends.

Let me, however, tell these " wolves in

[1] This astonishing piece of satire was composed after some weeks in the house of a Plymouth Brother. Almost every phrase used therein is a quotation, not a parody.
[2] See preface to " Hymns for the Little Flock," 1856, from which this stupefying sentence has been bodily taken.

sheep's clothing," these "clouds without water, carried about of winds; trees whose fruit withereth, without fruit, twice dead, plucked up by the roots; raging waves of the sea, foaming out their own shame; wandering stars, to whom is reserved the blackness of darkness for ever (Jude 12, 13), that they are "dogs, and sorcerers, and whoremongers, and murderers, and idolaters" (Rev. xxii. 15), and again, that they are "fearful and unbelieving, and abominable, and murderers, and whoremongers, and idolaters, and all liars" (Rev. xxi. 8), and that they "shall have their part in the lake which burneth with fire and brimstone, which is the second death" (Rev. xxi. 8), "where their worm dieth not, and the fire is not quenched" (Mark. ix. 44).

Let me only add that they are "a herd of many swine feeding" (Matt. viii. 30).

"Ye serpents, ye generation of vipers, how can ye escape the damnation of hell?" (Matt. xxiii. 33).

And now, belovèd brethren, with every prayer that this adaptation may prove of lasting blessing to You all, bringing forth "the fruits of the Spirit" (Gal. v. 22), especially "faith, hope and charity." "But the greatest of these is charity" (1 Cor. xiii. 13).

"ONWARD, PLYMOUTH BRETHREN."

Chorus.

ONWARD, Plymouth Brethren, marching as to war,
With the cross of jesus trampled on the floor;
Kelly, Lowe or Jewell [1] lead against the foe,
Forward into battle, see their followers go.
Onward, Plymouth Brethren, marching as to war,
With the cross of jesus trampled on the floor.

At the name of Barton, Raven's host doth flee,
On, M'Arthy's following, on to victory,

[1] These and others mentioned are or were great names among the contending "Brethren."

Stoney's scoundrels shiver at Our howls of rage,
Brothers, lift Your voices, Shriek aloud, Rampage!

Like a mighty army moves the Church of god.
Brothers, We are treading where the saints have trod.
We are all divided, fifty bodies We,
Fifty hopes and doctrines, nary charity.

Church and chapel perish! Open Plyms to hell!
But Our kind of Brethren still in safety dwell.
Raven's lot can never 'gainst the lord prevail,
We are his brave followers, you are Satan's tail.

Come then, outside peoples, join Our noble throng!
Blend with Ours your voices in the triumph song!
Glory, praise and honour unto Us alone!
Christians' necks our footstool, Heaven itself Our throne!

P.S.—BELOVED BRETHREN,—The spirit indeed is willing, but the flesh is weak. For I, like Balaam (in the old legend), was compelled to express our real feelings and not our pretended ones. This, of course, absolutely ruins the adaptation. In fact, I am not certain as to whether it does not rather give us away!

Alas! we are only poor, weak, failing creatures!

Your broken-hearted, broken-winded, broken-kneed brother,

JUDAS CAIAPHAS TRUELOVE.

[The man Truelove was at once put out of fellowship. He will be certainly damned. —PILATE CROSSPATCH.]

TO MRS O . . . . . N C . . . T.

*Written during the first session of the Licensing
Committee of the London County Council.*

I WILL not bring abuse to point my pen,
  Nor a sarcastic tongue.
Think only what you might be, before men,
  If you were young.

What fierce temptations might not lovers
    bring
  In London's wicked city?
Perhaps you might yourself have one wee
    fling,
  If you were pretty.

What might not hard starvation drive you to,
  With Death so near and sure?
Perhaps it might drive even virtuous you,
  If you were poor.

But is it just, or grateful to the One
  That keeps even you from wrong,
Or even humble to shriek, " Get you gone,
  For I am strong " ?

Temptation has not touched you, Mrs. C . . . t !
  Forsooth, I do not lie there,
For you are only not the thing you aren't
  Through being neither.

And since some fall in Life's tremendous
    storm,
  And you are on your feet,
Were it not better with a bosom warm
  And accents sweet

To help to raise (and no man will upbraid
    you)
  Your sisters fallen far ?
'Tis vain ! God's worst omission—Heart—
    has made you
  The thing you are !

THE LITTLE HALF-SOVEREIGN.[1]

RED is the angry sunset,
  Murk is the even grey,
Heavy the clouds that hover
  Over our Hell to-day.

" Say, in our dark Gomorrah,
  Lord, can an angel find
Fifty, but fifty, righteous—
  Body—I say not Mind."

Sadly the angel turneth—
  " Stay, ere thou fleest, stay ;
Canst thou not find me twenty ? "
  " Nay " is the answer, " nay."

" Are there not ten, bright spirit,
  Hidden, nor quickly seen,
Somewhere in Hell's dark alleys,
  Somewhere in Walham Green ?

" Speak, for I see thy forehead
  Sadden in dark denial,
Is there not one that standeth
  Tempter and longsome trial ?

" Is not a candle burning
  Somewhere amid the flame
Scorching the smoke of London
  With its eternal shame ?

" Is there no gate so stubborn
  That shall not find a key,
That with our Sovereign's image
  Graven in majesty ? "

[1] The occasion of this poem was the meeting
of the author with a fair and virtuous damsel
of pleasant address and conversation. She
politely asked him to call at her residence on
the following Sunday : but, on his doing so,
she straightway demanded half-a-sovereign,
and proffered a shameful equivalent. The
indignant boy went off and gave vent to his
feelings in the above rhymes.

Why not the Devil's portrait
Graven in Walham Green?
Why with the bare suggestion
Dare we insult our Queen?

Give me the golden trumpet
Blown at the judgment-day,
Closing the gate of mercy
Over the Cast Away.

Melt me its gold to money,
Coin me that small, small ring
Stamped with the Hoof of Satan,
Bearing the name of King.

Then, in the murky midnight,
Silently lead me down,
Down into Hell's dark portals,
Far in the West of Town.

Then to the shrieks of devils
Writhing in torments keen,
Sing me the song that tells me
Ever of Walham Green.

Sing of the little half-sovereign
Dancing in golden sheen ;
Leave me in Hell—or, better,
Leave me in Walham Green.

ODE TO SAPPHO.

O LESBIAN maiden !
O plumèd and snowlike in glory of white-
ness !
O mystical brightness
With love-lyrics laden !
Joy's fulness is fainting for passion and
sorrow.
To-night melts divine to the dawn of
to-morrow,
O Lesbian maiden !

The flame-tongue of passion
Is lambent and strong ;
In mystical fashion
Sucks sweetness from shade,
As the voice of thy song
In the halls of the dead,
Breaking fitful and wild,
Weird waking the slumber of Venus,
the sleep of her child,
O Lesbian maiden !

Thy tongue reaches red
On that pillar of might !
Flaming gold from thy head
Is a garland of light
On the forehead of night,
As we lie and behold
All the wonders untold
That the joys of desire
In their secrets enfold,
As the pillars of fire
On the ocean of old !
O Lesbian maiden !

The delight of thy lips
Is the voice of the Spring
That the nightingales sing
Over Winter's eclipse,
While my fingers enring
The white limbs of thy sleep
And my lips suck the lips
Of the house of my dream,
And press daintily deep,
Till the joys are supreme
That thine amorous mouth
On the home of thy love
Would exhaust the fierce drouth
Of the rivers thereof,
Till thy white body quiver
With mystic emotion
As the star-blossoms shiver
On silvery river
Rushed into the ocean !
O Lesbian maiden !

IN A LESBIAN MEADOW.

I.

UNDER the summer leaves
In the half-light
Love his old story weaves
Far out of sight.
Here we are lone, at last.
Heaven is overcast
Yet with no night.
Ere her immortal wings
Gather the thread of things
Into her might,
Up will the moon arise
Through the black-azure skies :
Birds shall sing litanies
Still of delight.

II.

Let my lips wander where
Tender moss grows,
Where through their dusky air
Beams a red rose.
Where the bee honey sips
Let my desirous lips,
Kissing, unclose
Delicate lips and chaste,
Sweetness divine to taste
While the sun glows ;
There in the dusk to dwell
By the sweet water-well
In the wood's deepest dell
Where—my love knows.

III.

Skies are grown redder far ;
Tempest draws nigher ;
Dark lowers a single star ;
Mars, like the fire !
Fiercer our lips engage ;
Limbs, eyes, ears, gather rage ;
Sharp grows desire.

Hear thy shoit bitter cries ?
Pity thine agonies ?
Loose, though love tire ?
Nay, neither hear nor spare ;
Frenzy shall mock at prayer ;
Torture's red torch shall flare
Till thou expire.

IV.

Stars stud a cloudless sky ;
Moon silvers blue ;
Breeze is content to die ;
Lightly falls dew.
Calm after strain and stress
Now to our weariness
Brings love anew.
Peace brings her balm to us,
Lying as amorous
Still, and as true,
Linked by new mystery,
Lovers confessed. A sigh
Sobs to the happy sky,
" Sorrow, go to ! "

" 'TIS PITY——"

—FORD.[1]

BLOW on the flame !
The charcoal's vaporous fume
Shall hide our shame !
Come, love, within the gloom !
For one last night, sweet sister, be the same ;
Come, nestle with me in sweet Death's
hot womb !

Two sunny eyes !
And this is all my ruin !
Two gleaming thighs !
And all to my undoing !
Far-swelling curves in ivory rapture rise
Warm and too white—bethink you of the
wooing !

[1] John Ford, author of " 'Tis Pity she's a
Whore," a drama of fraternal incest, and other
well-known plays.

A kiss of fire ;
A touch of passionate yearning
Steals higher and higher—
And kisses are returning !
The strong white grasp draws me still nigher
and nigher,
Our fusing forms in one fierce furnace
burning !

Fails to us speech
In Love's exultant leaping !
Each merged in each
The golden fruit is reaping !

.   .   .   .   .   .

Wilt slumber, dear ?   One last kiss, I beseech !

.   .   .   .   .   .

Come to us, Death !   My love and I are
sleeping !

EPILOGUE TO "GREEN ALPS."[1]

FAREWELL, my book, whose words I have
not given
One tithe of those fierce fires that in me
dwell !
Now, after these long nights that I have
striven,
Farewell !

My spirit burns to know, but may not
tell,
Whether thy leaves, by autumn breezes
driven,
Fly far away beyond the immutable ;

Whether thy soul shall find its home in
heaven,
Or dart far-flaming through the vaults of
hell—
To him that loveth much is much for-
given.
Farewell !

[1] *A volume which was never issued.* MSS.
and proofs have been carefully destroyed.
Several of the poems in this volume are taken
from that, viz. pp. 6-19.

TWO SONNETS IN PRAISE OF A PUBLISHER,

WHO SOUGHT TO INFECT OUR YOUTH WITH HIS NOXIOUS WARES.

The ordure of this goat, who is called
" Master Leonard."—ELIPHAZ LEVI.
He's the man for muck.—BROWNING.

I.

SMALL coffin-worms that burrow in thy brain
Writhe with delight ; thy rotten body teems
With all infesting vermin, as beseems
The mirror of an obscene mind.   In vain
Thy misbegotten brutehood shirks the pain
Of its avenging leprosies : death steams
In all thy rank foul atmosphere : the gleams
Of phosphorescent putrefaction wane.

Thy sordid hands reach through the filth to
snatch
The offal money of a prurient swarm.
Thy liar's tongue licks liquid dung to hatch
From fetid ulcers with its slimy warm
Venom some fouler vermin, in their nest
Thy rotten heart and thy polluting breast !

II.

Egg of the Slime !   Thy loose abortive lips
Mouth hateful things: thy shifty bloodshot eyes
Lurk craftily to snare some carrion prize,
The dainty morsel whence the poison drips
Unmarked : the maskèd infamy that slips
Into an innocent maw : corrupter wise !
Sly worm of hell ! that close and cunning lies
With sucking tentacles for finger-tips.

Earth spits on thee, contagious Caliban !
Hell spits on thee ; her sin is spiritual.
Only the awful slime and excrement
That sin sheds off will own thee for a man.
Only the worms in dead men's bowels that
crawl
To lick a loathlier brother are content.

MY WIFE DIES.

THE sun of love shone through my love's
    deep eyes
And made a rainbow of her tender tears,
And on her cheeks I saw a blush arise
When her lips opened to say, loverwise,
"I love"—and light broke through the
    cloud of fears
That hid her eyes.

The storm of passion woke in her red lips,
    When first they clung to mine and rested
        there ;
Lightnings of love were eager to eclipse
That earlier sunshine, and her whole soul
    clips
My soul—I kissed out life within her hair
Upon her lips.

We parted lips from lips and soul from soul
    To new strange passions in unholy lands,
Where love's breath chars and scorches like
    a coal.
So she is dead to-day—the sweet bells toll
    A lost, lost soul, a soul in Satan's bands,
    A lost, lost soul !

ODE TO VENUS CALLIPYGE.[1]

WHERE was light when thy body came
    Out of the womb of a perished prayer ?
    Where was life when the sultry air,
Hot with the lust of night and shame,
    Brooded on dust, when thy shoulders bare
Shone on the sea with a sudden flame
Into all Time to abundant fame ?

Daughter of Lust by the foam of the sea !
    Mother of flame ! Sister of shame !
    Tiger that Sin nor her son cannot tame !
Worship to thee ! Glory to thee !
Venus Callipyge, mother of me.

[1] A statue in Naples. Callipyge means
"having beautiful buttocks."

Fruitless foam of a sterile sea,
    Wanton waves of a vain desire,
    Maddening billows flecked with fire,
Storms that lash on the brine, and flee,
    Dead delights, insatiate ire
Broke like a flower to the birth of thee,
Venus Callipyge, mother of me !

Deep wet eyes that are violet-blue !
    Haggard cheeks that may blush no more !
    Body bruised daintily, touched of gore
Where the sharp fierce teeth have bitten
    through
    The olive skin that thy sons adore,
That they die for daily, are slain anew
By manifold hate ; for their tale is few.

Few are thy sons, but as fierce as dawn.
    Sweet are the seconds, weary the days.
    Nights ? Ah ! thine image a thousand ways
Is smitten and kissed on the fiery lawn
    Where the wash of the waves of thy native
        bays
Laps weary limbs, that of thee have drawn
Laughter and fire for their souls in pawn.

O thy strong sons ! they are dark as night,
    Cruel and barren and false as the sea.
    They have cherishèd Hell for the love of
        thee,
Filled with thy lust and abundant might,
    Filled with the phantom desire to free
Body and soul from the sound and sight
Of a world and a God that doth not right.

O thy dark daughters ! their breasts are
    slack,
    Their lips so large and as poppies red ;
    They lie in a furious barren bed ;
They lie on their faces ; their eyelids lack
    Tears, and their cheeks are as roses
        dead ;
White are their throats, but upon the back
Red blood is clotted in gouts of black.

All on their sides are the wounds of lust
  Wet, from the home of their auburn hair
Down to the feet that we find so fair ;
Where the red sword has a secret thrust,
  Pain, and delight, and desire they share.
Verily pain ! and thy daughters trust
Thou canst bid roses spring out of dust.

Mingle, ye children of such a queen,
  Mingle, and meet, and sow never a seed !
  Mingle, and tingle, and kiss, and bleed
With the blood of the life of the Lampsa-
  cene,[1]
  With the teeth that know never a pitiful
  deed
But fret and foam over with kisses obscene—
Mingle and weep for what years have been.

Never a son nor a daughter grow
  From your waste limbs, lest the goddess
  weep ;
  Fill up the ranks from the babes that
  sleep
Far in the arms of a god of snow.
  Conquer the world, that her throne may
  keep
More of its pride, and its secret woe
Flow through all earth as the rivers flow.

Which of the gods is like thee, our queen ?
  Venus Callipyge, nameless, nude,
  Thou with the knowledge of all indued,
Secrets of life and the dreams that mean
  Loves that are not, as are mortals', hued
All rose and lily, but linger unseen,
Passion-flowers purpled, garlands of green !

Who like thyself shall command our ways ?
  Who has such pleasures and pains for hire ?
  Who can awake such a mortal fire
In the veins of a man, that deathly days
  Have robbed of the masteries of desire ?
Who can give garlands of fadeless bays
Unto the sorrow and pain we praise ?

[1] Priapus.

Yea, we must praise, though the deadly
  shade
Fall on the morrow, though fires of hell
  Harrow our vitals ; a miracle
Springs at thy kisses, for thou hast made
  Anguish and sorrow desirable ;
Torment of hell as the leaves that fade
Quickly forgotten, despised, decayed.

They are decayed, but thou springest again,
  Mother of mystery, barren, who bearest
  Flowers of most comeliest children, who
  wearest
Wounds for delight, whose desire shall stain
  Star-space with blood as the price thou
  sharest
Sweet with thy lovers, whose passing pain
Ripens to marvellous after-gain.

Thou art the fair, the wise, the divine !
  Thou art our mother, our goddess, our
  life !
  Thou art our passion, our sorrow, our
  strife !
Thou, on whose forehead no lights ever
  shine,
  Thou, our redeemer, our mistress, our
  wife,
Thou, barren sister of deathlier brine,
Venus Callipyge, mother of mine !

Daughter of Lust by the foam of the sea !
Mother of flame ! Sister of shame !
Tiger that Sin nor her son cannot tame !
Worship to thee ! Glory to thee !
Venus Callipyge, mother of me.

THE CANNIBALS.

ALL night no change, no whisper. Scarce
  a breath,
But lips closed hard upon the cup of death
To drain its sweetest poison. Scarce a sigh
Beats the dead hours out ; scarce a melody

Of measured pulses quickened with the blood
Of that desire which pours its deadly flood
Through soul and shaken body ; scarce a
  thought,
But sense through spirit most divinely wrought
To perfect feeling ; only through the lips
Electric ardour kindles, flashes, slips
Through all the circle to her lips again,
And thence, unwavering, flies to mine, to
  drain
All pleasure in one draught. No whispered
  sigh ;
No change of breast ; love's posture perfectly
Once gained, we change no more. The
  fever grows
Hotter or cooler, as the night wind blows
Fresh gusts of passion on the outer gate.
But we, in waves of frenzy, concentrate
Our thirsty mouths on that hot drinking cup,
Whence we may never suck the nectar up
Too often or too hard ; fresh fire invades
Our furious veins, and the unquiet shades
Of night make noises in the darkened room.
Yet, did I raise my head, throughout the
  gloom
I might behold thine eyes as red as fire
A tigress maddened with supreme desire ;
White arms that clasp me ; fervent breast
  that glides
An eager snake, about my breast and sides ;
Teeth keen to bite, red tongue that never tires,
And lips ensanguine with unfed desires,
A very beast of prey ; hot hands caress,
And violent breath that surfeits not excess.
But raise no head ! I know thee, breast and
  thigh,
Lips, hair, and eyes, and mouth : I will not
  die
But thou come with me o'er the gate of death.
So, blood and body furious with breath
That pants through foaming kisses, let us stay
Gripped hard together to kiss life away,
Mouths drowned in murder, never satiate,
Kissing away the hard decrees of Fate,
Kissing insatiable in mad desire,
Kisses whose agony may never tire,
Kissing the gates of hell, the sword of God,
Each unto each a serpent or a rod,

A well of wine and fire, each unto each,
Whose lips are fain convulsively to reach
A higher heaven, a deeper hell. Ah ! day
So soon to dawn, delight to snatch away !
Damned day, whose sunlight finds us as with
  wine
Drunken, with lust made manifest divine
Devils of darkness, servants unto hell—
Yea, king and queen of Sheol, terrible
Above all fiends and furies, hating more
The high Jehovah, loving Baal Peor,
Our father and our lover and our god !
Yea, though he lift his adamantine rod
And pierce us through, how shall his anger
  tame
Fire that glows fiercer for the brand of shame
Thrust in it ; so, we who are all of fire,
One dull red flare of devilish desire,
The God of Israel shall not quench with tears,
Nor blood of martyrs drawn from myriad
  spheres,
Nor watery blood of Christ ; that blood shall
  boil
With all the fury of our hellish toil ;
His veins shall dry with heat ; his bones
  shall bleach
Cold and detested, picked of dogs, on each
Dry separate dunghill of burnt Golgotha.
But we will wrest from heaven a little star,
The Star of Bethlehem, a lying light
Fit for our candle, and by devils' might
Fix in the vast concave of hell for us
To lume its ghastly shadows murderous,
That in the mirror of the lake of fire
We may behold the image of Desire
Stretching broad wings upon us, and may leap
Each upon other, till our bodies weep
Thick sweet salt tears, till, perfected of
  shames,
They burn to one another as the flames
Of our hell fuse us into one wild soul :
Then, one immaculate divinest whole,
Plunge, fire, within all fire, dive far to death ;
Till, like king Satan's sympathetic breath,
Burn on us as a voice from far above
Strange nameless elements of fire and love ;
And we, one mouth to kiss, one soul to lure,
For ever wedded, one, divine, endure

Far from sun, sea, and spring, from love or
        light,
Imbedded in impenetrable night ;
Deeper than ocean, higher than the sky,
Vaster than petty loves that dream and die,
Insatiate, angry, terrible for lust,
Who shrivel God to adamantine dust
By our fierce gaze upon him, who would strive
Under our wrath, to flee away, to dive
Into the deep recesses of his heaven.
But we, one joy, one love, one shame for
        leaven,
Quit hope and life, quit fear and death and
        love,
Implacable as God, desired above
All loves of hell or heaven, supremely wed,
Knit in one soul in one delicious bed
More hot than hell, more wicked than all
        things,
Vast in our sin, whose unredeeming wings
Rise o'er the world, and flap for lust of death,
Eager as any one that travaileth ;
So in our lust, the monstrous burden borne
Heavy within the womb, we wait the morn
Of its fulfilment. Thus eternity
Wheels vain wings round us, who may never
        die
But cling as hard as serpent's wedlock is,
One writhing glory, an immortal kiss.

THE BLOOD-LOTUS.

THE ashen sky, too sick for sleep, makes my
        face grey ; my senses swoon.
Here, in the glamour of the moon, will not
        some pitying godhead weep

For cold grey anguish of her eyes, that look
        to God, and look in vain,
For death, the anodyne of pain, for sleep,
        earth's trivial paradise ?

Sleep I forget. Her silky breath no longer
        fans my ears ; I dream
I float on some forgotten stream that hath
        a savour still of death,

A sweet warm smell of hidden flowers whose
        heavy petals kiss the sun,
Fierce tropic poisons every one that fume
        and sweat through forest hours.

They grow in darkness ; heat beguiles their
        sluggish kisses ; in the wood
They breathe no murmur that is good, and
        Satan in their blossom smiles.

They murder with the old perfume that
        maddens all men's blood ; we die
Fresh from some corpse-clothed memory,
        some secret redolence of gloom,

Some darkling murmurous song of lust quite
        strange to man and beast and bird,
Silent in power, not overheard by any snake
        that eats the dust.

No crimson-hooded viper knows ; no silver-
        crested asp has guessed
The strange soft secrets of my breast ; no
        leprous cobra shall disclose

The many-seated, multiform, divine, essential
        joys that these
Dank odours bring, that starry seas wash
        white in vain ; intense and warm

The scents fulfil ; they permeate all lips, all
        arteries, and fire
New murmured music on the lyre that throbs
        the horrors they create.

Omniscient blossom ! Is thy red slack bosom
        fresher for my kiss ?
Are thy loves sharper ? Hast thou bliss in
        all the sorrow of the dead ?

Why art thou paler when the moon grows
        loftier in the troublous sky ?
Why dost thou beat and heave when I press
        lips of fire, hell's princeliest boon,

To thy mad petals, green and gold like angels'
        wings, when as a flood
God's essence fills them, and the blood
        throughout their web grows icy cold ?

To thy red centre are my eyes held fast and
    fervent, as at night
Some sad miasma lends a light of strange and
    silent blasphemies

To lure a soul to hell, to draw some saint's
    charred lust, to tempt, to win
Another sacrifice to sin, another poet's heart
    to gnaw

With dubious remorse. Oh ! flame of tortur-
    ing flower-love ! sacrament
Of Satan, triple element of mystery and love
    and shame,

Green, gold, and crimson, in my heart you
    strive with Jesus for its realm,
While Sorrow's tears would overwhelm the
    warriors of either part.

Jesus would lure me : from His side the
    gleaming torrent of the spear
Withdraws, my soul with joy and fear waits
    for sweet blood to pour its tide

Of warm delight—in vain ! so cold, so
    watery, so slack it flows,
It leaves me moveless as a rose, albeit her
    flakes are manifold.

He hath no scent to drive men mad ; no
    mystic fragrance from his skin
Sheds a loose hint of subtle sin such as the
    queen Faustina had.

Thou drawest me.   Thy golden lips are
    carven Cleopatra wise.
Large, full, and moist, within them lies the
    silver rampart, whence there slips

That rosy flame of love, the spring of blood
    at my light bidding spilt ;
And thy desires, if aught thou wilt, are softer
    at my suffering.

Fill up with Death Life's loving-cup ! Give
    me the knowledge, me the power
For some new sin one little hour, provoking
    Hell to belch us up.

So in some damned abyss of woe thy chant
    should dazzle as of old,
Thy kisses burn like molten gold, thy visions
    swing me to and fro.

Strange fascinations whirl and wind about
    my spirit lying coils ;
Thy charm enticeth, for the spoils of victory,
    all an evil mind.

Thy perfume doth confound my thought, new
    longings echo, and I crave
Doubtful liaisons with the grave and loves of
    Parthia for sport.

I think perhaps no longer yet, but dream and
    lust for stranger things
Than ever sucked the lips of kings, or fed
    the tears of Mahomet.

Quaint carven vampire bats, unseen in curious
    hollows of the trees,
Or deadlier serpents coiled at ease round
    carcases of birds unclean ;

All wandering changeful spectre shapes that
    dance in slow sweet measure round
And merge themselves in the profound, nude
    women and distorted apes

Grotesque and hairy, in their rage more
    rampant than the stallion steed ;
There is no help : their horrid need on these
    pale women they assuage.

Wan breasts too pendulous, thin hands
    waving so aimlessly, they breathe
Faint sickly kisses, and inweave my head in
    quiet burial-bands.

The silent troops recede ; within the fiery
    circle of their glance
Warm writhing woman - horses dance a
    shameless Bacchanal of sin ;

Foam whips their reeking lips, and still the
    flower-witch nestles to my lips,
Twines her swart lissome legs and hips, half
    serpent and half devil, till

My whole self seems to lie in her ; her kisses
   draw my breath ; my face
Loses its lustre in the grace of her quick
   bosom ; sinister

The raving spectres reel ; I see beyond my
   Circe's eyes no shape
Save vague cloud-measures that escape the
   dance's whirling witchery.

Their song is in my ears, that burn with their
   melodious wickedness ;
But in her heart my sorceress has songs more
   sinful, that I learn

As she sings slowly all their shame, and
   makes me tingle with delight
At new debaucheries, whose might rekindles
   blood and bone to flame.

The circle gathers. Negresses howl in the
   naked dance, and wheel
On poniard-blades of poisoned steel, and
   weep out blood in agonies ;

Strange beast and reptile writhe ; the song
   grows high and melancholy now ;
The perfume savours every brow with lust
   unutterable of wrong.

Clothed with my flower-bride I sit, a harlot
   in a harlot's dress,
And laugh with careless wickedness that
   strews the broad road of the Pit

With vine and myrtle and thy flower, my
   harlot-maiden, who for man
Now first forsakest thy leman, thy Eve, my
   Lilith, in this bower

Which we indwell, a deathless three, changeless and changing, as the pyre
Of earthly love becomes a fire to heat us
   through eternity.

I have forgotten Christ at last ; he may look
   back, grown amorous,
And call across the gulf to us, and signal
   kisses through the vast :

We shall disdain, clasp faster yet, and mock
   his newer pangs, and call
With stars and voices musical, jeers his
   touched heart shall not forget.

I would have pitied him. This flower spits
   blood upon him ; so must I
Cast ashes through the misty sky to mock
   his faded crown of power,

And with our laughter's nails refix his torn
   flesh faster to the wood,
And with more cruel zest make good the
   shackles of the Crucifix.

So be it ! In thy arms I rest, lulled into
   silence by the strain
Of sweet love-whispers, while I drain damnation from thy tawny breast :

Nor heed the haggard sun's eclipse, feeling
   thy perfume fill my hair,
And all thy dark caresses wear sin's raiment
   on thy melting lips—

Nay, by the witchcraft of thy charms to sleep,
   nor dream that God survive ;
To wake, this only to contrive--fresh passions
   in thy naked arms ;

And, at that moment when thy breath mixes
   with mine, like wine, to call
Each memory, one merged into all, to kiss,
   to sleep, to mate with death !

THE NATIVITY.

CHRISTMAS 1897.

THE Virgin lies at Bethlehem.
   (Bring gold and frankincense and myrrh !)
The root of David shoots a stem.
   (O Holy Spirit, pity her !)

She lies alone amid the kine.
   (Bring gold and frankincense and myrrh !)
The straw is fragrant as with wine.
   (O Holy Spirit, pity her !)

Mine host protects an honest roof.
(Bring gold and frankincense and myrrh !)
His spouse sniffs loud and holds aloof.
(O Holy Spirit, pity her !)

The Angel has not come again.
(Bring gold and frankincense and myrrh !)
Why did God deal her out such pain ?
(O Holy Spirit, pity her !)

Her love-hours held the Holy Ghost.
(Bring gold and frankincense and myrrh !)
Where is he now she needs him most ?
(O Holy Spirit, pity her !)

Joseph drinks deep outside the inn.
(Bring gold and frankincense and myrrh !)
She is half hated by her kin.
(O Holy Spirit, pity her !)

The agony increases fast.
(Bring gold and frankincense and myrrh !)
Each spasm is a holocaust.
(O Holy Spirit, pity her !)

There are three kings upon the road.
(Bring gold and frankincense and myrrh !)
She hath thrice cursed the name of God.
(O Holy Spirit, pity her !)

There stands her star above the sky.
(Bring gold and frankincense and myrrh !)
She hath thrice prayed that she may die.
(O Holy Spirit, pity her !)

Her bitter anguish hath sufficed.
(Bring gold and frankincense and myrrh !)
She is delivered of the Christ.
(The angels come to worship her.)

TRANSLATIONS FROM BAUDE-LAIRE.[1]

CAIN ET ABEL.

I.

SEED of Abel, eat, drink, sleep !
God shall smile complaisantly.
Seed of Cain, in the muck-heap
Crawl and miserably die !

[1] The original metres are in all cases closely imitated.

Seed of Abel, thine oblation
Sweet to Seraphim doth smell :
Seed of Cain, shall thy damnation
Ever find the bounds of Hell ?

Race of Abel, see thy seed
And thy cattle flourish more !
Race of Cain, for hunger's need,
Like a dog thy bowels roar.

Seed of Abel, warm thy paunch
At thy patriarchal hall !
Seed of Cain, on shivering haunch
Squat in cave, despised jackal !

Seed of Abel, love and swarm !
So thy gold shall also grow.
Seed of Cain, heart over-warm,
Guard thy lust and crush it low !

Seed of Abel, grow, well-faring
Like the bugs in forest beats !
Seed of Cain, at bay, despairing,
Throw thy children on the streets !

II.

Seed of Abel, carrion
Shall make fat the smoking soil.
Seed of Cain, on thee has none
Laid sufficient woes of toil.

Seed of Abel, this thy shame—
To the boar-spear yields the sword.
Seed of Cain, to heaven flame,
And to earth cast Heaven's Lord !

THE LITANY OF SATAN.

O thou, of Angels fairest and most wise,
God by Fate's treachery shorn of liturgies !
O Satan, have pity of my long misery !

O Prince of Exile, Sufferer of wrong,
Whose vengeance, conquered, rises triply strong !
O Satan, have pity of my long misery !

Who knowest all, of under earth the king,
Familiar healer of man's suffering !
O Satan, have pity of my long misery !

Who to the leper, even the cursed pariah,
Hast taught by love the taste of heavenly fire !
O Satan, have pity of my long misery !

Thou who on Death, thine old and strong
leman,
Begottest Hope—a charming madwoman !
O Satan, have pity of my long misery !

Who knowest in which caves of envious lands
God has hid precious stones with jealous
hands !
O Satan, have pity of my long misery !

Thou whose clear eye discerns the arsenals
deep,
Where the small folk of buried metals sleep!
O Satan, have pity of my long misery !

Whose broad hand hides the giddy precipice
From sleepers straying about some edifice !
O Satan, have pity of my long misery !

Whose skill makes supple the old bones, at
needs,
Of the belated sot, 'mid surging steeds !
O Satan, have pity of my long misery !

Who taught frail man, to make his suffering
lighter,
Consoling, to mix sulphur with salt nitre !
O Satan, have pity of my long misery !

O subtle complice, who as blatant Beast
Brandest vile Crœsus, him that pities least !
O Satan, have pity of my long misery !

Who in girls' eyes and hearts implantest deep
Lust for the wound, the twain that wound
bids weep !
O Satan, have pity of my long misery !

Staff of the exiled, the inventor's spark,
Confessor of hanged men and plotters dark !
O Satan, have pity of my long misery !

Adopted sire of whom black wrath and power
Of God the Father chased from Eden Bower !
O Satan, have pity of my long misery !

FEMMES DAMNÉES.

Like pensive cattle couched upon the sand
  They turn their eyes to ocean's distant ring ;
Feet seek each other, hand desires hand,
  With languor sweet and bitter shuddering.

Some, hearts love - captured with long
  whispering,
  Spell out the love of timorous childhood,
Where babbles in deep dell the gentle spring,
  And dive among the young trees of the
  green wood.

Others, like sisters, slowly, with grave eyes,
  Cross the rocks filled with apparitions dim,
Where Antony beheld, like lavers, rise
  The nude empurpled breasts that tempted
  him.

Some, by the dying torch-light, call thy name,
  In the dumb hollow of old pagan fanes,
To succour feverish shriekings of fierce flame,
  O Bacchus, soother of men's ancient pains.

Others, whose throat is thirsty for breast-
  blood,
  To hide a whip 'neath flowing robes are
  fain,
Mingling in lonely night and darksome wood
  The foam of pleasure and the tears of pain.

O virgins, demons, monsters, O martyrs !
  Great souls contemptuous of reality !
Seekers for the Infinite, satyrs, worshippers,
  Now mad with cries, now torn with agony !

You whom my soul has followed to your hell,
  Poor sisters, more beloved than wept by
  me,
For your fierce woes, your lusts insatiable,
  And the urns of love that fill the hearts
  of ye !

CARRION.

Recall, my soul, the sight we twain have
looked upon
This summer morning soft and sweet,
Beside the path, an infamous foul carrion,
Stones for its couch a fitting sheet.

Its legs stretched in the air, like wanton
whores
Burning with lust, and reeking venom
sweated,
Laid open, carelessly and cynically, the doors
Of belly rank with exhalations fœtid.

Upon this rottenness the sun shone deadly
straight
As if to cook it to a turn,
And give back to great Nature hundredfold
the debt
That, joining it together, she did earn.

The sky beheld this carcase most superb out-
spread
As spreads a flower, itself, whose taint
Stank so supremely strong, that on the grass
your head
You thought to lay, in sudden faint.

The flies swarmed numberless on this putres-
cent belly,
Whence issued a battalion
Of larvæ, black, that flowed, a sluggish liquid
jelly,
Along this living carrion.

All this was falling, rising as the eager seas,
Or heaving with strange crepitation—
Was't that the corpse, swollen out with a
lascivious breeze,
Was yet alive by copulation?

And all the carcase now sounded strange
symphonies
Like wind, or running water wan,
Or grain that winnower shakes and turns,
whene'er he plies
With motion rhythmical his fan.
VOL. II.

The shapes effaced themselves; no more
their images
Were aught but dreams, a sketch too slow
To tint the canvas, that the artist finishes
By memory that does not go.

Behind the rocks a bitch unquietly gazed on
Ourselves with eye of wrathful woe,
Watching her time to return unto the skeleton
For tit-bits that she had let go.

Yet you are like to it, this dung, this carrion,
To this infection doubly dire,
Star of my eyes that are, and still my nature's
sun,
You, O my angel! You, my own desire!

Yes! such will you be, queen, in graces that
surpass,
Once the last sacraments are said;
When you depart beneath wide-spreading
blooms and grass
To rot amid the bones of many dead.

Then, O my beauty! tell the worms, who
will devour
With kisses all of you to dust;
That I have kept the form and the essential
power
Divine of my distorted lust.

THE DENIAL OF ST. PETER.

I.

WHAT makes God then of all the curses deep
That daily reach his Seraphim divine?
Like to a tyrant gorged with meat and wine,
Our blasphemous music lulleth him to sleep.

II.

Tears of the martyrs, and saints torturèd,
Must prove intoxicating symphonies,
Since, spite of blood-price paid to gain
them ease,
The heavens therewith are not yet satiated.

B

III.

Jesus ! recall Gethsemane afresh,
  Where thy simplicity his pity sought
  Who in his heaven heard, and mocked for
    nought,
Coarse hangmen pierce with nails thy living
  flesh.

IV.

When on thy godhead spat the virulence
  Of scum of soldiery and kitchen-knaves ;
  When thou didst feel the thorns pierce
    bloody graves
Within thy brain where Manhood burnt in-
  tense ;

V.

When thy bruised broken body's horrid weight
  Racked thy stretched arms, that sweat and
    blood enow
  Coursed down the marble paleness of thy
    brow,
Lift up on high, a butt for all men's hate :—

VI.

Dreamedst thou then of those triumphant
    hours
  When, that the eternal promise might
    abide,
  Thy steed a mild she-ass, thou once didst
    ride
On roads o'erstrewn with branches and fresh
  flowers ;

VII.

When, thy heart beating high with hope and
    pride,
  Thou didst whip out those merchants vile
    with force,
  At last the master ? Did not keen remorse
Bite thy soul ere the spear had pierced thy
  side ?

VIII.

I, certes, I shall gladly quit this hell
  Where dream and action walk not hand-
    in-hand !
  May I use the brand and perish by the
    brand !
Saint Peter denied Jesus. He did well.

GLOIRE ET LOUANGE.

GLORY and praise to thee, O Satan, in the
    height
Of Heaven, where thou didst rule, and in
    the night
Of Hell, where conquered, dost dream
    silently !
Grant that one day my soul 'neath Know-
    ledge-Tree
Rest near thine own soul, when from thy
    forehead
Like a new temple all its branches spread.

THE FOUNT OF BLOOD.

SOMETIMES I think my blood in waves ap-
    pears,
Springs as a fount with music in its tears ;
I hear it trickling with long murmuring sound,
But search myself in vain to find the wound.

Across the city, as in closèd meres,
Making the pavements isles, it disappears ;
In it all creatures' thirst relief hath found ;
All nature in its scarlet hue is drowned.

I have often prayed these fickle wines to weep
For one day Lethe on my threatening fear—
Wine makes the ear more sharp, the eye more
    clear.

I have sought in Love forgetfulness and
    sleep—
My love's a bed of needles made to pierce,
That drink be given to these women fierce !

LA BEATRICE.

As I one day to nature made lament
In burnt-up lands, calcined of nutriment,
As in my musing thought's vague random dart
I slowly poised my dagger o'er my heart,
I saw in full noon o'er my forehead form
A deathly cloud far pregnant with the storm,
That bore a flock of devils vicious
Most like to dwarfs cruel and curious.

Coldly they set themselves to gaze on me,
Like passers-by a madman that they see—
I heard them laugh and chuckle, as I think,
Now interchange a signal, now a wink.
" Let us at leisure view this caricature,
This shade of Hamlet mimicking his posture,
The doubting look and hair flung wide to
wind !
A pity, eh? to see this merry hind,
This beggar, actor out of work, this droll,
Because he plays artistically his rôle,
Wishing to interest in his chanted woes
Brooks, eagles, crickets, every flower that
blows,
And even to us the rubric old who made
To howl out publicly his wild tirade?"
I could have (for my pride is mountains high,
And dominates cloud tops or demon's cry)—
I could have simply turned my sovereign
head,
Had I not seen, 'mid their obscene herd led,
Crime, that the sun has not yet brought to
book,
Queen of my spirit with the peerless look.
And she laughed with them at my dark
distress,
And turned them oft some dirtiest caress.

LE VIN DU SOLITAIRE.

THE strange look of a woman of the town,
Who glides toward us like the rays that slake
The wave-wrought moon within the trembling
lake,
Where she would dip her careless beauty
down ;
The last crowns unto which a gambler's
fingers cling ;
A libertine caress from hungry Adeline ;
The sound of music, lulling, silver, clean,
Like the far cry of human suffering :

All these, deep bottle ! are of little worth
Beside the piercing balm thy fertile girth
Holds in the reverent poet's lifted soul ;
To him thou givest youth, and hope, and life,
And pride, this treasure of all beggar's strife
That gives us triumph, Godhead, for its dole.

CHALDEAN FOOLS.

CHALDEAN fools, who prayed to stars and
fires,
Believed there was a God who punished liars.
These gods of theirs they often would
invoke,
Apparently with excellent effect :
They trusted to escape the penal smoke
By making Truth the trade-mark of their
sect.

How fortunate that we are Christian Folk,
And know these notions to be incorrect !

CALL OF THE SYLPHS.[1]

BEHOLD, I am ; a circle on whose hands
The twelvefold Kingdom of my Godhead
stands.
Six are the mighty seats of living breath,
The rest sharp sickles, or the horns of death,
Which are, and are not, save in mine own
power.
Sleep they? They rise at mine appointed
hour.
I made ye stewards in the primal day,
And set your thrones in my celestial way.
I gave ye power above the moving time
That all your vessels to my crown might climb.
From all the corners of your fortress caves
Ye might invoke me, and your wise conclaves
Should pour the fires of increase, life and
birth,
Continual dewfall to the thirsty earth.
Thus are ye made of Justice and of Truth,
The Souls of Fury, and the Lords of Ruth.
In His great Name, your God's, I say, arise !
Behold ! His mercies murmur in the skies.
His Name is mighty in us to the end.
In Him we cry : Move, answer, and descend !
Apply yourselves to us ; arise ! For why?
We are the Wisdom of your God most high !

[1] This Fragment is a paraphrase of one of
the elemental invocations given in Dr. Dee's
famous record of magical working.—A. C.

INVOCATION.[1]

O SELF Divine ! O Living Lord of Me !
Self-shining flame, begotten of Beyond !
Godhead immaculate ! Swift tongue of fire,
Kindled from that immeasurable light
The boundless, the immutable. Come forth,
My God, my lover, spirit of my heart,
Heart of my soul, white virgin of the Dawn,
My Queen of all perfection, come thou forth
From thine abode beyond the Silences
To me the prisoner, me the mortal man,
Shrined in this clay : come forth, I say, to me,
Initiate my quickened soul ; draw near,
And let the glory of thy Godhead shine
Through all the luminous aethers of the air
Even to earth, thy footstool ; unto me
Who by these sacred invocations draw
The holy influence within myself,
To strengthen and to purify my will
And holy aspiration to thy Life.
Purge me and consecrate until my heart
Burn through the very limits of the veil,
And rend it at the hour of sacrifice
That even the secret pillar in the midst
May be made manifest to mortal eyes.
Behold upon my right hand and my left
The mighty pillars of amazing fire,
And terrible cloud. Their tops in Heaven
    are veiled,
Whereon the everlasting lamps rejoice.
Their pedestals upon the Universe
Are set in rolling clouds, in thunder-gusts,
In vivid flame, and tempest : but to me,
Balanced between them, burns the holy light
Veilless, one liquid wheel of sacred fire,
Whirling immutably within itself
And formulating in the splendid sun
Of its white moony radiance, in the light
Of its immaculate eternity,
Thy glorious vision ! O thou Starlight face,
And crownèd diamond of my self and soul,

[1] Versified from the Manuscript called "ꙟ
of ꙟ in Z2."—A. C.
Z2 was a MS. of magical formulæ given to
advanced members of the Zelator Adeptus
Minor grade in the Hermetic Order of the
Golden Dawn.

Thou Queenly Angel of my Higher Will,
Form in my spirit a more subtle fire
Of God, that I may comprehend the more
The sacred purity of thy divine
Essence ! O Queen, O Goddess of my life,
Light unbegotten, Scintillating spark
Of the All-Self ! O holy, holy Spouse
Of my most godlike thought, come forth ! I
    say,
And manifest unto thy worshipper
In more candescent fulgours ! Let the air
Ring with the passion of my holy cry
Unto the Highest. For persistent will
And the continual fervour of my soul
Have led me to this hour of victory,
This throne of splendour. O thou Beauty's
    Self,
Thou holiest Crown thus manifest to me,
Come forth, I say, come forth ! With
    mightier cries
Than Jesus uttered on the quivering cross :
" Eli, Eli, lama sabachthani,"
Thee, thee, thee only I invoke ! O Soul
Of my own spirit, let thy fervid eyes
Give me their light : for thou dost stand, as
    God
Among the Holy Ones. Before the gods
Thy music moves, coequal, coeterne,
Thou, Lord of Light and Life and Love !
    Come forth !
I call thee in the holiest name of Him
Lord of the Universe, and by His Name,
Osiris perfected through suffering,
Glorious in trial : by His Holy Name,
Jesus, the Godhead passing through the gates
Of Hell, that even there the rescuers
Might find the darkness, and proclaim the
    light ;
For I invoke thee by the sacred rites
And secret words of everlasting power :
By the swift symbol of the Golden Dawn
And all its promise, by the Cross of Fire,
And by the Gleaming Symbol : by the Rose
And Cross of Light and Life : the holy Ankh,
The Rose of Ruby and the Cross of Gold.
By these I say, Come forth ! my holy
    Spouse,
And make me one with thine abundant ray

Of the vast ocean of the unmanifest
Limitless Negativity of Light
Flowing, in Jesus manifest, through space,
In equilibrium, upon the world
Illumined by the White Supernal Gleam
Through the red Cross of Calvary : Come
    forth,
My actual Self! Come forth, O dazzling one,
Wrapped in the glory of the Holy Place
Whence I have called thee : Come thou forth
    to me,
And permeate my being, till my face
Shine with thy light reflected, till my brows
Gleam with thy starry symbol, till my voice
Reach the Ineffable : Come forth, I say,
And make me one with thee : that all my
    ways
May glitter with the holy influence,
That I may be found worthy at the end
To sacrifice before the Holy Ones :
That in thy Glory, Strength, and Majesty,
And by the Beauty and Harmony of Heaven
That fills its fountains at the Well of Life,
I may be mighty in the Universe.
Yea, come thou forth, I mightily conjure
Thy radiant Perfection, to compel
All Spirits to be subject unto Me,
That every spirit of the Firmament
And of the Ether, and upon the Earth
And under Earth, and of the stable land,
Of water, of the whirling of the air,
Of the all-rushing fire ; and every Spell
And scourge of God the Vast One may be
    made
Obedient unto me, to the All-Good
And ultimate Redemption : Hear me, thou !

    Eca, zodacare, Iad, goho,
    Torzodu odo kikale qaa !
    Zodacare od zodameranu !
    Zodorje, lape zodiredo Ol
    Noco Mada, das Iadapiel !
    Ilas ! hoatahe Iaida ! [1]

O crowned with starlight ! Winged with
    emerald

[1] This conjuration is in the "angelic" language of Dr. Dee. See the edition of Goetia
published by the S.P.R.T.

Wider than Heaven ! O profounder blue
Of the abyss of water ! O thou flame
Flashing through all the caverns of the night,
Tongues leaping from the immeasurable
Up through the glittering Steeps unmanifest
To the ineffable ! O Golden Sun !
Vibrating glory of my higher self !
I heard thy voice resounding in the Abyss :
" I am the only being in the deep
Of Darkness : let me rise and gird myself
To tread the path of Darkness : even so
I may attain the light. For from the Abyss
I came before my birth : from those dim halls
And silence of a primal sleep ! And He,
The Voice of Ages, answered me and said :
Behold ! for I am He that formulates
In darkness ! Child of Earth ! the Light
    doth shine
In darkness, but the darkness understands
No ray of that initiating light ! "
Now, by Initiation's dangerous path
And groping aspiration, came I forth
Where the White Splendour shone upon the
    Throne,
Even to the Temple of the Holy Ones :
Now, by that Light, come forth, I say, to me,
My Lady of the Starlight and the Moon !
Come and be absolute within my mind,
That I may take no dim remembrance back
To drown this glory with earth's quivering
    gloom.
But, O abide within Me ! Every hour
I need the lofty and the limpid stream
Of that White Brilliance : Leave me not alone,
O Holy Spirit ! Come to comfort me,
To draw me, and to make me manifest,
Osiris to the weeping world ; that I
Be lifted up upon the Cross of Pain
And Sacrifice, to draw all human kind
And every germ of matter that hath life,
Even after me, to the ineffable
Kingdom of Light ! O holy, holy Queen !
Let thy wide pinions overshadow me !

I am, the Resurrection and the Life !
The Reconciler of the Light and Dark.
I am the Rescuer of mortal things.
I am the Force in Matter manifest.

I am the Godhead manifest in flesh.
I stand above, among the Holy Ones.
I am all-purified through suffering,
All-perfect in the mystic sacrifice,
And in the knowledge of my Selfhood
    made
One with the Everlasting Lords of Life.
The Glorified through Trial is My Name.
The Rescuer of Matter is My Name.
I am the Heart of Jesus girt about
With the Swift Serpent ! I, Osirified,
Stand in this Hall of Twofold Truth and
    say :
Holy art Thou, Lord of the Universe !
Holy art Thou, whom Nature hath not formed !
Holy art Thou, O Vast and Mighty One !
O Lord of Darkness and O Lord of Light !
Holy art Thou, O Light above all Gods !
O Holy, Holy, Holy, Holy King
Ineffable, O Consciousness Divine
In whose white Presence, even I, a god,
A god of gods, prostrate myself and say :
I am the spark of Thine abundant flame.
I am the flower, and Thou the splendid
    Sun
Wherefrom my Life is drawn ! All hail to
    Thee,
For Holy, Holy, Holy, is Thy Name !
Holy art Thou, O Universal Lord !
Holy art Thou, whom Nature hath not formed !
Holy art Thou, the Vast and Mighty
    One !
O Lord of Darkness and O Lord of Light !

I see the Darkness fall as lightning falls !
I watch the Ages like a torrent roll
Past Me : and as a garment I shake off
The clinging skirts of Time. My place is
    fixed
In the abyss beyond all Stars and Suns.
I AM, the Resurrection and the Life !

Holy art Thou, Lord of the Universe !
Holy art Thou, whom Nature hath not formed !
Holy art Thou, the Vast and Mighty One !
O Lord of Darkness and O Lord of Light !

HYMN TO APOLLO.

Written in the Temple of Apollo.

GOD of the golden face and fiery forehead !
Lord of the Lion's house of strength, exalted
In the Ram's horns ! O ruler of the vaulted
        Heavenly hollow !
Send out thy rays majestic, and the torrid
Light of thy song ! thy countenance most
        splendid
Bend to the suppliant on his face extended !
        Hear me, Apollo !

Let thy fierce fingers sweep the lyre forgotten !
Recall the ancient glory of thy chanted
Music that thrilled the hearts of men, and
        haunted
        Life to adore thee !
Cleanse thou our market-places misbegotten !
Fire in my heart and music to my pæan
Lend, that my song bow, past the empyrean,
        Phœbus, before thee !

All the old worship in this land is broken ;
Yet on my altar burns the ancient censer,
Frankincense, saffron, galbanum, intenser !
        Ornaments glisten.
Robes of thy colour bind me for thy token.
My voice is fuller in thine adoration.
Thine image holds its god-appointed station.
        Lycian, listen !

My prayers more eloquent than olden chants
Long since grown dumb on the soft forgetful
        airs—
My lips are loud to herald thee : my prayers
        Keener to follow.
I do aspire, as thy long sunbeam slants
Upon my crown ; I do aspire to thee
As no man yet—I am in ecstasy !
        Hear me, Apollo !

My chant wakes elemental flakes of light
Flashing along the sandal-footed [1] floor.
All listening spirits *answer and adore*
        Thee, the amazing !

    [1] Strewn with sandalwood (?)

I follow to the eagle-baffling sight,
Limitless oceans of abounding space ;
Purposed to blind myself, but know thy face,
    Phœbus, in gazing.

O hear me ! hear me ! hear me ! for my hands,
Dews deathly bathe them ; sinks the stricken
    song ;
Eyes that were feeble have become the strong,
    See thee and glisten.
Blindness is mine ; my spirit understands,
Weighs out the offering, accepts the pain,
Hearing the pæan of the unprofane !
    Lycian, listen !

God of the fiery face, the eyes inviolate !
Lord of soundless thunders, lightnings light-
    less !
Hear me now, for joy that I see thee sightless,
    Fervent to follow.
Grant one boon ; destroy me, let me die
    elate,
Blasted with light intolerant of a mortal,
That the undying in me pass thy portal !
    Hear me, Apollo.

Hear me, or if about thy courts be girded
Paler some purple softening the sunlight
Merciful, mighty, O divide the one light
    Into a million
Shattered gems, that I mingle in my worded
Measures some woven filament of passion
Caught, Phœbus, from thy star-girt crown, to
    fashion
    Poet's pavilion.

Let me build for thee an abiding palace
Rainbow-hued to affirm thy light divided,
Yet where starry words, by thy soul guided,
    Sing as they glisten,
Dew-drops diamonded from the abundant
    chalice !
Swoons the prayer to silence ; pale the altar
Glows at thy presence as the last words
    falter—
    Lycian, listen !

THE HERMIT'S HYMN TO SOLITUDE.

Namo Tassa Bhagavato Arahato Sammasambuddhasa.

Venerable Lord and Best of Friends,
  We, seeing the cycle in which Maha Brahma
is perhaps more a drifting buoy than ourselves,
knowing that it is called the walking in delusion,
the puppet show of delusion, the writhing of
delusion, the fetter of delusion, are aware that
the way out of the desert is found by going
into the desert. Will you, in your lonely
lamaserai, accept this hymn from me, who,
in the centre of civilisation, am perhaps more
isolated than you in your craggy fastness among
the trackless steppes of your Untrodden Land ?
               ALEISTER CROWLEY.

PARIS, A.B. 2446.

I.

MIGHTIEST Self !   Supreme in Self-Con-
    tentment !
Sole Spirit gyring in its own ellipse ;
Palpable, formless, infinite presentment
Of thine own light in thine own soul's eclipse !
Let thy chaste lips
Sweep through the empty aethers guarding
    thee
(As in a fortress girded by the sea
The raging winds and wings of air
Lift the wild waves and bear
Innavigable foam to seaward), bend thee
    down,
Touch, draw me with thy kiss
Into thine own deep bliss,
Into thy sleep, thy life, thy imperishable
    crown !
Let that young godhead in thine eyes
Pierce mine, fulfil me of their secrecies,
Thy peace, thy purity, thy soul impenetrably
    wise.

II.

All things which are complete are solitary ;
The circling moon, the inconscient drift of
    stars,
The central systems.   Burn they, change
    they, vary ?
Theirs is no motion beyond the eternal bars.
Seasons and scars

Stain not the planets, the unfathomed home,
The spaceless, unformed faces in the dome
Brighter and blacker than all things,
Borne under the eternal wings
No whither: solitary are the winter woods
And caves not habited,
And that supreme grey head
Watching the groves : single the foaming
     amber floods,
And O ! most lone
The melancholy mountain shrine and throne,
While far above all things God sits, the
     ultimate alone !

III.

I sate upon the mossy promontory
Where the cascade cleft not his mother rock,
But swept in whirlwind lightning foam and
     glory,
Vast circling with unwearying luminous shock
To lure and lock
Marvellous eddies in its wild caress ;
And there the solemn echoes caught the stress,
The strain of that impassive tide,
Shook it and flung it high and wide,
Till all the air took fire from that melodious
     roar ;
All the mute mountains heard,
Bowed, laughed aloud, concurred,
And passed the word along, the signal of
     wide war.
All earth took up the sound,
And, being in one tune securely bound,
Even as a star became the soul of silence
     most profound.

IV.

Thus there, the centre of that death that
     darkened,
I sat and listened, if God's voice should
     break
And pierce the hollow of my ear that
     hearkened,
Lest God should speak and find me not
     awake—
For his own sake.

No voice, no song might pierce or penetrate
That enviable universal state.
The sun and moon beheld, stood still.
Only the spirit's axis, will,
Considered its own soul and sought a deadlier
     deep,
And in its monotone mood
Of supreme solitude
Was neither glad nor sad because it did not
     sleep ;
But with calm eyes abode
Patient, its leisure the galactic load,[1]
Abode alone, nor even rejoiced to know that
     it was God.

V.

All change, all motion, and all sound, are
     weakness !
Man cannot bear the darkness which is death.
Even that calm Christ, manifest in meekness,
Cried on the cross and gave his ghostly breath,
On the prick of death,
Voice, for his passion could not bear nor dare
The interlunar, the abundant air
Darkened, and silence on the shuddering
Hill, and the unbeating wing
Of the legions of His Father, and so died.
But I, should I be still
Poised between fear and will ?
Should I be silent, I, and be unsatisfied ?
For solitude shall bend
Self to all selfulness, and have one friend,
Self, and behold one God, and be, and look
     beyond the End.

VI.

O Solitude ! how many have mistaken
Thy name for Sorrow's, or for Death's or
     Fear's !
Only thy children lie at night and waken—
How shouldst thou speak and say that no
     man hears?
O Soul of Tears !
For never hath fallen as dew thy word,
Nor is thy shape showed, nor as Wisdom's
     heard

[1] Via Lactea, the " Milky Way."

Thy crying about the city
In the house where is no pity,
But in the desolate halls and lonely vales of
sand :
Not in the laughter loud,
Nor crying of the crowd,
But in the farthest sea, the yet untravelled
land.
Where thou hast trodden, I have trod ;
Thy folk have been my folk, and thine abode
Mine, and thy life my life, and thou, who
art thy God, my God.

VII.

Draw me with cords that are not ; witch me
chanted
Spells never heard nor open to the ear,
Woven of silence, moulded in the haunted
Houses where dead men linger year by year.
I have no fear
To tread thy far irremeable way
Beyond the paths and palaces of day,
Beyond the night, beyond the skies,
Beyond eternity's
Tremendous gate ; beyond the immanent
miracle.[1]
O secret self of things !
I have nor feet nor wings
Except to follow far beyond Heaven and
Earth and Hell,
Until I mix my mood
And being in thee, as in my hermit's hood
I grow the thing I contemplate—that selfless
solitude !

THE STORM.

Written on the North Atlantic Ocean.

IN the sorrow of the silence of the sunset,
when the world's heart sinks to sleep,
And the waking wind arises from the wedding
of the aether and the deep,
There are perfumes through the saltness of
the even ; there are hints of flowers afar ;
And the God goes down lamented by the
lonely vesper star.

The monsters rise around us as we move in
moving mist,
Slow whales that swim as musing, and lo !
or ever we wist,
Looms northward in the grey, mysterious ice,
cathedral high,
Clad in transparent clouds of cold, as a ghost
in drapery.

The solemn dusk descending creeps around
us from the East ;
Clouded as with the ungainly head of a
mysterious beast.
Long wisps of darkness (even as fingers)
reach and hold
The sobbing West toward them, clasp the
barred Hesperian gold.

Still pale a rose reflection lingers, in pure
soft blue ;
Even above the tempest, where a lonely
avenue
Leads from the wan moon's image, shadowy
in the air,
Waning, half hidden from the sun—and yet
her soul is there.

So stand I looking ever down to the rolling
sea,
Breast-heaves of a sleeping mother, spouse of
Eternity :
The dark deep ocean mother, that another[1]
hath reviled,
Calling her bitter and barren—and am I not
her child ?

O mother sea, O beautiful, more excellent
than earth,
How is thy travail understood, except thou
give me birth ?
O waves of death, O saltness, O sorrow
manifold !
I see beneath thy darkness azure ; deeper
still, the heart of gold.

---

[1] The universe.

[1] It is not known to whom Crowley refers.

Am I not true, O mother, who hast held the
  lives of men
Sucked down to thy swart bosom—O render
  not again !
Keep thou our life and mix it with thine
  eternal sleep :
Rest, let us rest from passion there, deep !
  O how deep !

Deep calleth unto deep, Amen ! hast thou no
  passion, thou ?
Even now the white flames kindle on thy
  universal brow.
I hear white serpents hiss and wild black
  dragons roll ;
And the storm of love is on thee—ah ! shall
  it touch thy soul ?

Nay, O my mother, in eternal calm thy
  virginal depths lie.
The peace of God, that passeth understanding,
  that am I !
Even I, perceiving deeply beneath the eyes
  of flame
The soul that, kindling, is not kindled : I
  have known thy Name.

Awake, O soaring billows ! Lighten the
  raging dome,
Wrap the wide horizon in a single cloak of
  flaming foam,
Leap in your fury ! Beat upon the shores
  unseen ! Devour your food,
The broken cliff, the crumbled bank, the
  bar. I know the mood.

Even so I see the terror of universal strife :
Murderous war, and murderous peace, and
  miserable life :
The pang of childbirth, and the pain of
  youth, and the fear of age,
Life tossed and broken into dust in the
  elemental rage.

Is not God part of every the tiniest spark
  of man ?
Is He not moulded also in His own eternal
  plan ?

Even so ; as the woes of earth is the angry
  crested sea.
Even so ; as Her great peace abideth in the
  deep—so He !

What wreck floats by us ? What pale corpse
  rolls horribly above,
Tossed on the unbewailing foam, cast out of
  light and life and love ?
The sea shall draw thee down, O brother, to
  her breast of peace,
Her unimaginable springs, her bridal secrecies.

Even so draw me in life, O Mother, to thy
  breast !
Below the storm, below the wind, to the
  abiding rest !
That I may know thy purpose and understand
  thy ways :
So, weeping always for the woe, also the love
  to praise !

The darkness falls intensely : no light invades
  the gloom.
Stillness drops dew-like from the heaven's
  unreverberant womb.
Westward the ship is riding on the sable
  wings of night,
I understand the darkness—why should I
  seek the light ?

ASSUMPTA CANIDIA.

Written in Mexico City.

WATERS that weep upon the barren shore
  Where some lone mystery of man abides ;
  As if the wailing of forsaken brides,
Rapt from the kiss of love for evermore,
Impressed its memory on the desolate
  Sounds at its edge ; on such a ́strand of
    tears
I linger through the long forgetful years,
My sin for mother, and my woe for mate.
  I am a soul lost utterly—forbear !
  I am unworthy both of tear and prayer.

The mystic slumber of my sense forlorn
Stirs only now and then ; some deeper
    pang
Reminds despair there is a sharper fang,
Reminds my night of a tempestuous morn.
For I am lost and lonely : in the skies
    I see no hope of any sun or star ;
On earth there blooms no rose, no nenu-
    phar ;
No cross is set for hope of sacrifice.
    I cannot sleep, I cannot wake ; and death
    Passes me by with his desirèd breath.

No shadow in my mind to prove a sun ;
    No sorrow to declare that joy exists ;
    A cycle of dim spectres in the mists
Moves just a little ; lastly there is One,
One central Being, one elusive shape,
    Not to aspire to, not to love ; alas !
Only a memory in the agèd mass
Of chained ones bound to me without escape !
    Oh, doom of God ! Oh, brand how worse
        than Cain's !
    Divided being, undivided pains !

What is this life ? (To call it life that grows
    No inch throughout all time.) This bitter-
        ness
    Too weak and hateful to be called distress ?
Slow memory working backward only knows
There was some horror grown to it for kin ;
    Some final leprous growth that took my
        brain,
    Weaving a labyrinth of dullest pain
From the sweet scarlet thread I thought was
    sin.
    I cannot sin ! Alas, one sin were sweet !
    But sin is living—and we cannot meet !

So long ago, so miserably long !
    I was a maiden—oh how rich and rare
    Seemed the soft sunshine woven in my hair !
How keen the music of my body's song !
How white the blossom of my body's light !
    How red the lips, how languorous the eyes,
    How made for pleasure, for the sleepy
        sighs

Softer than sleep ; amorous dew-dreams of
    night
    That draw out night in kisses to the day !
    So was I to my seeming as I lay.

That soft smooth-moving ocean of the west
    Under the palm and cactus as it rolled,
    Immortal blue, fixed with immortal gold,
Moving in rapture with my sleeping breast !
The young delicious green, the drunken smell
    Of the fresh earth, the luxury of the glow
    Where many colours mingled into snow,
Song-marvels in the air desirable.
    So lazily I lay, and watched my eyes
    In the deep fountain's sun-stirred har-
        monies.

I loved myself ! O Thou ! (I cried) divine
    Woman more lovely than the flowers of
        earth !
    O Self-hood softer than the babe at birth,
Sweeter than love, more amorous than wine,
Where is thy peer upon the face of life ?
    I love myself, the daughter of the dawn.
    Come, silken night, in your deep wings
        withdrawn
Let me be folded, as a tender wife
    In my own arms imagined ! Let me sleep,
    Unwaking from the admirable deep !

My arms fell lazily about the bed.
    I lay in some delicious trance.   I fell
    Deep through sleep's chambers to the gate
        of Hell,
And on that flaming portalice I read
The legend, " Here is beauty, here delight,
    Here love made more desirable than thine,
    Fiercer than light, more dolorous than wine.
Here the embraces of the Sons of Night !
    Come, sister, come ; come, lonely queen
        of breath !
    Here are the lustres and the flames of
        death."

Hence I was whirled, as in a wind of light,
    Out to the fragrance of a loftier air,
    A keener scent, and rising unaware
Out of the Palace of Luxurious Night,

I came to where the Gate of Heaven shone,
  Battled with comet and with meteor.
  Behold within that crested House of War,
One central glory of a sapphire stone,
  Whereon there breathed a sense, a mist,
    a sun !
  I stood and laughed upon the Ancient One.

For He was silent as my body's kiss,
, And sleeping as my many-coloured hair,
  And living as my eyes and lips ; and where
The vast creation round him cried " He Is !",
No murmur reached Him ; He was set alone,
  Alone and central. Ah ! my eyes were dim.
  I worshipped even ; for I envied Him.
So, moving upward to the azure throne,
  I spread my arms unto that ambient mist ;
  Lifted my life and soul up to be kissed !

A million million voices roared aloud !
A million million sabres flashed between !
  Flamed the vast falchion ! Fiery Cherubin
Flung me astounded to the mist and cloud.
A stone, flung downward through eternal
    space,
  I dropped. What bitter curses and despair
  Rang through wide aether ! How the
    trumpet blare
Cursed back at me ! Thou canst not see His
    Face !
  Equal and Spouse ? Bring forth the Virgin
    Dower,
  Eternal Wisdom and Eternal Power !

I woke ! and in a well's untroubled pool
  I saw my face—and I was ugly now !
  Blood-spattered ebony eyelash and white
    brow !
Blood on my lips, and hair, and breast !
    " Thou fool ! "
A horrid torture in my heart—and then
  I licked my lips : the tigress tasted blood.
  My changèd features—wash them in the
    flood
Of murder ! This is power over men
  And angels. I will lift the twisted rod,
  And make my power as the power of God !

I made my beauty as it was before.
  I learned strange secrets ; by my love and
    skill
  I bent creation to my wanded will.
I tuned the stars, I bound the bitter shore
Beyond the Pleiads : until the Universe
  Moved at my mantra [1] : Heaven and Hell
    obeyed ;
  Creation at my orders stayed or swayed.
" Take back," I cried, " the mockery of a
    curse ! "
  " I wield Thy Power." With my magic rod
  Again I strode before the Throne of God.

" Forgone my Virgin Splendour ! I aspire
  No longer as a maiden to thy Love.
  We twain are set in majesty above :
My cloud is mighty as thy mystic Fire."
Vanished the mist, the light, the sense, the
    throne !
  Vanished the written horror of the curse ;
  Vanished the stars, the sun, the Universe.
I was in Heaven, lost, alone. Alone !
  A new curse gathered as a sombre breath :
  " Power without Wisdom is the Name of
    Death ! "

And therefore from my devastating hand
  (For I was then unwilling to be dead)
  I loosed the lightning, and in hate and
    dread
Despairing, did I break the royal wand.
Mortal, a plaything for a thousand fears,
  I found the earth ; I found a lonely place
  To gaze for ever on the ocean's face,
Lamenting through the lamentable years ;
  Without a god, deprived of life and death,
  Sensible only to that sombre breath.

Thus wait I on the spring-forgotten shore ;
  Looking with vain unweeping eyes, for aye
  Into the wedding of the sea and sky,
(That do not wed, ay me !) for evermore
Hopeless, forgetting even to aspire
  Unto that Wisdom ; miserably dumb ;
  Waiting for the Impossible to come,
Whether in mercy or damnation dire—

  [1] The Hindu equivalent for " spell."

I who have been all Beauty and all
Power !—
This is thine hour, Apollyon, thine Hour !

I, who have twice beheld the awful throne ;
And, as it were the vision of a glass,
Beheld the Mist be born thereon, and pass ;
I, who have stood upon the four-square stone !
I, who have twice been One——! Woe,
woe is me !
Lost, lost, upon the lifeless, deathless plane,
The desert desolate, the air inane ;
Fallen, O fallen to eternity !
I, who have looked upon the Lord of Light ;
I, I am Nothing, and dissolved in Night !

(THE SPIRIT OF GOD, DESCENDING,
ASSUMETH HER INTO THE GLORY
OF GOD.)

VENUS.

Written in the temple of the L.I.L., [1] *No. 9,
Central America.*

MISTRESS and maiden and mother, im-
mutable mutable soul !
Love, shalt thou turn to another? Surely
I give thee the whole !
Light, shalt thou flicker or darken? Thou
and thy lover are met.
Bend from thy heaven and hearken ! Life,
shalt thou fade or forget?

Surely my songs are gone down as leaves
in the dark that are blown ; .
Surely the laurel and crown have faded and
left me alone.
Vainly I cry in the sunlight ; moon pities
my passion in vain.
Dark to my eyes is the one light, aching in
bosom and brain.

Surely, O Mother, thou knowest ! Have I
not followed thy star ?
I have gone whither thou goest, bitterly
followed afar,

[1] A secret Order, probably established by
Crowley himself.

Buried my heart in thy sorrow, cast down
my soul at thy knees.
Thou, thou hast left me no morrow. Days
and desires, what are these ?

Nay, I have torn from my breast passion and
love and despair :
Sought in thy palaces rest, sleep that awaited
me there ;
Sleep that awaits me in vain : I have done
with the hope of things ;
Passion and pleasure and pain have stung
me, and lost their stings.

Only abides there a hollow, void as the
heart of the earth.
Echo may find it and follow, dead from the
day of her birth.
Life, of itself not insatiate ; death, not pre-
suming to be ;
Share me intense and emaciate, waste me,
are nothing to me.

Still in the desolate place, still in the bosom
that was
Even as a veil for thy face, thy face in a
breathed-on glass,
Hangs there a vulture, and tears with a beak
of iron and fire.
I know not his name, for he wears no
feathers of my desire.

It is thou, it is thou, lone maiden ! My heart
is a bird that flies
Far into the azure laden with love-lorn songs
and cries.
O Goddess of Nature and Love ! Thyself
is the lover I see.
But thou art in the above, and thy kiss is
not for me.

Thou art all too far for my kiss ; thou art
hidden past my prayer.
Thy wing too wide, and the bliss too sweet
for me to share.
Thou art Nature and God ! I am broken in
the wheelings of thy car ;
Thy love-song unheard or unspoken, and I
cannot see thy star.

Thou art not cold, but bitter is thy burning
cry to me.
My tiny heart were fitter for a mortal than
for thee.
But I cast away the mortal, and I choose the
tortured way,
And I stand before thy portal, and my face
is cold and grey.

Thou lovest me with a love more terrible
than death ;
But thou art in the above, and my wings feel
no wind's breath.
Thou art all too fierce and calm, too bitter
and sweet, alas !
Thou weavest a cruel charm on my soul that
is as glass.

I know thee not, who art naked ; I lie beneath thy feet
Who hast called till my spirit achèd with a
pang too deathly sweet.
Thou hast given thee to me dying, and made
thy bed to me.
I shiver, I shrink, and, sighing, lament it
cannot be.

I have no limbs as a God's to close thee in
and hold :
Too brief are my periods, and my hours are
barren of gold.
I am not thewed as Jove to kill thee in one
caress !
Not a golden shower is my love, but a child's
tear of distress.

Give me the strength of a panther, the tiger's
strenuous sides,
The lion's limbs that span there some thrice
the turn of the tides,
The mutinous frame, the terror of the royal
Minotaur,
That our loves may make a mirror of the
dreadful soul of war !

For love is an equal soul, and shares an
equal breath.
I am nought—and thou the whole ? It were
not love, but Death.

Give me thy life and strength, let us struggle
for mastery,
As the long shore's rugged length that battles
with the sea.

I am thine, I am thine indeed ! My form
is vaster grown,
And our limbs and lips shall bleed on the
starry solar throne.
My life is made as thine ; my blessing and
thy curse
Beget, as foam on wine, a different universe.

I foam and live and leap : thou laughest,
fightest, diest !
In agony swift as sleep thou hangest as the
Christ.
My nails are in thy flesh ; my sweat is on thy
brow ;
We are one, we are made afresh, we are
Love and Nature now.

I am swifter than the wind : I am wider
than the sea :
I am one with all mankind : and the earth
is made as we.
The stars are spangles bright on the canopy
of our bed,
And the sun is a veil of light for my lover's
golden head.

O Goddess, maiden, and wife ! Is the
marriage bed in vain ?
Shall my heart and soul and life shrink back
to themselves again ?
Be thou my one desire, my soul in day as in
night !
My mind the home of the Higher ! My
heart the centre of Light !

A LITANY.[1]

I.

BLACK thine abyss of noon
Flings forth the thunder-swoon.
Smite us, and slay, Amoun,
Amoun, Achiha !

[1] The Table of Correspondences will elucidate any doubtful point in this poem.

II.

Thoth, from the starry space
Flash out the splendid face !
Wisdom, immortal grace,
Thoth, turn to usward !

III.

Deep, deep thy sombre Sea,
Spouse of eternity !
Mother, we cry to Thee :
Hear us, Maut, Mother !

IV.

Sound, sistron, sound afar !
Shine, shine, O dawning Star !
Flame, flame, O meteor Car !
Isis, Our Lady !

V.

Strike, strike the louder chord !
Draw, draw the flaming sword,
Crowned child and conquering Lord :
Horus, avenger.

VI.

Dawn-star of flaming light,
Five rays in one unite,
Light, Life, Love, Mercy, Might,
Star of the Magi.

VII.

Lift, lift the Cross of Light,
Rose, golden, green, and white,
Rise, rise athwart the night !
Mighty Aeshuri !

VIII.

Flame, flame, thou Blazoned Sun !
Seal-Star of Solomon !
Seven Mysteries in One !
Godhead and Mankind !

IX.

Beauty and life and love !
Let fly thy darling dove !
Bend to us from above,
Lady Ahathor !

X.

Where light and darkness meet,
There shine thy flaming feet,
There is thy splendid seat ;
Mighty Anubi !

XI.

Swift-winged Stability,
Lifting the earth and sky,
Hold me up utterly,
Keep me, O Shuwe !

XII.

Virginal Queen of Earth,
Late love, and last of birth,
Loose, loose the golden girth,
Nephthys, the crowned one !

XIII.

Hail, crowned Harpocrates,
Show, show thy secrecies,
Lotus-throned silences,
Typhon's réplacer !

MARCH IN THE TROPICS.

Written near Manzanillo.

WHAT ails thee, earth ? Is not the breath
of Spring
Exultant on thy breast ? What aileth thee,
O many-mooded melancholy sea ?
I hear the swift rush of that triumphant wing !
Listen ! the world's whole heart is listening !
In England now the leaf leaps, and the tree
Gleams dewy, and the bird woos noisily.
Here in the tropics now is no such thing.

Dull heavy heat burns through the clouded
sky,
And yet no promise of the latter rains.
Earth bears her fruit, but unrefreshed of
death.
In winter is no sorrow, in the dry
Harsh spring no joy, while pestilence and
pains
Hover like wolves behind the summer's breath.

NIGHT IN THE VALLEY.

Written at the foot of Citlaltepetl.

I LAY within the forest's virgin womb
  Tranced in the sweetness, nuptial, indolent,
Of the faint breeze and tropical perfume,
  And all the music far lone waters lent
Unto the masses of magnolia bloom,
  Tall scarlet lilies, and the golden scent
Shed by strange clusters of more pallid flowers,
And purple lustre strewn amid the twilight
    bowers.

Far, far the pastureless, the unquiet sea
  Moaned ; far the stately pyramid of cold
Shrouding the stars, arose : sweet witchery
  That brought them in the drowsing eye,
    to fold
The picture in : the wingèd imagery
  That Hermes gathers with that floral gold
Whose triple flower or flame or pinioned light
Lends life to death, and love and colour unto
    light.

How flames that scarlet stronger than Apollo,
  Too swift and warm to know itself a bird !
How the light winds and waves of moonlight
    follow,
  Shot from the West, cadence of Daylight's
    word !
How flock the tribes of wings within the
    hollow,
  Even as darkness summons home the herd !
The still slow water slackens into sleep.
The rose-glow dies, leaves cold Citlaltepetl's [1]
    steep.

The chattering voices of the day depart.
  Earth folds her limbs and leans her loving
    breast
Even to all her children : the great heart
  Beats solemnly the requiem of rest.
The sea keeps tune ; the silent stars upstart
  Seeming to sentinel that sombre crest
Where of old time burst out the vulture fire
Cyclopean, that is dead, now, as a man's
    desire.

[1] Called by the Spaniards Orizaba.

The drowsy cries of night birds, then the
    song
  Lovely and lovelorn in the listening vale,
So wild and tender, swooping down in long
  Notes of despair, then lifting the low tale
In golden notes to skyward in one throng
  Of clustered silver, so the nightingale
Tunes the wild flute, as dryads he would
    gather
To roof with music in the palace of the
    weather,

With love despairing, dying as music dies ;
  With lost souls' weeping, and the bitter
    muse
Of such as lift their hearts in sacrifice
  On some strange cross, or shed Sicilian
    dews
Over a sadder lake than Sicily's—
  Hark ! they are leaping from the valley
    views
Into the light and laughter and deep grief
Of that immortal heart that sings beyond
    belief.

How pitiful, how beautiful, the faces !
  The long hair shed on shoulders ivory
    white !
Each note shoots down the dim arboreal
    spaces
  Like amber or like hyaline lit with light.
Each spirit glimmers in the shadowy places
  Like hyacinths or emeralds : or the night
Shows them as shadows of some antique
    gem
Where moonlight fills its cup and flashes into
    them.

So, in the moony twilight and the splendour
  Of music's light, the desolate nightingale
Fills all the interlunar air with tender
  Kisses like song, or shrills upon the scale,
Till quivering moonrays shake again, to send
    her
  Luminous tunes through every sleepy vale,
While the slow dancers rhythmically reap
The fairy amaranth, and silver wheat of
    sleep.

Now over all that scythe of sleep impending
Mows the pale flowers of vision following ;
Dryad and bird and fount and valley blending
Into one dreamy consciousness of spring ;
And all the night and all the world is ending,
And all the souls that weep and hearts
    that sing !
So, as the dew hides in the lotus blossom,
Sleep draws me with her kiss into her bridal
bosom.

METEMPSYCHOSIS.

Written at Vera Cruz.

DIM goes the sun down there behind the tall
And mighty crest of Orizaba's snow :
Here, gathering at the nightfall, to and fro,
Fat vultures, foul and carrion, flap, and call
Their ghastly comrades to the domèd wall
That crowns the grey cathedral. There they
    go—
The parasites of death, decay and woe,
Gorged with the day's indecent festival.

I think these birds were once the souls of
    priests.
They haunt by ancient habit the old home
Wherein they held high mass in days of old.
But now they soar above it—for behold !
God hath looked mercifully down on Rome,
Promoting thus her children to be beasts.

ADVICE OF A LETTER.[1]

THE Wingèd Bull that dwellèd in the north
Hath flown into the West, and uttered forth
His thunders in the Mountains. He shall
    come
Where blooms the sempiterne chrysanthe-
    mum.
The wingèd Lion, that wrought dire amaze
In the Dark Place, where Light was, did his
    ways

[1] With a letter to Ceylon, sent from Mexico
in duplicate for certainty by way both of England and Japan. The allusions are Hermetic
or Alchemical.

Take fiery to enkindle a new flame :
The Eagle of the High Lands yet that came
By the red sunset to an eastern sky
Shall plume himself and gather him and
    fly
Even as a Man that rideth on a Beast
Trained, to the Golden Dawn-sky of the
    East.
Therefore his word shall seek the Ivory
    Isle
By double winds and by the double Style,
Twin doorways of the Sunset and the Dawn.
And thou who tak'st it, shalt be subtly drawn
Into strange vigils, and shalt surely see
The ancient form and memory of me,
Nor me distinct, but shining with that Light
Wherein the Sphinx and Pyramid unite.

ON WAIKIKI BEACH.[1]

UPHEAVED from Chaos, through the dark
    sea hurled,
    Through the cleft heart of the amazèd sea,
    Sprang, 'mid deep thunderous throats of
        majesty,
Titanic, in the waking of the world ;
    Sprang, one vast mass of spume and
        molten fire,
    Lava, tremendous waves of earth ; sprang
        higher
    Than the sea's crest volcano-torn, to be
    Written in Cyclopean charactery,
        Hawaii.   Here she stands
        Queen of all laughter's lands
    That dance for dawn, lie tranced in
        leisured noon,
        Dreaming through day towards
            night,
        Craving the perfumed light
    Of the stars lustrous, and the gem-born
        moon.
        Dewy with clustered diamond,
The long land swoons to sleep ; the sea
    sleeps and yet wakes beyond.

[1] Near Honolulu.

C

Here, in the crescent beach and bay, the sea,
Curven and carven in warm shapes of
dream,
Answers the love-song of the lilied
stream,
And moves to bridal music. Stern and free,
The lion-shapen headland guards the
shore ;
The ocean, the bull-throated, evermore
Roars ; the vast wheel of heaven turns
above,
Its rim of pain, its jewelled heart of
love ;
Sun-waved, the eagle wing
Of the air of feathered spring
Royally sweeps, and on the musical marge
Watches alone the man.
O silvern shape and span
Of moonlight, reaching over the grey,
large
Breast of the surf-bound strand,
Life of the earth, God's child, Man's bride,
the light of the sweet land !

Are emeralds ever a spark of this clear green,
Or sapphires hints of this diviner blue,
Or rubies shadows of this rosy hue,
Or light itself elsewhere so clear and clean ?
For all the sparkling dews of heaven
fallen far
Crystalline, fixed, forgotten (as a star
Forgets its nebulous virginity)
Are set in all the sky and earth and sea.
Shining with solar fire,
The single-eyed desire
Of scent and sound and sight and sense
perfuses
The still and lambent light
Of the essential night ;
And all the heart of me is fain, and muses,
As if for ever doomed to dream
Or pass in peace Lethean adown the grey
Lethean stream.

So deep the sense of beauty, and so keen !
The calm abiding holiness of love
Reigns ; and so fallen from the heights
above

Immeasurable, the influence unseen
Of music and of spiritual fire,
That the soul sleeps, forgotten of desire,
Only remembering its God-like birth
Reflected in the deity of earth,
Becometh even as God.
The pensive period
Of night and day beats like a waving fan
No more, no more : the years,
Reft of their joys and fears,
Pass like pale faces, leave the life of man
Untroubled of their destinies,
Leave him forgotten of life and time, im-
mortal, calm and wise.

Only the ceaseless surf on coral towers,
The changeless change of the unchanging
ocean,
Laps the bright night, with unsubstantial
motion
Winnowing the starlight, plumed with
feathery flowers
Of foam and phosphor glory, the strange
glow
Of the day's amber fallen to indigo,
Lit of its own depth in some subtle
wise,
A pavement for the footsteps from
the skies
Of angels walking thus
Not all unseen of us,
Nor all unknown, nor unintelligible,
When with souls lifted up
In the Cadmean cup, [1]
As incense lifted in the thurible,
We know that God is even as we,
Light from the sky, and life on earth, and
love beneath the sea.

THE TRIADS OF DESPAIR.

Written off the Coast of Japan.

I.

I LIE in liquid moonlight poured from the
exalted orb.
Orion waves his jewelled sword ; the tingling
waves absorb

----
[1] See Euripides, *Bacchae.*

Into their lustre as they move the light of
all the sky.
I am so faint for utter love I sigh and long
to die.
Far on the misty ocean's verge flares out the
Southern Cross,
And the long billows on the marge of coral
idly toss,
This night of nights! The stars disdain a
lustre dusk or dim.
Twin love-birds on the land complain, a
wistful happy hymn.
I turn my face toward the main : I laugh
and dive and swim.

Now fronts me foaming all the light of surf-
bound waters pent ;
Now from the black breast of the night the
Southern Cross is rent.
I top the mighty wall of fears ; the dark
wave rolls below.
A tall swift ship on wings appears, a cataract
of snow
Plunging before the white east wind ; she
meets the eager sea
As forest green by thunder thinned meets
fire's emblazonry.
Then I sink back upon the breast of mighty-
flinging foam,
Ride like a ghost upon the crest, the silver-
rolling comb ;
Float like a warrior to his rest, majestically
home.

But oh ! my soul, what seest thou, whose
eyes are open wide ?
What thoughts inspire me idling now, lone
on the lonely tide ?
Here in the beauty of the place, hope laughs
and says me nay ;
In nature's bosom, in God's face, I read
Decay, Decay.
Here in the splendour of the Law that built
the eternal sphere,
Beauty and majesty and awe, I fail of any
cheer.
Here, in caprice, in will divine, I see no
perfect peace ;

Here, in the Law's impassive shrine, no hope
is of release.
All things escape me, all repine, all alter,
ruin, cease.

II.

But thou, O Lord, O Apollo,
Must thou utterly change and pass ?
Thy light be lost in the hollow ?
Thy face as a maid's in a glass
Go out and be lost and be broken
As the face of the maid is withdrawn,
And thy people with sorrow unspoken
Wait, wait for the dawn ?

But thou, O Diana, our Lady,
Shall it be as if never had been ?
The vales of the sea grown shady
And silver and amber and green
As thy light passed over and kissed them ?
Shall thy people lament thee and swoon,
And we miss thee if thy love missed them,
Awaiting the moon ?

But thou, who art Light, and above them,
Who art fire and above them as fire,
Shall thy sightless eyes not love them
Who are all of thine own desire ?
Immaculate daughters of passion,
Shalt thou as they pass be past ?
And thy people bewail thee, Thalassian,
Lost, lost at the last ?

III.

Nay, ere ye pass your people pass,
As snow on summer hills,
As dew upon the grass,
As one that love fulfils,
If he in folly wills
Love a lass.

Yet on this night of smiles and tears
A maiden is the theme.
The universe appears
An idle summer dream
Lost in the grey supreme
Mist of years.

For she is all the self I own,
And all I want of will.
She speaks not, and is known.
Her window shining chill
Whispers " He lingers still.
I am alone."

IV.

But to-night the lamp must be wasted,
And the delicate hurt must ache,
And the sweet lips moan untasted,
My lady lie lonely awake.
The night is taken from love, and love's
    guerdon
Is life and its burden.

To-night if I turn to my lover
I must ask : If she be ? who am I ?
To-night if her heart I uncover
No heart in the night I espy.
I am grips with the question of eld, and the
    sphinx holds fast
My eyes to the past.

Who am I, when I say I languish ?
Who is she, if I call her mine ?
And the fool's and the wise man's anguish
Are burnt in the bitter shrine.
The god is far as the stars, and the wine and
    fire
Salt with desire.

Desunt cetera.

THE DANCE OF SHIVA.[1]

*Written at the House of Sri Parananda
Swami, Ceylon.*

WITH feet set terribly dancing,
    With eyelids filled of flame,
Wild lightnings from Him glancing,
    Lord Shiva went and came.
The dancing of His feet was heard
And was the final word.

[1] The MS. of this Hymn most mysteriously (for I am very careful) disappeared two days after being written. I can remember no more of it than the above ; nor will inspiration return. —A. C.

He danced the measure golden
    On dead men . . .
His Saints and Rishis [1] olden,
    The yogins that . . .
He trampled them to dust and they
Were sparks and no more clay.

The dust thrown up around Him
    In cycles whirled and twined,
Dim sparks that fled and found Him
    Like mist beyond the mind.
The universe was peopled then
With little gods, and men.

In that ecstatic whirling
    He saw not nor . . .

He knew not in His fervour
    Creation's sated sigh ;
The groan of the Preserver,
    Life's miserable lie.
I broke that silence, and afraid
I knew not what I prayed.

.   .   .   .   .

Let peace awaken for an hour
And manifest as power.

.   .   .   .   .

Cease not the dance unceasing,
    The glance nor swerve nor cease,
Thy peace by power increasing
    In me by power to peace.

Desunt cetera.

SONNET FOR A PICTURE.

*Written in the woods above Kandy. Inscribed
to T. Davidson.*

LURED by the loud big-breasted courtesan
    That plies trained lechery of obedient eyes,
He sits, holds bed's last slattern-sweet
    surprise,
Late plucked from gutter to grace groves
    of Pan.

[1] The seven Rishis are the great Sages of India. They received from the Gods the sacred Books.

The third one, ruddy as they twain are wan,
  Hungrily gazes, sees her tower of lies
Blasted that instant in some wizard wise—
The frozen look—the miserable man !

What sudden barb of what detested dart
  Springs from Apollo's bowstring to his
    heart ?
On sense-dulled ears what Voice rings the
    decree ?
  "For thee the women burn : the wine is
    cool :
For thee the fresco and the fruit—thou
    fool !
This night thy soul shall be required of thee !"

THE HOUSE.

A NIGHTMARE.[1]

Written at Anuradhapura.

I MUST be ready for my friend to-night.
  So, such pale flowers as winter bears
    bedeck
The old oak walls : the wood-fire's cheerful
    light
  Flashes upon the fire-dogs silver-bright.
    Wood ? why, the jetsam of yon broken
      wreck
  Where the white sea runs o'er the sandy
    neck

That joins my island to the land when tides
  Run low. What curious fancies through
    my brain
Run, all so wild and all so pleasant ! Glides
No phantom creeping from the under sides
  Of the grey globe : no avatar of pain
Gathering a body from the wind and rain.

[1] This, with slight variations, was one of the
regular dreams of Allen Bennett Macgregor,
just as the "flying" dream, the "naked in
church" dream, the "taken in adultery"
dream, the "lost tooth" dream, the "being
shaved" dream, and many others of specific
type recur from time to time in the life of most
people.—A. C.

So the night fell, and gently grew the
    shades
  In firelight fancies taking idle form ;
Often a flashing May-day ring of maids,
Or like an army through resounding glades
  Glittering, with martial music, trumpet,
    shawm,
Drum—so I build the echoes of the storm

Into a pageant of triumphant shapes.
  So, as the night grows deeper, and no
    moon
Stirs the black heaven, no star its cloud
    escapes,
I sit and watch the fire : my musing drapes
  My soul in darker dreams ; the storm's
    wild tune
Rolls ever deeper in my shuddering swoon :

Whereat I start, shudder, and pull together
  My mind. Why, surely it must be the
    hour !
My friend is coming through the wet wild
    weather
Across the moor's inhospitable heather
  To the old stately tower—my own dear
    tower.
He will not fail me for a sudden shower !

My friend ! How often have I longed to
    see
  Again his gallant figure and that face
Radiant—how long ago we parted !—we
The dearest friends that ever were ! Ah me !
  I curse even now that hateful parting-
    place.
But now—he comes ! How glad I am !
    Apace

Fly the glad minutes—There he is at last !
  I know the firm foot on the marble floor.
The hour-glass turns ! What miseries to cast
For ever to the limbo of the past !
  He knocks—my friend ! O joy for ever-
    more !
He calls ! "Open the door ! Open the
    door !"

You guess how gladly to the door I rushed
And flung it wide. Why ! no one's there !
      Arouse !
I am asleep. What horror came and crushed
My whole soul's life out as some shadow
      brushed
My body and passed in ? All sense allows
At last the fearful truth—This is the house !

This is my old house on the marsh, and here,
Here is the terror of the distant sea
Moaning, and here the wind that wails, the
      drear
Groans like a ghost's, the desolate house of
      fear
Whence I fled once from my great enemy—
This is the house ! O speechless misery !

Here the great silver candlesticks illume
The agèd book, the blackness blazoned o'er
With golden characters and scarlet bloom
Twined in the blue-tinged sigils wrought for
      doom,
And dreadful names of necromancer's lore
Written therein : so stood my room before

When the hissed whisper came, " Beware !
      Beware !
They're coming !" and " They're coming !"
      when the wind
Bore the blank echoes of their stealthy care
To creep up silently and find me there,
Hid in the windowless old house, stark
      blind
For fear—and then—what horrors lurked
      behind

The door firm barred !—and thus they cried
      in vain :
" Open the door ! " Then crouched I mad
      with fear
Till at the dawn their footsteps died again.
They can do nothing to me—that is plain—
While the door bars them ! What is it
      runs clear
Truth in my mind ? Once more they may
      be near ?

And then came memory. Wide the portal
      stood
And—what had brushed me as it passed ?
      What froze
My dream to this awakening—fearful flood
Of horror loosed, loosing a sweat of blood,
An agony of terror on these brows ?
God ! God ! Indeed, indeed this is the
      house !

The candles sputtered and went out. I stood
Fettered by fear, and heard the lonely wind
Lament across the marsh. A frenzied flood
Of hate and loathing swept across my mood,
And with a shudder I flung the door to.
      Mind
And body sank a huddled wreck behind.

Nought stirred. Draws hither the grim doom
      of Fate ?

A long, long while.

                  Now—in the central core
Of my own room what accent of keen hate,
Triumphant malice, mockery satiate,
Rings in the voice above the storm's wild
      roar ?
It cries " Open the door ! Open the door ! "

ANIMA LUNAE.

*Written partly under the great rock Sigiri, in
      Ceylon, partly in Arabia, near Aden.*

ZÔHRA the king by feathered fans
Slept lightly through the mid-day heat.
Swart giants with drawn yataghans
Guard, standing at his head and feet,
Zôhra, the mightiest of the khans !

Each slave Circassian like a moon
Sits smiling, burning with young bloom
Of dawn, and weaves an airy tune
Like a white bird's song bright and bold
That dips a fiery plume.
So the song lulled, lazily rolled
In tubes of silver, lutes of gold ;

And all the palace drowsed away
The hours that fanned with silken fold
The progress of the Lord of Day.
Yet, as he slept, a grey
Shadow of dream drew near, and stooped
And glided through the ranks of slaves,
Leaving no shadow where they drooped,
No echo in the architraves
As silent as the grave's.
That shape vibrated to the tune
Of thought lulled low ; the stirless swoon
Half felt its fellow gather close,
Yet stirred not : now the intruder moves,
Turns the tune slowlier to grave rows
Of palm trees, losing life in loves
Less turbid than the mildest dream
That ever stirred the stream
Whereon night floats, a shallop faint,
Ivory and silver bow and beam,
Dim-figured with the images
Divinely quaint
Of gold engraved, forth shadowing sorceries.
So the king dreamed of love : and passing on
The shape moved quicker, winnowing with
    faint fans
The soundless air of thought : the noonday sun
Seemed to the mightiest of a thousand khans
Like to a man's
Brief life—a thousand such dream spans !—
And so he dreamed of life : and failing
    plumes
Wrought through ancestral looms
In the man's brain : and so he dreamed of
    death.
And slower still the grey God wrought
Dividing consciousness from breath,
And life and death from thought.
So the king dreamed of Nought.

Yet subtly-shapen was this Nothingness,
Not mere negation, as before that dream
Drew back the veil of sleep ;
But strange : the king turned idly, sought to
    press
The bosom where love lately burnt supreme,
And found no ivory deep.
He turned and sought out life ; and nothing
    lived :

Death, and nought died. The king's brow
    fell. Sore grieved
He rose, not knowing : and before his will
Swan's throat, dove's eyes, moon's breast,
    and woman's mouth,
And form desirable
Of all the clustered love drew back : grew
    still
" O turn, my lover, turn thee to the South !"
The girl's warm song of the Siesta's hour.
Heedless of all that flower,
Eager to feel the strong brown fingers close
On the unshrinking rose
And pluck it to his breast to perish there ;
With neither thought nor care
Nor knowledge he went forth : none stay,
    none dare
Proffer a pavid prayer.

There was a pavement bright with emerald
Glittering on malachite
Clear to the Sun : low battlements enwalled
With gold the ground enthralled,
Sheer to the sight
Of sun and city : thither in his trance
The king's slow steps advance.
There stood he, and with eyes unfolded far
(Clouds shadowing a star
Or moonlight seen through trees—so came
    the lashes
Over—and strong sight flashes !)
Travelled in thought to life, and in its gleam
Saw but a doubtful dream.

His was a city crescent-shaped whose wall
Was brass and iron : in the thrall
Of the superb concave
Lay orbed a waveless wave.
Four moons of liquid light revolved and threw
Their silvery fountains forth, whose fruitful
    dew
Turned all the plain to one enamelled vale
Green as the serpent's glory, and—how still !
—To where the distant hill
Shaped like an Oread's [1] breast arose beyond,
Across the starless pond

    [1] Mountain nymph.

Silent and sleeping—O the waters wan
That seem the soul of man !—
Suddenly darkness strikes the horizon round
With an abyss profound
That blots the half-moon ere the sun be set.
A mountain of pure jet
Rears its sheer bulk to heaven ; and no snows
Tinge evening with rose.
No blaze of noon invades those rocks of night,
Nor moon's benignant might.
And looking downward he beheld his folk
Bound in no tyrant's yoke ;
Knowing no God, nor fearing any man ;
Life's enviable span
Free from disease and vice, sorrow and age.
Only death's joys assuage
A gathering gladness at the thought of sleep.
Never in all the archives, scroll on scroll,
Reaching from aeons wrote they " Women weep,
Men hate, the children suffer." In the place
Where men most walked a tablet of fine brass
Was set on marble, with an iron style
That all might carve within that golden space
If one grief came—and still the people pass,
And since the city first began
None wrote one word thereon till one—a man
Witty in spite of happiness—wrote there :
" I grieve because the tablet is so fair
And still stands bare,
There being none to beautify the same
With the moon-curved Arabian character."
Whereat the king, " Thy grief itself removes
In its own cry its cause." And thence there came
Soft laughter that may hardly stir
The flowers that shake not in the City of Loves.
(For so men called the city's name
Because the people were more mild than doves,
More beautiful than Gods of wood or river ;
And so the city should endure for ever.)

But the king's mood was otherwise this day.
Along time's river, fifty years away,
There was a young man once
Ruddier than autumn suns

With gold hair curling like the spring sun's gold,
And blue eyes where stars lurked for happiness,
And lithe with all a young fawn's loveliness.
Such are the dwellers of the fire that fold
Fine wings in wanton ecstasy, and sleep
Where the thin tongues of glory leap
Up from the brazen hold
And far majestic keep
Of Djinn, the Lord of elemental light.
But he beheld some sight
Beyond that city's joy : his gentle word
The old king gently heard.
(This king was Zôhra's father) " Lord and king
Of love's own city, give me leave to wing
A fervid flight to yonder hills of night.
Not that my soul is weary of the light
And lordship of thy presence ; but in tender dream
I saw myself on the still stream
Where the lake goes toward the mountain wall.
These little lives and loves ephemeral
Seemed in that dream still sweet : yet even now
I turned the shallop's prow
With gathering joy toward the lampless mountains.
I heard the four bright fountains
Gathering joy of music—verily
I cannot understand
How this can be,
Yet—I would travel to that land."
So all they kissed him—and the boy was gone.
But when the full moon shone
A child cried out that he had seen that face
Limned with incomparable grace
Even in the shape of splendour as she passed.
The king's thought turned at last
To that forgotten story : and desire
Filled all his heart with aureate fire
Whose texture was a woman's hair ; so fine
Bloomed the fair flower of pleasure :
Not the wild solar treasure
Of gleaming light, but the moon's shadowy pearl,
The love of a young girl

Before she knows that love : so mused the
    king ;
" I am not weary of the soul of spring,"
He said, " none happier in this causeless
    chain
Of life that bears no fruit of pain,
No seed of sorrow," yet his heart was stirred,
And, wasting no weak word
On the invulnerable air, that had
No soul of memories sad,
He passed through all the palace : in his
    bowers
He stooped and kissed the flowers ;
And in his hall of audience stayed awhile,
And with a glad strange smile
Bade a farewell to all those lords of his ;
And greeted with a kiss
The virgins clustered in his halls of bliss.
Next, passing through the city, gave his hand
To many a joyous band
Flower-decked that wandered through the
    wanton ways
Through summer's idle days.
Last, passing through the city wall, he came
Out to the living flame
Of lambent water and the carven quay,
Stone, like embroidery !
All the dear beauty of art's soul sublime
He looked on the last time,
And trod the figured steps, and found the ledge
At the white water's edge
Where the king's pinnace lodged ; but he
    put by
That shell of ivory,
And chose a pearl-inwoven canoe, whose
    prow
Bore the moon's own bright brow
In grace of silver sculptured ; and therein
He stepped ; and all the water thin
Laughed to receive him ; now the city faded
Little by little into many-shaded
Clusters of colour. So his boat was drawn
Subtly toward the dawn
With little labour ; and the lake dropped
    down
From the orb's utter crown
O'er the horizon ; and the narrowing sides
Showed him the moving tides

And pearling waters of a tinier stream
Than in a maiden's dream
She laves her silken limbs in, and is glad.
Then did indeed the fountains change their
    tune,
Sliding from gold sun-clad
To silver filigree wherethrough the moon
Shines—for the subtle soul
Of music takes on shape, and we compare
The cedar's branching hair,
The comet's glory, and the woman's smile,
To strange devices otherwise not heard
Without the lute's own word.

So on the soul of Zôhra grew
A fashioned orb of fiery dew :
Yet (as cool water on a leaf)
It touched his spirit not with grief,
Although its name was sorrow.
" O for a name to borrow "
(He mused) " some semblance for this subtle
    sense
Of new experience !
For on my heart, untouched, my mind not
    used
To any metre mused,
Save the one tranquil and continuous rhyme
Of joy exceeding time,
Here the joy changes, but abides for ever,
Here on the shining river
Where the dusk gathers, and tall trees begin
To wrap the shallop in,
Sweet shade not cast of sun or moon or
    star,
But of some light afar
Softer and sweeter than all these—what light
Burns past the wondrous night
Of yonder crags ?—what riven chasm hides
In those mysterious sides ?
Somewhere this stream must leap
Down vales divinely steep
Into some vain unprofitable deep ! "

So mused the king. Mark you, the full
    moon shone !
Nay, but a little past the full, she rose
An hour past sunset : as some laughter gone,
After the bride's night, lost in subtler snows

Rosy with wifehood. Now the shallop glides
On gloomier shadier tides,
While the long hair of willows bent and kissed
The stream, and drew its mist
Up through their silent atmosphere.
Some sorrow drawing near
That slow, dark river would for sympathy
Have found its home and never wandered out
Into the sunlight any more. A sigh
Stirred the pale waters where the moonlight
      stood
Upon the sleepy flood
In certain bough-wrought shapes of mystic
      meaning,
As if the moon were weaning
The king her babe from milk of life and love
To milk new-dropped above
From her sweet breast in vaporous light
Into the willowy night
That lay upon the river. So the king
Heard a strange chant—the woods began to
      sing ;
The river took the tune ; the willows kept
Time ; and the black skies wept
Those tears, those blossoms, those pearl drops
      of milk
That the moon shed : and looking up he saw
As if the willows were but robes of silk,
The moon's face stoop and draw
Close to his forehead : at the tears she shed
He knew that he was dead !
Thus he feared not, nor wondered, as the
      stream
Grew darker, as a dream
Fades to the utter deep
Of dreamless sleep.
The stream grew darker, and the willows
      cover
(As lover from a lover
Even for love's sake all the wealth of love)
The whole light of the skies : there came to
      him
Sense of some being dim
Bent over him, one colour and one form
With the dark leaves ; but warm
And capable of some diviner air.
Her limbs were bare, her face supremely
      fair,

Her soul one shapely splendour,
Her voice indeed as tender
As very silence : so he would not speak,
But let his being fade : that all the past
Grew shadowy and weak,
And lost its life at last,
Being mere dream to this that was indeed
Life : and some utter need
Of this one's love grew up in him : he knew
The spirit of that dew
In his own soul ; and this indeed was love.
The faint girl bent above
With fixed eyes close upon him ; oh ! her face
Burned in the rapturous grace
Feeding on his ; and subtly, without touch,
Grew as a flower that opens at the dawn
Their kiss : for touch of lips is death to love.
Even as the gentle plant one finger presses,
However soft the tress is
Of even the air's profane caresses,
It closes, all its joy of light withdrawn ;
The sun feels sadness in his skies above,
Because one flower is folded. Thus they
      floated
Most deathlessly devoted
Beyond the trees, and where the hills divide
To take the nighted tide
Into a darker, deeper, greener breast,
Maybe to find—what rest ?
Now to those girdling mountains moon-exalted
Came through the hills deep-vaulted
That pearly shallop : there the rocks were
      rent,
And the pale element
Flowed idly in their gorges : there the night
Admits no beam of light ;
Nor can the poet's eye
One ray espy.
Therefore I saw not how the voyage ended,
Only wherethrough those cliffs were rended
I saw them pass : and ever closer bent ·
The lady and the lover ; ever slower
Moved the light craft, and lower
Murmured the waters and the wind com- ·
      plained ;
And ever the moon waned ;
Not wheeling round the world,
But subtly curved and curled

In shapes not seen of men, abiding ever
Above the lonely river
Aloft : no more I saw than this,
The shadowy bending to the first sweet kiss
That surely could not end, though earth
    should end.
Therefore my shut eyes blend
With sleep's own secret eyes and eyelashes,
Long and deep ecstasies,
Knowing as now I know—at last—how this
Foreshadows my own bliss
Of falling into death when life is tired.
For of all things desired
Not one as death is so desirable,
Seeing all sorrows pass, all joys endure,
All lessons last. Not heaven and not hell
(My spirit is grown sure)
Await the lover
But death's veil draws, life's mother to dis-
    cover,
Nature ; no longer mother, but a bride !
Ay ! there is none beside.

O brothers mightier than my mightiest word
In the least sob that stirred
Your lyres, bring me, me also to the end !
Be near to me, befriend
Me in the moonlit, moonless deeps of death,
And with exalted breath
Breathe some few flames into the embers dull
Of these poor rhymes and leave them
    beautiful.

"SABBÉ PI DUKKHAM."

(Everything is Sorrow.)

A LESSON FROM EURIPIDES.

Written in Lamma Sayadaw Kyoung, Akyab.

LAUGHTER in the faces of the people
Running round the theatre of music
When the cunning actors play the Bacchae,
Greets the gay attire and gait of Pentheus,
Pentheus by his blasphemy deluded,
Pentheus caught already in the meshes
Of the fate that means to catch and crush him,
Pentheus going forth with dance and revel,
Soon by Bassarids (wild joys of Nature)
To be hunted. Ai ! the body mangled
By the fatal fury of the Maenads
Led by Agave his maddened mother
(Nature's self). But this the people guess not,
Only see the youth in woman's raiment,
Feignèd tresses drooping from his forehead,
Awkward with unwonted dress, rude waving
Aye the light spear tipped with mystic pine-
    cone ;
Hear his boast who lifts the slender thyrsus :
" I could bear the mass of swart Cithaeron,
And themselves the Maenads on my shoul-
    ders."
So the self-willed's folly lights the laughter
Rippling round the theatre. But horror
Seizes on the heart of the judicious.
They see only madness and destruction
In the mockery's self innate, implicit.
Horror, deeper grief, most dreadful musings
Theirs who penetrate the poet's purpose !
So in all the passing joys of nature,
Joys of birth, and joys of life, in pleasures
Beautiful or innocent or stately,
May the wise discern the fact of being—
Change and death, the tragedy deep-lurking
Hidden in the laughter of the people,
So that laughter's self grows gross and hateful.
Then the Noble Truth of Sorrow quickens
Every heart, and, seeking out its causes,
Still the one task of the wise, their wisdom
Finds desire, and, seeking out its medicine,
Finds cessation of desire, and, seeking
How so fierce a feat may be accomplished,
Finds at first in Truth a right foundation,
Builds the walls of Rightful Life upon it,
Four-square, Word and Act and Aspiration
Folded mystically across each other,
Crowns that palace of enduring marble
With sky-piercing pinnacles of Will-power
Rightly carven, rightly pointed ; strengthens
[Mind sole centred on the single object]
All against the lightning, earthquake, thunder,
Meteor, cyclone with strong Meditation.
There, the sacred spot from wind well-
    guarded,
May the lamp, the golden lamp, be lighted

To illume the whole with final Rapture
And destroy the House of pain for ever,
Leave its laughter and its tears, and shatter
All the causes of its mockery, master
All the workings of its will, and vanish
Into peace and light and bliss, whose nature
Baffles so the little tongues of mortals
That we name it not, but from its threshold,
From the golden word upon its gateway,
Style " Cessation "; that whose self we guess
   not.
Thus the wise most mystically interpret
Into wisdom the worst folly spoken
By the mortal of a god deluded.
So, the last wise word rejected, Pentheus
Cries, " ἄγ' ὡς τάχιστα, τοῦ χρόνου δέ
σοι φθονῶ?" — " Why waste we time in
   talking ?
Let us now away unto the mountains ! "
So the wise, enlightened by compassion,
Seeks that bliss for all the world of sorrow,
Swears the bitter oath of Vajrapani :
" Ere the cycle rush to utter darkness
Work I so that every living being
Pass beyond this constant chain of causes.
If I fail, may all my being shatter
Into millions of far-whirling pieces ! "
Swears that oath, and works, and studies
   silence,
Takes his refuge in the triple jewel,
Strangles all desires in their beginning,
Leaves no egg of thought to hatch its serpent
Thrice detested for unnatural breeding—
Basilisk, to slay the maddened gazer.
Thus the wise man, for no glory-guerdon,
Hope of life or joy in earth or heaven,
Works, rejecting all the flowers of promise
Dew-lit that surround his path ; but keepeth
Steady all his will to one endeavour,
Till the light, the might, the joy, the sorrow,
Life and death and love and hate are broken :
Work effaces work, avails the worker.
Strength, speed, ardour, courage and endur-
   ance
(Needed never more) depart for ever.
All dissolves, an unsubstantial phantom,
Ghost of morning seen before the sunrise,
Ghost of daylight seen beyond the sunset.

All hath past beyond the soul's delusion.
All hath changèd to the ever changeless.
Name and form in nameless and in formless
Vanish, vanish and are lost for ever.

DHAMMAPADA.[1]

I.

ANTITHESES.   (THE TWINS.)

ALL that we are from mind results, on mind
   is founded, built of mind.
Who acts or speaks with evil thought, him
   doth pain follow sure and blind : [2]
So the ox plants his foot and so the car-wheel
   follows hard behind.

All that we are from mind results, on mind
   is founded, built of mind.
Who acts or speaks with righteous thought,
   him happiness doth surely find.
So failing not, the shadow falls for ever in
   its place assigned.

" Me he abused and me he beat, he robbed
   me, he defeated me."
In whom such thoughts find harbourage
   hatred will never cease to be.

" Me he abused and me he beat, he robbed
   me, he defeated me."
In whom such thoughts no harbourage may
   find, will hatred cease to be.

" The state of hate doth not abate by hate in
   any clime or time,
But hate will cease if love increase," [3] so
   soothly runs the ancient rhyme.

[1] An attempt to translate this noblest of the
Buddhist books into the original metres.   The
task soon tired.—A. C.
[2] Blind, i.e., operated by law, not by caprice
of a deity.
[3] Crowley has imitated the punning of the
Pali by the repeated rhymes, which further
gives the flavour of the Old English proverbial
saw.

The truth that "here we all must die" those others do not comprehend ;
But some perceiving it, for them all discords find an utter end.

Sodden [1] with passion, unrestrained his senses (such an one we see),
Immoderate in the food of sense, idle and void of energy :
Him surely Mara [2] overcomes, as wind throws down the feeble tree.

Careless of passion, well restrained his senses, such an one we find
Moderate in pleasure, faithful, great in mighty energy of mind :
Him Mara shakes not ; are the hills thrown down by fury of the wind ?

He, void of temperance and truth, from guilt, impurity, and sin
Not free, the poor and golden robe he hath no worth to clothe therein. [3]

Regarding temperance and truth, from guilt, impurity, and sin
Freed, he the poor and golden robe indeed hath worth to clothe therein.

They who see falsehood in the Truth, imagine Truth to lurk in lies,
Never arrive to know the Truth, but follow eager vanities.

To whom in Truth the Truth is known, Falsehood in Falsehood doth appear,
To them the Path of Truth is shown ; right aspirations are their sphere !

[1] Sodden — the habitual — who *lives* unrestrained, etc.
[2] The Indian power of evil.
[3] Alternative reading !—
Who is not free from dirty taint, and temperate and truthful ain't,
He should not wear the garment quaint that marks the Arahat or Saint.—A. C.

An ill-thatched house is open to the mercy of the rain and wind.
So passion hath the power to break into an unreflecting mind.

A well-thatched house is proof against the fury of the rain and wind.
So passion hath no power to break into a rightly-ordered mind.

Here and hereafter doth he mourn, him suffering doth doubly irk,
Who doeth evil, seeing now at last how evil was his work.

The virtuous man rejoices here, hereafter doth he take delight,
Both ways rejoices, both delights, as seeing that his work was right.

Here and hereafter suffers he : the pains of shame his bosom fill
Who thinks "I did the wrong," laments his going on the Path of Ill.

Here and hereafter hath he joy : in both the joy of rectitude
Who thinks "I did the right" and goes rejoicing on the Path of Good.

A-many verses though he can recite of Law, the idle man who doth it not
Is like an herd who numbereth cows of others, Priesthood him allows nor part nor lot.

Who little of the Law can cite, yet knows and walks therein aright, and shuns the snare
Of passion, folly, hate entwined : Right Effort liberates his mind, he doth not care
For this course done or that to run : surely in Priesthood such an one hath earned a share.

II.

EARNESTNESS.

Amata's[1] path is Earnestness, Dispersion
    Death's disciples tread :
The earnest never die, the vain are even as
    already dead.

Who understand, have travelled far on con-
    centration's path, delight
In concentration, have their joy, knowing the
    Noble Ones aright.

In meditation firmly fixed, by constant strenu-
    ous effort high,
They to Nibbana[2] come at last, the incom-
    parable security.

Whose mind is strenuous and reflects ; whose
    deeds are circumspect and pure,
His thoughts aye fixed on Law, the fame of
    that concentred shall endure.

By Earnestness, by centred thought, by self-
    restraint, by suffering long,
Let the wise man an island build against the
    fatal current strong.

Fools follow after vanity, those men of evil
    wisdom's sect ;
But the wise man doth earnestness, a precious
    talisman, protect.

Follow not vanity, nor seek the transient
    pleasures of the sense :
The earnest one who meditates derives the
    highest rapture thence.

When the wise man by Earnestness hath
    Vanity to chaos hurled
He mounts to wisdom's palace, looks serene
    upon the sorrowing world.

[1] Sanskrit, Amrita, the " Elixir of Life "
and food of the gods.
[2] Sanskrit, Nirvana. See Childers' Pali
Dictionary for etymological discussion. The
signification is too difficult a question to settle
offhand in a note.

Mighty is wisdom : as a man climbs high
    upon the hills ice-crowned,
Surveys, aloof, the toiling folk far distant
    on the dusty ground.

Among the sleepers vigilant, among the
    thoughtless eager-eyed
The wise speeds on ; the racer so passes the
    hack with vigorous stride.

By earnestness did Maghava[1] attain of Gods
    to be the Lord.
Praise is one-pointed thought's reward ; Dis-
    persion is a thing abhorred.

The Bhikkhu who in Earnestness delights,
    who fears dispersions dire,
His fetters all, both great and small, burning
    he moves about the fire.

The Bhikkhu who in Earnestness delights,
    Dispersion sees with fear,
He goes not to Destruction ; he unto Nibbana
    draweth near.

III.

THE ARROW.

Just as the fletcher shapes his shaft straightly,
    so shapes his thought the saint,
For that is trembling, weak, impatient of
    direction or restraint.

Mara's dominion to escape if thought im-
    petuously tries
Like to a fish from water snatched thrown on
    the ground it trembling lies.

Where'er it listeth runneth thought, the tame-
    less trembling consciousness.
Well is it to restrain :—a mind so stilled and
    tamed brings happiness.

Hard to perceive, all-wandering, subtle and
    eager do they press,
Thoughts ; let the wise man guard his
    thoughts ; well guarded thoughts bring
    happiness.

[1] Indra, the Indian Zeus.

Moving alone, far-travelling, bodiless, hidden
  i' th' heart, who trains
His thought and binds it by his will shall be
  released from Mara's chains.

Who stills not thought, nor knows true laws;
  in whom distraction is not dumb,
Troubling his peace of mind ; he shall to
  perfect knowledge never come.

His thoughts concentred, unperplexed his
  mind renouncing good and ill
Alike, for him there is no fear if only he
  be watchful still.

Knowing this body to be frail, making this
  thought a fortalice, do thou aright
Mara with wisdom's shaft assail !   Watch
  him when conquered. Never cease thou
  from the fight.

Alas ! ere long a useless log, this body on
  the earth will lie
Contemned of all, and void of sense and
  understanding's unity.

What foe may wreak on foe, or hate work
  on the hated from the hater,
Surely an ill directed mind on us will do
  a mischief greater.

Father and mother, kith and kin, of these
  can none do service kind
So great to us, as to ourselves the good
  direction of the mind.

IV.

FLOWERS.

O who shall overcome this earth, the world
  of God's and Yama's [1] power !
Who find the well taught Path as skill of
  herbist finds the proper flower ?

---

[1] Hades plus Minos; he both rules and
judges the dead, according to Hindu mythology.

The seeker shall subdue this earth, the world
  of God's and Yama's power ;
The seeker find that Path as skill of herbist
  finds the proper flower.

Like unto foam this body whoso sees, its
  mirage-nature comprehends aright,
Breaking dread Mara's flower-pointed shaft
  he goes, Death's monarch shall not meet
  his sight.

Like one who strayeth gathering flowers, is
  he who Pleasure lusteth on ;
As the flood whelms the sleeping village, so
  Death snaps him—he is gone.

Like one who strayeth gathering flowers is
  he whose thoughts to Pleasure cling ;
While yet unsatisfied with lusts, there con-
  quereth him the Iron King.

As the bee gathers nectar, hurts not the
  flower's colour, its sweet smell
In no wise injureth, so let the Sage within
  his hamlet dwell.

To others' failures, others' sins done or good
  deeds undone let swerve
Never the thought ; thine own misdeeds,
  omissions,—these alone observe.

Like to a lovely flower of hue bright, that
  hath yet no odour sweet,
So are his words who speaketh well, fruitless,
  by action incomplete.

Like to a lovely flower of hue delightful and
  of odour sweet
So are his words who speaketh well, fruitful,
  by action made complete.

As from a heap of flowers can men make
  many garlands, so, once born,
A man a-many noble deeds by doing may
  his life adorn.

Travels the scent of flowers against the wind?
Not Sandal, Taggara, nor Jasmine scent!
But the odour of the good doth so, the good
pervadeth unto every element.

When Sandal, Lotus, Taggara and Vassiki
their odour rare
Shed forth, their fragrant excellence is verily
beyond compare.

Yet little is this fragrance found of Taggara
and Sandal wood:
Mounts to the Gods, the highest, the scent of
those whose deeds are right and good.

Perfect in virtue, living lives of Earnestness,
Right Knowledge hath
Brought into liberty their minds, that Mara
findeth not their path.

As on a heap of rubbish thrown by the way-
side the Lotus flower
Will bloom sweet scented, delicate and ex-
cellent to think upon;
So 'mid the slothful worthless ones, the
Walkers in Delusion's power,
In glory of Wisdom, light of Buddh forth
hath the True Disciple shone.

Desunt cetera.[1]

ST. PATRICK'S DAY, 1902.

Written at Delhi.

O GOOD St. Patrick, turn again
Thy mild eyes to the Western main!
Shalt thou be silent? thou forget?
Are there no snakes in Ireland yet?

> *Death to the Saxon! Slay nor spare!*
> *O God of Justice, hear us swear!*

[1] The reader will kindly note such important
changes of metre as occur in the two last verses
of "The Twins" and elsewhere. The careless
might suppose that these do not scan; they do,
following directly or by analogy a similar
change in the Pali.

The iron Saxon's bloody hand
Metes out his murder on the land.
The light of Erin is forlorn.
The country fades: the people mourn.

Of land bereft, of right beguiled,
Starved, tortured, murdered, or exiled;
Of freedom robbed, of faith cajoled,
In secret councils bought and sold!

Their weapons are the cell, the law,
The gallows, and the scourge, to awe
Brave Irish hearts: their hates deny
The right to live—the right to die.

Our weapons—be they fire and cord,
The shell, the rifle, and the sword!
Without a helper or a friend
All means be righteous to the End!

Look not for help to wordy strife!
This battle is for death or life.
Melt mountains with a word—and then
The colder hearts of Englishmen!

Look not to Europe in your need!
Columbia's but a broken reed!
Your own good hearts, your own strong hand
Win back at last the Irish land.

Won by the strength of cold despair
Our chance is near us—slay nor spare!
Open to fate the Saxons lie:—
Up! Ireland! ere the good hour fly!

Stand all our fortunes on one cast!
Arise! the hour is come at last.
One torch may fire the ungodly shrine—
O God! and may that torch be mine!

But, even when victory is assured,
Forget not all ye have endured!
Of native mercy dam the dyke,
And leave the snake no fang to strike!

They slew our women: let us then
At least annihilate their men!
Lest the ill race from faithless graves
Arise again to make us slaves.

Arise, O God, and stand, and smite
For Ireland's wrong, for Ireland's right!
Our Lady, stay the pitying tear!
There is no room for pity here!

What pity knew the Saxon e'er?
Arise, O God, and slay nor spare,
Until full vengeance rightly wrought
Bring all their house of wrong to nought!

Scorn, the catastrophe of crime,
These be their monuments through time!
And Ireland, green once more and fresh,
Draw life from their dissolving flesh!

By Saxon carcases renewed,
Spring up, O Shamrock virgin-hued!
And in the glory of thy leaf
Let all forget the ancient grief!

Now is the hour! The drink is poured!
Wake! fatal and avenging sword!
Brave men of Erin, hand in hand,
Arise and free the lovely land!

Death to the Saxon! Slay nor spare!
O God of Justice, hear us swear!

THE EARL'S QUEST.

Written at Camp Despair, 20,000 ft., Chogo
Ri Lungma, Baltistan.

So now the Earl was well a-weary of
The grievous folly of this wandering.
Had he been able to have counted Love

Or Power, or Knowledge as the sole strong
thing
Fit to suffice his quest, his eyes had gleamed
With the success already grasped. The sting

Of all he suffered, was that he esteemed
His quest partook of all and yet of none.
So as he rode the woodlands out there beamed
VOL. II.

The dull large spectre of a grim flat sun,
Red and obscure upon the leaden haze
That lapped and wrapped and rode the
horizon.

The Earl rode steadily on. A crest caught
rays
Of that abominable sunset, sharp
With needles of young pines, their tips ablaze,

Their feet dead black; the wind's dark
fingers warp
To its own time their strings, a sombre mode
Found by a ghost on a forgotten harp

Or (still more terrible!) the lost dread ode
That used to call the dead knights to their
chief
To the lone waters from the shadowy road.

So deemed the weary Earl of the wind's grief,
And seemed to see about him form by form
Like mighty wrecks, wave-shattered on a reef,

Moulded and mastered by the shapeless storm
A thousand figures of himself the mist
Enlarged, distorted: yet without a qualm

(So sad was he) he mounted the last
twist
Of the path's hate, and faced the wind, and
saw
The lead gleam to a surly amethyst

As the sun dipped, and Night put forth a paw
Like a black panther's, and efface the East.
Then, with a sudden inward catch of awe

As if behind him sprang some silent beast,
So shuddered he, and spurred his horse, and
found
A black path towards the water; he released

The bridle; so the way went steep, ill bound
On an accursed task, so dark it loomed
Amid its yews and cypresses, each mound
D

About each root, a grave, where Hell en-
  tombed
A vampire till the night broke sepulchre
And all its phantoms desperate and doomed

Began to gather flesh, to breathe, to stir.
Such was the path, yet hard should find the
  work
Glamour, to weave her web of gossamer

Over such eyesight as the Earl's for murk.
He had watched for larvæ by the midnight
  roads,
The stake-transpiercèd corpse, the caves
  where lurk

The demon spiders, and the shapeless toads
Fed by their lovers duly on the draught
That bloats and blisters, blackens and cor-
  rodes.

These had he seen of old ; so now he laughed,
Not without bitterness deep-lying, that erst
He had esteemed such foolish devil's craft

Part of his quest, his quest when fair and first
He flung the last, the strongest horseman back
With such a buffet that no skill amerced

Its debt but headlong in his charger's track
He must be hurled, rib-shattered by the shock ;
And the loud populace exclaimed " Alack ! ",

Their favourite foiled.   But oh ! the royal
  stock
Of holy kings from Christ to Charlemagne
Hailed him, anointed him, fair lock by lock,

With oil that drew incalculable gain
From those six olives in the midst whereof
Christ prayed the last time, ere the fatal Wain [1]

Stood in the sky reversed, and utmost Love
Entered the sadness of Gethsemane.
So did the king ; so did the priest above

---

[1] Charles' Wain—Ursa Major. There is a
silly legend to this effect.

Place his old hands upon the Earl's, decree
The splendid and the solemn accolade
That he should go forth to the world and be

Knight-errant ; so did then the fairest maid
Of all that noble company keep hid
The love that melted her ; she took the blade

Blessed by a mage, who slew the harmless kid
With solemn rite and water poured athwart
In stars and sigils,—fire leapt out amid,

And blazed upon the blade ; and stark cold
  swart
Demons came hurtling to enforce the spell,
Until the exorcisms duly wrought

Fixed in the living steel so terrible
A force nor man nor devil might assail,
Nay—might approach the wary warrior well,

So long as he was clothed in silver mail
Of purity, and iron-helmeted
With ignorance of fear : so through the hail

Of flowers, of cries, of looks, of white and red,
Fear, hatred, envy, love—nay, self-conceit
Of girls that preened itself and masqued in-
  stead

Of love—he rode with head deep bowed—
  too sweet,
Too solemn at that moment to respond,
Or even to lift his evening eyes to greet

The one he knew was nearest—too, too fond !
He dared not—not for his sake but for hers.
So he bent down, and passed away beyond

In space, in time. [The myriad ministers
Of God, seeing her soul, prayed God to send
One spirit yet to turn him—subtly stirs

The eternal glory of God's mouth ; " The end
Is not, nor the beginning." Such the speech
Our language fashions down — to compre-
  hend.]

The wood broke suddenly upon the beach,
Curved, flat ; the water oozing on the sand
Stretched waveless out beyond where eye
    might reach,

A grey and shapeless place, a hopeless land !
Yet in that vast, that weary sad expanse
The Earl saw three strange objects on the
    strand

His keen eye noted at the firstborn glance,
And recognised as pointers for his soul ;
So that his soul was fervid in the dance,

Knowing itself one step more near the goal,
Should he but make the perfect choice of
    these.
Farthest, loose tethered, at a stake's control,

A shallop rocked before the sullen breeze.
Midway, a hermit's hut stood solitary,
A dim light set therein.   Near and at ease

A jolly well-lit inn—no phantom airy !
Solid and warm, short snatches of light song
Issuing cheery now and then.   " Be wary ! "

Quoth the wise Earl, " I wander very long
Far from my quest, assuredly to fall
Sideways each step towards the House of
    Wrong,

" Were but one choice demented.   Choice
    is small
Here though.   (A flash of insight in his mind)
Which of these three gets answer to its call ?

" Yon shallop ?—leave to Galahad !   Re-
    signed
Yon hermit be to welcome Lancelot !
For me—the inn—what fate am I to find ?

" Who cares ?   Shall I seek ever—do ye
    wot ?—
But in the outré, the obscure, the occult ?
My Master is of might to lift me what

" Hangs, veil of glamour, on my ' Quisque
    vult,'
The morion's motto : to exhaust the cross,
Bidding it glow with roses—the result

" What way he will : may be adventure's loss
Is gain to common sense ; whereby I guess
Wise men have hidden Mount Biagenos[1]

" And all its height from fools who looked no
    less
For snows to lurk beneath the roots of yew,
Or in the caverns grim with gloominess

" Hid deep i' the forests they would wander
    through,
Instead of travelling the straightforward road.
I call them fools—well, I have been one too.

" Now then at least for the secure abode
And way of luck — knight-errantry once
    doffed,
The ox set kicking at his self-set goad,

" Here's for the hostel and the light aloft !
Roderic, my lad !   there's pelf to pay the score
For ale and cakes and venison and a soft

" Bed we have missed this three months—
    now no more
Of folly !   Avaunt, old Merlin's nonsense
    lore !
Ho there !   Travellers !   Mine host !   Open the
    door ! "

Desunt cetera.

In the second part—a joyous inn fireside
—the Earl refuses power, knowledge, and
love (offered him by a guest) by the symbolic
drink of ale and the cherry cheeks of the
maid.

In part three she, coming secretly to him,
warns him he must destroy the three vices,
faith, hope, and charity.   This he does
easily, save the love of the figure of the
Crucified ; but at last conquering this, he
attains.   [These were never written.]

[1] The mystic mountain of the Rosicrucians.

EVE.

Written in the Mosque of Omar.

HERS was the first sufficient sacrifice
That won us freedom, hers the generous
  gift
That turned herself upon the curse adrift
Sailless and rudderless, to pay the price
Of permanence with pain, of love with vice,
Like a tall ship swan-lovely, swallow-swift,
That makes upon the breakers. So the rift
Sprang and the flame roared.   Farewell,
  Paradise !

How shall a man that is a man reward
Her priceless sacrifice, rebuke the Lord ?
  Why, there's Convention's corral ; ring her
  round !
Here's shame's barbed wire ; push out the
  unclean thing !
Here's freedom's falconry ; quick, clip her
  wing !
There, labour's danger—thrust her under-
  ground !

THE SIBYL.

CROUCHED o'er the tripod the pale priestess
  moans
  Ambiguous destiny, divided fate.
  Sibylline oracles of woe create
Roars as of beasts, majestic monotones
Of wind, strong cries of elemental thrones,
  All sounds of mystery of the Pythian state !
  O woman without change or joy or date
I await thy oracle as the Delphian stone's !

Desunt cetera.

LA COUREUSE.

Written in the Quartier Latin, Paris.

A FADED skirt, a silken petticoat,
  A little jacket, a small shapely shoe,
  A toque.   A symphony in gray and blue,
The child ripples, the conquering master-note

Subtlety. Faint, stray showers of twilight float
  In shadows round the well-poised head ;
  dark, true,
  Joyous the eyes laugh—and are weeping
  too,
For all the victory of her royal throat.

She showed her purse with tantalising grace :
  Some sous, a franc, a key, some stuff, soft
  grey.
The mocking laughter trills upon her tongue :
" There's all my fortune."   " And your
  pretty face !
What do you do ? "   Wearily, " I am gay."
" What do you hope for ? "   Simply, " To
  die young."

SONNET FOR A PICTURE.[1]

" ποικιλοθρον', ἀθανατ' 'Αφροδιτα."
                                    Σαπφω.

   " ——We have seen
  Gold tarnished, and the gray above——"
                                    —SWINBURNE.

As some lone mountebank of the stage may
  tweak
  The noses of his fellows, so Gavin [2]
Tweaks with her brush-work the absurd
  obscene
Academicians.   How her pictures speak !
Chiaroscuro Rembrandtesque, form Greek !
  What values !   What a composition clean !
  Breadth shaming broadness !   Manner
  epicene !
Texture superb !   Magnificent technique !

Raphael, Velasquez, Michael Angelo,
  Stare, gape, and splutter when they see
  thy colour,
  Reds killing roses, greens blaspheming
  grass.
O thou art simply perfect, don't you know ?
  Than thee all masters of old time are duller,
  O artiste of the Quartier Montparnasse !

[1] A parody on his own appreciations of
Rodin's sculpture.
[2] An art student in Paris at this time.

TO " ELIZABETH."

WITH A COPY OF TANNHÄUSER.

Written in the Akasa.[1]

THE story of a fool.   From love and death
Emancipate, he stands above.   The goal
Is in the shrines of misty air : there roll
The voices and the songs of One who saith :
" There is no peace for him who lingereth."
Love is a cinder now that was a coal :
Either were vain.   The great magician's soul
Is far too weak to risk Elizabeth.

All this is past and under me.   Above,
Around, the magian tree of knowledge waves
Its rosy flowers and golden fruit.   I know
Indeed that he is caught therein who craves ;
But I, desiring not, accept the glow
And blossom of that Knowledge that is Love.

RONDELS (AT MONTE CARLO).

Written in the Casino, Monte Carlo.

I.

THERE is no hell but earth : O coil of fate
Binding us surely in the Halls of Birth,
The unsubstantial, the dissolving state !
There is no hell but earth.

Vain are the falsehoods that subserve to mirth.
Dust is to dust, create or uncreate.
The wheel is bounded by the world's great
girth.

By prayer and penance unregenerate,
Redeemed by no man's sacrifice or worth,
We swing : no mortal knows his ultimate.
There is no hell but earth.

II.

In all the skies the planets and the stars
Receive us, where our fate in order plies.
Somewhere we live between the savage bars
In all the skies.

[1] Space or Ether.   The Hindus say that all
actions, especially important (*i.e.* spiritual)
ones, are written therein.   It is an Automatic
Recording Angel.

Let God's highest heaven receive the man
who dies—
All hath an end : he falls : the stains and
scars
Are his throughout unwatched eternities.

The roses and the scented nenuphars
Give hope—oh ! monolith ! oh house of
lies !
We change and change and fade, strange
avatars
In all the skies.

III.

One way sets free.   That way is not to tread
Through fire or earth or spirit, air or sea.
That secret is not gathered of the dead.
One way sets free.

Not to desire shall lead to *not to be.*
There is no hope within, none overhead,
None by the chance of fate's august decree.

It is a path where tears are ever shed.
There is no joy—is that a path for me ?
Yea ! though I track the ways of utmost dread,
One way sets free.

IN THE GREAT PYRAMID OF GHIZEH.[1]

I SAW in a trance or a vision the web of the
ages unfurled, flung wide with a scream of
derision, a mockery mute of the world.   As
it spread over sky I mapped it fair on a
sheet of blue air with a hurricane pen.   I
copy it here for men.   First on the ghostly
adytum of pale mist that was the abyss of
time and space (the stars all blotted out,
poor faded nenuphars on the storm-sea of
the infinite :) I wist a shapeless figure arise
and cover all, its cloak an ancient pall,
vaster and older than the skies of night,
and blacker than all broken years—aye !
but it grew and held me in its grasp so that

[1] If this poem be repeatedly read through,
it falls into a subtly rhymed and metrical form.

I felt its flesh, not clean sweet flesh of man but leprous white, and crawling with innumerable tears like worms, and pains like a sword-severed asp, twitching, and loathlier than all mesh of hates and lusts, defiling; nor any voice it had, nor any motion, it was infinite in its own world of horror, irredeemably bad as everywhere sunlit, being this world, forget not ! being this world, this universe, the sum of all existence ; so that opposing fierce resistance to the all-law, stood loves and joys, delicate girls, and beautiful strong boys, and bearded men like gods, and golden things, and bright desires with wings, all beauties, and all truths of life poets have ever prized. So showed the microscope, this agèd strife between all forms; but seen afar, seen well drawn in a focus, synthesised, the whole was sorrow and despair ; agony biting through the fair ; meanness, contemptibility, enthroned ; all purposeless, all unatoned ; all putrid of an hope, all vacant of a soul. I called upon its master, as who should call on God. Instead, arose a shining form, sweet as a whisper of soft air kissing the brows of a great storm ; his face with light was molten, musical with waves of his delight moving across : his countenance utterly fair ! then was my philosophic vision shamed: conjecture at a loss ; and my whole mind revolted ; then I blamed the vision as a lie ; yet bid that vision speak how he was named, being so wonderfully desirable. Whereat he smiled upon me merrily, answering that whoso named him well, being a poet, called him Love ; or else being a lover of wisdom, called him Force ; or being a cynic, called him Lust ; or being a pietist, called him God. The last—thou seest !—(he said), a lie of Hell's, and all a partial course of the great circle of whirling dust (stirred by the iron rod of thought) that men call wisdom. So I looked deep in his beauty, and beheld its truth. The life of that fair youth was as a whiz of violent little whirls, helical coils of emptiness, grey curls of misty and impalpable stuff, torn, crooked, all ways

and none at once, but ever pressed in idiot circles ; and one thing he lacked, now I looked from afar again, was rest. Thence I withdrew my sight, the eyeballs cracked with strain of my endeavour, and my will struck up with subtler skill than any man's that in fair Crete tracked through the labyrinth of Minos, and awoke the cry to call his master ; grew a monster whirlwind of revolving smoke and then, mere nothing. But in me arose a peace profounder than Himalayan snows cooped in their crystalline ravines. I saw the ultimation of the one wise law. I stood in the King's Chamber, by the tomb of slain Osiris, in the Pyramid and looked down the Great Gallery, deep, deep into the hollow of earth ; grand gloom burned royally therein ; I was well hid in the shadow ; here I realised myself to be in that sepulchral sleep wherein were mirrored all these things of mystery. So the long passage steeply sliding ever up to my feet where I stood in the emptiness ; at last a sure abiding only in absolute ceasing of all sense, and all perceived or understood or knowable ; thus, purple and intense, I beheld the past that leads to peace, from royal heights of mastery to sleep, from self-control imperial to an end, therefore I shaped the seven tiers of the ascending corridor into seven strokes of wisdom, seven harvests fair to reap from seven bitter sowings.[1] Here ascend the armies of life's universal war chasing the pious pilgrim. First, his sight grew adamant, sun-bright, so that he saw aright. Second, his heart was noble, that he would live ever unto good. Third, in his speech stood tokens of this will, so pitiful and pure he spake, nor. ever from him brake woe-winged words, nor slaver of the snake. Fourth, in each noble act of life he taught crystalline vigour of thought, so in each deed he was aright ; well-wrought all the man's work ; and fifth, this hero strife grew one with his whole life, so harmonised to the one after-end his every

[1] Compare the Noble Eightfold Path, as described in "Science and Buddhism," *infra*.

conscious and unconscious strain, his peace and pleasure and pain, his reflex life, his deepest-seated deed of mere brute muscle and nerve! Thence, by great Will new-freed, the ardent life leaps, sixth, to Effort's tower, invoking the occult, the secret power, found in the void when all but Will is lost; so, seventh, he bends it from its bodily station into the great abyss of Meditation, whence the firm level is at last his own and Rapture's royal throne is more than throne, sarcophagus! an end! an end! Resounds the echo in the stone, incalculable myriads of tons poised in gigantic balance overhead, about, beneath. O blend your voices, angels of the awful earth! dogs! demons leaping into hideous birth from the imprisoned deserts of the Nile! And thou, O habitant most dread, disastrous crocodile, hear thou the Law, and live, and win to peace!

THE HILLS.

TO OSCAR ECKENSTEIN.

WHENCE the black lands shudder and darken,
  Whence the sea birds have empire to range,
Whence the moon and the meteor hearken
  The perpetual rhythm of change,
On earth and in heaven deluded
  With time, that the soul of us kills,
·I have passed. I have brooded, fled far to the wooded
  And desolate hills.

Not there is the changing of voices
  That lament or regret or are sad,
But the sun in his strength rejoices,
  The moon in her beauty is glad.
As timeless and deathless time passes,
  And death is a hermit that dwells
By the imminent masses of ice, where the grasses
  Abandon the fells.

There silence, arrayed as a spectre,
  Is visible, tangible, near,
To the cup of the man pours nectar,
  To the heart of the coward is fear:
Though the desolate waste be enchaunted
  By a spell that bewilders and chills,
To me it is granted to worship the haunted
  Delight of the hills.

To me all the blossoms are seedless,
  Yet big with all manner of fruit:
And a voice in the waste is needless
  Since my soul in its splendour is mute.
Though the height of the hill be deserted,
  The soul of a man has its mate;
With the wide sky skirted his heart is reverted
  To commune with Fate.

Far flings out the spur to the sunset;
  Its help to the hope of the sun
That all be unfolded if one set,
  That none be apart from the One;
And the sweep of the wings of the weather,
  Marked bright with the silvery ghylls
For flickering feather, brings all things together
  To nest in the hills.

Like a great bird poised in the æther,
  The mountain keeps watch over earth,
On the child that lies sleeping beneath her
  Wild-eyed from a terrible birth.
But by noise of the world unshaken,
  By dance of the world not bedinned,
The hill bides forsaken, yet only to waken
  Her lover, the wind.

Like a lion asleep in his fastness,
  Or a warrior leant on his spear,
The hill stands up in the vastness,
  And the stars grow strangely near;
For the secret of life and its gladness
  Are hidden in strength that distils
A potion of madness from berries of sadness
  Grown wild in the hills.

Though the earth be disparted and rended,
  Thus only the great peaks change
That their image is moulded and blended
  Into all that a fancy may range ;
And the silence my song could refigure
  To the note of a bird did I will,
Of glory or rigour, of passion or vigour—
  The change were to ill !

For silence is better than singing
  Though a Shelley wove songs in the sky,
And hovering is sweeter than winging ;
  To live is less good than to die.
The secret of secrets is hidden
  Not in lives nor in loves, but in wills
That are free and unchidden, that wander
    unbidden
  To home in the hills.

A strength that is more than the summer
  Is firm in that silence and rest,
Though stiller the rocks be and dumber
  That the soul of its slumber oppressed.
For stronger control is than urging,
  And mightier the heart of the sea
Than her waves deep-merging and striving
    and surging
  That deem they are free.

In spirit I stand on the mountain,
  My soul into God's withdrawn,
And look to the East like a fountain
  That shoots up the spray of the dawn.
And the life of the mountain swims through
    me
  (So the song of a thrush in me thrills)
And the dawn speaks to me, of old for it
    knew me
  The soul of the hills.

I stand on the mountain in wonder
  As the splendour springs up in the East,
As the cloud banks are rended asunder,
  And the wings of the Night are released.
As in travail a maiden demented,
  Afraid of the deed she hath done,
By no man lamented, springs up the sweet-
    scented
  Pale flower of the sun.

So change not the heights and the hollows ;
  The hollows are one with the heights
In that pallid grave dawn of Apollo's
  Confusion of shadows and lights.
Unreal save to sense that can sense her
  That maiden of sunrise refills
The air's grey censer with perfumes intenser
  The higher the hills.

So, vague as a ghost swift faded,
  Steals dawn, and so sunset may see
How her long long locks deep-braided
  Fall down to her breast and her knee.
So night and so sunrise discover
  No light and no darkness to heed.
Night is above her, and brings her no lover ;
  And day, but no deed.

Such a sense is up and within me,
  A tongue as of mystical fire !
Love, beauty, and holiness win me
  To the end of the great desire,
Where I cease from the thirst and the labour,
  As the land that no ploughman tills
Lest the robber his neighbour unloosen the
    sabre
  From holds in the hills.

From love of my life and its burden
  Set free in the silence remote,
Grows a sorrow divine for my guerdon,
  A peace in my struggling note.
Compassion for earth far extended
  Beneath me, the swords and the rods,
My Spirit hath bended, bowed me and
    blended
  My self into God's.

But God—what divinity rises
  To me in the mountainous place ?
What sun beyond suns, and surprises
  Mine eyes at the dawn of His face ?
No God in this silence existing,
  No heaven and no earth of Him skills,
Save the blizzards unresting, whirling and
    twisting
  Adrift on the hills.

So witless and aimless and formless
  I count the Creator to be ;
Not strong as who rides on the stormless
  And tames the untamable sea.
But motion and action distorted
  Are marks of the paths He hath trod.
Hated or courted, aided or thwarted :—
  Lo, He is your God !

But mine in the silence abideth ;
  Her strength is the strength of rest ;
Not on thunders or clouds She rideth
  But draweth me down to Her breast :
No maker of men, but dissolving
  Their life from its burden of ills,
Ever resolving the circle revolving
  To peace of the hills.

And dark is Her breast and unlighted ;
  But a warm sweet scent is expressed,
And a rose as of sunset excited
  In the strength of Her sunless breast.
Her love is like pain, but enchanted :
  Her kiss is an opiate breath
Amorously panted : Her fervours last granted
  Are sorrow, and death.

Nor death as ye name in derision
  The change to a cycle of pain,
To a cycle of joy as a vision
  Ye chase, and may capture in vain.
Endeth you peace, and your change is
  Like the change in a measure that shrills
And slackens and ranges ; your passion
    estranges
  The love of the hills !

Nay ! death is a portal of passing
  To miseries other but sure.
Yet the snow on the hills amassing
  The wind of an hour may endure ;
But as day after day grows the summer
  The crystals melt one after one.
The hill—shall they numb her ? Their frost
    overcome her ?
  Demand of the sun !

That uttermost death of my lady
  Revealed in the heart of the range
Is as light in the groves long shady
  As peace in the halls of change.
The web of the world is rended ;
  Stayed are the causal mills ;
Time is ended ; space unextended.
  An end of the hills !

ALICE: AN ADULTERY

1903

INTRODUCTION[1] BY THE EDITOR.

YOKOHAMA, *April*, 1901.

IT has often been pointed out how strange are the prophecies made from time to time by writers of what purports to be merely fiction.

Of all the remarkable tales with which Mr. R. Kipling has delighted the world, none is more striking than that of McIntosh Jellaludin[2] and his mysterious manuscript. And now, only a few years after reading that incredible tale, I myself, at Yokohama, come across a series of circumstances wonderfully analogous. But I will truthfully set down this history just as it all happened.

I went one memorable Wednesday night to No. 29.[3] For my advent in this most reputable quarter of the city, which is, after all, Yama,[4] and equally handy for the consul, the chaplain, and the doctor, readers of Rossetti will expect no excuse; for their sakes I may frankly admit that I was actuated by other motives than interest and solicitude for my companion, a youth still blindly groping for Romance beneath the skirts of tawdry and painted Vice. Perhaps I may have hoped to save him from what men call the graver and angels the lesser consequences of his folly. This for the others.

As to the character of the mansion at

which we arrived, after a journey no less dubious than winding, I will say that, despite its outward seeming, it was, in reality, a most respectable place; the main occupation of its inhabitants seemed to be the sale of as much "champagne" as possible; in which inspiring preface my friend was soon deeply immersed. . . .

Golden-haired, a profound linguist, swearing in five Western and three Oriental languages, and comparable rather to the accomplished courtesans of old-time Athens than to the Imperial Peripatetics of the *Daily Telegraph* and Mr. Raven-Hill,[1] her looks of fire turned my friend's silky and insipid moustache into a veritable Burning Bush. But puppy endearments are of little interest to one who has just done his duty by No. 9[2] in distant Yoshiwara; so turned to the conversation of our dirty old Irish hostess, who, being drunk, grew more so, and exceedingly entertaining.

Of the central forces which sway mankind, her knowledge was more comprehensive than conventional. For thirty years she had earned her bread in the capacity of a Japanese Mrs. Warren;[3] but having played with fire in many lands, the knowledge she had of her own subject, based on indefatigable personal research, was as accurate in detail as it was cosmopolitan in character. Yet she had not lost her ideals; she was a devout Catholic, and her opinion of the human understanding, despite her virginal innocence of Greek, was identical with that of Mr. Locke.[4]

On occasions I am as sensitive to inexplic-

---

[1] This and the "Critical Essay" (now omitted) were the result of collaboration. Some omissions, &c., in the text of the First Edition were intended to aid the illusion of this introduction.

[2] A dissipated but gifted European who became unified with the Indian native, and wrote a book about him.

[3] Disinclination to marry is congenital in the elect: the Pauline alternative is discountenanced by my doctor.—ED.

[4] The Bluff, or European quarter.

[1] A talented artist, who published a book of amusing sketches of the loose women who promenaded the "Empire" Music Hall.

[2] Called "Nectarine," a famous brothel.

[3] A bawd. From Shaw's play, "Mrs. Warren's Profession."

[4] The philosopher.

able interruption as Mr. Shandy,[1] and from behind the hideous yellow partition came sounds as of the constant babbling of a human voice. Repeated glances in this direction drew from my entertainer the information that it was "only her husband," indicating the yellow-haired girl with the stem of her short clay pipe. She added that he was dying.

Curiosity, Compassion's Siamese twin, prompted a desire to see the sufferer.

The old lady rose, not without difficulty, lifted the curtain, and let it fall behind me as I entered the gloom which lay beyond. On a bed, in that half-fathomed twilight, big with the scent of joss-sticks smouldering in a saucer before a little bronze Buddha-rupa,[2] lay a man, still young, the traces of rare beauty in his face, though worn with suffering and horrid with a week's growth of beard.

He was murmuring over to himself some words which I could not catch, but my entrance, though he did not notice me, seemed to rouse him a little.

I distinctly heard—

" These are the spells by which to re-assume
An empire o'er the disentangled doom."

He paused, sighing, then continued—

" To suffer woes which hope thinks infinite;
To forgive wrongs darker than death or night ;
To defy power which seems omnipotent ;
To love, and bear ; to hope till hope creates
From its own wreck the thing it contem-plates ;
Neither to change, nor falter, nor repent :
This, like thy glory, Titan, is to be
Good, great, and joyous, beautiful, and free :
This is alone Life, Joy, Empire, and Vic-tory." [3]

The last phrase pealed trumpet-wise : he sank back into thought. "Yes," he said slowly, "neither to change, nor falter, nor repent." I moved forward, and he saw me. "Who are you?" he asked.

"I am travelling in the East," I said. "I love Man also ; I have come to see you. Who are you?"

[1] See "Tristam Shandy," by Laurence Sterne, Chap. I.
[2] Image of Buddha.
[3] Shelley, "Prometheus Unbound," iv.

He laughed pleasantly. "I am the child of many prayers."

There was a pause.

I stood still, thinking.

Here was surely the very strangest outcast of Society. What uncouth bypaths of human experience, across what mapless tracks beyond the social pale, must have led hither—hither to death in this Anglo-Saxon-blasted corner of Japan, here, at the very outpost of the East. He spoke my thought.

" Here I lie," he said, " east of all things. All my life I have been travelling eastward, and now there is now no further east to go."

" There is America," I said. I had to say something.

" Where the disappearance of man has followed that of manners : the exit of God has not wished to lag behind that of grammar. I have no use for American men, and only one use for American women."

" Of a truth," I said, "the continent is accursed—a very limbo."

" It is the counterfoil of evolution," said the man wearily. There was silence.

" What can I do for you ?" I asked. " Are you indeed ill ?"

" Four days more," he answered, thrilling with excitement, " and all my dreams will come true—until I wake. But you can serve me, if indeed— Did you hear me spouting poetry ?"

I nodded, and lit my pipe. He watched me narrowly while the match illuminated my face.

" What poetry ?"

I told him Shelley.

" Do you read Ibsen ?" he queried, keen-ing visibly. After a moment's pause : " He is the Sophocles of manners," I said, re-warded royally for months of weary waiting. My strange companion sat up transfigured. " The Hour," he murmured, " and the Man ! . . . What of Tennyson ?"

" Which Tennyson ?" I asked.

The answer seemed to please him.

" In Memoriam ?" he replied.

" He is a neurasthenic counter-jumper."

" And of the Idylls ?"

" Sir Thomas[1] did no wrong ; can im-potence excuse his posthumous emascula-tion ?" [2]

[1] Sir T. Malory : author of the true " Morte d' Arthur."
[2] See A. C. Swinburne, " Under the Micro-scope."

He sank back contented. "I have prayed to my God for many days," he said, "and by one of the least of my life's miracles you are here; worthy to receive my trust. For when I knew that I was to die, I destroyed all the papers which held the story of my life—all save one. That I saved; the only noble passage, perhaps—among the many notable. Men will say that it is stained; you, I think, should be wiser. It is the story of how the Israelites crossed the Red Sea. They were not drowned, you know (he seemed to lapse into a day-dream), and they came out on the Land of Promise side. But they had to descend therein."

"They all died in the wilderness," I said, feeling as if I understood this mystical talk, which, indeed, I did not. But I felt inspired.

"Ay me, they died—as I am dying now."

He turned to the wall and sought a bundle of old writing on a shelf. "Take this," he said. "Edit it as if it were your own: let the world know how wonderful it was." I took the manuscript from the frail, white hand.

He seemed to forget me altogether.

"Namo tassa Bhagavato arahato sammasambuddhasa,"[1] he murmured, turning to his little black Buddha-rupa.

There was a calm like unto—might I say, an afterwards?

"There is an end of joy and sorrow,
Peace all day long, all night, all morrow,"

he began drowsily.

A shrill voice rose in a great curse. The hoarse anger of drunken harlotry snarled back. "Not a drop more," shouted my friend, adding many things. It was time for my return.

"I will let them know," I whispered. "Good-bye."

"'There is not one thing with another;
But Evil saith to Good: "My brother—"'"[2]

he went on unheeding.

I left him to his peace.

My re-appearance restored harmony. The

fulvous and fulgurous lady grew comparatively tranquil; the pair withdrew. The old woman lay sprawled along the divan sunk in a drunken torpor.

I unrolled the manuscript and read.

Brutal truth-telling humour, at times perhaps too Rabelaisian; lyrics, some of enchanting beauty, others painfully imitative; sonnets of exceedingly unequal power, a perfectly heartless introduction (some fools would call it pathetic),[1] and, as a synthesis of the whole, an impression of profound sadness and, perhaps, still deeper joy, were my reward. Together with a feeling that the writer must have been a philosopher of the widest and deepest learning and penetration, and a regret that he showed no more of it in his poetry. First and last, I stood amazed, stupefied: so stand I still.

Dramatic propriety forbade me seeing him again; he was alone when he started.

Let us not too bitterly lament! He would hate him who would "upon the rack of this tough world stretch him out longer."

To the best of my poor ability I have executed his wishes, omitting, however, his name and all references sufficiently precise to give pain to any person still living.[2] His handwriting was abominably difficult, some words quite indecipherable. I have spent long and laborious hours in conjecture, and have, I hope, restored his meaning in almost every case. But in the Sonnets of the 12th, 18th, 23rd, 24th, 29th, 35th, 41st, 43rd, and 48th days, also in "At Last," "Love and Fear," and "Lethe," one or more whole lines have been almost impossible to read. The literary student will be able readily to detect my patchwork emendations. These I have dared to make because his whole pattern (may I use the word?) is so elaborate and perfect that I fear to annoy the reader by leaving any blanks, feeling that my own poverty of diction will be less noticeable than any actual hiatus in the sense or rhythm. I attempt neither eulogy nor criticism here. Indeed, it seems to me entirely uncalled for. His words were: "Let the world know how wonderful it was," that is, his love and hers; not "how wonderful it is," that is, his poem.

The poem is simple, understandable, direct, not verbose. More I demand not,

---

[1] "Glory to the Blessed One, the Perfected One, the Enlightened One." It is the common Buddhist salute to their Master.

[2] These quotations are from Swinburne's "Ilicet."

---

[1] The MS. has been lost.—ED.

[2] The *essential* facts are, of course, imaginary.

seeing it is written (almost literally so) in blood; for I am sure that he was dying of that love for Alice, whose marvellous beauty it was his mission (who may doubt it?) to reveal. For the burning torch of truth may smoke, but it is our one sure light in passion and distress. *The jewelled silence of the stars* is, indeed, the light of a serener art; but love is human, and I give nothing for the tawdry gems of style when the breast they would adorn is that of a breathing, living beauty of man's love, the heart of all the world. Nor let us taint one sympathy with even a shadow of regret. Let us leave him where

" Sight nor sound shall war against him more,
 For whom all winds are quiet as the sun,
 All waters as the shore."[1]

NOTE.—The sudden and tragic death of the Editor has necessitated the completion of his task by another hand. The introduction was, however, in practically its present form.

WHAT LAY BEFORE.

WHITE POPPY.

AMID the drowsy dream,
Lit by some fitful beam
    Of other light
Than the mere sun, supreme
On all the glint and gleam
    Shooting through night,
Above the water-way
Where my poor corpse must stay,
I bend and float away
    From human sight.

Unto the floral face,
Carven in ancient grace
    Of Gods or Greeks,
The whole sky's way gives place :
Open the walls of space,
    And silence speaks.

[1] Swinburne, " Ave atque Vale."

See ! I am floating far
Beyond space and sun and star,
As drifts a nenuphar
    Down lilied creeks.

Beyond the heavens I see
The pale embroidery
    Of some wan child
Wasted by earth and sea,
Whose kisses were too free,
    Too swift and wild ;
A Maenad's floating tress
Lost in the wilderness
Of death's or my caress,
    Discrowned, defiled.

Clad in pale green and rose,
Her thin face flickers, glows,
    Tempestuous flame.
Horrid and harsh she goes,
Speaks, trembles, wakes and knows
    How frail is shame !
Grows vast and cloudy and is
The whole mouth's sobbing kiss,
And crushes me with bliss
    Beyond a name.

Then fall I from excess
Of bitter ecstasies,
    Pale ghosts of blood,
To worlds where palaces
Shine through dim memories
    Of flower and flood,
Shine in pale opal and pearl,
Void of bright boy or girl,
Desolate halls that furl
    Their shapes subdued.

And wide they sunder, wide
They fall into the tide
    Of fallen things.
Me, me, O meek-browed bride,
Horrible faces hide
    And devilish wings.

Me the grim harpies hold
In kisses slaver-cold,
Mute serpent-shapes of gold
    With serpent stings.

The dreadful bridal won,
The demon banquet done,
    My flesh let loose :—
Rises a strange red sun,
A sight to slay or stun ;
    Sepulchral dews
Fall from the rayless globe,
Whose sightless fingers probe
My golden-folded robe,
    My soul's misuse.

And in that thankless shape
Vines grow without a grape,
    Thorns roseless spring.
Nay ! There is no escape :—
The yawning portals gape,
    The orbèd ring
As by a whirlpool drawn
Into that devil-dawn :—
I sink and shriek and fawn
    Upon the thing.

Ha ! in the desperate pang
And subtle stroke and fang
    Of hateful kisses
Whence devilish laughter sprang,
Close on me with a clang
    The brazen abysses.
The leopard-coloured paw
Strikes, and the cruel jaw
Hides me in the glutless maw—
    Crown of ten blisses !

For all the vision world
Is closed on me and curled
    Into the deep
Of my slow soul, and hurled
Through lampless lands, and furled,
    Sharp folds and steep :
Till all unite in one,
Seven planets in the sun,
And I am deeplier done
    Into full sleep.

MESSALINE.

BENEATH the living cross I lie
And swoon towards eternity :
Prodigious sinewy shapes, and lean
And curving limbs of Messaline.
    The deep arched eyes, the floating mane,—
One pierces, one wraps-in my brain.
A crown of thorn, a spear of clean
Cold fire of dying Messaline.
    Swart tangles of devouring hair,
The scorpion labyrinth and snare,
Leprous entanglements of sense,
The Imminence of the Immense.
And in the deep hard breath I draw
Kissed from her strangling mouth and maw,
I feel the floating deaths that dwell
About that citadel of hell ;
A soft lewd flavour, an obscene
Mysterious self of Messaline.
    Or, in the kisses that swoop low
To catch my breath and kill me so,
I feel the ghostliness of this
Unreal shuttle-game—the kiss !
Her moving body sobs above,
And calls its lechery true love.
Out from the flame of heart she plucks
One flower of fiery light, and sucks
Its essence up within her lips,
And flings it into mine, and dips
And bends her body, writhes and swims
To link the velvet of our limbs,
My drouthy passion worn and keen,
And lusty life of Messaline.
    The heart's blood in her boiling over
She sucked from many a dying lover :
The purple of her racing veins
Leapt from some soul's despairing pains ;
She drinks up life as from a cup ;
She drains our health and builds it up
Into her body ; takes our breath,
And we—we dream not it is death !
Arm unto arm and eye to eye,
Breast to great breast and thigh to thigh,
We look, and strain, and laugh, and die.
I see the head hovering above
To swoop for cruelty or love ;

I feel the swollen veins below
The knotted throat ; the ebb and flow
Of blood, not milk, in breasts of fire ;
Of deaths, not fluctuants, of desire ;
Of molten lava that abides
Deep in the vast volcanic sides ;
Deep scars where kisses once bit in
Below young mountains that be twin,
Stigmata cruciform of sin,
The diary of Messaline.
　The moving mountains crater-crowned ;
The valleys deep and silver-bound ;
The girdle treacherously wound ;
One violet-crested mounded mole,
Some blood-stain filtered from the soul ;
The light and shadow shed between
My soul and God from Messaline.
　And even as a dark and hidden
Furnace roars out in woods forbidden,
A sullen tide of molten steel
Runs from deep furrows in the wheel ;
So from afar one central heat
Sends the loud pulse to fever beat ;
So from one crown and heart of fire
Spring the vast phantoms of desire,
Impossible and epicene,
Familiar souls of Messaline.
　And as, when thunder broods afar
Imperial destinies of war,
Men see the haze and heat, and feel
The sun's rays like a shaft of steel,
Seeing no sun ; even so the night
Clouds that deep miracle from sight :
Until this destiny be done
Hangs the corona on the sun ;
And I absorbed in those unclean
Ghost-haunted veins of Messaline.

CALIFORNIA.

FORGED by God's fingers in His furnace,
　　Fate,
My destiny drew near the glowing shore
Where California hides her golden ore,
Her rubies and her beryls ; gross and great,

Her varied fruits and flowers alike create
Glories most unimaginable, more
Than Heaven's own meadows match ; yet
　　this is sore,
A stain ; not one of these is delicate.

Save only the clear green within the sea—
　Because that rolls all landless from Japan.
I did not know until I missed it here
How beautiful that beauty is to me,
　That life that bears Death's sigil [1] traced
　　too clear,
Blue lines within the beauty that is man.

MARGARET.

THE moon spans Heaven's architrave ;
　Stars in the deep are set ;
Written in gold on the day's grave,
　" To love, and to forget ; "
And sea-winds whisper o'er the wave
　The name of Margaret.

A heart of gold, a flower of white,
　A blushing flame of snow,
She moves like latticed moons of light—
　And O ! her voice is low,
Shell-murmurs borne to Amphitrite,
　Exulting as they go.

Her stature waves, as if a flower
　Forgot the evening breeze,
But heard the charioted hour
　Sweep from the farther seas,
And kept sweet time within her bower,
　And hushed mild melodies.

So grave and delicate and tall—
　Shall laughter never sweep
Like a moss-guarded waterfall
　Across her ivory sleep ?
A tender laugh most musical ?
　A sigh serenely deep ?

[1] Signature, usually applied to the supposed
signatures of divine beings.

She laughs in wordless swift desire
A soft Thalassian tune ;
Her eyelids glimmer with the fire
That animates the moon ;
Her chaste lips flame, as flames aspire
Of poppies in mid-June.

She lifts the eyelids amethyst,
And looks from half-shut eyes,
Gleaming with miracles of mist,
Gray shadows on blue skies ;
And on her whole face sunrise-kissed,
Child-wonderment most wise.

The whitest arms in all the earth
Blush from the lilac bed.
Like a young star even at its birth
Shines out the golden head.
Sad violets are the maiden girth,
Pale flames night-canopied.

O gentlest lady ! Lift those eyes,
And curl those lips to kiss !
Melt my young boyhood in thy sighs,
A subtler Salmacis !
Hide, in that peace, these ecstasies ;
In that fair fountain, this !

She fades as starlight on the stream,
As dewfall in the dell ;
All life and love, one ravishing gleam
Stolen from sleep's crucible ;
That kiss, that vision is a dream :—
And I—most miserable !

Still Echo wails upon the steep,
" To love—and to forget ! "
Still sombre whispers from the deep
Sob through Night's golden net,
And waft upon the wings of sleep
The name of Margaret.

ALICE: AN ADULTERY.

" Commit not with man's sworn spouse."
                King Lear.

\GAINST the fiat of that God discrowned,
Unseated by Man's justice, and replaced,
By Law most bountiful and maiden-faced
And mother-minded : passing the low
bound

Of man's poor law we leapt at last and
found
Passion ; and passing the dim halls dis-
graced
Found higher love and larger and more
chaste,
A calm sphinx waiting in secluded ground.

Hear the sad rhyme of how love turned to
lust,
And lust invigorated love, and love
Shone brighter for the stain it rose above,
Gathering roses from the quickening dust ;
And faith despoiled and desecrated trust
Wore pearlier plumes of a diviner dove.

THE FIRST DAY.

" Who ever loved that loved not at first sight ? "
              As You Like It.

THE waving surf shone from the Peaceful
Sea.[1]
Young palms embowered the house
where Beauty sate
Still but exultant, silent but elate
In its own happiness and majesty
Of a mild soul unstirred by rivalry
Of any life beyond its own sweet state.
I looked around me, wondered whether
Fate
Had found at last a woman's love for me.

I had no hope : she was so grave and
calm,
So shining with the dew-light of her
soul,
So beautiful beyond a woman's share.
Yet—here ! Soft airs, and perfume through
the palm,
And moonlight in the groves of spice,
control
The life that would not love and yet be
fair.

---

[1] *I.e.* the Pacific.

THE SECOND DAY.

" Keep you in the rear of your affection
Out of the shot and danger of desire."
Hamlet.

I WAS so hopeless that I turned away
And gave my love to foul oblivion, .
Shuttered my bosom's window from the
sun,
Kindled a corpse-light and proclaimed
" The day ! " ;
Lurked in Aeaean [1] fens to elude the ray
Whose beauty might disturb me : I did
shun .
The onyx eyes that saw me not as one
Possible even for a moment's play.

Thus I was tangled in some house of hell,
Giving mine own soul's beauty up to lust,
Hoping to build some fort impregnable
Against my love : instead the deep disgust
Of my own beasthood crushed it into
dust,
And left my manhood twisted in her
. spell.

THE THIRD DAY.

" My love is most immaculate white and red. "
Love's Labour's Lost.

SHE was more graceful than the royal palm ;
Tall, with imperial looks, and excellence
Most simply swathed in spotless ele-
gance,
And holy and tuneful like some stately
psalm.
Her breath was like a grove of myrrh and
balm,
And all the sight grew dim before the
sense
Of blind attraction toward ; an influence
Not incompatible with her own calm.

[1].Circe, who dwelt on the island of Aeaea,
transformed men into swine.

All the red roses of the world were blended
To give the lively colour of her face ;
All the white lilies of the sea shone
splendid
Where the blue veins afforded them a space ;
Like to the shapely fragrance of dawn's
shrine
She gleamed through mist, enchanting,
Erycine.[1]

THE FOURTH DAY.

"Amen, if you love her ; for the lady is very
well worthy."
Much Ado about Nothing.

I TOOK another way to shield my love.
I turned my thoughts to the abyss of sky,
Pierced the frail veil, and sought Eter-
nity ;
Where the Gods reign most passionless
above
All foolish loves of men, and weary of
The slow procession of Earth's mystery ;
Where worlds, not men, are born and
live and die,
And aeons flit unnoticed as a dove.

Thither I fled, busied myself with these ;
When—lo ! I saw her shadow following !
In every cosmic season-tide of spring
She rose, being the spring : in utter peace
She was with me and in me : thus I saw
Ours was not love, but destiny, and law.

REINCARNATION.

IN Life what hope is always unto men ?
Stories of Arthur that shall come again
To cleanse the Earth of her eternal stain,
Elias, Charlemagne, Christ.   What
matter then ?

[1] At Eryx, in Sicily, was a famous temple of
Venus.

E

What matter who, or how, or even when?
  If we but look beyond the primal pain,
  And trust the Future to write all things
    plain,
  Graven on brass with the predestined pen.

This is the doom. Upon the blind blue sky
  A little cloud, no larger than an hand !
  Whether I live and love, or love and die,
I care not : either way I understand.
  To me—to live is Christ ; to die is gain :
  For I, I also, I shall come again.

THE FIFTH DAY.

"Thine eyes, sweet lady, have infected mine."
                                      Richard III.

ALL thought of work is almost cast aside.
  I followed like a dog the way she went,
  Speaking but seldom, very well content
  To day-dream, oft imagining a bride,
A wife, a lover, even a sister, tied
  By some soft bond of twinning : thus
    I blent
  A real joy with a brighter element
  Of fancy free to wander far and wide.

For as I followed by the shore and bended
  Over her footsteps in the wood, my will
  Rose to high strength assertive and
    transcended
The petty forms of the seducer's skill.
  Chaste love strode forth, a warrior's
    stern and splendid
  Determined footsteps on the Arcadian
    Hill.

THE SIXTH DAY.

                        " Are there not charms
By which the property of youth and maidhood
May be abused?"
                                      Othello.

I DREW a hideous talisman of lust
  In many colours where strong sigils
    shone ;
  Crook'd mystic language of oblivion,
  Fitted to crack and scorch the terrene
    crust

And bring the sulphur steaming from the
    thrust
  Of Satan's winepress, was ill written on
  The accursèd margin, and the orison
  Scrawled backwards, as a bad magician
    must.

By these vile tricks, abominable spells,
  I drew foul horrors from a many hells—
  Though I had fathomed Fate ; though
    I had seen
Chastity charm-proof arm the sea-gray eyes
  And sweet clean body of my spirit's
    queen,
  Where nothing dwells that God did not
    devise.

THE SEVENTH DAY.

" This word 'love,' which greybeards call
    divine,
Be resident in men like one another
And not in me : I am myself alone."
                                  3 *Henry VI.*

THEREFORE I burnt the wicked pantacle,
  And cast my love behind me once
    again.
  I mused upon the mystery of pain,
  Where the Gods taught me by another
    spell
Not chosen from the armoury of Hell,
  But given of Mercury to cleanse the
    stain
  Of the old planet : thus I wrote me
    plain
  Secrets divine—tremendous, terrible !

Thus I forgot my soul and dwelt alone
  In the strong fortress of the active
    mind
  Whose steady flame burned eager in the
    night ;
Yet was some shadow on the starry throne,
  Some imperfection playing hoodman-
    blind
  So that I saw not perfectly aright.

THE EIGHTH DAY.

"A certain aim he took
At a fair Vestal thronèd by the West."
Midsummer Night's Dream.

HERE in the extreme west of all the earth
This Vestal sate ; and I from Cupid's
  bow
Loosed a fair shaft of verses shapen so
As to fling love through the chaste girdle's
  girth,
And show my love how meek was my love's
  birth,
How innocent its being : thus arow
Stood the mild lines, immaculate, to
  show
My harmless passion and her own great
  worth.

She could not be offended : and moreover—
When at the nightfall I sought Heaven's
  light,
All my work grew unspotted, done
  aright !
The high Gods came above my head to hover,
Because I worked with a diviner might,
The perfect sage being the perfect lover.

THE NINTH DAY.

"How canst thou tell she will deny thy suit
Before thou make a trial of her love?"
                    1 *Henry VI.*

I WAS most weary of my work : the mind
  Shuddered at all the wonders it had
    written,
  And the whole body by the spirit smitten
  Groaned : so I went and left my love
    behind,
Danced the gross "hula," [1] hardly disinclined,
  By a new lust emphatically bitten ;
  And so in flames at harlot glances litten
  I sought that solace I shall never find.

[1] The indecent dance of the South Sea
Islands.

Fool ! not to tell her. Triple fool to fly
  The sunny glance, the moonlight medi-
    tation,
  For even the light of heaven. How
    much worse
The dark antithesis, the coarser curse
  Of Eden ! Pass, O shadows of crea-
    tion,
  Into the daybreak of Eternity !

THE TENTH DAY.

"O God ! I could be bounded in a nutshell,
and count myself king of infinite space, were
it not that I have bad dreams."
                    Hamlet.

THE mere result of all this was a dream.
  The day passed damned, void of my
    love's dear light,
  And stole accursèd to the endless night,
  Forgotten (as I trust) by God : no
    beam
Of memory lighting it down Time's dark
    stream.
  I dreamt : my shrine was broken and
    my might
  Defiled, and all my Gods abased, in
    sight
  Of all blind Heaven exenterate [1] and
    extreme. [2]

The foulest traitor of all womankind
  I ever knew, became my friend : [3] un-
    clean
  Sexual abominations floated through,
More foul because a golden cord did wind
  Unspotted through that revel epicene,
  The pure faith of one woman that was
    true.

[1] Disembowelled.
[2] Used here to mean "at the last gasp."
[3] This circumstance was later fulfilled : I
having judged her actions on insufficient evidence.—AUTHOR.

THE ELEVENTH DAY.

" What win I if I gain the thing I seek?"
                              Rape of Lucrece.

THERE is much sorcery in the word eleven.
   I took my lover's image pale and clear,
   Fixed in my mind ; I saw her standing
      near,
   Wooed her, conjured her by the power
      of heaven,
Of my own mind, the Genii of the Seven,
   To come and live with me and be my
      dear,
   To love me in the spirit without fear ;—
   Leaving the body's love to follow at
      even.

Seemeth it not absurd ? to use the thought,
   The utterly divine impersonal
   Mind of a man, the pure, the spiritual,
To such a purpose rather less than nought,
   A woman's love—considering that all
   Wise men assure us that it may be
      bought !

THE TWELFTH DAY.

" I grant thou wert not married to my Muse
And therefore mayst without attaint o'erlook
The dedicated words which writers use
Of their fair subjects."
                              The Sonnets.

I LEARNT at last some sort of confidence,
   Called me the fool I was, knowing my
      skill
   Proven of old, all women's native will
   To do all things soever that lack sense,
Especially if evil : thoughts immense
   Like this I thought : plumes of my
      amorous quill
   I tickled her withal : then grave and still
   Waited secure : the silence grew intense.

She read—and saw me but a beardless boy,
   Too young to fear, too gentle not to pity,
   Not overbold ; quite powerless to destroy
Her life's long peace, the ten-year-wallèd city.[1]
   Why be too cruel, check such baby joy ?
   She said " I think the poem very pretty."

RED POPPY.[2]

I HAVE no heart to sing.
What offering may I bring,
      Alice, to thee ?
My great love's lifted wing
Weakens, unwearying,
      And droops with me,
Seeing the sun-kindled hair
Close in the face more fair,
The sweet soul shining there
      For God to see.

Surely some angel shed
Flowers for the maiden head,
      Ephemeral flowers !
I yearn, not comforted.
My heart has vainly bled ·
      Through age-long hours.
To thee my spirit turns ;
My bright soul aches and burns,
As a dry valley yearns
      For spring and showers.

Splendid, remote, a fane
Alone and unprofane,
      I know thy breast.
These bitter tears of pain
Flood me, and fall again
      Not into rest.
Me, whose sole purpose is
To gain one gainless kiss,
And make a bird's my bliss,
      Shrined in that nest.

[1] She had been married ten years.
[2] The poem in question.

O fearful firstling dove !
My dawn and spring of love,
Love's light and lure !
Look (as I bend above)
Through bright lids filled thereof
Perfect and pure,
Thy bloom of maidenhood.
I could not : if I could,
I would not : being good,
Also endure !

Cruel, to tear or mar
The chaliced nenuphar ;
Cruel to press
The rosebud ; cruel to scar
Or stain the flower-star
With mad caress.
But crueller to destroy
The leaping life and joy
Born in a careless boy
From lone distress.

More cruel then art thou
The calm and chaste of brow,
If thou dost this.
Forget the feeble vow
Ill sworn : all laws allow
Pity, that is
Kin unto love, and mild.
List to the sad and wild
Crying of the lonely child
Who asks a kiss.

One kiss, like snow, to slip,
Cool fragrance from thy lip
To melt on mine ;
One kiss, a white-sail ship
To laugh and leap and dip
Her brows divine ;
One kiss, a starbeam faint
With love of a sweet saint,
Stolen like a sacrament
In the night's shrine !

One kiss, like moonlight cold
Lighting with floral gold
The lake's low tune ;
One kiss, one flower to fold,

On its own calyx rolled
At night, in June !
One kiss, like dewfall, drawn
A veil o'er leaf and lawn—
Mix night, and noon, and dawn,
Dew, flower, and moon !

One kiss, intense, supreme !
The sense of Nature's dream
And scent of Heaven
Shown in the glint and gleam
Of the pure dawn's first beam,
With earth for leaven ;
Moulded of fire and gold,
Water and wine to fold
Me in its life, and hold !—
In all but seven !

I would not kiss thee, I !
Lest my lip's charactery
Ruin thy flower.
Curve thou one maidenly
Kiss, stooping from thy sky
Of peace and power !
Thine only be the embrace !—
I move not from my place,
Feel the exultant face
Mine for an hour !

THE THIRTEENTH DAY.

"If it be a sin to make a true election, she is
damned."

Cymbeline.

IN the dim porchway where the sea's deep
boom
Under our very feet made ceaseless song,
We sate, remote, the lone lanai [1] along
Sequestered from the young moon in
the gloom

[1] The South Sea word for balcony, or rather
verandah.

Of early even : then the tender bloom
 Shone on her cheek and deepened as
  the strong
 Arms gathered round her, more than
  shame or wrong,
 And the soft question murmured " Love
  you—whom ? "

The deepening rose ; the heart's pulse
  quickening ;
 The fear ; the increasing ecstasy of this—
A little cloud lifted a sombre wing
Shadowing our secret breath from Artemis—
 Breasts met and arms enclosed, and all
  the spring
 Grew into summer with the first long
  kiss.

THE FOURTEENTH DAY.

" Some there be that shadows kiss ;
 Such have but a shadow's bliss ;
 There be fools alive, I wis."
    Merchant of Venice.

ALL day we chose each moment possible
 When to the other's face each face
  might cling,
 Each kiss burn forth, a double fiery
  sting
 Exalting us in joy foreseen to swell
A mighty exultation ; it befell,
 However, that I saw the shadowy thing
 Lurk behind love, and flap a scornful
  wing,
 Seeing our honour stood a citadel.

I saw the foolishness of love that saith :
 " I am exalted over shame and death,
 But will not take my fill of death and
  shame."
For each kiss leaps, a more insistent breath,
 And adds fresh fuel to the amorous
  flame,
 Not quells it—Is not honour but a name?

THE FIFTEENTH DAY.

" Were kisses all the joys in bed,
 One woman would another wed."
  Sonnets to Sundry Notes of Music.

ANOTHER day rose of unceasing fire:
 Kisses made monstrous for their sterile
  storm
 Maddening with sea-sounds, as of lute
  or shawm
 Fluting and clashing in extreme desire ;
The silly " Thus far and no farther," nigher
 Each hour to break (poor arbitrary
  form !)
 As each kiss bade our bodies wed and
  warm
 Give love one chance before its wave
  retire.

Not so : this trial was the tiniest
 Man ever knew, confronted afterward
 With giant fears and passions ;—long to
  fight
And last to yield a Maenad-swelling breast
 Unto a furious Dionysian horde
 Drunk not with wine, but with aveng-
  ing night.

THE SIXTEENTH DAY.

" My chastity's the jewel of our house
 Bequeathèd down from many ancestors,
 Which were the greatest obloquy i' th' world
For me to lose."
    All's Well.

THERE was no secret cave of the wood's
  womb
 Where we might kiss all day without a
  start
 Of fear that meant to stay and must
  depart,
 Nor any corner where the sea's perfume

Might shelter love in some wave-carven tomb.
    But Maytime shone in us ; with words
        of art
I drew her down reluctant to my heart,
    When night was silence and my bed
        the gloom.

So without sin we took strange sacrament,
    Whose wine was kisses, and whose bread
        the flower
    Of fast and fervent cleaving breast to
        breast.
As lily bends to lily we were bent,
    Not as mere man to woman : all the
        dower
    Of martyred Virgins crowned our dan-
        gerous quest.

ALICE.

THE roses of the world are sad,
    The water-lilies pale,
Because my lover takes her lad
    Beneath the moonlight veil.
No flower may bloom this happy hour—
Unless my Alice be the flower.

The stars are hidden in dark and mist,
    The moon and sun are dead,
Because my love has caught and kissed
    My body in her bed.
No light may shine this happy night—
Unless my Alice be the light.

So silent are the thrush, the lark !
    The nightingale's at rest,
Because my lover loves the dark,
    And has me in her breast.
No song this happy night be heard !—
Unless my Alice be the bird.

The sea that roared around the house
    Is fallen from alarms,
Because my lover calls me spouse,
    And takes me to her arms.
This night no sound of breakers be !—
Unless my Alice be the sea.

Of man and maid in all the world
    Is stilled the swift caress,
Because my lover has me curled
    In her own loneliness.
No kiss be such a night as this !—
Unless my Alice be the kiss.

No blade of grass awaiting takes
    The dew ,fresh-fallen above,
Because my lover swoons, and slakes
    Her body's thirst of love.
This night no dewfall from the blue !—
Unless my Alice be the dew.

This night—O never dawn shall crest
    The world of wakening,
Because my lover has my breast
    On hers for dawn and spring.
This night shall never be withdrawn—
Unless my Alice be the dawn.

THE SEVENTEENTH DAY.

          " Now I want
   Spirits to enforce, art to enchant."
                    Tempest.

LAST night—but the boy shrieked in's sleep
    —then, there
    I had ended all ! Having ingressed the
        track
    That leads from green or white-crowned
        hours to black,
    The pleasant portals of the scorpion
        snare,
First gleaming toils of an enchantress' hair
    That afterward shall change their fer-
        vours slack
    To strong gripe of a devil-fish : go back ?
    The hand is put forth to the plough—
        beware !

I took my shrine down :[1] at the night we lay
    Four hours debating between fear and sin:
    Whether our love went deeper than the
        skin,

[1] Meaning that spiritual work was abandoned for the moment, and that he wished to
use the room for a profane purpose.

Or lower than the lips : love won the day.
  We nestled like young turtles that be
    twin
  Close till the morn-star chased the moon
    away.

LOVE AND FEAR.

THE rose of the springtime that bended
  Its delicate head to the breeze
Is crimson and stately and splendid
  Now summer is here and at ease ;
Love risen as the sun hath transcended its
  passion and peace.

In a garden of dark foliage that clusters
  Round your face as a rosebud with-
    drawn,
  New splendour springs carmine and
    lustres
    Your cheeks with the coming of
      dawn,
Love's light as an army that musters its
  plumes—and is gone.

For fear as a fountain, that trembles
  With wind, is arisen, and hides
The light of your love, and dissembles
  The roar of the passionate tides ;
Though a flickering flame it resembles, love
  is, and abides.

I see through the moonlight that covers
  (As a mist on the mountain) your
    head
The flame of your heart as a lover's
  Shine out in your face and be shed,
A ruby that flashes and hovers and droops
  and is dead.

As a saint in a vision half hidden
  I see the sweet face in a mist,
A nimbus of glory unbidden
    That shades you or shows as you
      list.
But I, as a bridegroom, unchidden, may
  kiss—and am kissed.

In the light and the manifest splendour
  That shows you in darkness a bride,
Pale blossom of moonlight and slender,
  A lily that sways in the tide,
A star that falls earthward to bend her sweet
  breast to my side :—

No depth of the darkness may shield you
  From eyes that with love are aflame,
No darkness, but light, as you yield you
  To love that is stronger than shame,
No music but kisses, that pealed you their
  pæan, proclaim :

That the light of the heaven is shaded,
  The sound of the sea is made still,
The climax shall come unupbraided
  Obedient alone to our will,
And the flowers that were fallen and faded
  drink dew to their fill :

Dew filling your eyes and their lashes
  With tender mirage of a tear ;
Dew fallen on the mouth as it flashes,
  The kiss that is master of fear ;
Dew covering the body that dashes and
  clings to me here.

O fairest, O rose among roses !
  O flower of the innermost fire !
O tune of my soul that encloses
  All life, the tempestuous lyre !
O dawn of my dawn that reposes and darts
  in desire !

And death and its portals are rifted,
  Life listens our kisses that weep ;
Love hears, and his measure is shifted,
  Grows solemn and deadly and deep ;
Love's ship droops its sails and is drifted in
  silence to sleep.

And soft as a seal on our slumber
  Dreams drift of Aurorean dew ;
Dreams shapen of flames that encumber
  The shrine of the morn in the blue ;
Flames shapen of lips that outnumber our
  kisses anew.

THE EIGHTEENTH DAY.

" Touches so soft still conquer chastity."
Passionate Pilgrim.

SHE grew most fearful, starting at slight noise ;
  As knowing that the sting of shame was
    hers
  Worse than a guilty love administers,
Since our pure shame unworthily destroys
The love of all she had, her girls and boys,
  Her home, their lives : and yet my
    whisper stirs
Into live flame her passion, and deters
  Her fear from spurning all the day's
    due joys.

She had not dared to speak one word, to tell
  How deep and pure a fountain sunward
    leapt
In her life's garden : but to-night she lay
In my intense embraces : so the spell
  Moved her : " I love you," said she. So
    we kept,
Remurmuring that one phrase until the
    day.

THE NINETEENTH DAY.

" The boy is foolish, and I fear not him."
Richard III.

SHE dared not come into my room to-night.
  So ? I was acquiescent, sharp despair
And nervous purpose mixing in me there
The while I waited : then I glided light
(Clad in the swart robe of an eremite) [1]
  Across the passage. Now, all unaware
  My kisses underneath the veil of vair
Woke her : she turned and sighed and
    held me tight.

Her child slept gently on the farther side.
  But we took danger by the throat, de-
    spised
All but the one sole splendour that we
    prized ;

[1] Crowley was accustomed to wear a black
robe of a magical pattern as a *robe de
chambre.*

And she, whose robe was far too slight to hide
  The babe-smooth breasts, was far too
    frail to cover
Her heart's true fire and music from her
    lover.

THE TWENTIETH DAY.

" *Val.* How long hath she been deformed?
  Speed. Ever since you loved her."
Two Gentlemen of Verona.

AGAIN the unveiled goddess of delight
  Watched us at midnight : there my
    lover lay
Child-breasted, maiden as the rose of day
Dawning on snowy mountains : through
    deep night
Her body gleamed self-luminously white
  With the sweet soul that sundered the
    quick clay,
  And all her being was a sense of May ;—
Scent conquering colour, soul out-
    running sight.

Not with the Lysian, [1] nor Iacchian dew
  Of frenzy covered, but with warmer
    flakes
Of Aphrodite shed upon our life,
We clung still closer, till the soul ran through
  Body to body, twined like sunny snakes,
Sinlessly knowing we were man and wife.

THE TWENTY-FIRST DAY.

" *Mal.* Dispute it like a man.
  Macd.   I shall do so.
But I must also feel it as a man."
Macbeth.

I HAD a fearful dream (on going away)
  Of scorpion women curled in my caress,
  And twenty days they closed on my
    distress
Not giving me relief, but gold and gray,

[1] Cornelius Agrippa distinguishes three
frenzies ; of Apollo, Dionysus, and Aphrodite ;
song, wine, and love.

Cold and intense ; the one-and-twentieth day
  They drew my life out, one exceeding
    stress,
  Volcanic anguish !—Here's the strange
    excess :
  I called, ere waking, on the name
    Eheieh !

Solve me the riddle of the dream who can !
  That night I sought a new toy for a lure,
  And she would not : but knew how hard
    to endure
Is love like ours, the love of purity.
  So she : " Dispute it like a man ! " and I :
  " But I must also feel it as a man ! "

  Note. Eheieh is the Hebrew for " I am that
I am." Its numerical value is 21. I was not
aware at the time that this was the 21st day.—
AUTHOR.[1]

THE TWENTY-SECOND DAY.

" I'll have her : but I will not keep her long."
                                    Richard III.

IT was impossible that she should come
  Over the leagues of summer-coloured sea
  Alone with love and laughter and tears
    and me
  To the toy land[2] of the chrysanthemum,
Where. all the flowers lack scent, the birds
    are dumb,
  The fruits are tasteless : where the
    jewelled lea
  And all the many-leavèd greenery
  Is dwarf : French gem-work on a baby's
    thumb.

The Yankee God[3] frowned also on the plan.
  We had enough, no more. But I insist,
  Still thinking I was master of my heart :
Saying, " Another month to be a man,
  Another month to kiss her and be kissed,
  And then—all time to Magic and to
    Art ! "

  [1] That is, the imaginary author.
  [2] Japan.   [3] The dollar.

THE TWENTY-THIRD DAY.

          " He has strangled
          His language in his tears."
                              K. Hen. VIII.

MY comedy has changed its blithe aspect
  To bitterest face of tragedy ; she said :
  "Alas ! O soul of mine ! I am surely
    dead,
  Seeing my life is by a serpent wrecked
Of sore disease : but spare me, and reflect
  That in few months I die : but were I
    • wed—
  O lover ! O desire discomfited !
  I die at once : consider, and elect."

How could I otherwise than spare my wife ?
  With tender lips and fingers one strong
    kiss
  Swooned slave-wise even before the gate
    of bliss,
No more : for I rose up and cursed my life,
  Hating the God that made us to dissever
  So soon so sweet a love, and that for ever.

  Ut. Canc. sublatum iri dixisse. Vae Capri-
corno ![1] (Author's Note.)

THE TWENTY-FOURTH DAY.

  " She having the truth of honour in her, hath
made him that gracious denial which he is
most glad to receive."
                            Measure for Measure.

OF course I might have known it was a lie.
  Nathless, I wept all morning and de-
    spaired.
  Nothing for any life of earth I cared,
  Neither for heaven : I railed against the
    sky,

  [1] This intentionally obscure note means that
she said she had cancer. Now Capricorn, the
opposite to Cancer in the Zodiac, is called " the
symbol of gross passion."

Hating the earth, the sea, the witchery
    Of all the universe : my breast I bared
    And cursed God, hoping lightning ; and
        I dared
    Not ask my love "In very truth—you
        die !"

    I could not bear it longer ; then she
      spake :
    " I lied indeed, love, for mine honour's
      sake,"
    And I reproached her for her love's dis-
      trust, ·
Saying " I would not so in any wise
    Have lowered love unto the level of lust
    But now—" I hid my thought in tears
    and sighs.

THE TWENTY-FIFTH DAY.

" I am in health, I breathe, and see thee ill."
                     Richard II.

ALICE was desperately ill at morn.
    Hour by sweet hour I watched her
      sorrowing,
    While the strong fever fought uncon-
      quering
    With native coolness of her life, o'er-
      worn
Or poisoned ; thus I fought the long forlorn
    Battle all day, until the evening
    Brought back sweet health on sleep
      and noiseless wing :
    Strong love of the long battle was re-
      born.

The child slept elsewhere that she might
    sleep well.
    Therefore, not fearing anything, I came ;
    Lit my love's candle at her body's flame,
And fought not with the fevers now that
    swell
    Our burning lips and bosoms, until
      shame
    Nearly surrendered the sweet citadel.

THE TWENTY-SIXTH DAY.

" I think the devil will not have me damned
· · · he would never else cross me thus."
          Merry Wives of Windsor.

THIS time she set her will against my will ;
    Swore that she would not come : in my
      despair
    I half believed her an enchantress fair
    Cruel as hell and dowered with subtle
      skill
To strain my life out with her love, and kill
    My soul with misery : suddenly a rare
    Swift smile set shimmering all the am-
      bient air,
    And then I knew she was my true love
      still.

She would not come? Why, were Hell's
    portals fast
    Shut, as to Orpheus on Eurydice,
    Their brass would break before love's
      gold and steel,
The sharpness inlaid with sweet tracery
    Of talismans of virtue : she is leal
    To come and live and be my love at
      last.

UNDER THE PALMS.

THE woodland hollows know us, bird-
    enchanted,
    Likewise the spaces of the ghostly sea,
The lake's abundant lilies, the pale slanted
    Moonlight on flowers, the wind's low
      minstrelsy ;
For all the tropic greenery is haunted
    By you and me. . . . . . .

The tall palms bend and catch love's tender
    ditty
    To learn a sweeter song to lure their
      mate.
The soft wind sighs in amorous self-pity,
    Having no love wherein to laugh elate,
And turns to the cold harbour and the city,
    Wailing its fate . . . .

Two faces and two bosoms, breathing slowly
   In tune and time with the sea's hymn
     below,
Breathing in peace of love, mighty and holy,
   Fearing to fuse, and longing—be it so !
And the world's pulse stops, as God bends
   him lowly
     To hear and know. . . . . . .

For not the heights of heaven shall exalt her
   Whose heart is full of love's dumb deity,
Nor harp-strings lift me, nor the sound of
   psalter,
   Whose love is merged and molten into
   thee,
Nor incense sweeter be by shrine or altar
     For you and me. . . . .

But like dove's eyes where glamour lies
   a-dwelling,
   Like sweet well-water rising in the well,
Strong steep black currents thrust up,
   flooding, welling,
   Into the moonlight, swift, adorable,—
So kisses cluster, so our bosoms swelling
     Abide and dwell. . . . .

Yet the twin faces, like Madonnas, meeting,
   Fear and draw back and gaze a little
     space ;
Fear, lest they lose the moonlight frail and
   fleeting,
   Lose their own beauty in their own
   embrace,
But feel how gladdening hearts and bosoms
   beating
     Kindle the face . . . .

But not for long shall lilies strive with roses,
   Nor fear be fearful, nor delight repose,
Nor love retire ; the woodland cleaves and
   closes
   Round heads an aureole hides, a rainbow
   shows.
A swifter shape of fire cleaves us, encloses
     Rosebud and rose. . . . .

Mouth unto mouth ! O fairest ! Mutely lying,
   Fire lambent laid on water,—O ! the
     pain !
Kiss me, O heart, as if we both were dying !
   Kiss, as we could not ever kiss again !
Kiss me, between the music of our sighing,
     Lightning and rain !

Not only as the kiss of tender lovers—
   Let mingle also the sun's kiss to sea,
Also the wind's kiss to the bird that hovers,
   The flower's kiss to the earth's deep
   greenery.
All elemental love closes and covers
     Both you and me.

All shapes of silence and of sound and seeing,
   All lives of Nature molten into this,
The moonlight waking and the shadows
   fleeing,
   Strange sorcery of unimagined bliss,
All breath breathing in ours ; mingled all
   being
     Into the kiss.

THE TWENTY-SEVENTH DAY.

  " The ship is in her trim ; the merry wind
   Blows fair from land."
               Comedy of Errors.

QUITE careless whether golden gales of wind
   Fling our boat forward, or the storm
   and spark
   Of lightning lamp or shroud us in the
   dark,
   Careless if ever land again we find,
Careless of all things (this love being blind),
   We put to sea. O gladly stand and mark
   The diamond headland fall behind our
   barque,
   Wrapped in shrine - shadow of love's
   central mind !

We are alone to-day on the strange sea,
   Divider of the dawn's divinity
   From sunset's splendour : our eternal
   noon

Of love recks little of eternity—
　And though the moon is dying, ourselves
　　may swoon,
　One deathless shape of the large-
　　breasted moon.

THE TWENTY-EIGHTH DAY.

"But I perceive in you so excellent a touch
of modesty that you will not extort from me
what I am willing to keep in."
　　　　　　　　　　　　Twelfth-Night.

A CURIOUS conflict this of love and fear,
　Honour and lust, and truth and trust
　　beguiled;
　One in the semblance of a rose-bright
　　child :—
　The other in a shape more gross and
　　clear,
A fiercer woman-figure crowned severe
　With garlands woven of scourges, but
　　whose wild
　Breast beat with splendour of sin, whose
　　looks were mild,
　Hiding the cruel smile behind a tear.

So she: "I know you never would ; " yet did
　Such acts that no end otherwise might be,
　So I: "I will not ever pluck the
　　flower ; "
Yet strayed enchanted on the lawns forbid,
　And bathed enamoured in the secret sea,
　Both knowing our words were spoken—
　　for an hour.

THE TWENTY-NINTH DAY.

"Persever in that clear way thou goest,
And the gods strengthen thee."
　　　　　　　　　　　　Pericles.

LINKED in the tiny shelf upon the ship,
　My blind eyes burned into her mild
　　ones : limbs
　Twined to each other while fine dew
　　bedims
　Their quivering skins : lip fastened unto
　　lip :

Whole soul and body frenzied meet and clip ;
　And the breath staggers, and the life-
　　blood swims !
　Terrible gods chant black demoniac
　　hymns
　As the frail cords of honour strain and
　　slip.

For in the midst of that tremendous tide
　The mighty vigour of a god was mine !
　Drunk with desire, her lamentations
　　died.
The dove gave place a moment to the swine !
　Rapturous draughts of madness ! Out
　　she sighed
　Uttermost life's love, and became a
　　bride.

THE THIRTIETH DAY.

"For God's sake, lords, convey my tristful
　Queen,
For tears do stop the floodgates of her eyes."
　　　　　　　　　　　　King Henry IV.

BITTER reproaches passed between us twain,
　Hers real, mine with sneering logic sewn
　Proving my trespass hardly half her own,
　Its cause ; I proved her how she made
　　me fain
And left me mad, and led through joy and
　　pain
　To that unthinkable thing : I might atone
　No whit in this way : then that stubborn
　　stone
　My heart grew tears : we were good
　　friends again.

Therefore at night I added nothing new :
　Only a little while I lay with her
　And with mere kisses sucked her soul
　　away,
And made my banquet of immortal dew,
　Demanding nothing but to minister
　To her desire until the dawn grew grey.

THE DAY WITHOUT A NUMBER.

" O never shall the sun that morrow see."
Macbeth.

WE lost a day ! [1]   Nor kisses, nor regret,
   Nor fear, nor pain, nor anything at all !
   The day was lost, evanished past recall,
   That saw no sunrise, never saw sun set—
For East and West invisibly were met
   In gateways neither glad nor musical
   Nor melancholy nor funereal.
Nought is there to remember nor forget.

Yet in my westward journey many hours
   I stole, and now must pay them back
      again.
   I plucked not one flower, but an hundred
      flowers ;
I bore an hundred passions in my brain—
   King Solomon had three hundred para-
      mours.
   I quite agree that everything is vain.

THE THIRTY-FIRST DAY.

" You whoreson villain ! will you let it fall?"
Taming of the Shrew.

THE inexpiable fate whose shuddering wing
   Fear fled from, changed the native deed
      of sin
   Into a spasmic kiss too salt and keen,
   Windless, that ended with a sterile sting
The earlier hour whose heart was full of
      spring ;
   And the large love grew piteously lean ;
   Dreadful, like death ; withdrawn and
      epicene
   At the mad crisis of the eventful thing.

O that such tender fondness like a flower's
   Should take such nameless infamy !
      That we
   Should pluck such bitter bloom, rooted
      in fear,

[1] On the westward voyage across the Pacific
a day is " lost " on the 180th degree.

Salt with the scurf of some diseasèd sea,
   Foul with the curse of God : that we
      are here,
   Hating the night's inexorable hours.

THE THIRTY-SECOND DAY.

" Me of my lawful pleasure she restrained
   And prayed me oft forbearance."
Cymbeline.

HOW sweet the soft looks shot, endearing
      shame
   With their warm fragrance of love's
      modest eyes !
   The secret knowledge of our secrecies
   Shone from their distance with a subtle
      flame,
And gave to pudency a rosier name
   When the long lashes drooped, and
      saintlier sighs
   Took softer meanings, till my arteries
   Throbbed with the glad desire that went
      and came.

" I charge you in the very name of love."
   Quoth she : " We have all day to steal
      below
   And snatch short kisses out of danger's
      throat.
Why beg you night : is not the day enough?"
   But I : " The night is panting and aglow
   To feel our hair distraught and limbs
      afloat."

THE THIRTY-THIRD DAY.

" Clubs, clubs ! These lovers will not keep the
   peace."
Titus Andronicus.

NATHLESS she locked her cabin-door to me.
   All lovers guess the piteous night I
      passed—
   Shuddering phantoms, hideous and
      aghast,
   Loomed, lust of hate ! toward me : how
      did she ?

She never told: but I might surely see
   In the drawn face and haggard eyes
      what vast
Voices of misery had held her fast,
And made her curse her own lock's
      cruelty.

So by her beauty and my love we swore,
   And by the light within mine eyes, by
      her
Sweet shame: that never so we sunder
      again.
But she: "You swear 'by thy bright face'
      in vain;
   'By thy sweet self' you grow a perjurer;
Who have shamed my face and made
   me but an whore."

THE THIRTY-FOURTH DAY.

" *Ben.* Stop there, stop there.
   Mer. Thou desirest me to stop in my tale
      against the hair."
                           Romeo and Juliet.

SWEET are the swift hard struggles ere the
      kiss,
   When the frail body blushes into tears,
   And short breaths cancel the long sighs,
      and fears
Constrain delight, until their import is
Made foolish when the struggle's synthesis
   Leads to hot armistice, as dewy spheres
   Glow, and increase the fury that reveres
No God, no heaven but its own hell's
      bliss.

So after desperate shifts of modesty
   We could no more; loosened and lax
      we lay
Breathing and holding: then in amorous
      play
She laughed and left her body's love to me,
   And kissed one kiss holding the heart
      of May,
   And kissed again, and kissed our lives
      away.

THE THIRTY-FIFTH DAY.

"I cannot kiss, that is the humour of it, but
   adieu."
                           King Henry V.

THE third time bitterly came reason back.
   Is it a fault in love when mornings find
   The soul grown sober and rethroned the
      · mind?
Or is it mere necessity to track
The candid chequer cross-wise to the black,
   And love, not mutable, yet well inclined
   To take his pleasure in becoming blind
After such sight mere day is wont to lack?

So we were angry with ourselves and said
   We would not kiss—two days, and we
      would part.
   And she prayed heaven that she might
      be dead,
And I cursed heaven and my foolish head.
   I strove to turn towards old shapes of
      Art;
   She, to some phantom faded from her
      heart.

THE THIRTY-SIXTH DAY.

" 'Twas not their infirmity,
   It was married chastity."
                           Phœnix and Turtle.

YET ere the stars paled slowly in the east
   I could not sleep: and she—how else?
      What rest
   May a man know until his quiet breast
Beats to her tune? I garbed me as a
      priest
And moved towards my Host—on God I
      feast!
   We lay in naked chastity, caressed
   Child-like or dreaming, till the dawn
      repressed
Our sighs: that nuptial yet hath never
      ceased.

That was the best : far sundered by the tide
    Dolorous, endless as Oceanus,[1]
    A serpent-river girdling the large earth,
Still in that pure embrace we bring to birth
    A thousand pleasant children born of us,
    Sacred and sinless, if unsanctified.

LETHE.

WE have forgotten all the days of fear,
    The nights of torment when the kiss
      expired,
    Lost upon lips with love not overtired,
    But fearing many things—the after year,
The end, the man—O no, not him ! the
      tear,
    The children's sorrow, and our own
      shame fired
    Not less in doing all that love desired :
We have forgotten, surely—being here !

We have forgotten every shape of sorrow,
    Knowing no end to one night's ecstasy
    In the night's kiss from morning that
      we borrow,
From the hard usurer, Eternity—
    Seeing we have it in our power to die
    Before the new kiss kindle for the
      morrow.

THE THIRTY-SEVENTH DAY.

" By long and vehement suit I was seduced
    To make room for him in my husband's
      bed."
                    King John.

MORTALS are not for nectar all the time :
    Ambrosia feeds not men ; nepenthe's sip
    Is only for a moment : then we dip
    Back to the earth and leave the bed
      sublime,

---

[1] The imaginary river of the Ancients, which
formed the circumference of the world-disk.

And tune our kisses to a terrene rhyme.
    So, once again before we left the ship
    With right good will our bodies cling
      and slip,
    And the life's flame sinks as the kisses
      climb.

There never has been such a supreme kiss
    Since heaven and earth began to be as
      this !
    Doubt nothing of it ! yet our spirits
      knew
Its savour was as roses fallen to dust :
    Our proper food was of Selenian dew,
    And love without a battle conquered lust.

THE THIRTY-EIGHTH DAY.

"The carcass of a beauty spent and done."
                    Lover's Complaint.

ONE day from landing. Kamakura sees
    Pass to the mighty shrine and shape of
      bronze[1]
    Me, pilgrim, murmuring pious orisons,
    Taking my refuge in that House of
      Peace,
And after, sees my love, and doth not please.
.   She was too young to know that shrine
      the Son's,
    Or see the Virgin's House in Kwan-
      se-on's ;[1]
    And when I told her, flushed, and bade
      me cease.

I ceased indeed ! All hope of mental flower
    She shattered in five minutes : following
      lust,
    All intellectual communing did pass,
And all respect of mind : but love's high
      tower,
    Stricken of lightning, stood : not fallen
      in dust,
    Beautiful fragments as of a Greek vase.

---

[1] The Dai-Butsu, a vast statue of Buddha.
[2] The Goddess. Her function is variously
identified with that of Isis, Bhavani, or the
Kundalini.

THE THIRTY-NINTH DAY.

" Had I no eyes but ears, my ears would love
That inward beauty and invisible."
Venus and Adonis.

NOTE from this day no possible event.
All secrets told, and all desires fulfilled
Primitive passion of our soul have killed.
.We dwell within a calmer element
Perfectly pure and perfectly content.
The subtler splendour of our love has
stilled
Those sombre glories that it never willed,
Those giant meanings that it never
meant.

Fire only is our substance ; there we dwell,
The Salamandrine with the Salamander.
No fuel to crack, no water to make
tunes,
No air to blow us hither and thither ; well !
At our own will through cosmic space
we wander
Alive, the sun's beam mixing with the
moon's.

THE FORTIETH DAY.

" Away, you rascally Althea's dream, away ! "
2 King Henry IV.

MERE terror struck into our souls, one shaft
Sudden and swift ; our punishment was
here.
The shapeless form of an avenging fear
Shuddered within her ; from the deep
rich draught
Of lively labour that her nights had quaffed
Rises a serpent : prescience of next year,
The springtide ; may the Minotaur[1]
appear,
Prodigious offspring of the fatal graft ?

---

[1] The offspring of Europa and of Jupiter
under the form of a bull.

The worst has happened.   Time must now
discover
What love had hidden from the wittol's[1]
eyes
(What hate may tell him if he read my
song,
If he be subtle : not if he be wise).
In our despair came laughter to my
lover :
" All's well as yet. I calculated wrong."

THE FORTY-FIRST DAY.

" I am sick."
Antony and Cleopatra.

How things are changed since Alice was so
ill !
I, being in high fever, lay in bed,
While my love smoothed the pillows
for my head :
Her calm looks christened me with dew
to still
All chance of fever to the soul, and fill
My heart with pure love like a snowfall
shed
Meekly, a blossom where frail white and
red
Were never frenzied at some mad god's
will.

She sat and gazed upon me all day long.
Sometimes she held my hands ; then
she would weep,
And then stoop tenderly and kiss my
lips,
Or lull me with some chaste and gentle
song
Of angel love. Night's plume its dew
fall drips
As she still sits and watches me to sleep.

---

[1] Cuckold.

F

THE FORTY-SECOND DAY.

" *Pol.* No longer stay.
Leon. One seven-night longer.
Pol. Very sooth, to-morrow."
Winter's Tale.

I COULD not let her leave me the day after.
Also we *must* wait till the month decide
Whether the mother stood behind the
    bride.
In any other case what love and laughter
Such tidings of an angel's birth would waft
    her ;
Now, what a fear ! And so she would
    abide
Another vessel and another tide,
Until we held the key of the hereafter.

But this sad spectre could not change our
    calm.
The day went by more peaceful than a
    dream
Dreamt by a maiden in pure winds of
    balm ;
Love's sweet still music like a far-off psalm
Thrilled our quiet pulses : with the in-
    tent supreme :
" This one week more a century shall
    seem."

AT LAST.

O TEARLESS sorrow of long years, depart !
O joy of minutes that be ages long,
Come ! Let the choral pulse and
    strength of song
Quicken, and the fire of lute and lyre dart,
An arrow red with blood and bright with
    art,
And cover all the fiery bloom of wrong
With blossoms blacker where the blood
    runs strong
As our lips pale, their life fled to the heart.

Surely we are as dead, we loving so,
    So bitterly, so keenly : let no breath
    Persuade us we are living and must die !

Better believe eternal kisses flow
    Under the strong rude current miscalled
        death,
    The lotus-river where our bodies lie !

THE FORTY-THIRD DAY.

" O theft most base
That we have stolen what we do fear to keep."
Troilus and Cressida.

IMPOSSIBLE that we shall ever part !
    The heart shrinks back from thinking it,
        the mind
    Hates it, and prays as love is to be blind.
    Yet we know well that no magician's art
Can keep our two selves near their single
        heart.
    Self-mocked I urged her " Come and
        leave behind
    All fear and friends and children : we
        shall find
    Love risen sole without a counterpart."

Even while I begged her, I well knew she
        must.
    We could not, loving to see her children
        laugh,
    Let cowards twit them with their
        mother's lust.
Even our own purity confirmed the trust.
    How long, O Lord, how long? Too
        long by half
    Till men read, wondering, wedlock's
        epitaph.

THE FORTY-FOURTH DAY.

" lips, O you
The doors of breath, seal with a righteous kiss
A dateless bargain to engrossing death."
Romeo and Juliet.

SLEEP, O deep splendour of disastrous years,
    Gone like a star fallen at the fall of night !
    Wake, O mute mouth and majesty of
        light,
    Made of no sound that even silence
        hears,

But born of strings intangible, of spheres
    Shaken of love, a mightier music's might
    Frailer to sound than dewfall is to sight !
Wake, O sweet soul incorporate of tears !

Or else dream on and let no tears begem
    Love's crown of thorns, ensanguine
        diadem,
    But let pale kisses blossom, starry shrine
Of lips most deathlike, that endure divine
    Past sleep's, or parting's, or death's spoil
        of them
    In the pomegranate walks of Proser-
        pine ![1]

THE FORTY-FIFTH DAY.

    "Peace, fool ! I have not done."
            Troilus and Cressida.

THOU knowest, O Love, how tired our
    bodies grow
    Forgotten in quick converse, love to
    love ;
    How the flame flickers of the ghost
        above,
The spirit's kiss ; the sleepless to-and-fro
Movement of love's desire too strong to know
    Or care for that it takes its substance
        of—
    As if life's burden were not drear enough
Or death's deliverance not so far and
    slow.

Our bodies almost perish, with one thought
    Crowned and completed, consecrate and
        shrined :
    A perfect temple of fine amber wrought,
Whose shrine's the body and whose lamp
    the mind.
    The heart is priest and sacrifice in one ;
    And, where it sinned or sorrowed, shall
        atone.

[1] Proserpine, ravished by Hades, was sought
by her mother Demeter. But as she had eaten
(a pomegranate) in Hell, Hades retained a
claim upon her for half the year. See Forty-
eighth Day.

THE FORTY-SIXTH DAY.

    " Because I love you, I will let you know :
    . . . . my wife . . . .
    . . . like a fountain with a hundred spouts
    Did run pure blood."
            Julius Cæsar.

WAS it a sense of uttermost relief
    We gladdened with, and bade our fears
        forget ?
    Was there no subtle fragrance of regret ?
    For me, at least, a pang of perfect grief ?
Had it been otherwise, I would be chief
    And drive her to abandon all things yet
    In mere despair, that by-and-by shall
        get
    Young comfort in a babe beyond belief.

God would not curse and bless us to such
    measure ;
    We were not sad enough nor glad
        enough !
    A little time of misery and pleasure ;
Pain strangling half the ecstasy thereof—
    Such all our gain, who gained the
        utmost treasure,
    Gift of the wizard wand and cup of love.

THE FORTY-SEVENTH DAY.

    "Thou ever young, fresh, lov'd, and delicate
    wooer."
            Timon of Athens.

THE little money that we had to spend
    Was gone long since : the little more I
    stole
    Followed : I pledged then all things but
    my soul
    (On which the usurers refused to lend)
To raise our utmost, till a ship should send
    Much plenty from the Sunset : to control
    And stop her yet a little while, the whole
    I meant to waste before the week should
    end.

Thus we went Northward to the capital,
　　Desolate huts and ways funereal,
　　An hateful town; earthquake and heat
　　　　and rain
Made the place wretched, did not love enchain
　　There even as here: what mattered
　　　　aught at all
　　While love was hovering and our lips
　　　　were fain?

THE FORTY-EIGHTH DAY.

　　　　" Let us return
And strain what other means is left to us
In our dear peril."
　　　　　　　　Timon of Athens.

OUR love takes on a tinge of melancholy,
　　The six months glory of life past on earth
　　About to yield to Hades' bridal birth,
　　The world's sad sympathy with Perse-
　　　　phone.
Yet I myself, while tuning to her key
　　My sighs of sorrow, mused in secret mirth:
　　" I am convinced at last of money's
　　　　worth,
　　For lack of which she cannot cross the
　　　　sea."

I told her, like a fool, a day too soon.
　　She went and told her story to the priest;
　　She wept, and borrowed money of the
　　　　beast.
She told me she would go: June fell from June.
　　I, left in limbo; she, to front the elate
　　Cuckoldy lawyer in the Lone Star State.

THE FORTY-NINTH DAY.

　　　　" Let me twine
Mine arms about that body."
　　　　　　　　Coriolanus.

I STOLE her money, even then to prove
　　She had no wings to fly with: but I
　　　　knew
　　What to her hateful duty there was due,
　　And how the hateful system stank there-
　　　　of:

I let her go, both weeping, both enough
　　Heart-broken: no farewell went ever
　　　　through—
　　Words came not: only ever: " I love
　　　　you !"
　　With broken kisses and stained cheeks
　　　　of love.

So all day long and half the night we wan-
　　　　dered
　　Down deep lanes and in gardens, like
　　　　lost souls.
　　Strong kisses that had surfeited a score
Of earthly bridals in an hour we squandered ;
　　And tears like fire, and looks like burn-
　　　　ing coals,
　　Without a word passed on for evermore.

THE FIFTIETH DAY.

Suffolk.　　" If I depart from thee I cannot live."
Margaret.　　　　" let me hear from thee,
　　For whereso'er thou art in this world's
　　　　globe
　　I have an Iris that shall find thee
　　　　out."
　　　　　　　　2 *King Henry VI.*

I.

AT noon she sailed for home, a weeping
　　　　bride
　　Widowed before the honeymoon was
　　　　done.
　　Always before the rising of the sun
　　I swore to come in spirit to her side
And lie like love ; and she at eventide
　　Swore to seek me and gather one by one
　　The threads of labyrinthine love new
　　　　spun,
　　Cretan[1] for monstrous shadows serpent-
　　　　eyed.

So the last kiss passed like a poison-pain,
　　Knowing we might not ever kiss again.
　　Mad tears fell fast: " Next year !" in
　　　　cruel distress

1 The reference is still to the Minotaur, who
dwelt in a labyrinth in Crete.

We sobbed, and stretched our arms out, and
    despaired,
    And—parted. Out the brute-side of
    truth flared ;
    " Thank God I've finished with that
    foolishness ! "

II.

AH ! there be two sides to all shapes of
    truth !
    I might indeed go back to bitter toil,
    Prune the mind's vine, and gather in the
    spoil
    Rough-conquered from books, men,
    fields, without ruth
Pillaging Nature, pawning strength and
    youth
    For some strange guerdon (or its counter-
    foil)
    Gainless or not-to-be-gained, priestly or
    royal,
    Profane, canaille—I know not, in good
    sooth !

I might do this ; or else I might repose
    Wrapped in the urned leaves of my
    love's blown rose,
    Seek her in spirit, and commune, and
    wait
Her freedom and the rapture to enclose
    In my own house her beauty intimate.
    I am a fool, tossing a coin with Fate.

III.

Is love indeed eternal ? Otherwise
    Is evolution an eternal plan ?
    Must I move upward in the stream of
    Man,
    God-ward : my life as Christ to sacrifice,

As Buddha to repress : to grow so wise,
    Space, time shall lie within my finger-
    span ?
    I know not which I wish : either I can ;
    Not both, unless all meditation lies.

I am not sure : if love as great as ours
    May not be God to part of us at least,
    Leaving the rest to find its heights and
    powers
In other spheres ; that, night's enamoured
    priest ;
    This, on the lake the dewy lotus-flowers
    That lift their jewelled hearts toward
    the East.

AFTER.

Now, when the sun falls in the dismal sky
    And no light leaps beneath the plunging
    prow,
    I know the fulness of my sorrow now :—
    That all my talk and laughter was a lie ;
That as each hour widens the gulfs that sigh
    Between us ; the truth scores upon my
    brow
    Sigils of silence, burns in me the vow
    " I love you, and shall love you till I
    die."

Whether next year, as fondly we made oath,
    Shall see us meet at least, whether as
    wife
    I shall at last gather the whole vow's
    breath—
Not heaven nor hell shall break our solemn
    troth.
    I love you, and shall love you all my
    life.
    I love you, and shall love you after
    death.

THE ARGONAUTS *

1904

ARGONAUTAE.

ACTUS PRIMUS.

JASON.

PELIAS. JASON. *Semi-chorus of Iolchian*
Men. *Semi-chorus of Iolchian* Women.

SCENE: *The Throne-chamber of* KING
PELIAS.

SEMI-CHORUS OF MEN.

THE prophecies are spoken in vain,
    The auguries vainly cast,
Since twenty years of joyous reign
    In peace are overpast ;
And those who cursed our King's desires
Are branded in the brow for liars.

SEMI-CHORUS OF WOMEN.

We heard the aged prophet speak
    The doom of woe and fear.
We wait with blanched and icy cheek
    The one-and-twentieth year :
For Justice lies, as seeds lie, dead,
But lifts at last a Gorgon head !

MEN.

What fear can reach our Thessaly ?
    What war disturb our peace ?
Long stablished is young amity
    Maid-blushing over Greece :
And fair Iolchus stands sublime,
A monument to lesson time.

WOMEN.

But if such fear were come indeed,
    Who reads the riddle dread
Spoken in frenzy by the seer
    Against the royal head ?
We know the Rhyme's involving spell—
Its purport ? Irresolvable !

MEN.

We heard his foolish maundering :
    But, bred in wiser ways,
We have forgotten : do ye sing
    The rune of ancient days !
To-day his curse cacophonous
Shall earn at least a laugh from us !

WOMEN.

"O ! when the armèd hand is nigh,
    Iolchus shall not see
Peace shining from Athena's sky
    Until the Fleece be free ;
Until the God of War shall scorn
The sting, and trust him to the horn.

"Until the Sun of Spring forsake
    His eastern home, and rise
Within our temple-walls and make
    One glory of the skies—
Until the King shall die and live,
Athena never shall forgive."

MEN.

Surely, O friends, at last 'tis clear
    The man was mad indeed !
Such nonsense we did never hear
    As this prophetic screed !
More, as 'tis never like this land
Should ever see an armèd hand.

* This play, written when Crowley was studying Hindu religion, derives much of its colour
and philosophical import from Pataiyali, the Upanishads and Sankarachariya's commentary,
Shaivite mysticism, the Bhagavat Purana, Bhagavat Gita, and Vedantist literature *in general.*

86

JASON.

Where is the son of Tyro and Poseidon?

MEN.

Iolchus' King has here a dwelling-place.

WOMEN.

See you the sword shake—and the iron hand
Not shaking? The man's mood is full of wrath.

MEN.

Peace, foolish! Were it so, we would not see.

WOMEN.

Ay me! this stranger seems most ominous.

JASON.

Where is the son of Tyro and Poseidon?

MEN.

This is the Palace-place of Pelias,
Son of Poseidon, of Iolchus King.

JASON.

Iolchus' King is here, in very truth.
Where is the son of Tyro?

MEN.

Who art thou?

JASON.

Know me for Jason and great Aeson's heir.

MEN.

We learn good news, most enviable sir:
That Aeson hath such grand inheritance.

JASON.

You have grown fat beneath an evil rule.
Your period is at hand. Go, one of you,
And drag the impious wretch before my sight!

MEN.

Aeson? Thy father?

JASON.

Play not with my wrath!
My mood is something dangerous.

MEN.

Dangerous sir,
I go indeed, to bring some danger more
Hither.

JASON.

Poltroonery dislikes the wise.
Fair maidens, I salute you pleasantly.

WOMEN.

Welcome, O welcome to the land,
Young heir of prophecy!
The armèd hand, the glittering brand,
The scabbard's jewellery!
That wealth avails not : cast it down!
The sword alone may win the crown!

JASON.

Ye languish wretched in the tyrant's rule?

WOMEN.

Most happy are we, King. But change is sweet.

JASON.

A short-lived omen of success to me.

WOMEN.

Nay, but adventure and the prophecy!

JASON.

I see I have but small support in you.

WOMEN.

Not so, great Jason! Had I suffered much,
My spirit had been broken to the scourge.
Now, being strong and happy, with what joy
I cry: Evohe! Revolution!
I have grown weary of this tiresome peace.

JASON.

I promise you intense unhappiness.

WOMEN.

Here is the ugly monster ! Out ! To think
We once believed him reverend and refined,
Saw majesty in all that tottering gait,
And honour in the goat-like beard of him !

FIRST WOMAN.

A week ago your blue eyes were in tears,
Sidelong regarding the old mountebank.

SECOND WOMAN.

To-day I would not be his concubine
For all Iolchus—for all Thessaly !

THIRD WOMAN.

I see the same glance seek out Jason now.

SECOND WOMAN.

Ay, there's a man ! What muscles ! What
    fine fire
In the quick eye ! What vigour and warm
    strength !

FIRST WOMAN.

Yes, in your wishes. But indeed he is
A proper man. Away, you ancient egg !

PELIAS.

With what audacious foot and impious voice
Strides this young man and talks? Let him
    advance,
Trembling at our offended majesty.
Who art thou whose rude summons startles us
From work of state to listen a young mouth
Beardless? Speak, man, for shortly thou
    shalt die.

JASON.

Athena speaks.

WOMEN.

Ah, there's a fine retort !

PELIAS.

Goddesses speak and men list reverently.
Could he not find a fitter messenger ?

JASON.

Her cause is Jason's. Jason therefore
    speaks.

PELIAS.

Aha ! A suppliant to our clemency !
I did mistake the gesture and the sword
Angrily gripped, the foot flung terribly
Foremost, the fierce, constrainèd attitude.
But—as a suppliant ! Tell thy woeful tale,
Sad youth ! Some woman thou hast loved
    and lost ?

JASON.

Thou hast robbed me of this kingdom.
    Thou hast kept
My father (poor half-witted man !) a slave
And parasite about thy court (one grief
The more I add to this account of thine !)
Myself a babe thou didst seek out to slay,
And, I being hid, with fish-hooks bent with
    lies
And gilded with most spacious promises,
Cunningly angled for old Chiron's [1] grace
To catch me yet. Athena hears me swear
To right all this—nay, answer me before
Anger get all the spoil of me, and drink
Thy life-blood in one gulp ! Descend that
    daïs !
Bend thou a suppliant at my awful knee,
And thus—perhaps—at least get grace of life.

. PELIAS.

And if I say I will not yield the throne ?

JASON.

I am of force to take it.

PELIAS.

                    Are my friends
Not faithful ? Who draws sword for Pelias ?

MEN.

Shall we not slay thee this presumptuous
    fool ?

[1] A Centaur who hid the child Jason.

JASON.

I am of force, I say.   I wrestled once
From sunrise to sunset with Heracles,
Great Heracles !   Not till the full moon
    rose
Availed his might to lay me prone.   Be-
    ware !
Ye weakling knaves !   I am of force, I say.

PELIAS.

Rebellious youth, the justice of thy cause
And force I will admit—where force goes
    far.
But think'st thou wait no wild Erinyes
For thee a guest in these my halls, for thee
Whose hands are dipped not yet in blood
    so deep
As to have murdered an old man, and him
Thy father's brother ?

JASON.

                            Justice covers all.
The Furies cannot follow if a man
To his own heart be reconciled.   They feed
On his own bosom, nay ! are born thereof.
An alien clan he might elude, but these,
Blood of his blood, he shall nor slay nor
    'scape.
My heart hath never pastured on regret
Or pang for thee.   My justice covers all.

PELIAS.

That one word " justice " covers all indeed
To thine own self.   But think'st thou for a
    word
To ruin many years of commonweal,
And poison in an hour the politics
Of states and thrones for—justice ?   Thou
    art just ;
But wisdom, but the life of innocents,
The happiness of all, are better served
By solemn thought and weighty counsel
    held.

JASON.

This is more simple.   I abolish thee—
One sword-sweep—and assume thy "politics."

PELIAS.

Thou art this " simple " !   Will my liege
    allies
(Willing with age and wisdom to accord)
Not tremble at thy firebrand breed, not
    think
Who hath in blood, an old man's blood,
    made fast
A perilous footing, may betimes discover
More " justice "—and invasion footing it
Hard after ?   Wilt thou plunge all Thessaly,
All Greece, in haste and sudden armament,
Fury of thought and frenzy of deed, at once
For justice ?   Wouldst thou be so violent
For justice, save in thine own cause, O boy ?
And wilt thou pity not the happy days
And storm-unshatterèd abodes of Greece ?

JASON.

Athena, who is Justice, also is
Wisdom : and also " She who buildeth
    towns."

PELIAS.

Think also, I am born of deity.
I am inured to majesty ; I know
How venerable is the sight of kings,
And how the serpent Treason writhes
    beneath
The royal foot, conscious of its own shame,
And how the lion of Rebellion cowers
Before the presence of a king unarmed,
Quelled by one mild glance of authority.

JASON.

A king unjust is shorn of majesty.

PELIAS.

Still the one fool's word—justice—answers
    all.
Would thou wert older and more politic !

JASON.

Would I were liar with thine own foul
    brand !
The gods are weary of thy cozening.

PELIAS.

To proof, then, boy. I lay my sceptre by,
Put off my crown, descend the steps to thee.
Here is my breast. Look firmly in my
face,
And slay me. Is there fear writ large and
deep
In mine old eyes? Or shudderest thou
with fear?

JASON.

More hate than fear. In sooth, I cannot
strike.

PELIAS.

A king is not so slain—except a madman
May fall upon him with averted head.[1]
Indeed, I conquer. [*Aside.*] Even so,
beware !
Victory ill-nurtured breeds the babe defeat.
[*Aloud.*] Listen, my brother's son ! Nay,
stoop not so,
Bending ashamèd brows upon the earth !
I am well weary of the world of men.
I grow both old and hateful to myself,
Most on the throne : power which to youth
is sweet
To age looks fearful. Also I have wept—
Alas ! how often !—and repented me
Of those unkingly deeds whereby I gained
This throne whose joy is turned to bitterness.
I will make peace with thee, and justice
still
Shall have a home and shrine in Thessaly.
Be patient notwithstanding ! Prove thyself
Valiant and wise—and reign here ! If in
sooth
An aged counsellor, whose reverend hair
Commands a hearing, may assist at all,
Wisdom to wisdom added, I am here.
Yet would I rather slide into my grave,
Untroubled with the destinies of states,
Even of such an one so dear to me
Who thus a score of years have nurtured it.

[1] These two lines are directly taken from
Eliphaz Levi.

JASON.

I hear thee. Thou art grown like royal
wine
Better with age. Forgive my violence !

PELIAS.

[*Aside.*] The fish bites hard. [*Aloud.*] There
is a prophecy :
" Once stirred, Iolchus never shall know
peace
Till in its temple hangs the Golden Fleece."
Now thou hast so disquieted our days,
The time is come : seek thou Aea's[1] isle,
And hang this trophy on our temple walls !

JASON.

Tell me what is this fleece.

PELIAS.
Let women sing.

WOMEN.

In Ares' grove, the sworded trees,
The world's heart wondering,
Hangs evermore the Golden Fleece,[2]
The glory of the spring,
The light of far Aea's coast.
Such glamour as befits a ghost.

Before that glittering woof the Sun
Shrinks back abashed in shame,
The splendour of the shining one,
One torrent-fleece of flame !
What heart may think, what tongue may
sing
The glory of the golden thing ?

[1] Colchis, a county of Asia, bounded on the
W. by the Euxine, on the N. by the Caucasus,
and on the E. by the Iberia. Distinguish from
Aeaea.
[2] The symbolism of the Fleece and its
guardians is curious. The Fleece is of (♈) Aries
the Ram, the sign of the spring. The sun
being exalted in this sign, the fleece is called
golden. Ares or Mars (♂) is in Astrology
the ruler of this sign. His other house is
Scorpio (♏) the Dragon. The whole legend is
thus a glyph of the Magnum Opus. That
Crowley neglects this is a significant mark of
the change to his maturer manner.

About the grove the scorpion coils
　　Inextricably wind
Within the wood's exceeding toils,
　　The shadow hot and blind ;
There lurk his serpent sorceries,
The guardian of the Golden Fleece.

The dragon lifts his nostrils wide
　　And jets a spout of fire ;
The warrior questing turns aside,
　　Not daring to desire ;
And Madness born of Ares lurks
Behind the wonder of his works.

Be sure that were the woodland way
　　Tracked snakewise to the core,
The dragon slain or driven away,
　　The good Fleece won by war,
Not yet should Ares sink his spear,
Or fail of flinging forth a fear.

The torch of Madness should be lit,
　　And follow him afar :
Upon his prow should Madness sit,
　　A baleful beacon-star ;
And in his home Despair and Strife
Lie in his bosom for a wife !

But oh, the glory of the quest,
　　The gainless goodly prize !
The fairest form man e'er caressed,
　　The word he heard most wise ;—
All lures of life avoid and cease
Before the winning of the Fleece !

O nameless splendour of the Gods,
　　Begotten hardly of Heaven !
Unspoken treasure of the abodes
　　Beyond the lightning levin !
No misery, no despair may pay
・ The joy to hold thee for a day !

JASON.

Athena's servant recks not much of Ares.

PELIAS.

Are thine eyes kindled at the golden
　　thought ?

JASON.

Mine eyes see farther than the Fleece of
　　Gold.

PELIAS.

What heroes can attain so fair a thing ?

JASON.

I have some friends who would esteem this
　　quest
Lightly—a maiden's pleasure-wandering
Through lilied fields a summer's afternoon.

PELIAS.

The Gods give strength ! I pray them send
　　thee back
Safe to this throne.

JASON.

　　　　　　　I will not see thy face
Ever again until the quest be won.
Rule thou with justice in my sacred seat
Until I come again.

PELIAS.

　　　　　　　The Gods thy speed.

MEN.

　The hardy hero goes to find
　　The living Fleece of Gold ;
　Or else, some death may chance to bind
　　Those limbs of manly mould.
　In sooth, I doubt if I shall earn
　The singer's fee for his return.

PELIAS.

Think now—I feared that fool. It must be
　　true
That guilt is timorous. Ay ! when danger's
　　none !
Let but swords flash—and guilt grows God
　　for might !
Indeed I rule—until he come again.
Ay, when the stars fall, Jason shall be king !

EXPLICIT ACTUS PRIMUS.

ARGONAUTAE.

ACTUS SECUNDUS.

ARGO.

ARGUS *the son of* PHRIXUS, JASON, HERACLES, CASTOR, POLLUX, THE- SEUS, ORPHEUS. *Chorus of* Heroes. *Chorus of* Shipbuilders.

SCENE : *An open place near Iolchus.*

CHORUS OF SHIPBUILDERS.

THE sound of the hammer and steel !
The song of the level and line !
The whirr of the whistling wheel !
The ring of the axe on the pine !

The joy of the ended labour,
As the good ship plunges free
By sound of pipe and tabor
To front the sparkling sea !

The mystery-woven spell !
The voyage of golden gain !
The free full sails that swell
On the swell of the splendid main !

The song of the axe and the wedge !
The clang of the hammer and chain !
Keen whistle of chisel and edge !
Smooth swish of the sliding plane !

Hail to the honour of toil !
Hail ! to the ship flown free !
Hail ! to the golden spoil,
And the glamour of all the sea !

HERACLES.

A good stout song, friend Argus, matching well
The mighty blows thou strikest : yet me-
thinks
One blow should serve to drive yon nail well home
Where thou with tenfold stroke—

THESEUS.
Good Heracles !
Not all men owe thy strength——

ARGUS.
Nay, let him try !
Take my toy hammer !

HERACLES.
I have split the wood !

THESEUS.
Vexation sits tremendous on his brow.
Beware a hero's fury ! Thou art mad,
Argus, to play so dangerous a trick.

ARGUS.
True, Theseus—if he had but hit his thumb !

CASTOR.
Cease this fool's talk. The moon waits not the work.

POLLUX.
The sun will sink no later for your pleasure.
On to thy work, man.

THESEUS.
He that traps a lion
And baits him for an hour, and lets him go,
Does well to think before he tempt again
The forest paths.

HERACLES.
The wise man wisely thinks
That nothing is but wisdom—and myself
Think strongly that no other thing exists
But strength : so with his subtleties of mind
He baffles me ; and I lift up my club,
And with one blow bespatter his wise brains.

JASON.
Ay, not for nothing did the darkness reign
Those eight-and-forty hours,[1] O Zeus-begot !

[1] Zeus caused a night to extend to this length, that he might efficiently beget Hercules.

THESEUS.

Tell me, friend master, how the work goes on.
When shall our gallant vessel breast the deep?
When shall we see the sun sink o'er the poop,
And look toward moonrise, and the land be lost,
And the perched watcher on the mast behold
The melting mirror of the ocean meet
The crystallising concave of the sky?

ARGUS.

All this shall happen when the work is done.

JASON.

How many moons, friend fool, before that day?

ARGUS.

These things are known not even to the Gods,
Except the Father only.[1]

HERACLES.

Fools must talk.

ARGUS.

I talk, divulging nothing.

HERACLES.

I strike thee,
Yet act not.

ARGUS.

Hero, stay that heavy hand!
The ship shall sail ere spring.

THESEUS.

But now you talk
More as befits a workman to a king.

[1] The satire is on Matthew xxiv. 36.

JASON.

Be gentle now, my friends! These ship-builders,
Reared in the rugged borders of the North,[1]
Have northern manners; surly if attacked,
But genial when——

ARGUS.

The proper treatment is
Kindness—like lions whom Demeter tamed.

THESEUS.

I promise thee, the next time thou art wroth,
A second kindness from Alcides' hand.

ARGUS.

Spare me that, King, and take, thyself, a club.

JASON.

King Theseus, thou art far reputed wise.
Hast thou not learnt a lesson from the hap
Of Heracles supreme in—shipbuilding?
I by my meekness will abash thy strength.
Good Argus, thou art unsurpassed in art
To curve the rougher timbers, to make smooth
The joints and girders, and to plane and work
The iron and the nailheads, and to lift
Row after row the tiers of benches thrice
In triple beauty, and to shape the oars,
To raise the mast——

ARGUS.

Thy knowledge staggers me!
How wast thou thus instructed?

JASON.

By much thought.
To clamp the decks——

[1] Argus is wittily characterised as a Scottish shipbuilder.

ARGUS.

I stand with brows abashed.
Thou art the master—build the ship thyself.

JASON.

Nay, but my knowledge is of mind alone.
I cannot so apply it as to build
An Argo.

ARGUS.

Yet I verily believe
Such mind must pierce far deeper than these
names,
Seeking the very nature of the things
Thou namest thus so pat. Perchance to
thee
These logs, nails, bolts, tools, have some
life of sense,
Some subtle language. Tell us what they
say![1]

THESEUS.

'Tis but a giber—leave the churl alone.

JASON.

Indeed I spake of things I knew not of.

ARGUS.

You speak more wisely when you float away
Into pure dream, and talk of mystic things
That no man born of woman understands,
And therefore does not dare to contradict.

JASON.

He who speaks much and bitterly at last
Lays himself open to retort. I think
I never heard such contradictions fly
As when men talk of gods—that never
were!

ARGUS.

Thou wouldst do better to leave men alone.
The wisest talk is folly when work waits.
Look! how these sturdy villains gape around,
Fling down their task, and hang upon the
words
That flow like nectar from your majesty.

[1] The gibe in these twenty lines is against
Rudyard Kipling's silly vitalisation of machinery,
and his ignorance even of the correct terms.

CASTOR.

In truth, my friend, if you would wear your
crown
This side of Orcus, you should go away.

POLLUX.

Ay! let the men work! For a mind as yours
Is good, and skill as theirs is also good.

CASTOR.

But mix the manual and the mental—well,
No ship was built by pure philosophy.

POLLUX.

Nor yet designed by artisans.

JASON.

Enough!
Come, great Alcides, it is time to go.

ARGUS.

A fool allows a moment's irritation
To move the purpose of a thousand years.
Go, go!

HERACLES.

Remember! We are met this day
To call upon the name with praise and
prayer
Of great Athena, since our ship is built
With sculptured olive pregnant in the prow,
And all the length of pine is coiled and
curled
With the swift serpent's beauty, and the owl
Sits in huge state upon the midmost bench.
Thus, therefore, by the manifest design,
Joining the wisdom to the power and will,
We build the Argo.

ARGUS.

What a heavy club
We carry! And how well becomes our figure
The lion's skin!

HERACLES.

Be still, thou art an ass!

ARGUS.

The fabled ass, O Zeus-descended one ?

HERACLES.

What ass ?

ARGUS.

The one that wore the lion's skin !

THESEUS.

This fellow were beneath a man's contempt.
How should a God-born heed him ?

JASON.

We are here,
Men, to invoke Athena, immolate
The sacred cock upon her altar-stone,
That She, who sprang in armour from the brain
Of the All-Father, may descend to bless
Our labours, since delay grows dangerous,
Haply by Her power and subtlety
She please to aid the work, and to perform
A prodigy to save us ! Mighty Queen,
That art the balance and the sword alike
In cunning Argus' brain——

HERACLES.

Ay ! Mighty Wisdom,
Who thus can overshadow such a fool,
And make him capable to build a ship.

ARGUS.

O Thou ! Athena, whose bright wisdom shone
In this beef-witted fellow, making him
Competent even to sweep a stable out !
Glorious task !—I shall return anon.

JASON.

Nay, follow not ! The Goddess were displeased,
Coming, to find our greatest hero gone.

THESEUS.

This is the midmost hour of day.

JASON.

Arise,
All heroes, circling round the sacred stone
In beautiful order and procession grave,
While our chief priest, our mightiest in song,
The dowered of Phoebus, great Oeager's heir,
Invokes that glory on the sacrifice
That kindles all its slumber into life
And vivid flame descending on the wheel
And chariot of lightning, licking up
The water of the loud-resounding sea
Lustral, poured seven times upon the earth,
And in one flash consuming wood and stone
And the sweet savour of the sacrifice.

ORPHEUS.

But when the flame hath darted from the eye
Of my divine existence, and hath left
Nothing, where was the altar and the earth,
The water and the incense and the victim—
Nothing of all remains ! Then look to it
That ye invoke not Wisdom by the Name
Of bright Athena !

JASON.

We are here to call
Upon that Wisdom by that mighty Name !

ORPHEUS.

Who calleth upon Wisdom is not wise.
Is it not written in the Sibyl's book [1]
That Wisdom crieth in the streets aloud
And none regardeth her ? Obey my voice.

JASON.

O master of Apollo's lyre and light !
We are not wise—and for that very cause
We meet to-day to call on Wisdom.

ORPHEUS.

Well !
The altar stands, shadowing the Universe
That with my fire of Knowledge I destroy—
And there is Wisdom—but invoke Her not,
Friends, Who is only when none other is.

[1] Actually Proverbs i. 20.

JASON.

Let us begin : the hour draws on apace.
Drive off the demons from the sacrifice !

ORPHEUS.

Let all the demons enter and dwell therein !
My friends, ye are as ignorant as priests !
Let there be silence while the sleeper [1]
    wakes !

O coiled and constricted and chosen !
  O tortured and twisted and twined !
Deep spring of my soul deep frozen,
  The sleep of the truth of the mind !
    As a bright snake curled
    Round the vine of the World !

O sleeper through dawn and through day-
    light,
  O sleeper through dusk and through
    night !
O shifted from white light to gray light,
  From gray to the one black light !
    O silence and sound
    In the far profound !

O serpent of scales as an armour
  To bind on the breast of a lord !
Not deaf to the Voice of the Charmer,
  Not blind to the sweep of the sword !
    I strike to the deep
    That thou stir in thy sleep !

Rise up from mine innermost being !
  Lift up the gemmed head to the heart !
Lift up till the eyes that were seeing
  Be blind, and their life depart !
    Till the Eye that was blind [2]
    Be a lamp to my mind !

[1] The Hindus hold that the Kundalini, the
spring of spiritual power, lies coiled and sleeping upon a lotus-flower at the base of the spine.
She may be aroused by various methods.
[2] The "third eye," that rudimentary eye
called the pineal gland.

Coil fast all thy coils on me, dying,
  Absorbed in the sense of the Snake !
Stir, leave the flower-throne, and up-
    flying
Hiss once, and hiss thrice, and awake !
    Then crown me and cling !
    Flash forward—and spring !

Flash forth on the fire of the altar,
  The stones, and the sacrifice shed ;
Till the Three Worlds [1] flicker and falter,
  And life and her love be dead !
    In mysterious joy
    Awake—and destroy !

JASON.

It is enough !

HERACLES.

Too great for a god's strength !

THESEUS.

Speak !

CASTOR.

Change !   Not to be borne !

POLLUX.

But this is death !

ORPHEUS.

Let the light fade.   The oracle is past.

JASON.

The Voice is past.   We are alive again.

ORPHEUS.

What spake That Silence ?

HERACLES.

"This is not a quest
Where strength availeth aught."   I shall not
    go.

[1] Of gods, men, and demons.

JASON.

Nay, brother. The voice was : "The end is sorrow !"

THESEUS.

Ye heard not, O dull-witted ! Unto me
(Alone of all ye wise) the great voice came,
"The Gates of Hell shall not in all prevail."

CASTOR.

I heard, "Regret not thy mortality !
Love conquers death !"

POLLUX.

But I, "Regret not thou
Thine immortality ! Love conquers life !"[1]

ORPHEUS.

A partial wisdom to a partial ear.

JASON

But what speech came to thee ?

ORPHEUS.

I heard no voice.

ARGUS.

What means this ? Here's my labour thrown away,
My skill made jest of, all my wage destroyed
At one fell stroke.

JASON.

What ? Is the Argo burnt ?

[1] Pollux being immortal, and Castor mortal, at the former's request Zeus allowed them to pool their fates, and live alternate days in Hades and Olympus.

ARGUS.

Burnt ! Should I then complain ? The ship is finished.

JASON.

The Goddess, furious at thine absence, Argus,
Hath frenzied thee with some delusion.

HERACLES.

Calm !
Control thy madness ! I am sorry now
My pungent wit so shamed his arrogance
As made him seem to scorn Athena.

ARGUS.

Thou !
But see me, I am ruined. The good ship
Is finished ! Where's my daily wage ?

JASON.

Be sure
I pay thee treble if thy tale be true.

ARGUS.

Ay ! treble nothing ! I shall buy a palace.

JASON.

Treble thine utmost wish.

ARGUS.

Two evils then
Thou pilest on one good ! But come and see !

[*The Argo is discovered.*

CHORUS OF HEROES.

By Wisdom framed from ancient days
   The stately Argo stands above ;
Too firm to fear, too great to praise,
   The might of bright Athena's love !
Oh ! ship of glory ! tread the foam,
And bring our guerdon from its home !

G

The silent thought, the hand unseen,
  The rayless majesty of light
Shed from the splendour of our Queen
  Athena! mystery and might ;
These worked invisibly to bring
The end of triumph to our King.

Great Jason, wronged by hate of man,
  Shall pass the portals of the deep ;
Shall seek the waters wide and wan ;
  Shall pass within the land of sleep ;
And there the guardians of the soil
Shall rest at last from pain and toil.

O ruler of the empyréan,
  Behold his fervour conquering
The fury of the breed Cadmean,
  The dragons of the Theban king ;
And armèd men shall spring from earth
In vain to ward the gloomy girth !

But thou, Athena, didst devise
  Some end beyond our mortal ken,
Thy soul impenetrably wise
  Shines not to us unthinking men.
O guard the warrior band of Greece,
And win for us the Golden Fleece !

By miracle this happy day
  The ship is finished for our quest.
Bring thou the glory from the gray !
  Bring thou our spirits into rest !
O Wisdom, that hast helped so far,
  Sink never thou thy guiding star !

CHORUS OF WORKMEN.

Then let us gather one and all,
  And launch our dragon on the main
With paeans raised most musical,
  Until our heroes come again.
With watching and with prayer we wait
The imperious Destinies of Fate !

EXPLICIT ACTUS SECUNDUS.

ARGONAUTAE.

ACTUS TERTIUS.

MEDEA.

AEETES, JASON, MEDEA, Messengers,
Chorus of Heroes.

SCENE : *The Palace of* AEETES.

AEETES.

Were this man son of Zeus, beloved of
    Heaven,
And skilled with very craft of Maia's son,
Stronger than Phoebus, subtler than the
    Sphinx,
This plague should catch him, nor my
    wisdom spare.

CHORUS OF HEROES.

Thus hast thou sent him unto Hades, king.

AEETES.

Not otherwise were such gain possible.
Ye are the witnesses that with much skill,
And eloquence of shining words, and
    thought
Darkling behind their measured melody,
I did dissuade him.

CHORUS.

          Such an enterprise
After such toils no man should lightly leave.
Remember all the tasks impossible
This hero hath already done, befòre
He ever touched this sounding coast of
    thine.

AEETES.

Alas! but now his weird is loneliness !

CHORUS.

Was that from Destiny, or will of thine ?

AEETES.

I love him little.   Yet my words were true,
Nor would it skill him aught if myriad mēn
Bucklered his back and breast.   For when
     a man
Batters with sword-hilt at the frowning
     gates
That lead to the Beyond, not human force—
Hardly the favour of the gods themselves—
Shall stead him in that peril.

CHORUS.
                    Yet we know
Courage may conquer all things.

AEETES.
                    Such a man
Is greater than the gods !

CHORUS.
                    If only he
Know who he is—that all these gods and
     men
And things are but the shadows of himself !

AEETES.

I cannot give you hope.   Await the end.

CHORUS.

We fear indeed that in the trap
   Of wiles our king is taken.
Lachesis shakes a careless lap
   And dooms divine awaken !
A desolate and cruel hap
   In this sad hour is shaken.

The desperate son and violent
   Of Helios hath designed
A fate more hard than Pelias meant,
   Revolving in his mind
Mischief to catch the coiled ascent
   Of groaning humankind.

O bright Athena, hitherto
   Protectress of the quest,
Divide the deep descending blue !
   Be present, ever-blest !
Bring thou the hero Jason through
   To victory—and rest !

MEDEA.

Not by Athena's calm omnipotence,
O heroes, look for safety !   Little men,
Looking to God, are blinded ; mighty ones,
Seeking His presence, reel before the glance ;
And They, the greatest that may be of men,
Become that Light, and care no whit for
     earth.
But all your prayers are answered by your-
     selves,
As I myself achieve this thought of mine.

CHORUS.

To me thou seemest to blaspheme the gods.

MEDEA.

Belike I seem, O ye of little wit.

CHORUS.

Surely thy tender years and gentle looks
Belie such hatred to our king !   I scorn
To triumph on an enemy once fallen.

MEDEA.

Fools always !   I am tenderer than my years,
And gentler than my glances.

CHORUS.
                    Sayst thou—what ?

MEDEA.

Ye know me a most powerful sorceress.

CHORUS.

So I have heard, O lotus-footed [1] one !
Nathless I see not any miracle.

MEDEA.

Last night the heavy-hearted audience
Broke up, and Jason wended wearily
His way, oppressed by direful bodements of
The fate of this forenoon.   I saw him go
Sad, and remembered how sublime he stood,

   [1] An epithet common in the East, conveying
a great compliment.

Bronzed with a ruder sun than ours, and
  scarred
(Rough tokens of old battles) yet so calm
And mild (with all that vigour) that to me
Came a swift pity—the enchanter's bane.
That I flung from me. But my subtle soul
Struck its own bosom with the sword of
  thought,
So that I saw not pity, but desire !

CHORUS.

Surely a bane more potent than the first.

MEDEA.

Love is itself enchantment !

CHORUS.
                              Some kind god
Whispers from this a little light of hope.

MEDEA.

Only the hopeless are the happy ones.[1]

CHORUS.

But didst thou turn him from his gleaming
  goal ?
Cover that shame with sweeter shame than
  this ?

MEDEA.

Thou knowest that his vigil was to keep,
Invoking all Olympus all the night,
And then to yoke the oxen, and to plough
The fearful furrow, sow the dreadful seed,
Smite down the armies, and assuage the
  pest
Of slime thrice coiled about the sacred grove.

CHORUS.

Thy bitter love disturbed that solitude ?

MEDEA.

Not bitter, heroes. See ye yet the end ?

1 "The hopeless are happy, like the girl
Pingala " (Buddhist Proverb). Pingala waited
for her lover, and mourned because he came
not. But, giving up hope at last, she regained
her cheerfulness. *Cf.* 2 Samuel xii. 15-23.

CHORUS.

Our good quest ended by thy father's hate,
And by thy own hour's madness ! This
  see.

MEDEA.

But if he gain the Fleece ?

CHORUS.
                              A blissful end.

MEDEA.

This end and that are moulded diversely.

CHORUS.

Riddle no more, nor ply with doubtful hope
Hearts ready to rejoice and to despair
Equally minded.

MEDEA.
                  At the midmost hour,
His mind given up to sleepless muttering
Of charms not mine—decrees Olympian—
All on a sudden he felt fervent arms
Flung round him, and a hot sweet body's
  rush
Lithe to embrace him, and a cataract
Of amber-scented hair hissing about
His head, and in the darkness two great
  eyes
Flaming above him, and the whole face filled
With fire and shapen as kisses. And those
  arms
And kisses and mad movements of quick
  love
Burnt up his being, and his life was lost
In woman's love at last !

CHORUS.
                          Unseemly act !
Who dared thus break on meditation ?

MEDEA.
                                          I.

CHORUS.

Surely thy passion mastered thee, O queen !

MEDEA.

I tell you—thus the night passed.

CHORUS.

Verily,
The woman raves.

MEDEA.

Such victory as this
Outsails all shame. Before the dawn was up
I bound such talismans about his breast
That fire and steel grow dew and flowery
    wreaths
For all their power to hurt him. Presently
I made a posset, drugged with somnolence,
Sleepy with poppy and white hellebore,
Fit for the dragon. This was my design.

CHORUS.

Beware thy father's anger when he finds
His plans thus baffled ! He will murder us.

MEDEA.

Heroes indeed ye are, and lion hearts.

CHORUS.

No woman need school me in bravery.

MEDEA.

Rather a hare.

CHORUS.

Most impudent of whores !

MEDEA.

But when my husband comes victorious
Fleece-laden, he will rather——

CHORUS.

Wilt thou then
Further my ruin, making known this shame !

MEDEA.

Here is the Argive sense of gratitude.
Let me stir up its subtler thought, and show
What favours ye may gather afterward
From hands and lips ye scorn—not courte-
    ously.

CHORUS.

What ? Canst thou save us from this newer
    doom ?

MEDEA.

I love your leader with no mortal love,
But with the whole strength of a sorceress.

CHORUS.

It seems indeed thy hot will can bewitch
Our chaste one with one action impudent.

MEDEA.

I will not leave him ever in the world.

CHORUS.

Persistence in these ills—will cure them not.
" Worst " is the hunter, " worse " the hound,
    when " bad "
Is the stag's name.

MEDEA.

We rule Iolchus' land.

CHORUS.

Indeed the hunter follows. I despise
Lewd conduct in the lowest, and detest
Spells hurtful to the head, when ancient
    hags
Brew their bad liquors at the waning moon,
Barking their chants of murder. But to rule
A land, and wive a king, and breed to him
Kings—then such persons are unsuitable.

MEDEA.

Unless these words were well repented of
I might transform ye into——

CHORUS.

Stay, great queen !

MEDEA.

Well for your respite comes this messenger.

MESSENGER.

Queen and fair mother of great kings un-
born,
And mighty chosen of the land of Greece,
A tidings of deep bliss is born to you.

CHORUS.

Tell me that Jason has achieved the quest.

MESSENGER.

Truth is no handmaid unto happiness.

CHORUS.

What terror dost thou fill my heart withal?

MEDEA.

O timorous heroes! Let the herald speak!
Who meets fear drives her back; who flees
from fear
Stumbles; who cares not, sees her not.
Speak on!

THE MESSENGER.

Terrible bellowings as of angry bulls
Broke from the stable as the first swift shaft
Of dawn smote into it: and stampings fierce
Resounded, shaking the all-mother earth.
Whereunto came the calm and kingly man,
Smiling as if a sweet dream still beguiled
His waking brows; not caring any more
For spring or summer; heeding least of all
That tumult of ox-fury. Suddenly
A light sprang in his face; the great hand shot
Forth, and broke in the brass-bound door;
the day
Passed with him inwards; then the brazen
hoofs
Beat with a tenfold fury on the stone.
But Jason, swiftly turned, evaded these,
And chose two oxen from that monstrous herd
To whose vast heads he strode, and by the
horns
Plucked them. Then fire, devouring, sprang
at him
From furious nostrils: and indignant breath,
Fountains of seething smoke, spat forth at him.

But with no tremor of aught that seemed like
fear
Drew them by sheer strength from their
place, and yoked
Their frenzy to his plough, and with the goad
Urged them, thrice trampling the accursèd field
Until the furrows flamed across the sun,
Treading whose glory stood Apollo's self
As witness of the deed. Then a last thrust
Savage, drove them less savage to their stalls,
And Jason turned and laughed. Then drew
he out
The dreadful teeth of woe, Cadmean stock
Of Thebes' old misery, and presently
Pacing the furrowed field, he scattered them
With muttered words of power athwart the
course
Of the bright moon, due path of pestilence
And terror. Ere the last bone fell to earth
The accursèd harvest sprang to life. Armed
men,
Fiery with anger, rose upon the earth
While Jason stood, one witnessing a dream,
Not one who lives his life. The sword and
spear
Turn not to him, but mutual madness strikes
The warriors witless, and fierce wrath invades
Their hearts of fury, and with arms engaged
They fell upon each other silently
And slew, and slew. As in the middle seas
A mirage flashes out and passes, so
The phantoms faded, and the way was clear.
Thus, stepping ever proud and calm, he went
Unto the grove of Ares, where the worm,
Huge in his hatred, guarded all. But now
Sunk in some stupor, surely sent of Zeus,
He stirred not. Stepping delicately past
The dragon, then came Jason to the grove
And saw what tree umbrageous bore the fruit
That he had saddened for so long. And he,
Rending the branches of that wizard Oak,
With a strong grasp tore down the Fleece of
Gold.
Then came a voice: "Woe, woe! Aea's isle!
The glory is departed!" And a voice
Answered it "Woe!" Then Jason seemed
to see
Some Fear behind the little former fears;

And his face blanched a moment, as behold-
ing
Some Fate, some distant grief.   Then,
    catching sight
Now of the glory of his gain, he seemed
Caught in an ecstasy, treading the earth
As in a brighter dream than Aphrodite
Sent ever to a man, he turned himself
(We could not see him for the golden flame
Burning about him !) moving hitherward.
But I took horse and hasted, since reward
May greet such tidings, and for joy to see
Your joy exceed my joy.

MEDEA.

           Reward indeed
Awaits thee from such folk as us, who stand
In fear of life, when great Aeetes hears
This news, and how all came.

MESSENGER.

           My lady's smile
Is the reward I sought, not place nor gold.

MEDEA.

Thou hast it, child.

SECOND MESSENGER.

           The hero is at hand.

CHORUS.

O happy of mortals !
O fronter of fear,
The impassable portals !
Ye heavens, give ear !
Our song shall be rolled in the praise of the
    gold, and its glory be told where the
    heavenly fold rejoices to hold the stars
    in its sphere.

O hero Iolchian !
Warrior king !
From the kingdom Colchian
The Fleece dost bring !
Our song shall be sung and its melody flung
    where the Lyre and the Tongue are
    fervid and young, all islands among
    where the Sirens sing.

Thou bearest, strong shoulder,
The sunbright fleece !
Glow swifter and bolder
And brighter—and cease !
O glory of light ! O woven of night ! O
    shining and bright ! O dream of de-
    light ! How splendid the sight for the
    dwellers of Greece !

Gained is the guerdon !
The prize is won.
The fleecy burden,
The soul of the sun !
The toil is over; the days discover high joys
    that hover of lover and lover, and fates
    above her are fallen and done.

JASON.

Queen of this people ! O my heart's desire
Spotless, the Lady of my love, and friends
By whose heroic ardours I am found
Victor at last, well girded with the spoil
Of life in gleaming beauty, and this prize
Thrice precious, my Medea—all is won !
Needs only now the favouring kiss of Eurus,
Bright-born of Eos, to fulfil for us
The last of all the labours, to inspire
The quick-raised sail, and fill that flushing
    gold
With thrice desirèd breath, that once again
Our prow plunge solemn in the Argive waters
To strains of music—victory at peace
Mingling with sweeter epithalamy—
To tell our friends how happy was the quest.

MEDEA.

But not those strains of music, though divine
From Orpheus' wingèd lyre, exalt at all
Our joy to joy, beyond all music's power !

CHORUS.

I fear Aeetes, and the Pelian guile.

JASON.

Fear is but failure, herald of distress !

MEDEA

What virtue lives there in the coward's hrate ?

CHORUS.

In sooth, I have no fear at all—to flee.

JASON.

Night, like a mist, steals softly from the East.
The hand of darkness gathers up the folds
Of day's gold garment, and the valleys sink
Into slow sadness, though the hills retain
That brilliance for a little.

CHORUS.
Let us go !
Methinks that under cover of the night
I may escape Aeetes.

JASON.
If he chase,
Our Argo is not battered by rough winds
So far but what some fight were possible.

MEDEA.   [*Leads forward* ABSYRTUS.]
I know a better way than that, my lord.
This boy shall come with us.

JASON.
Ah, not to Greece !
Aea needs to-morrow's king.

MEDEA.
" With us "
I said.   " To Greece "—I said not.

CHORUS.
What is this?
Thou hintest at some dangerous destiny.

MEDEA.
Come love, to the long years of love with
me !
JASON.
Form, heroes, and in solemn order stride ;
The body-guardians of the Golden Fleece !

MEDEA.
Guarding your king and queen on every
side —

CHORUS.

We sail triumphant to the land of Greece.

MEDEA.

A woman's love, a woman's power be told
Through ages, gainers of the Fleece of Gold.

EXPLICIT ACTUS TERTIUS.

ARGONAUTAE.

ACTUS QUARTUS.

SIRENAE.

JASON, MEDEA, ORPHEUS, THESEUS, HER-
ACLES, *Chorus of* Heroes, *the* Sirens.

SCENE : *The Argo.*

MEDEA.

Ay ! I would murder not my brother only,
But tear my own limbs, strew them on the
sea,[1]
To keep one fury from the man I love !

CHORUS.

This act and speech are much akin to madness.

MEDEA.

Remember that your own skins pay the price.

CHORUS.

I now remember somewhat of the voice
Of the oracle, that Madness should hunt hard
On the thief's furtive track, upon the prow
Brooding, and at the table president,
And spouse-like in the bed.

[1] The Argonauts being pursued by Aeetes,
Medea threw the severed limbs and trunk of
Absyrtus upon the sea, so that the father, stop-
ping to perform the sacred duties of burial, was
left behind.

MEDEA.

　　　　　　But this is like
That Indian fable [1] of a king: how he,
Taking some woman—an indecent act
Not proper to be done!—against the will
Of priests or princes, sought the nuptial bed
And
　" Climbed the bed's disastrous side,
　He found a serpent, not a bride ;
　And scarcely daring to draw breath,
　He passed the dumb night-hours with
　　death,
　Till in the morning cold and gray
　The hooded fear glided away.
　Which morning saw ten thousand pay
　The price of jesting with a king ! "—

JASON.

Indeed these toils and dangerous pursuits,
Labours and journeys, go to make one
　mad.
Well were it to beguile our weariness
With song.

MEDEA.

　　And here is the sole king of song.

ORPHEUS.

My song breaks baffled on the rocks of
　time
If thy bewitching beauty be the theme.

MEDEA.

Sing me thy song, sweet poet, of the sea,
That song of swimming when thy love lost
　sense
Before the passion of the Infinite.

JASON.

The more so as my master warns me oft
Of late how near that island is, where dwell
The alluring daughters of Melpomene.

[1] The " fable " is Crowley's own.

ORPHEUS. [1]

Light shed from seaward over breakers bend-
　ing
　Kiss-wise to the emerald hollows : light
　　divine
　Whereof the sun is God, the sea his
　　shrine ;
Light in vibrations rhythmic ; light unending ;
　Light sideways from the girdling crags
　　extending
　Unto this lone and languid head of
　　mine ;
　Light, that fulfils creation as with wine,
Flows in the channels of the deep : light,
　　rending
　The adamantine columns of the night,
　Is laden with the love-song of the light.

Light, pearly-glimmering through dim gulf
　and hollow,
　Below the foam-kissed lips of all the sea ;
　Light shines from all the sky and up to
　　me
From the amber floors of sand : Light calls
　　Apollo !
The shafts of fire fledged of the eagle follow
　The crested surf, and strike the shore,
　　and flee
　Far from green cover, nymph-enchanted
　　lea,
Fountain, and plume them white as the sea-
　　swallow,
　And turn and quiver in the ocean, seem-
　　ing
　The glances of a maiden kissed, or
　　dreaming.

Light, as I swim through rollers green and
　gleaming,
　Sheds its most subtle sense to penetrate
　This heart I thought impervious to Fate.
Now the sweet light, the full delight, is
　　beaming

[1] The song describes Waikiki Beach, near
Honolulu.

Through me and burns me: all my flesh is
teeming
With the live kisses of the sea, my mate,
My mistress, till the fires of life abate
And leave me languid, man-forgotten, deem-
ing
I see in sleep, in many-coloured night,
More hope than in the flame-waves of
the light.

Light ! ever light ! I swim far out and follow
The footsteps of the wind, and light in-
vades
My desolate soul, and all the cypress
shades
Glow with transparent lustre, and the hollow
I thought I had hidden in my heart must
swallow
The bitter draught of Truth ; no Nereid
maids
Even in my sea are mine ; the whole
sea's glades
And hills and springs are void of my Apollo—
The Sea herself my tune and my desire !
The Sun himself my lover and my lyre !

CHORUS.

This song is sweeter than the honeycomb.

MEDEA.

Nearly as sweet as good friends quarrelling.

JASON.

Look, friends, methinks I see a silvern shape
Like faint mist floating on the farthest sea.

MEDEA.

I see a barren rock above the tides.

JASON.

I hear a sound like water whispering.

MEDEA.

I hear a harsh noise like some ancient crone
Muttering curses.

JASON.

Now I hear a song.
'Tis like some shape of sleep that moans for
joy,
Some bridal sob of love !

MEDEA.

O Son of God !
My poet, swiftly leap the live lyre forth !
Else we are all enchanted—yet to me
This song is nowise lovely. But in him
I note the live look of the eyes leap up,
And all his love for me forgotten straight
At the mere echo of that tune.

ORPHEUS.

Hark, friends !
Aea's tune—my Colchian harbour-song ![1]

I hear the waters faint and far,
And look to where the Polar Star,
Half hidden in the haze, divides
The double chanting of the tides ;
But, where the harbour's gloomy mouth
Welcomes the stranger to the south,
The water shakes, and all the sea
Grows silver suddenly.

As one who standing on the moon
Sees the vast horns in silver hewn,
Himself in darkness, and beholds
How silently all space unfolds
Into her shapeless breast the spark
And sacred phantom of the dark ;
So in the harbour-horns I stand
Till I forget the land.

Who sails through all that solemn space
Out to the twilight's secret place,
The sleepy waters move below
His ship's imaginary flow.
No song, no lute, so lowly chaunts
In woods where still Arisbe haunts,
Wrapping the wanderer with her tresses
Into untold caresses.

[1] The harbour in which this lyric was written
was that of Vera Cruz.

For none of all the sons of men
That hath known Artemis, again
Turns to the warmer earth, or vows
His secrets to another spouse.
The moon resolves her beauty in
The sea's deep kisses salt and keen;
The sea assumes the lunar light,
And he—their eremite !

In their calm intercourse and kiss
Even hell itself no longer is ;
For nothing in their love abides
That passes not beneath their tides,
And whoso bathes in light of theirs,
And water, changes unawares
To be no separate soul, but be
Himself the moon and sea.

Not all the wealth that flowers shed,
And sacred streams, on that calm head ;
Not all the earth's spell-weaving dream
And scent of new-turned earth shall seem
Again indeed his mother's breast
To breathe like sleep and give him rest;
He lives or dies in subtler swoon
Between the sea and moon.

So standing, gliding, undeterred
By any her alluring word
That calls from older forest glades,
My soul forgets the gentle maids
That wooed me in the scarlet bowers,
And golden cluster-woof of flowers ;
Forgets itself, content to be
Between the moon and sea.

No passion stirs their depth, nor moves ;
No life disturbs their sweet dead loves ;
No being holds a crown or throne ;
They are, and I in them, alone :
Only some lute-player grown star
Is heard like whispering flowers afar ;
And some divided, single tune
Sobs from the sea and moon.

Amid thy mountains shall I rise,
O moon, and float about thy skies?
Beneath thy waters shall I roam,
O sea, and call thy valleys home ?

Or on Daedalian oarage fare
Forth in the interlunar air ?
Imageless mirror-life ! to be
Sole between moon and sea.

CHORUS.

No song can lure us while he sings so well.

JASON.

But look ! I see entrancing woman-forms
That beckon—fairy-like and not of earth.
So, fitter than the bed of this my queen
To rest heroic limbs !

MEDEA.

                    The wretched one !
Thou knowest that their kiss is death !

JASON.

                              Perhaps.
It were their kiss.

MEDEA.

                    Are not my kisses sweet ?

JASON.

Listen, they sing.   This time the words ring
    true,
Sailing across that blue abyss between.
Like young birds winging their bright flight
    the notes
Glimmer across the sea.

MEDEA.

                    They sing, they sing !

PARTHENOPE.

O mortal, tossed on life's unceasing ocean,
    Whose waves of joy and sorrow never
    cease,
Eternal change—one changeless thing,
    commotion !
    Even in death no hint of calm and
    peace !—

Here is the charm, the life-assuaging
    potion,
  Here is a better home for thee than
    Greece !
Come, lover, to my deep, soft, sleepy
    breast !
        Here is thy rest !

O mortal, sad is life ! But in my kisses
  Thou may'st forget its fever-parchèd
    thirst.
Age, death, and sorrow fade in slender
    blisses :
  My swoon of love drinks up the draught
    accurst.
And all thy seasons grow as sweet as this
    is,
  One constant summer in sleep's bosom
    nursed.
All storm and sunlight, star and season,
    cease,
        Here is thy peace.

O mortal, sad is love ! But my dominion
  Extends beyond love's ultimate abode.
Eternity itself is but a minion,
  Lighting my way on the untravelled
    road.
Gods shelter 'neath one shadow of my
    pinion.
  Thou only tread the path none else hath
    trode !
Come, lover, in my breast all blooms
    above,
        Here is thy love !

MEDEA.

My poet, now ! The one song in the world !

ORPHEUS.

Above us on the mast is spread
  The splendour of the fleece !
Before us, Argive maidens tread
  The glowing isles of Greece !
Behind us, fear and toil are dead :
  Below, the breakers cease !
The Holy Light is on my head—
  My very name is Peace !

The water's music moves ; and swings
  The sea's eternal breast.
The wind above us whistles, rings,
  And wafts us to the West.
Greece lures us on with beckonings
  And sighs of slumber blest.
I am not counted with the kings—
  My very name is Rest !

Medea shoots her sweetest glance
  And Jason bends above—
Young virgins in Iolchus dance,
  Hearing the news thereof.
The heroes—see their glad advance !
  Hath Greece not maids enough ?
I lie in love's ecstatic trance.
  My very name is Love !

LIGIA.

Come over the water, love, to me !
  Come over the little space !
Come over, my lover, and thou shalt see
  The beauty of my face !
Come over the water ! I will be
A bride and a queen and a lover to thee !

Come over the water, love, and lie !
  All day and all night to kiss !
Come over, my lover, an hour to die
  In the language-baffling bliss !
Come over the water ! Must I sigh ?
Thy lover and bride and queen am I !

Come over the water, love, and bide
  An hour in my swift caress !
So short is the space, and so smooth the
    tide—
  More smooth is my loveliness !
Come over the water, love, to my side !
I am thy lover and queen and bride !

MEDEA.

Sing, poet, ere the rash fool leap !

JASON.

Ah, Zeus !

ORPHEUS.

The hearts of Greeks with sharper flames
Burn than with one fire of all fire,
We have the Races and the Games,
The song, the chisel, and the lyre ;
We have the altar, we the shrine,
And ours the joy of love and wine.

Why take one pleasure, put aside
The myriad bliss of life diverse?
Unchanging joy will soon divide
Into the likeness of a curse.
Have we no maidens, slender, strong,
Daughters of tender-throated song?

I swear by Aphrodite's eyes
Our Grecian maids are fairer far !
What love as sweet as theirs is lies
In Sun or planet, moon or star?
What nymphs as sweet as ours are dwell
By foreign grove and alien well ?

With every watchman's cheery cry,
"Land ho !" through all the journeying
years
Our ever-hoping hearts reply,
"A land of bliss at last appears."
But what land laps a foreign foam
So sweet as is the hero's home?

At every port the novel sights
Charm for an hour—delusive bliss.
On every shore the false delights
Of maidens ply the barbarous kiss.
But where did hero think to stay
Lulled in their love beyond a day ?

No shoreland whistles to the wind
So musically as Thrace : no town
So gladdens the toil-weary mind
As brave Athenae : no renown
Stands so divine in war and peace
As the illustrious name of Greece.

This island of the subtle song
Shall vanish as the shaken spray
Tossed by the billow far and strong
On marble coasts : we will not stay !
Dreams lure not those who ply the sail
Before, the home ! behind, the gale !

JASON.

Ah ! I am torn, I am torn !

MEDEA.

God's poet, hail !
Help us, Apollo ! Light of Sun, awake !
This is the desperate hour.

JASON.

I have no strength.

MEDEA.

Beware the third, the awful ecstasy !

ORPHEUS.

A higher spell controls a lower song.
Listen, they sing !

JASON.

Joy ! Joy ! they sing, they sing !

LEUCOSIA.

O lover, I am lonely here !
O lover, I am weeping !
Each pearl of ocean is a tear
Let fall while love was sleeping.

A tear is made of fire and dew
And saddened with a smile ;
The sun's laugh in the curving blue
Lasts but a little while.

The night-winds kiss the deep : the stars
Shed laughter from above ;
But night must pass dawn's prison bars :
Night hath not tasted love.

With me the night is fallen in day ;
The day swoons back to night ;
The white and black are woven in gray,
Faint sleep of silken light.

A strange soft light about me shed
Devours the sense of time :
Hovers about my sleepy head
Some sweet persistent rhyme.

Beneath my breast my love may hear
Deep murmur of the billows—
O gather me to thee, my dear,
On soft forgetful pillows !

O gather me in arms of love
As maidens plucking posies,
Or mists that fold about a dove,
Or valleys full of roses !

O let me fade and fall away
From waking into sleep,
From sleep to death, from gold to gray,
Deep as the skies are deep !

O let me fall from death to dream,
Eternal monotone ;
Faint eventide of sleep supreme
With thee and love alone !

A jewelled night of star and moon
Shall watch our bridal chamber,
Bending the blue rays to the tune
Of softly-sliding amber.

Dim winds shall whisper echoes of
Our slow ecstatic breath,
Telling all worlds how sweet is love,
How beautiful is death.

MEDEA.
Sing, Orpheus, this doth madden them the
most.
Should one man leap—This tune is terrible !

ORPHEUS.
I am not moved, although I am a man.
So strong a safeguard is cool chastity.

MEDEA.
But love thou me ! My husband is distraught.

ORPHEUS.
Madness is on him for thy punishment.

MEDEA.
Sing, therefore !

ORPHEUS.
This last song of theirs was sweet.

MEDEA.
Thine therefore should be sweeter.

ORPHEUS.
The Gods grant it !

Lift up this love of peace and bliss,
The starry soul of wine,
Destruction's formidable kiss,
The lamp of the divine :
This shadow of a nobler name
Whose life is strife, whose soul is fame !

I rather will exalt the soul
Of man to loftier height,
And kindle at a livelier coal
The subtler soul of Light.
From these soft splendours of a dream
I turn, and seek the Self supreme.

This world is shadow-shapen of
The bitterness of pain.
Vain are the little lamps of love !
The light of life is vain !
Life, death, joy, sorrow, age and youth
Are phantoms of a further truth.

Beyond the splendour of the world,[1]
False glittering of the gold,
A Serpent is in slumber curled
In wisdom's sacred cold.
Life is the flaming of that flame.
Death is the naming of that name.

[1] The theory of these verses is that of certain
esoteric schools among the Hindus.

The forehead of the snake is bright
  With one immortal star,
Lighting her coils with living light
  To where the nenuphar
Sleeps for her couch. All darkness dreams
The thing that is not, only seems.

That star upon the serpent's head
  Is called the soul of man :
That light in shadows subtly shed
  The glamour of life's plan.
The sea whereon that lotus grows
Is thought's abyss of tears and woes.

Leave Sirenusa ! Even Greece
  Forget ! they are not there !
By worship cometh not the Peace,
  The Silence not by prayer !
Leave the illusions, life and time
And death, and seek that star sublime—

Until the lotus and the sea
  And snake no longer are,
And single through eternity
  Exists alone the Star,
And utter Knowledge rise and cease
In that which is beyond the Peace !

JASON.
Those isles have faded : was this vision true?

HERACLES.
I know not what hath passed : I seem asleep
Still, with the dream yet racing in my brain.

THESEUS.
There was a sweetness : whether sight or
    song
I know not.

JASON.
  But my veins grew strong and swollen
And madness came upon me.

MEDEA.
           You are here,
Let that suffice. Remember not !

ORPHEUS.
          But now
I see the haze lift on the water-way,
And hidden headlands loom again.

JASON.
            I know
The pleasant portals.

CHORUS.
    Here is home at last.

ORPHEUS.
The sunset comes : the mist is lifted now
To let the last kiss of the daylight fall
Once ere night whisper. " Sleep ! "

JASON.
          And see ! the ship
Glides between walls of purple.

MEDEA.
          The green land
Cools the tired eyes.

CHORUS.
    The rocks stand sentinel.

MEDEA.
Let still the song that saved us gladden us.
Lift up thy lyre, sweet Orpheus, on the sea.

ORPHEUS.[1]
Over a sea like stainèd glass
At sunset like a chrysopras :—
  Our smooth-oared vessel over-rides
  Crimson and green and purple tides.
Between the rocky isles we pass;
And greener islets gay with grass ;
  Between the over-arching sides
  Our pinnace glides.

[1] The song describes the approach to Hong
Kong Harbour.

Just by the Maenad-haunted hill
Songs rise into the air, and thrill,
Like clustered birds at evening
When love outlingers rain and spring.
Faint faces of strange dancers spill
Their dewy scent ; and sweet and chill
The wind comes faintly whispering
On wanton wing.

Between the islands sheer and steep
Our craft treads noiseless o'er the deep,
Turned to the gold heart of the west,
The sun's last sigh of love expressed
Ere the lake glimmer, borrow sleep
From clouds and tinge their edges ; weep
That night brings love not to his breast,
But only rest.

We move toward the golden track
Shed in the water : we look back
Eastward, where rose is set to warn
Promise and prophecy of dawn
Reflected, lest the ocean lack
In any space serene or slack
Some colour, blushing o'er the fawn
Dim-lighted lawn.

And under all the shadowy shapes
Of steep and silent bays and capes
The water takes its darkest hue ;
Catches no laughter from the blue ;
No purple ray or gold escapes,
But dim green shadow comes and drapes
Its lustre : thus the night burns through
Tall groves of yew.

Thither, ah thither ! Hollow vales
Trembling with early nightingales !
Languish, O sea of sleep ! Young moon !
Dream on above in maiden swoon !
None daring to invoke the gales
To shake our sea, and swell our sails.
Not song, but silence, were a boon—
Save for this tune.

Round capes grown darker as night falls,
We see at last the splendid walls
That ridge the bay ; the town lies there
Lighted (the temple's hour for prayer)

At grave harmonious intervals.
The grand voice of some seaman calls,
Just as the picture fades, aware
How it was fair.

JASON.

A thousand victories bring us to the shore
Whence we set out : look forth ! The people
come
Moving with lights about the anchorage
To greet the heroes of the Golden Fleece.
My Queen ! Medea ! Welcome unto Greece !

EXPLICIT ACTUS QUARTUS.

ARGONAUTAE.

ACTUS QUINTUS.[1]

ARES.

JASON, MEDEA, PELIAS, ACASTUS, AL-
CESTIS *and her* Sisters, MADNESS.

SCENE : *The Palace at Iolchus.*

MADNESS.

Black Ares hath called
Me forth from the deep !
Blind and appalled,
Shall the palace high-walled
Shake as I leap
Over the granite,
The marble over,
One step to span it,
One flight to hover,
Like a moon round a planet,
A dream round a lover !

[1] The legend is grotesque, and the poet's
power is strained—perhaps overstrained—to
be faithful without being ridiculous. Only the
tragic necessity of avenging the indignity done
to Ares compelled this conclusion of the
drama, and the somewhat fantastic and unreal
machinery of the catastrophe.

How shall I come?
  Shrieking and yelling?
Or quiet and dumb
  To the heart of the dwelling?
Silently striding,
  Whispering terror
Into their ears;
Watching, abiding,
  Madness and error,
Brooder of fears!

Thus will I bring
  Black Ares to honour,
Draw the black sting
  Of the serpent upon her!
How foolish to fight
  With the warrior God
Who brings victory bright
  Or defeat with a nod,
Who standeth to smite
  With a spear and a rod!
Here is the woman,
  Thinking no evil,
Wielding the human
  By might of a devil!
But I will mock her
  With cunning design,
In my malice lock her.
  The doom is divine!

MEDEA.

Ai! Ai! This rankles sorely in my mind
That Pelias should wander, free to slide
His sidelong looks among our courtiers
Ripe ever for some mischief. Yet methinks
There is a wandering other than this present—
Say, by the Stygian waves, unburied corpse!—
But, for the means? It ill befits our power
And grace—my husband's honour—to stretch
  forth
The arm of murder o'er the head of age.
But surely must be means——

MADNESS.

          The prophecy!

MEDEA.

Happy my thought be! I have found it.
  Ha!
" Athena shall relent not till the king
Shall die and live." Vainly the prophet
  meant
Mere transference of the crown. I'll twist
  his saying
To daze the children—fools they are! So mask
Evil beneath the waxen face of Good,
Trick out Calamity in robes of Luck—
Come, children! Is the sun bright? And
  your eyes?

ALCESTIS.

Dear queen, all's well with us. Such happiness
Crowds daylight—even sleep seems sorrowful,
Though bright with dainty dreams!

FIRST DANAID.

          But you are sad!

MEDEA.

I meditate the ancient prophecy.
Thus a foreboding is upon my heart,
Seeing some danger follow yet, o'erhang
Our heads, poised gaily in incertitude!

SECOND DANAID.

Nay, grieve not, dear Medea! All men say
The prophecy is well fulfilled.

MEDEA.

          Ay me!
" Until the king shall die and live again."

ALCESTIS.

What means that?

MEDEA.

          I have meditated long.

SECOND DANAID.

To what sad end?

MEDEA.

At the full end I see
Allusion to my magic—to that spell
Whereby an old man may renew his youth.

ALCESTIS.

Our father!

MEDEA.

You have guessed aright, my child.
Your father must abandon his old age
And—by my magic—find sweet youth again!

DANAIDES.

But this is very difficult to do.

MEDEA.

For me such miracles are merely play,
Serving to while away the idle hours
While Jason hunts——

ALCESTIS.

How grand it were to see
Our aged father rival the strong youths
In feats of great agility!

MEDEA.

Agreed!
But surely you should work the charm your-
selves.
For children magic is a blithesome game!

DANAIDES.

Dear lady! teach us how to say the spell!

MEDEA.

Words must be aided by appalling deeds!

ALCESTIS.

O! O! you frighten us.

MEDEA.

Be brave, my child!
I too passed through unutterable things!

ALCESTIS.

Let me fetch father!

MEDEA.

Nay, consider first.
Would he consent? The process is severe!

DANAIDES.

We know the sire is not exactly brave,
Though very wise and good.

MEDEA.

'Tis clear to me;
Without his knowledge we must do the deed.

ALCESTIS.

What is this "deed"?

MEDEA.

A caldron is prepared;
And, having hewn your father limb from
limb,
We seethe him in a broth of magic herbs.

ALCESTIS.

And then?

MEDEA.

The proper incantations said,
There rises from the steam a youthful shape
More godlike than like man. And he will
fall
In kind embraces on his children's necks.

ALCESTIS.

O queen, this process seems indeed severe.

MEDEA.

Without his knowledge must the thing be
done.

DANAIDES.

This also seems to us no easy task.

MEDEA.

He sleeps through noon, while others are
abroad.

ALCESTIS.

Let us make haste! Dear queen, how good
you are!

MEDEA.

One thing remember ! While you say the
  spell—
Here is the parchment !—let no thought arise
In any of your minds ![1]

ALCESTIS. [*To her Sisters.*]
Remember that !

MEDEA.

Else—Ototototoi !

FIRST DANAID.
What woe is this ?

MEDEA.

The charm is broken.

SECOND DANAID.
And our father——

MEDEA.
Lost !

DANAIDES.
Ai Ai ! Ai Ai ! Ai Ai !

MEDEA.
Ai Ai ! Ai Ai !

ALCESTIS.

Be brave, dear sisters, pluck your courage up !
Easy this one condition ! All is safe.

MEDEA.

Haste then ! Good luck attend you ! When
  the hunt
Returns, how joyful——

[1] It is a common jest among the Hindus to
play this trick on a pupil, *i.e.*, to promise him
magical powers on condition that during a
given ceremonial he abstains from thinking of
a certain object (*e.g.*, a horse). He fails, because only the training of years can enable a
student so to control his mind as to accomplish
this feat of suppressing involuntary thought.

FIRST DANAID.

Striding vigorous,
The man renewed grasps Jason in embrace
Worthy of Heracles.

ALCESTIS.
Thanks, thanks, dear queen !
We go, we go !

MEDEA.
The Goddess be your speed !
Thus will the danger pass ! That vicious fool
Shall cease his plots against my best beloved.
No taint of fell complicity shall touch
My honour in this matter. I will sleep
Through the delicious hours of breezy noon,
Lulled by sweet voices of my singing maids ;
Secure at least that no one will attempt
To wreck my virtue or—restore my youth !

CHORUS.

O sleep of lazy love, be near
  In dreams to lift the veil,
And silence from the shadowy sphere
To conjure in our lady's ear !—
  The voices fall and fail ;
The light is lowered. O dim sleep,
Over her eyelids creep !

The world of dreams is shapen fair
  Beyond a mortal's nod :
A fragrant and a sunny air
Smiles : a man's kisses vanish there,
  Grow kisses of a god ;
And in dreams' darkness subtly grows
No Earth-flowered bloom of rose.

O dreams of love and peace, draw nigh,
  Hover with shadowy wings !
Let shining shapes of ecstasy
Cover the frail blue veil of sky,
  And speak immortal things !
Dream, lady, dream through summer noon,
Lulled by the sleepy tune !

The sense is riven, and the soul
Goes glimmering to the abode,
Where aeons in one moment roll,
And one thought shapes to its control
Body's forgotten load.
Our lady sleeps ! Our lady smiles
In far Elysian isles !

FIRST WOMAN.

Thrice have I crept towards the bed, and
thrice
An unseen hand has caught the uplifted knife,
A grinning face lurked out from the blank
air
Between me and that filthy sorceress.

SECOND WOMAN.

Daily I poison the she-devil's drink,
And nothing harms her !

THIRD WOMAN.

I have a toad whose breath
Destroys all life——

CHORUS.

Thou dealest in such arts?

THIRD WOMAN.

Ay ! for this hate's sake. Are we sisters all
Herein ?

CHORUS.

True sisters !

THIRD WOMAN.

The familiar soul
Sucks at her mouth—She sickens not nor
dies ;
More poisonous than he.

FIRST WOMAN.

Ah ! beast of hell !
What may avail us ?

SECOND WOMAN.

Jason is quite lost
In her black sorceries.

FOURTH WOMAN.

Our chance gone !

FIRST WOMAN.

Our life
Degraded to her service.

SECOND WOMAN.

We, who are
Born nobly, are become her minions.

THIRD WOMAN.

Slaves, not handmaidens !

ALCESTIS.

Otototototoi !
Ai Ai ! What misery !

FIRST WOMAN.

See ! the lady weeps !

ALCESTIS.

Ai Ai ! the black fiend, how he dogs my
feet !
The fatal day ! Ai ! Ai !

CHORUS.

What sorrow thus,
Maiden, removes the feet of fortitude ?

ALCESTIS.

Who shall arouse him ?

CHORUS.

Peace, our lady sleeps.

ALCESTIS.

Ah me ! but she must wake ! A black, black
deed
Hangs on the house.

MEDEA.

What meets my waking ear ?
Alcestis !

ALCESTIS.
Ah, dear queen, lament, lament!
I am undone by my own——

MEDEA.
What! the work?

ALCESTIS.
Alas! Alas! the work!

MEDEA.
Thy father?

ALCESTIS.
Slain!

CHORUS.
Ai Ai! the old man slain!

MEDEA.
Ai Ai!

ALCESTIS.
Ai Ai!

MEDEA.
The strong spell broken?

ALCESTIS.
Nay, but thoughts arose,
So many thoughts—or ever I was ware—
And he—the caldron seethes——

MEDEA.
He rises not?

ALCESTIS.
Nought but moist smoke springs up.

MEDEA.
Alas! for me!
All is but lost.

ALCESTIS.
Canst thou do anything?

MEDEA.
Nothing. Ai Ai!

ALCESTIS.
Ai Ai!

CHORUS.
Ai Ai! Ai Ai!

JASON.
What! Shall the hunter find his joy abroad,
And sorrow in his house?

MEDEA.
Thy very hearth
Polluted with the old man's blood!

ACASTUS.
What blood?
Answer me, woman!

MEDEA.
To thy knees, false hound,
Fawning to snap!

ACASTUS.
What misery, pale slaves,
Lament ye?

CHORUS.
Ah! the ill omen! Ah, the day!
Alcestis hath her sire in error slain.

ACASTUS.
Sister!

ALCESTIS.
O brother, bear thine anger back!

ACASTUS.
Speak!

ALCESTIS.
Ah, the prophecy! Ai Ai!

CHORUS.
Ai Ai!

ACASTUS.

What folly masks what wickedness? Speak
on !

ALCESTIS.

I cannot speak.

JASON.

Speak thou, Medea !

MEDEA.

The child
Hath hewn her sire asunder, seething him
In herbs of sacred power.

ACASTUS.

By thy decree?

MEDEA.

Nay !

MADNESS.

Safer is it to admit to these
Fools—charge the child with lack of fortune !

MEDEA.

Yea !
I bade her take a waxen shape, carved well
To look like the old man——

ALCESTIS.

Nay ! nay ! the Sire
Himself we stole on sleeping——

CHORUS.

Hewn apart !
Ai Ai !

MEDEA.

I said not thus !

ALCESTIS.

I am so wild,
Bewildered with these tears.

ACASTUS.

Enough of this !
It is the malice of that sorceress
Disguised —she well knows how.

CHORUS.

Thus, thus it is !
We know the witch's cunning.

JASON.

Dogs and fools !
For this ye die.

MADNESS.

Nobility and love
Urge my own sanction to support the wife !

JASON.

I bade my queen prepare this spell. Disputes
Your arrogance my kingship?

ACASTUS.

Ay, indeed !
Now justice turns against thee, fickle jade
As fortune. Mine is a boy's arm, but I
Advance against thee an impervious blade,
And give thee in thy throat and teeth the
lie !

JASON.

Boy's bluster !

MADNESS.

Justice will be satisfied.
It will be best to flee !

JASON.

But what is this?
A sword? I scorn a sword. I scorn a boy.
Let none suppose me fearful !

MEDEA.

Give not back !

MADNESS.

It will be finer far to go away
As those disdaining aught but their own love.

MEDEA.

Ay ! let us leave these folk's ingratitude,
My husband ! in thy love alone I rest.
This splendour and this toil alike resume
Our life from the long honeymoon of love
We wish at heart.

JASON.

To Corinth !

MEDEA.

Creon bears
The name of favourable to suppliants.

ACASTUS.

How virtue tames these tameless ones !
To-day
I am indeed a man.

MEDEA.

Thou brainless boy !
Thus, thus, and thus I smite thee on the
cheek—
Thus, thus I spit upon thy face.   Out, dog !

SEMICHORUS I.

His patience shows as something marvellous.

SEMICHORUS 2.

Virtue takes insult from the fortuneless.

MEDEA.

The curse of Ares dog you into Hades !
I have my reasons [*doubtfully*], ay, my reasons
plain !
Going, not forced.

CHORUS.

Yet going—that is good !

JASON.

To Corinth ! Bride of my own heart, Medea,
Well hast thou put thy power off for the
time
Preferring love to pomp, and peace to revel—

MEDEA.

And the soft cushions of the moss-grown
trees
To royal pillows, and the moon's young light
To gaudy lamps of antique workmanship—

JASON.

And music of the birds to harps of gold
Struck by unwilling fingers for gold coin.

MEDEA.

Come ! lest the curse I call upon this house
Eat us up also ! May the red plague rot
Their bones ! I lift my voice and prophesy :
The curse shall never leave this house of
fear ;
But one by treachery shall slay another,
And vengeance shall smite one, and one
lay bare
Her breasts in vain for love : until the
house
Perish in uttermost red ruin.

CHORUS.

Bah !
Speared wild-cats bravely spit !

JASON.

To Creon, come !

MADNESS.

Black Ares hath chosen
Me wisely, to send
A doom deep-frozen
From now to the end.
Never the curse
Shall pass from the house,
But gather a worse
Hate for a spouse.
The lovers are better
Escaped from my toils
Than these in the fetter
Of the golden spoils.

Yet still lies a doom
For the royal lovers.
Time bears in her womb
That darkness covers
A terror, and waits
The hour that is Fate's.

The work is done.   Let miracle inspire
Iolchian voices to the holy hymn,
Praise to black Ares, echo of this doom.

CHORUS.

So fearful is the wrath divine,
    That once aroused it shall not sleep,
Though prostrate slaves before the shrine
    Pray, praise. do sacrifice, and weep.
Ten generations following past
Shall not exhaust the curse at last.

From father unto son it flees,
    An awful heritage of woe.
Wives feel its cancerous prodigies
    Invade their wombs ; the children know
The inexpiable word, exhaust
Not by a tenfold holocaust.

Thus let mankind abase in fear
    Their hearts, nor sacrilege profane
The awful slumber of the seer,
    The dread adytum of the fane ;
Nor gain the mockery of a fleece,
Losing reality of peace.

Hail to wild Ares ! Men, rejoice
    That He can thus avenge his shrine !
One solemn cadence of that voice
    Peal through the ages, shake the spine
Of very Time, and plunge success
False-winged into sure-foot distress !

Hail to black Ares ! Warrior, hail !
    Thou glory of the shining sword !
What proven armour may avail
    Against the vengeance of the Lord ?
Athena's favour must withdraw
Before the justice of thy law !

Hail to the Lord of glittering spears,
    The monarch of the mighty name,
The Master of ten thousand Fears
    Whose sword is as a scarlet flame !
Hail to black Ares ! Wild and pale
The echo answers me : All Hail !

EXPLICIT ACTUS QUINTUS.

AHAB

AND OTHER POEMS

DEDICACE.

TO G. C. J.

PILGRIM of the sun, be this thy scrip!
The severing lightnings of the mind
Avail where soul and spirit slip,
And the Eye is blind.

PARIS, *December* 9, 1902.

RONDEL.

BY palm and pagoda enchaunted o'er-
shadowed, I lie in the light
Of stars that are bright beyond suns that
all poets have vaunted
In the deep-breathing amorous bosom of
forests of amazon might
By palm and pagoda enchaunted.

By spells that are murmured and rays of my
soul strongly flung, never daunted ;
By gesture of tracery traced with a wand
dappled white ;
I summon the spirits of earth from the gloom
they for ages have haunted.

O woman of deep-red skin ! Carved hair
like the teak ! O delight
Of my soul in the hollows of earth—how
my spirit hath taunted—
Away ! I am here, I am laid to the breast of
the earth in the dusk of the night,
By palm and pagoda enchaunted.

AHAB.

PART I.

THE polished silver flings me back
Dominant brows and eyes of bronze,
A curling beard of vigorous black,
And dusky red of desert suns
Burnt in my cheeks. Who saith me Nay ?
Who reigns in Israel to-day ?

Samaria in well-ordered ranks
Of houses stands in honoured peace :
Sweet nourishment from Kenah's banks
Flows, and the corn and vine increase.
In two pitched fields the Syrian hordes
Fled broken from our stallion swords.

Ay me ! But that was life ! I see
Now, from that hill, the ordered plain ;
The serried ranks like foam flung free,
Long billows, flashing on the main.
Past the eye's grip their legions roll—
Anguish of death upon my soul !

For, sheltered by the quiet hill,
Like two small flocks of kids that wait,
Going to water, ere the chill
Blow from the East's forsaken gate,
Lie my weak spears : O trembling tide
Of fear false-faced and shifty-eyed !

God ! how we smote them in the morn !
Their ravening tides rolled back anon,
As if the cedared crest uptorn
Roared from uprooted Lebanon
Down to the sea, its billows hurled
Back, past the pillars of the world !

Ah, that was life !   I feel my sword
  Live, bite, and shudder in my hand,
Smite, drink, the spirit of its lord
  Exulting through the infinite brand !
My chariot dyed with Syrian blood !
My footmen wading through the flood !

Ay ! that was life !   Before the night
  Dipped its cool wings, their hosts were
    stricken
Like night itself before the light.
  An hundred thousand corpses sicken
The air of heaven.   Yet some by speed
Escape our vengeance—ours, indeed !

Fate, the red hound, to Aphek followed.
  Some seven and twenty thousand died
When the great wall uprising hollowed
  Its terror, crashed upon its side,
And whelmed them in the ruin.   Strife,
Strength, courage, victory—that is Life !

Then—by my father's beard !   What seer
  Promised me victory ?   What sage
Now in my triumph hour severe
  Spits out red oracles of rage ?
Jehovah's.   The fanatic churl
Stands—see his thin lips writhe and curl !

" Because thou hast loosed the kingly man,
  To uttermost destruction's dread
In my almighty power and plan
  Appointed, I will have thy head
For his, thy life for his make mine,
And for his folk thou hast spared, slay thine."

But surely I was just and wise !
  Mercy is God's own attribute !
Mercy to noble enemies
  Marks man from baser mould of brute.
To fight their swordsmen—who would shirk ?
To slay a captive—coward's work !

" I have loved mercy," that He said ;
  Nor bade me slay the Syrian Chief.
Yet my head answers for his head ;
  My people take his people's grief.
Sin, troth, to spare one harmless breath,
Sith all my innocents earn death !

By timely mercy peace becomes,
  And kindly love, and intercourse
Of goodly merchandise, that sums
  Contention in united force.
" Praise who, relenting, showeth pity ;
Not him who captureth a city ! "

A wild strong life I've made of mine.
  Not till my one good deed is done—
Ay ! for that very deed divine—
  Comes the fierce mouth of malison.
So grows my doubt again, so swell
My ancient fears for Israel.

I hurled Jehovah's altars down ;
  I slew and I pursued his priests ;
I took a wife from Zidon Town ;
  I gave his temples to the beasts ;
I set up gods and graven shapes
Of calves and crocodiles and apes.

Myself to sorceries I betook ;
  All sins that are did I contrive,
Sealed in the Thora's dreadful book—
  I live, and like my life, and thrive !
Doth God not see ?   His ear is dull ?
Or His speech strangled, His force null ?

Nay, verily !   These petty sins
  His mercy and long-suffering pardon.
What final crime of horror wins
  At last His gracious heart to harden ?
What one last infamy shall wake
His anger, for His great Name's sake ?

Is there one sin so horrible
  That no forgiveness can obtain,
That flings apart the bars of hell,
  For which repentance shall be vain ?
Ay ! but there is !   One act of ruth
Done in my rash unthinking youth !

Who wonders if I hold the scale
  Poised in my deep deliberate mind,
Between the weight of Zidon's Baal
  And Judah's God—*each in his kind*
A god of power—each in his fashion
The hideous foeman of compassion ?

The blood alike of man and beast
  The worship of each God demands.
All priests are greedy—gold and feast
  Pour from the poor folk to their hands.
The doubtful power from heaven to strike
The levin bolt they claim alike.

I take no heed of trickery played
  By cunning mad Elijah's skill,
When the great test of strength was made
  On Carmel's melancholy hill,
And on the altar-stone the liar
Cried "Water," and poured forth Greek fire !

Then while the fools peer heavenward,
  Even as he prays, to see the skies
Vomit the flash, his furtive sword
  Fast to the flinty altar flies.
Whoof ! the wild blaze assures the clods
Jehovah is the God of gods !

Nor do I set peculiar store
  By tricks twin-born to this they show
When, with well-simulated lore
  Of learning, Baal's great hierarchs go
Into the gold god's graven shell
And moan the ambiguous oracle.

In my own inmost heart I feel,
  Deep as a pearl in seas of Ind,
A vision, keen as tempered steel,
  Lofty and holy as the wind,
And brighter than the living sun :
If these be gods, then there is none !

Baal and Jehovah, Ashtoreth
  And Chemosh and these Elohim,
Life's pandars in the brothel, Death !
  Cloudy imaginings, a dream
Built up of fear and words and woe.
All, all my soul must overthrow.

For these are devils, nothing doubt !
  Yet nought should trouble me : I see
My folk secure from foes without,
  Worship in peace and amity
Baal and Jehovah, sects appeased
By peace assured and wealth increased.

Yet am I troubled.   Doubt exists
  And absolute proof recoils before me.
Truth veils herself in awful mists,
  And darkness wakens, rolling o'er me
When I approach the dreadful shrine,
In my own soul, of the divine.

And what cries laughing Jezebel ?
  Golden and fragrant as the morn,
Painted like flames adorning Hell,
  Passions and mysteries outworn,
Ever enchanting, ever wise,
And terror in her wondrous eyes !

Her fascination steals my strength,
  Her luxury lures me as she comes ;
Reaches her length against my length,
  And breaks my spirit ; life succumbs—
A nameless avatar of death
Incarnate in her burning breath.

I know her gorgeous raiment folded
  In snaky subtle draperies,
All stalwart captains mighty-moulded
  To lure within her sorceries,
Within her bed   and I, who love,
See, and am silent, and approve !

Strange ! Who shall call the potter knave
  Who moulds a vessel to his will ?
One, if he choose, a black-browed slave :
  One, if he choose, a thing of ill,
Writhing, misshapen, footless, cruel :
One, like a carved Assyrian jewel ?

Shame on the potter heavy sit,
  If he revenge his own poor skill
That marred a work by lack of wit,
  By heaping infamy and ill
On the already ruined clay.
Shame on the potter, then, I say !

But what cries laughing Jezebel ?
  Scornful of me as all her lovers,
More scornful as we love her well !
  " Good king, this rage of doubt discovers
The long-hid secret ! All thy mind
A little shadow lurks behind."

Hers are the delicate sorceries
  In black groves : hers the obscure, obscene
Rites in dim moonlight courts ; the wise
  Dreadful occasions when the queen
Like to a bat, flits, flits, to gloat
Blood-drunk upon a baby's throat !

Therefore : all doubt, this fierce unrest
  Between that knowledge self bestows
And leaves of palm, and palimpsest,
  Scrawled sacred scrolls, whose legend goes
Beyond recorded time, and founds
Its age beyond all history's bounds ;

Therefore : all search for truth beyond
  The doubtful canon of the law,
The bitter letter of the bond
  Given when Sinai shook with awe,
They swear ; all wit that looks aslant
Shamed at the shameful covenant ; [1]

Therefore : this brooding over truth
  She much avers cuts short my day,
Steals love and laughter from my youth,
  Will dye my beard in early grey.
" Go forth to war ! Shall Judah still
Set mockery to thy kingly will ? "

May be. I often feel a ghost
  Creeping like darkness through my brain ;
Sensed like uncertainty at most,
  Nowise akin to fear or pain.
Yet it is there. To yield to such
And brood, will not avail me much.

Ho ! harness me my chariot straight,
  My white-maned horses fleet and strong !
Call forth the trumpeters of state !
  Proclaim to all Samaria's throng :
The King rides forth !   Hence, slaves !
    Away !
Haste ye ! The King rides forth to-day.

[1] Circumcision, medically commendable, is
both ridiculous and obscene if considered as a
religious rite. Gen. xvii. 9-14.

PART II.

WOULD God that I were dead ! Like Cain,
  My punishment I cannot bear.
There is a deep corrosive pain
  Invades my being everywhere.
Sprung from a seed too small to see,
A monster spawns and strangles me.

'Tis scarce a week ! In power and pride
  I rode in state about the city ;
Took pleasure in the eager ride,
  Saw grief, took pleasure in my pity ;
Saw joy, took pleasure in the seeing,
And the full rapture of well-being.

Would God that I had stayed, and smote
  My favourite captain through the heart,
Caught my young daughter by the throat,
  And torn her life and limbs apart,
Stabbed my queen dead : remorse for these
Might ape, not match, these miseries.

For, hard behind the palace gate,
  I spied a vineyard fair and fine,
Hanging with purple joy, and weight
  Of golden rapture of the vine :
And there I bade my charioteer
Stay, and bid Naboth to appear.

The beast ! A gray, deceitful man,
  With twisted mouth the beard would hide,
Evil yet strong : the scurril clan
  Exaggerate for its greed and pride,
The scum of Israel ! At one look
I read my foe as in a book.

The beast ! He grovelled in the dust.
  I heard the teeth gride as he bowed
His forehead to the earth. Still just,
  Still patient, passionless, and proud,
I ruled my heavy wrath. I passed
That hidden insult : spake at last.

I spake him fair. My memory held
  Him still a member of my folk ;
A warrior might be bold of eld,
  My hardy spearman when we broke
The flashing lines of Syrians. Yea !
I spake him fair. Alas the day !

" Friend, by my palace lies thy field
   Fruitful and pleasant to the sight.
Therefore I pray thee that thou yield
   Thy heritage for my delight.
Wilt thou its better ? Or its fee
In gold, as seemeth good to thee ?

" Content thyself ! " As by a spell
   He rears his bulk in surly rage.
" The Lord forbid that I should sell
   To thee my father's heritage ! "
No other word.   Dismissal craves ?[1]
Nay, scowls and slinks among his slaves.

Hath ever a slave in story dared
   Thus to beard openly his lord ?
My chariot men leapt forth and flared
   Against him with indignant sword.
Why wait for king's word to expunge
Life so detested with one lunge ?

" Cease ! "   My strong word flamed out.
   The men
   Shook with dead fear.   They jumped and
     caught
With savage instinct, brutal ken,
 . At what should be my crueller thought :
Torture !   And trembled lest their haste
Had let a dear life run to waste.

They argued after their brute kind.
   I have two prides ; in justice, one :
In mercy, one : " No ill I find
   In this just man," I cried ; " the sun
Is not defiled, and takes no hurt
When the worm builds his house of dirt.

" Curse ye Jehovah ! He abides,
   Hears not, nor smites ; the curse is pent
Close with the speaker ; ill betides
   When on himself the curve is bent,
And like the wild man's ill-aimed blow,[2]
Hits nought, swerves, swoops, and strikes
     him low.

---

[1] In the East the inferior dare not leave the
presence of his superior without permission.
[2] Another reference to the boomerang.

" Let the man go ! "   The short surprise
   Sinks in long wonder : angrily
Yet awed they spurn him forth. " Arise !
   O swine, and wallow in thy sty !
The King hath said it."   Thus the men
Turned the beast free—to goad again.

For now the little shadow shapes
   An image ever in my brain ;
Across my field of sight there gapes
   Ever a gulf, and draws the pain
Of the whole knowledge of the man
Into its vague and shifting span.

Moreover, in that gulf I see
   Now the bright vineyard sweet and clean,
Now the dog Naboth mocking me
   With rude curt word and mouth obscene
Wried in derision—well relied
Dog's insolence on monarch's pride.

Ah, friend ! Some winds may shake a city !
   Some dogs may creep too near a feast !
Thou, reckoning on my scorn, my pity,
   Thine own uncleanness as a beast :
Wilt thou not take thy count again ?
Seest thou the shadow on my brain ?

It grows, it grows.   Seven days slide past :
   I groan upon an empty bed :
I turn my face away : I fast :
   There cometh in my mouth no bread.
No man dare venture near to say :
" Why turns the King his face away ? "

It grows.   Ah me ! the long days slide ;
   I brood ; due justice to the man
Dogging desire.   A monarch's pride
   Outweighs his will : yet slowlier ran
To-day the thought : " I will no wrong : "
" The vines are cool," more sweet and strong

There is no sleep.   All natural laws
   Suspend their function : strange effects
And mighty for so slight a cause !
   What whim of weakling strength protects
This dog of Satan at my gate
From the full whirlwind of my hate ?

What mighty weakness stays the king
  If he arise, and cast desire
Far from its seat and seed and spring
  To Hinnom the detested fire?
Ay! both were wise. Madness alone
Sits throned on the king's vacant throne.

Dogs! Who dares break on me? " Dread
    lord !
  Mightiest of monarchs!"—"Cease, thou
    crow !
Thine errand ! ere the eunuch's sword
  Snatch thy bald head off at a blow."
" Mercy, World's Light ! " Swings clear and
    clean
The call " Room for the Queen! The Queen!"

Strong as a man, the Queen strides in.
  Even she shrank frighted !—my àspect
More dreadful than all shapes of sin
  Her dreams might shape or recollect',
Hideous with fasting, madness, grief,
Beyond all speaking or belief.

But the first glance at those bold eyes !
  Ah ! let me fling me at her feet !
Take me, O love ! Thy terror flies.
  Kiss me again, again, O sweet !
O honeyed queen, old paramour,
So keen our joy be and so sure !

" The king would be alone ! " Fast fly
  The trembling lackeys at her voice.
Lapped in her billowy breasts I lie,
  And love, and languish, and rejoice,
And—ah—forget ! The ecstatic hour
Bursts like a poppy into flower.

Back ! thou black spectre ! In her arms
  Devouring and devoured of love,
Feeding my face in myriad charms,
  As on a mountain feeds a dove,
Starred with fresh flowers, dew-bright, and
    pearled
With all the light of all the world :

Back ! With the kisses ravening fast
  Upon my panting mouth, the eyes
Darting hot showers of light, the vast
  And vicious writhings, the caught sighs
Drunk with delight, on love's own throne,
The moment where all time lies prone :

Back ! At the very central shrine,
  Pinnacled moment of excess
Of immolation's blood divine :
  Back ! from the fleshly loveliness:
Back ! loved and loathed ! O face concealed !
Back ! One hath whispered " Naboth's
    field."

I am slain. Her body passion-pearled
  Dreams her luxurious lips have drawn
My spirit, as the dust wind-whirled
  Sucks up the radiance of the dawn
In rainbow beauty [1]—yet remains
Mere dust upon the barren plains.

Reluctance to reveal my grief
  Is of my sickness a strange feature.
Yea, verily ! beyond belief
  Is the machinery of man's nature !
If thus spake Solomon in kind
Of body, I of soul and mind !

The lazy accents stir at last
  The scented air : " Oh, wherefore, lord,
Is thy soul sad ? This weary fast
  Strikes to my heart a lonely sword ! "
In brief words stammered forth I spoke
My secret ; and the long spell broke.

And now the gilded sin of her
  Leapt and was lambent in a smile :
" Give me but leave to minister
  This kingdom for a little while !
The vineyard shall be thine. O king,
This trouble is a little thing ! "

[1] " Dust-devils " show opalescence in certain
aspects of light.

I gave to her the signet's gold
  Carved in the secret charactery,
Whose flowers of writing bend and fold
  The star of Solomon, the eye
Whence four rays run—the Name ! the seal
Written within the burning wheel.

And now I lean with fevered will
  Across the carven screen of palm.
All nature holds its function still ;
  The sun is mild ; the wind is calm ;
But oh my ear the voices fall
Distant, and irk me, and appal.

Two men have sworn the solemn oath :
  "God and the king this dog blasphemed,"
Two judges, just, though little loth,
  Weigh, answer. As on one who dreamed
Comes waking—in my soul there groaned :
"Carry forth Naboth to be stoned ! "

Nine days ! And still the king is sad,
  And hides his face, and is not seen.
The tenth ! the king is gaily clad ;
  The king will banquet with the queen ;
And, ere the west be waste of sun,
Enjoy the vineyard he hath won.

All this I hear as one entranced.
  The king and I are friend and friend,
As if a cloud of maidens danced
  Between my vision and the end.
I see the king as one afeared,
Hiding his anguish in his beard.

I laugh in secret, knowing well
  What waits him in the field of blood ;
What message hath the seer to tell ;
  What bitter Jordan holds its flood
Only for Ahab, sore afraid
What lurks behind the vine's cool shade.

Yet—well I see—the fates are sure,
  And Ahab will descend, possess
The enchanting green, the purple lure,
  The globes of nectared loveliness,
And, as he turns ! who wonders now
The grim laugh wrinkles on my brow ?

I see him, a fantastic ghost,
  The vineyard smiling white and plain,
And hiding ever innermost
  The little shadow on his brain ;
I laugh again with mirthless glee,
As knowing also I am he.

A fool in gorgeous attire !
  An ox decked bravely for his doom !
So step I to the great desire.
  Sweet winds upon the gathering gloom
Bend like a mother, as I go,
Foreknowing, to my overthrow.

NEW YEAR, 1903.

O FRIENDS and brothers ! Hath the year
  deceased,
And ye await the bidding to fare well ?
How shall ye fare, thus bound of fate in hell ?
How, whom no light hath smitten, and
  released ?
Ye trust perchance in God, or man, or priest ?
Ay ! Let them serve you, let them save you !
  Spell
The name that guards the human citadel,
And answer if your course hath checked or
  ceased.

Path of the eightfold star ! Be thou revealed !
Isle of Nirvana, be the currents curled
About thee, that the swimmer touch thy
  shore !
Thought be your sword, and virtue be your
  shield !
Press on ! Who conquers shall for evermore
Pass from the fatal mischief of the world.

MELUSINE.

TO M. M. M.

HANGS over me the fine false gold
  Above the bosom epicene
    That hides my head that hungereth.
The steady eyes of steel behold,
  When on a sudden the fierce and thin
    Curled subtle mouth swoops on my breath,

And like a serpent's mouth is cold,
    And like a serpent's mouth is keen,
    And like a serpent's mouth is death.

Lithe arms, wan with love's mysteries,
    Creep round and close me in, as Thule
        Wraps Arctic oceans ultimate ;
Some deathly swoon or sacrifice,
    This love—a red hypnotic jewel
        Worn in the forehead of a Fate !
And like a devil-fish is ice,
    And like a devil-fish is cruel,
    And like a devil-fish is hate.

Beneath those kisses songs of sadness
    Sob, in the pulses of desire,
        Seeking some secret in the deep ;
Low melodies of stolen gladness,
    The bitterness of death ; the lyre
        Broken to bid the viol weep :
And like a Maenad's chants are madness,
    And like a Maenad's chants are fire,
    And like a Maenad's chants are sleep.

A house of pain is her bedchamber.
    Her skin electric clings to mine,
        Shakes for pure passion, moves and
            hisses ;
Whose subtle perfumes half remember
    Old loves, and desolate divine
        Wailings among the wildernesses ;
And like a Hathor's skin is amber,
    And like a Hathor's skin is wine,
    And like a Hathor's skin is kisses.

Gray steel self-kindled shine her eyes.
    They rede strange runes of time defiled,
        And ruined souls, and Satan's kin.
I see their veiled impurities,
    An harlot hidden in a child,
        Through all their love and laughter lean ;
And like a witch's eyes are wise,
    And like a witch's eyes are wild,
    And like a witch's eyes are Sin.

She moves her breasts in Bacchanal
    Rhymes to that music manifold
        That pulses in the golden head,

Seductive phrase perpetual,
    Terrible both to change or hold ;
        They move, but all their light is fled ;
And like a dead girl's breasts are small,
    And like a dead girl's breasts are cold,
    And like a dead girl's breasts are dead.

Forests and ancient haunts of sleep
    See dawn's intolerable spark
        While yet fierce darkness lingereth.
So I, their traveller, sunward creep,
    Hail Ra uprising in his bark,
        And feel the dawn-wind's sombre breath.
Strange loves rise up, and turn, and weep !
    Our warm wet bodies may not mark
        How these spell Satan's shibboleth
And like a devil's loves are deep,
    And like a devil's loves are dark,
    And like a devil's loves are death.

THE DREAM.

BEND down in dream the shadow-shape
    Of tender breasts and bare !
Let the long locks of gold escape
And cover me and fall and drape,
    A pall of whispering hair !
And let the starry eyes look through
    That mist of silken light,
And lips drop forth their honey-dew
And gentle sighs of sleep renew
    The scented winds of night !
As purple clusters of pure grapes
    Distil their dreamy wine
Whose fragrance from warm fields escapes
On shadowy hills and sunny capes
    In lands of jessamine !
So let thy figure faintly lined
    In pallid flame of sleep
With love inspire the dreamer's mind,
Young love most delicate and kind,
    With love—how calm and deep !
Let hardly half a smile revive
    The thoughts of waking hours.
How sad it is to be alive !
How well the happy dead must thrive
    In green Elysian bowers !

A sleep as deep as theirs bestow,
Dear angel of my dreams !
Bid time now cease its to-and-fro
That I may dwell with thee, and know
The soul from that which seems !
The long hair sobs in closer fold
And deeper curves of dawn ;
The arms bend closer, and the gold
Burns brighter, and the eyes are cold
With life at last withdrawn.
And all the spirit passing down
Involves my heart with gray :
So the pale stars of even crown
The glow of twilight ; dip and drown
The last despairs of day.
Oh ! closer yet and closer yet
The pearl of faces grows.
The hair is woven like a net
Of moonlight round me : sweet is set
The mouth's unbudded rose.
Oh never ! did our lips once meet
The dream were done for ever,
And death should dawn, supremely sweet,
One flash of knowledge subtle and fleet
Borne on the waveless river.

And therefore in the quiet hour
I rose from lily pillows
And swiftly sought the jasmine bower
Still sleeping, moonlight for a dower,
And bridal wreaths of willows.
And there I laid me down again :
The stream flowed softly by :
And thought the last time upon pain,
Earth's joy—the sad permuted strain
Of tears and ecstasy.
And there the dream came floating past
Borne in an ivory boat,
And all the world sighed low " At last."
The shallop waited while I cast
My languid limbs afloat
To drift with eyelids skyward turned
Up to the shadowy dream
Shaped like a lover's face, that burned ;
To drift toward the soul that yearned
For this—the hour supreme !
So drifting I resigned the sleep
For death's diviner bliss ;
As mists in rain of springtide weep,
Life melted in the dewfall deep
Of death's kiss in a kiss.

THE GOD-EATER *

A TRAGEDY OF SATIRE

1903

[The idea of this obscure and fantastic play is as follows :—
By a glorious act human misery is secured (History of Christianity).
Hence, appreciation of the personality of Jesus is no excuse for being a Christian.
Inversely, by a vile and irrational series of acts human happiness is secured (Story of the play).
Hence, attacks on the Mystics of History need not cause us to condemn Mysticism.
Also, the Knowledge of Good and Evil is a Tree whose fruit Man has not yet tasted : so that the Devil cheated Eve indeed ; or (more probably) Eve cheated Adam. Unless (most probable of all) God cheated the Devil, and the fruit was a common apple after all. Cf. H. Maudsley, " Life in Mind and Conduct."]

PERSONS.

CRIOSDA, aged 33.
MAURYA, his sister, aged 16.
RUPHA, the Hag of Eternity.

The scene of the Tragedy is laid in an ancient Scottish Hall, very remote.

The time is the One-and-Twentieth Century after Christ.

The action of the play occupies many years.

THE GOD-EATER.

ACT I.

CRIOSDA, MAURYA.

[The Scene is an old Baronial Hall, elaborately, yet somewhat grotesquely (from the incongruity), fitted up as an antique Egyptian temple. Centre : an altar between two obelisks ; on it a censer vomits smoke in great volumes. Above at back of stage is a stately throne, square and simple, on steps. In it sits MAURYA, quiet and silent. She is dressed in sombre green robes, lightened with old rose facings. She is heavily braceleted and ankleted with gold, and her crown is a gold disc, supported in silver horns, rising from her forehead. Above her is a rude painted board, representing the Winged Globe in many colours. Before the altar CRIOSDA is kneeling; he is dressed in a white robe fastened by a blue sash. A leopard's skin is over his shoulders, clasped with a golden clasp about his neck. He bears an "ankh" in his left hand, in his right a caduceus[1] wand. On his head is the winged helmet of Mercury, and his sandals are winged also. He is muttering low some fervent prayer, and anon casts incense upon the censer. The low muttering continues for a considerable time, MAURYA remaining quite still, as one rapt in her own thoughts. Suddenly, with startling vehemence, the song breaks out.

CRIOSDA.

    HAIL ! HAIL ! HAIL !

[MAURYA, startled, looks up and half rises. Then sits again, with a strange sweet smile of innocence and tenderness.

CRIOSDA. [Lower.]
The world is borne upon thy breast
  Even as the rose.

<hr>

[1] The wand of Mercury.

<hr>

* For the foundations of this play the student may consult any modern treatises on Sociology.

Wilt thou not lull it into rest,
  Some strong repose
More satisfying than pale sleep ;
Than death more long, more deep?

Hail ! at the twilight as at dawn !
  The sunset close
Even on the lake as on the lawn !
  The red ray glows
Across the woven stardrift's ways
In mystery of Maurya's praise.

Hear me, thy priest, at eventide !
  These subtler throes
Than love's or life's, invade, divide
  The world of woes.
Thy smile, thy murmur of delight, be enough
To fill the world with life and love !
      [*He bends over into deep reverence,
      yet with the air of one expecting
      a grace.*

      [MAURYA, *like one in trance, rises
      slowly, gathers her robes about her,
      and descends to the altar. Reaching
      over it, she bends and lifts him by
      his outstretched arms. She puts
      her lips to his forehead, and he,
      with a deep gasp, as of one in ecstasy
      not to be borne, drops back, breath-
      ing deeply. She lifts her hands,
      and brings them slowly, very for-
      cibly, forward, and says solemnly :*
The Blessing of Maurya.
Blessed be the House of the Servants of
  Maurya.
Blessed be the Stones of the House.
Blessed be the Tree of the House.
Blessed be the Food of the House.
Blessed be the Men of the House.
Blessed be all the Universe for their sakes.
The Blessing of Maurya.
      [*A short silence.*

      [MAURYA *goes back and lays her
      crown and robes on the throne.
      She is now dressed in wonderful
      close-fitting crimson silk, trimmed
      with ermine. Her bronze-gold hair
      is coiled wonderfully about her head.*

She comes down stage to CRIOSDA,
*who rises on one knee and takes
her thereon. She removes his
helmet and strokes gently his hair.*
Criosda, my brother !
  CRIOSDA. Maurya, little sister !
      [*He smiles with deep tenderness ;
      suddenly a pang catches him ; he
      strikes at his throat, and cries
      sharply :*
Ah !   [*Shivers with terrible emotion.*
  MAURYA. Criosda, ever the same ! The
    old world runs
On wheels of laughter for us little ones ;
To you, whose shoulders strain, the chariot
    seems
A poised fiend flogging you to hell.
  CRIOSDA.   These thoughts,
Maurya,—Maurya ! they become you not.
Child, to see sorrow is to taste it.
  MAURYA.   No ;
For such a sorrow is its own calm joy.
But—share me now your pain.
  CRIOSDA. [*In agony.*] No ! no ! not that !
  MAURYA. [*Smiling.*] The priest has
    secrets from the goddess?
  CRIOSDA.
[*With a cry as of physical pain, deadly sharp.*
                         Stop !
No jesting there.
  MAURYA.   I did not mean to jest.
As brother to sister ?
  CRIOSDA.   Ah ! that hurts, that hurts.
  MAURYA. I am heavy ?
  CRIOSDA. Heavy as my own heart's fear,
  MAURYA. You fear ? Am I in fault ? Is
    Maurya maid
The foe to Maurya goddess ?
  CRIOSDA.   Ah, indeed !
  MAURYA. Is not the work nigh ready ?
      [CRIOSDA *grips his caduceus, which
      he has dropped, and presses it
      savagely to his breast. Then, with
      a mingled burst of ferocity and joy,
      dashes* MAURYA *aside to the ground,
      reaches his hand towards the empty
      throne, apostrophising it, and cries
      with a strident laugh :*

CRIOSDA.					Ay, to-night!
[*A spasm overcomes him and he falls prone.*
MAURYA.	Criosda!	You are ill, ill!
Help!
[*He is silent; she unclasps the leopard's skin, and busies herself in trying to restore him.*
Janet! Angus! Angus!
[*Under her breath.*
Angus is the man—he saved poor Kenneth!
[*Aloud.*
Angus! Oh, miserable! No help comes here.
Criosda! wake! wake!—
Oh, I must take him out—no man may enter here!—It is ill luck. Old Andrew found the passage! and the next day he was dead —murdered, murdered! Oh, how horrible! —what a horrible place this is with all its beauty and love! and my worship—oh, how strange it all is. Criosda! come!
[*She begins to carry him to the great door, then notices his white robe.*
This must come off: they must not see the holy robes.
Criosda! my darling dear brother, do look at me!
[*She has removed the robes.* CRIOSDA *is now seen to be dressed in a dark-green tartan kilt and quasi-military tunic with silver buttons. A dirk hangs at his side. Its hilt is of unusual shape, being surmounted by the circle and cross familiar to visitors to Iona.*
Criosda! Ah yes, look up, look up!
How pale you are! There is no blood in your lips.
CRIOSDA.
[*Starting violently from her arms.*
Blood! Blood!
MAURYA. Lie still, dear, you are ill. Now! That is better. Come—can you walk a little?—we will get Angus to help.
CRIOSDA. No! No! I am well! I am well! Go, go!
If you love me, go.	I cannot bear it longer.

Your presence is my pain. There is nothing here.
Nothing—leave me!.
MAURYA.		Criosda, my own brother!
CRIOSDA. Go! O devil! Devil! Maurya!
[*He reaches out a threatening arm against the empty throne. Suddenly, with an inarticulate noise in his throat, he again collapses.*
MAURYA. Oh! Oh! he must come out and be tended. Where is the lever? Here—
[*Still supporting him on one arm, she raises a ponderous knocker and lets it fall. A clang, sombre, and of surprising volume, resounds. The door slowly opens of itself.*
CRIOSDA. [*Recovering.*] Who is at the door? Back, back. It is ill luck, ill luck, I say. Where is old Andrew? The faithful fool—Oh, the last dreadful look of his glazed eyes! What am I saying? Maurya, girl, go! I must tend the temple. I must be alone. It is not fitting—
MAURYA. You are ill; come and be tended yourself, first.
CRIOSDA. No! I am well. You are a girl, not a God.
MAURYA. Oh! Oh! Have I done amiss? Am I not——
CRIOSDA. Stop, don't!
[*Aside.*] I must be man—tut! tut!—
[*Aloud.*] Why, little sister, know
Those whom we worship as our gods are gods.
The power is mine: that art no skill resists.
No God dethrones himself; none can.
Will he, nill he, God must be God: it is a luckless fate for a girl's dower, a thankless way for a maiden's feet.
MAURYA. Why, then, am I not the Goddess Maurya?
CRIOSDA. Yes! yes! of course, but only by my making.
MAURYA. Was not my birth miraculous? and strange
The death of the old people of this house
That left you guardian?
CRIOSDA.		Yes, girl, that was strange.

MAURYA. Then, is the power that makes
   me in the end
True Goddess Maurya, yours, yours only?
CRIOSDA. [*Solemnly.*] No!
Stop! ask no more! There lies the awful crux.
Blind are fate's eyes, and pinioned are will's
   wings.
In you the whole chance lies.
MAURYA.   In me?
CRIOSDA.   In you.
MAURYA. I will do all to win!
CRIOSDA.   Do all?
MAURYA.   Do all.
CRIOSDA. Ah then! No, no, it is not yet
   enough.
Not definite yet. Stop! fool, shall I hint
   and ruin all with a word? Backwards
   or forwards, the blow goes home either
   way. [*Looks at her with keen fierce eyes.*]
   Ah!
MAURYA. [*A little frightened.*] Come,
   O my brother!
It is time to go.
CRIOSDA. No! leave me. It is but an hour.
   [MAURYA *smiles; leaves her hand a
   little in his, and so passes out
   slowly through the open door with
   her eyes fixed in love and trust on
   him.* CRIOSDA *starts up and pulls
   fiercely at a second lever, and the
   door clangs to with the same nerve-
   shattering shock.* CRIOSDA *staggers
   to altar; and, with his hand on it,
   turns towards door.*
Mouths of God's mercy! I would her eyes
were bleeding wounds in my heart! Ah
though! If she were a dog I could not do
it. She is my sister——
   [*Turns with a cry to throne and
   flings up his hands.*
and I will!
Death! Death!
It is a year to-night. I arrayed her first
In yon gold ornaments—My brain is sick!
I want coffee—or hashish—No! That is for
   her!
I must be very clear and calm, very clear,
   very calm,

How I must be ill—
   [*Correcting himself with effort.*] Ill I
   must be. Ha!
   [*Goes to altar, opens it, takes out a
   flask filled with a clear pale blue
   liquor with rosy stars of light in
   it, pours it into a long vial, and
   holds it to the light. The room
   is lighted by electricity, the globes
   being the eyes of strange sculpturea
   stone beasts on the walls.*
So far the story is true.
                 [*Drinks a little.*
Why, that is better already. I am again
the priest of Maurya—who is the brother
of Maurya? A trivial ape o' the time!—
cold, logical to a fault!—Ay! and a crime,
a crime at which the stars shake in the
heaven, men might think. Yet the stars,
I will wager, are indifferent. True, the
news has not reached them: true, that star
I see is not a star; it was so six, ten, twenty
thousand years ago—logical, I say!—and I
will drink, for parenthetical is a poor
substitute—
                    [*Drinks.*
Why, how thou fir'st me! with that icy fire
Of adamant thought. It well befits this hour
If I recoil the chain whose last smooth link
Slides o'er Time's cogwheel. In the be-
   ginning then
The vastness of the heavens and the earth
Created the idea of God. So Levi once
Sarcastic in apostasy; *à rebours.*
So Müller, mythopoeic in his mood
Of the unmasking mythopoeia. Now
Profounder science, Spencer's amplitude,
Allen's too shallow erudition, Frazer's
Research, find men have made—since men
   made aught—
Their Gods, and slain, and eaten. Sur-
   face! I,
Criosda of the Mist, see truth in all
Rather than truth in none. Below the rite,
The sight! Beyond the priest, the power!
   Above
The sense, the soul! So men who made
   their gods

Did make in very deed : so I will make
In uttermost truth a new god, since the old
Are dead, or drunk with wine, and soma-
    juice
And hemp and opium ! Maurya, thou shalt be!
So for long years I have dared. First the
    twin death
Of the dotards, slow constraint of Maurya's
    mind
To the one end. Next, study : next, research
In places long-forgotten of the West,
Deep hidden of the East : the perfect rite
Dragged by laborious hand and brain to shape
And this [*Raises glass*] the first fruits ! Hail,
    thou fount of wit,
Light liquor, child of cares how heavy! Drink!
The peace of the Priest !
                    [*He drinks up the liquor.*
                    Be thou my light !
Uncloud the misty channels of the mind !
Off, horror ! Off, compassion ! Be the brain
The almighty engine of the Will—and those
Subtler and deeper forces grimly guessed,
Terribly proven—be they strong thereby !
Awake, O sleeping serpent of the soul,
Unhinted skills, and unimagined powers,
And purposes undreamed of !
        [*He goes now calmly about the temple,
        arranging all the ornaments. He
        empties the censer.*
                    Shadowy influence
Of smoke ! Where lies its physiologic act ?
What drug conceals the portent ? Mystery !
Mystery ninefold closed upon itself
That matter should move mind—Ay ! darker
    yet
That mind should work on matter? And
    the proof
Extant, implicit in the thought thereof !
Else all our work were vain. These twain
    be one ;
And in their essence? Deeper, deeper yet
I dive.
        [*He draws the dirk and tests the point.*
        And will to-morrow show me aught ?
        [*He extinguishes the lamps, goes to
        the door and opens it. The clang
        startles him.*

I hate that door ! Strange that the outer
    air
Should bring back manhood ! Man, thou
    pitiest her !
Man, thou art whelmed in that red tide of
    lust
That rolls over strong loathing by vast will,
Hideous rapture of death. That's for thee,
    man !
Thine are the scalding tears of sympathy,
The tender love for the young flower. And
    these
Are none of the priest's. Enough !
        [*Exit. The door clangs again. The
        curtain falls ; a scene drops.
        RUPHA, an aged and wizened hag,
        of gigantic stature, is discovered
        seated, C. The scene represents a
        lonely hill-top covered with stones.
        A little coarse grass grows in places.
        Three great menhirs stand up, C.
        Moonlight.*
RUPHA. The rune of the breath.
        The saga of death.
        The secret of earth.
        The beginning of birth.
        The speech of woe.
        Ho ! Ho !

I scent the prey.
I sniff the air.
The dawn of day
Makes Maurya May
The Goddess rare.
The light of the stars
Be hers ; go, go,
Ye silent folk,
Harness your cars !
Brace the yoke !
It is time to Know.
Ho ! Ho !

Desolate deeds !
She bleeds, she bleeds.
The golden head
Is drooped for aye.
She is dead, she is dead.
She is God, and I ?

I am might.
I am power.
I am light
For an hour.
I am strong, I grow.
Ho! Ho!

I taught Criosda
The evil runes.
Mine were the tunes
His passion sang.
Mine is the clang
Of the olden door.
Half the secret
I gave : no more !
Half the secret
Hidden I keep.
Hide it deep !
That is mine !
I will work.
He is nought.
The runes divine
Awry be wrought.
Hail to the murk !
            [*A distant whine is heard.*
Cover me ! Lurk,
Rupha, lurk !
'Tis a foe.
Ho! Ho!
[*Clouds have been obscuring the moon ;
it is now dark. A fox passes over
the stage.*
Crafty ! Crafty !
That is the omen.
Fear not the foemen !
                [*She rises up.*
Mine is the spoil
Of the grimly toil.
Gloomy, gloomy !
Ah ! but I laugh.
He is but a fool.
He has lost !
He is lost !
Take the staff !
Trace the rule
Of the circle crossed !
[*She makes a circle and a cross therein.*

No light therein !
Mother of sin,
Thou hast won !
Death to the sun !
Hail to the glow
Of the corpse decayed !
Hail to the maid !
Ho! Ho!
[*She rambles about the stage, mutter-
ing savage runes with dismal
laughter. Her words are inarticu-
late, when with a last* Ho ! Ho !
the curtain falls.
[*The scene rises, and we again see
the stage as in* Scene I. MAURYA
and CRIOSDA *as in the opening.*
CRIOSDA *is, however, absolutely
calm.*

MAURYA. Criosda, answer !
CRIOSDA.   I obey, having heard.
MAURYA. This dawn shall see me take
    the final flight ?
CRIOSDA.   It shall.
MAURYA. I shall be taken utterly from
    earth ?
CRIOSDA. So.
MAURYA. Yet abide with thee, my priest.
CRIOSDA.   Ay ! Ay !
MAURYA. I feel no early prompting thither.
CRIOSDA.   No.
It is sudden.
MAURYA. What then lacks ?
CRIOSDA.   A draught : a word.
MAURYA. Where is the draught ?
CRIOSDA.   This incense in my hand.
MAURYA. What is the word ?
                [CRIOSDA *is silent.*
                Criosda, answer me.
CRIOSDA. To invoke death it were to
    answer this.
MAURYA. Ah, then, forbear !
                [CRIOSDA *is silent.*
                How shall I know the word ?
CRIOSDA. Good luck may bring it to the
    light.
MAURYA. Ill luck ?
CRIOSDA. A year's delay.
MAURYA.   Ah, let me gain one gift

Whose sweet reversion hangs above me now :
To order luck !
CRIOSDA.   Skill orders luck !
MAURYA.   _   The draught !
CRIOSDA. Hither, O Maurya !
MAURYA.   I will come to thee.
        [CRIOSDA, *taking hashish, throws it
        upon the glowing censer.* MAURYA
        comes down stage and bends over it.
        CRIOSDA *lifts it up and offers it
        reverently.*
MAURYA. Methinks anticipation o' the
        event
Shoots in my veins, darting delight.
Why, this is strange !
I am losing myself. Criosda !
The walls of the world fall back with a crash.
Where is all this? I am out of myself: I expand
O Maurya, where art thou, little phantom
        of myriads of ages ago ?   What a
        memory ! Ah ! Ah ! She is falling.
        [MAURYA *staggers.* CRIOSDA, *who
        has been watching her narrowly,
        catches her and lays her tenderly on
        the altar.*
Oh, what happiness, what happiness ! Cri-
        osda, dear brother, how I love you !
I wish to sleep for ever—I wish to die !
        [CRIOSDA, *who has been bending over
        her, leaps up, shrieks.*
CRIOSDA. The luck of Maurya !
        [*He draws quickly his dirk ; it flashes
        on high, he leaps on to the body of*
        MAURYA, *and plunges it into her
        heart.*

                CURTAIN.

                ACT II.

        FORTY YEARS AFTERWARDS.

The scene is an open and stormy sea. RUPHA,
        *with her staff, wave-riding in a cockle-
        shell.*

RUPHA.   Ha ! Ha !
                In the storm
                I ride.

The winds bear me.
The waves fear me.
I appal ; I inform
Their pride.
Let him hither,
Drifting ever
Wrecked and lost !
His life shall wither.
The dirk shall sever
His rune ill-crossed.

I hear him come
Across the foam
With a bang and a boom.
The winds, hum, hum.
The billows comb.
Ho ! Ho ! the doom !
Ho ! Ho ! I have won.
I shall win.
Death to the sun !
Life to sin !
They reap who sow.
Ho ! Ho !
        [*A boat drifts in, L. In it the aged*
        CRIOSDA, *his white hair afloat in
        the storm, is standing with folded
        arms. His eyes are dull, as seeing
        inward.*
RUPHA. Ha ! Ha !
'Tis the priest.
Dost think
O' the feast ?
Criosda, shrink !
The rune is woe.
Ho ! Ho !
CRIOSDA. Mother of Sin !
RUPHA.   Ho ! Ho !
CRIOSDA. Thus then at last the Luck of
        Maurya throws
A double-six to lost Criosda.
RUPHA. Ho !
        The Luck of Maurya !
        The power of the deed.
CRIOSDA. I find thee, mother, at last.
        Life's final flash
Gleams through the storm.
RUPHA. I am found !
        Ho ! Ho !

CRIOSDA. What of the power? I bid
these waves be calm
In Maurya's name.
[*The storm increases momently in vio-*
lence. RUPHA *mutters on.* CRIOSDA
shows with a gesture that he knows
his words avail nothing.
RUPHA. Ho! Ho!
CRIOSDA. I wittingly and well resumed
the rite
Learnt at thy breast, old wolf!
RUPHA. Ho! Ho!
The might is mine
O' the rune divine.
Silence, winds!
Peace, ye waves!
The spell binds
Their wrath
In the graves
Below ocean.
Clear the path!
Cease your motion?
Swift, be slow!
Ho! Ho!
[*The storm ceases.*
CRIOSDA. *Thy* words avail then?
RUPHA. Ha! Ha!
They avail.
I avail.
Did Rupha fail,
All would be done.
Death to the sun!
I know.
Ho! Ho!
CRIOSDA. All this I did for thee?
RUPHA. Ha! Ha!
What didst thou do?
Ha! Ha!
Ha! Ha!
CRIOSDA. What did I not do? All!
RUPHA. Tell! Tell!
'Tis a spell.
CRIOSDA. I will tell all. O sea, swallow
me up
With the last word!
RUPHA. It obeys?
No! No!
Ho! Ho!

CRIOSDA. Thou sinister one! Thy rite
I duly did;
That drugged (and dancing with delight
thereof
The maiden's mind) the maiden's body prone
Lay on her altar. Then she gave consent,
And I smote once.
RUPHA. Ha! Ha!
What came then?
CRIOSDA. I tore out her heart,
And held its flame aloft. The blackening
blood
Gushed on my arms—and then—
RUPHA. Ho! Ho!
CRIOSDA. With red lips reeking from the
sweet foul feast,
I sang in tuneless agony the spell;
Rolled athwart space the black words: then
some force
Tore me: I heard the tears drop in my
heart.
I heard the laughter of some utmost God
Hid in the middle of matter. That was I,
The hideous laugher of the maniac laugh
When loathing makes the bed to lust, and
twine
The limbs of agony about the trunk
Of torture — rapture stabbing through—
Maurya!
Ay, that was I; and I the weeping wolf
That howls about this hell that is my heart;
And I the icy and intangible
That beholds all, and is not.
RUPHA. Three in one!
One in three!
Death to the sun!
Glory to thee!
Thou wast there!
Enough!
It will grow.
Ho! Ho!
CRIOSDA. In English, I was mad. But
no new portents
Confound the course of the sun. I left my
home
To seek thee out. When skill availed me
not,
I put to sea to try the Luck of Maurya.

RUPHA. Thou shouldst have tried that
first of all.

CRIOSDA.   Why then
The Luck may avail if that wried tongue
can speak
Straight ! Hast thou aught to bid me do ?
To me naught matters more. My life I cast
On the one throw ; and, having lost, I have
lost.
I am indifferent to my fate as the stars
Are to my curses, were I fool enough
To curse.

RUPHA. Destiny has strange ways.

CRIOSDA.   I care not.

RUPHA. How long hast thou left home ?

CRIOSDA.   Seven years.

RUPHA.   Return !

CRIOSDA.   How can I ?

RUPHA. Stamp the boat beneath thy feet
Down wallowing in the trough !

CRIOSDA.   It is done !
   [*The boat sinks from under* CRIOSDA.
      He would sink did he not grasp the
      staff extended to him.

RUPHA. Now, stand alone !

CRIOSDA.   I stand.

RUPHA.   Then break, O vision
Of sea ; awake, O vision of the shrine !

CRIOSDA. All is illusion ?

RUPHA.   All.   Murder a mode
And love a mode of the unknown that is,
That nor thyself nor I can ever see.
Yet, so far as may be, awake, O shrine !
   [*She strikes the sea with her staff ;*
      the storm rises; it grows bitter
      dark ; only their shapes are dimly
      seen against the dark background
      of cloud. The scene rises.

RUPHA. Break, break, O mist of morning!
   [*The stage, which is full of mist,*
      gradually clears. It shows the
      Temple as in Scene I. *On the*
      throne the embalmed body of
      MAURYA *is seated. The altar*
      flames with glowing charcoal, and
      a thin steam of incense arises.
      RUPHA *and* CRIOSDA *are in front,*
      R. *Two priests minister ; a goodly*

crew of choristers intone low litanies.
A few young folk are at a barrier
by the footlights (centre) in prayer.
An old woman enters and brings
an offering of flowers, which the
priests receive and cast before the
throne. RUPHA *motions* CRIOSDA
to be silent.

1st PRIEST. Glory unto thee, Maurya,
secret Lady of the Stars !

CHORISTERS. Who wast born on earth !

2nd PRIEST. Glory unto thee, Maurya,
Lady of Life !

CHORISTERS. Who didst die for us !

ALL. Glory for ever unto Maurya !

THE WORSHIPPING FOLK. Maurya, hear
us !
   [*All bend deeper and deeper in adora-*
      tion. Silence awhile. They rise,
      and the priests see RUPHA *and*
      CRIOSDA.

1st PRIEST. [*Whispers.*] It is the Mother
of our Lady.

2nd PRIEST. [*Whispers.*] Who is with her ?

1st PRIEST. [*Whispers.*] The first disciple.

2nd PRIEST. [*Whispers.*] Blessed is this
day, O brother !

1st PRIEST. [*Whispers.*] Let us go and
do them reverence.
   [*They approach* RUPHA *and* CRIOSDA,
      and bend low before them.

RUPHA. Criosda ! Of one act the ultima-
tion
Rings through eternity past the poles of space.
Choose then what spangle on the robe of time
Shall glitter in thine eyes : for the hour
strikes.

CRIOSDA. Mother ! I would see the Luck
of Maurya stand
Two thousand years from now.

RUPHA. Good priest, bring forth
The globe of crystal.

1st PRIEST.   Hearing is enough.
   [*The priest takes a crystal from out*
      the altar, and places it thereupon.
      RUPHA *and* CRIOSDA *advance.*

RUPHA. Look ! I uplift the veil.
      [*She unveils the crystal.*

CRIOSDA. I see a lofty pyramid sun-white
Blaze in immaculate glory to the stars ;
Its splendour of itself, since all is dark
About, above.   Thereon a countless folk,
Multitudes many-coloured, grave and tall,
Beautiful, make a beautiful murmur, move,
In infinite musical labyrinths about.
Them doth the soul of love inhabit, them
The light of wisdom doth inform, them
    peace
Hath marked and sealed her own.   But on
    their lips
Is one imagined silence like a sigh.
Unanimous the hushèd harmony
Flows forth from heart to mouth ; and
    mouths bloom red
With ripe and royal repetition ; kisses
Flow like thick honey-drops in honeysuckle.
That is their worship.
    RUPHA. Whom then worship they ?

CRIOSDA.   Maurya !
    [*Recalled to himself, he perceives the
        meaning of this ; with a great cry
        breaks forward and stands before
        the throne, raises himself up and
        says in triumph and knowledge of
        peace :*
Then—I have lived !
    [*Reaches out his hand towards the
        enthroned mummy.*
                    Maurya !
    [*With the last terrible cry he collapses,
        and falls dead with his head on
        MAURYA'S knees.*
RUPHA. As it was in the beginning, is
    now, and ever shall be : world with-
    out end.
    [*She deliberately breaks her staff in
        her hands.   The report is sharp
        and very loud, like a pistol shot.*

CURTAIN.

THE SWORD OF SONG

CALLED BY CHRISTIANS

THE BOOK OF THE BEAST

1904

[This book is so full of recondite knowledge of various kinds that it seems quite ineffective to annotate every obscure passage. Where references and explanations can be concisely given, this has been done.]

"You are sad!" the Knight said, in an anxious tone ; "let me sing you a song to comfort you." *

"Is it very long?" Alice asked.

"It's long," said the Knight, "but it's *very very* beautiful. The name of the song is called 'The Book of the Beast.'"

"Oh! how ugly!" cried Alice.

"Never mind," said the mild creature. "*Some* people call it 'Reason in Rhyme.'"

"But which *is* the name of the song?" Alice said, trying not to seem too interested.

"Ah, you don't understand," the Knight said, looking a little vexed. "That's what the name is *called*. The name really *is* 'Ascension Day and Pentecost ; with some Prose Essays and an Epilogue,' just as the title is 'The Sword of Song' you know, just in the same way, just in the same way, just in the same way . . ."

Alice put her fingers in her ears and gave a little scream. "Oh, dear me! That's

harder than ever!" she said to herself, and then, looking determinedly intelligent : "So *that's* what the song is called. I see. But what *is* the song?"

"You must be a perfect fool," said the Knight, irritably. "The song is called 'Stout Doubt ; or the Agnostic's Anthology,' by the author of 'Gas Manipulation,' 'Solutions,' 'The Management of Retorts,' and other physical works of the first order—but that's only what it's *called*, you know."

"Well, what *is* the song then?" said Alice, who was by this time completely bewildered.

"If I wished to be obscure, child," said the Knight, rather contemptuously, "I should tell you that the Name of the Title was 'What a man of 95 ought to know,' as endorsed by eminent divines, and that . . ." Seeing that she only began to cry, he broke off and continued in a gentler tone : "it *means*, my dear . . ." He stopped short, for she was taking no notice ; but as her figure was bent by sobs into something very like a note of interrogation : "You want to know what it *is*,

* This passage is a parody on one in "Alice through the Looking-Glass."

I suppose!" continued the Knight, in a superior, but rather offended voice.

"If you would, please, sir!"

"Well, *that*," pronounced the Knight, with the air of having thoroughly studied the question and reached a conclusion absolutely final and irreversible, "*that*, Goodness only knows. But I will sing it to you."

PRELIMINARY INVOCATION.

NOTHUNG.*

THE crowns of Gods and mortals wither ;
    Moons fade where constellations shone ;
Numberless aeons brought us hither ;
    Numberless aeons beckon us on.
The world is old, and I am strong—
Awake, awake, O Sword of Song !

Here, in the Dusk of Gods, I linger ;
    The world awaits a Word of Truth.
Kindle, O lyre, beneath my finger !
    Evoke the age's awful youth !
To arms against the inveterate wrong !
Awake, awake, O Sword of Song !

Sand-founded reels the House of Faith ;
    Up screams the howl of ruining sect ;
Out from the shrine flits the lost Wraith ;
    "God hath forsaken His elect !"
Confusion sweeps upon the throng—
Awake, awake, O Sword of Song !

Awake to wound, awake to heal
    By wounding, thou resistless sword !
Raise the prone priestcrafts that appeal
    In agony to their prostrate Lord !
Raise the duped herd—they have suffered
        long !
Awake, awake, O Sword of Song !

My strength this agony of the age
    Win through ; my music charm the old
Sorrow of years : my warfare wage
    By iron to an age of gold :—
The world is old, and I am strong—
Awake, awake, O Sword of Song !

* The name of Siegfried's sword.

INTRODUCTION TO "ASCENSION DAY AND PENTECOST."

NOT a word to introduce my introduction ! Let me instantly launch the Boat of Discourse on the Sea of Religious Speculation, in danger of the Rocks of Authority and the Quicksands of Private Interpretation, Scylla and Charybdis. Here is the strait ; what God shall save us from shipwreck ? If we choose to understand the Christian (or any other) religion literally, we are at once overwhelmed by its inherent impossibility. Our credulity is outraged, our moral sense shocked, the holiest foundations of our inmost selves assailed by no ardent warrior in triple steel, but by a loathly and disgusting worm. That this is so, the apologists for the religion in question, whichever it may be, sufficiently indicate (as a rule) by the very method of their apology. The alternative is to take the religion symbolically, esoterically ; but to move one step in this direction is to start on a journey whose end cannot be determined. The religion, ceasing to be a tangible thing, an object uniform for all sane eyes, becomes rather that mist whereon the sun of the soul casts up, like Brocken spectre, certain vast and vague images of the beholder himself, with or without a glory encompassing them. The function of the facts is then quite passive : it matters little or nothing whether the cloud be the red mist of Christianity, or the glimmering silver-white of Celtic Paganism ; the hard grey dim-gilded of Buddhism, the fleecy opacity of Islam, or the mysterious medium of those ancient faiths which come up in as many colours as their investigator has moods.*

* "In order to get over the ethical difficulties presented by the naïve naturalism of many parts of those Scriptures, in the divine authority of which he firmly believed, Philo borrowed from the Stoics (who had been in like straits in respect of Greek mythology) that great Excalibur which they had forged with infinite pains and skill—the method of allegorical interpretation. This mighty ' two-handed engine at the door ' of the theologian is warranted to make a speedy end of any and every moral or intellectual difficulty, by showing that, taken allegorically, or, as it is otherwise said, ' poetically ' or ' in a spiritual sense,' the plainest words mean whatever a pious interpreter desires they should mean" (Huxley, "Evolution of Theology").—A. C.

If the student has advanced spiritually so that he can internally, infallibly perceive what is Truth, he will find it equally well symbolised in most external faiths.

It is curious that Browning never turns his wonderful faculty of analysis upon the fundamental problems of religion, as it were an axe laid to the root of the Tree of Life. It seems quite clear that he knew what would result if he did so. We cannot help fancying that he was unwilling to do this. The proof of his knowledge I find in the following lines :—

"I have read much, thought much, experienced much,
Yet would die rather than avow my fear
The Naples' liquefaction may be false . . .
I hear you recommend, I might at least
Eliminate, decrassify my faith
Since I adopt it : keeping what I must
And leaving what I can ; such points as this . . .
Still, when you bid me purify the same,
To such a process I discern no end . . .
First cut the liquefaction, what comes last
But Fichte's clever cut at God himself ? . . .
I trust nor hand, nor eye, nor heart, nor brain
To stop betimes : they all get drunk alike.
The first step, I am master not to take."

This is surely the apotheosis of wilful ignorance ! We may think, perhaps, that Browning is "hedging" when, in the last paragraph, he says : "For Blougram, he believed, say, half he spoke," [*] and hints at some deeper ground. It is useless to say, "This is Blougram and not Browning." Browning could hardly have described the dilemma without seeing it. What he really believes is, perhaps, a mystery.

That Browning, however, believes in universal salvation, though he nowhere (so far as I know) gives his reasons, save as they are summarised in the last lines of the below-quoted passage, is evident from the last stanza of "Apparent Failure," and from his final pronouncement of the Pope on Guido, represented in Browning's masterpiece as a Judas without the decency to hang himself.

"So (i.e., by suddenness of fate) may the truth be flashed out by one blow,
And Guido see one instant and be saved.
Else I avert my face nor follow him
Into that sad obscure sequestered state
Where God unmakes but to remake the soul
He else made first in vain : which must not be."

* Probably a record for a bishop.—A. C.

This may be purgatory, but it sounds not unlike reincarnation.

It is at least a denial of the doctrine of eternal punishment.

As for myself, I took the first step years ago, quite in ignorance of what the last would lead to. God is indeed cut away—a cancer from the breast of truth.

Of those philosophers, who from unassailable premisses draw by righteous deduction a conclusion against God, and then for His sake overturn their whole structure by an act of will, like a child breaking an ingenious toy, I take Mansel as my type. [*]

Now, however, let us consider the esoteric idea-mongers of Christianity, Swedenborg, Anna Kingsford, Deussen and the like, of whom I have taken Caird as my example. I wish to unmask these people : I perfectly agree with nearly everything they say, but their claim to be Christians is utterly confusing, and lends a lustre to Christianity which is quite foreign. Deussen, for example, coolly discards nearly all the Old Testament, and, picking a few New Testament passages, often out of their context, claims his system as Christianity. Luther discards James. Kingsford calls Paul the Arch Heretic. My friend the "Christian Clergyman" accepted Mark and Acts—until pushed. Yet Deussen is honest enough to admit that Vedanta teaching is identical, but clearer ! and he quite clearly and sensibly defines Faith—surely the most essential quality for the adherent to Christian dogma —as "being convinced on insufficient evidence." Similarly the dying-to-live idea of Hegel (and Schopenhauer) claimed by Caird as the central spirit of Christianity is far older, in the Osiris Myth of the Egyptians. These ideas are all right, but they have no more to do with Christianity than the Metric System with the Great Pyramid. But see Piazzi Smyth ! [†] Henry Morley has even the audacity to claim Shelley—Shelley !—as a Christian "in spirit."

Talking of Shelley :—With regard to my open denial of the personal Christian God, may it not be laid to my charge that I have dared to voice in bald language what Shelley

* As represented by his Encyclopædia article ; not in such works as "Limits of Religious Thought."—A. C.

† An astronomer whose brain gave way. He prophesied the end of the world in 1881, from measurements made in the Great Pyramid.

sang in words of surpassing beauty: for of course the thought in one or two passages of this poem is practically identical with that in certain parts of " Queen Mab " and " Prometheus Unbound." But the very beauty of these poems (especially the latter) is its weakness: it is possible that the mind of the reader, lost in the sensuous, nay ! even in the moral beauty of the words, may fail to be impressed by their most important meaning. Shelley himself recognised this later: hence the direct and simple vigour of the " Masque of Anarchy."

It has often puzzled atheists how a man of Milton's genius could have written as he did of Christianity. But we must not forget that Milton lived immediately after the most important Revolution in Religion and Politics of modern times: Shelley on the brink of such another Political upheaval. Shakespeare alone sat enthroned above it all like a god, and is not lost in the mire of controversy.* This also, though " I'm no Shakespeare, as too probable," I have endeavoured to avoid: yet I cannot but express the hope that my own enquiries into religion may be the reflection of the spirit of the age; and that plunged as we are in the midst of jingoism and religious revival, we may be standing on the edge of some gigantic precipice, over which we may cast all our impedimenta of lies and trickeries, political, social, moral, and religious, and (ourselves) take wings and fly. The comparison between myself and the masters of English thought I have named is unintentional, though perhaps unavoidable; and though the presumption is, of course, absurd, yet a straw will show which way the wind blows as well as the most beautiful and elaborate vane: and in this sense it is my most eager hope that I may not unjustly draw a comparison between myself and the great reformers of eighty years ago.

* So it is usually supposed. Maybe I shall one day find words to combat, perhaps to overthrow, this position. *P.S.* As, for example, page 185. As a promise-keeper I am the original eleven stone three Peacherine.—A. C.

I must apologise (perhaps) for the new note of frivolity in my work: due doubtless to the frivolity of my subject: these poems being written when I was an Advaitist and could not see why—everything being an illusion—there should be any particular object in doing or thinking anything. How I have found the answer will be evident from my essay on this subject.* I must indeed apologise to the illustrious Shade of Robert Browning for my audacious parody in title, style, and matter of his " Christmas Eve and Easter Day." The more I read it the eventual anticlimax of that wonderful poem irritated me only the more. But there is hardly any poet living or dead who so commands alike my personal affection and moral admiration. My desire to find the Truth will be my pardon with him, whose whole life was spent in admiration of Truth, though he never turned its formidable engines against the Citadel of the Almighty.

If I be appealed of blasphemy or irreverence in my treatment of these subjects, I will take refuge in Browning's own apology, from the very poem I am attacking:

" I have done: and if any blames me,
Thinking that merely to touch in brevity
The topics I dwell on were unlawful—
Or worse, that I trench with undue levity
On the bounds of the holy and the awful—
I praise the heart and pity the head of him,
And refer myself to Thee, instead of him,
Who head and heart alike discernest,
Looking below light speech we utter
Where frothy spume and frequent splutter
Prove that the soul's depths boil in earnest ! "

But I have after all little fear that I am seriously wrong. That I show to my critics the open door of the above city of refuge may be taken as merely another gesture of contemptuous pity, the last insult which may lead my antagonists to that surrender which is the truest victory.

PEACE TO ALL BEINGS.

* *Vide infra*, " Berashith."

ASCENSION DAY

I FLUNG out of chapel [1] * and church,
Temple and hall and meeting-room,
Venus' Bower and Osiris' Tomb,[2]
And left the devil in the lurch,
While God[3] got lost in the crowd of gods,[4]   5
And soul went down [5] in the turbid tide
Of the metaphysical lotus-eyed,[6]
And I was—anyhow, what's the odds?

The life to live? The thought to think? Shall I take refuge
In a tower like once Childe Roland ‡ [7] found, blind, deaf, huge, 10
Or in that forest of two hundred thousand
Trees,[8] fit alike to shelter man and mouse, and—
Shall I say God? Be patient, your Reverence,[9]
I warrant you'll journey a wiser man ever hence!
Let's tap (like the negro who gets a good juice of it,   15
Cares nought if that be, or be not, God's right use of it),[10]
In all that forest of verses one tree [11]
Yclept " Red Cotton Nightcap Country " :
How a goldsmith, between the Ravishing Virgin
And a leman too rotten to put a purge in,   20
Day by day and hour by hour,
In a Browningesque forest of thoughts having lost himself,
Expecting a miracle, solemnly tossed himself
Off from the top of a tower.
Moral : don't spoil such an excellent sport as an   25
Ample estate with a church and a courtesan !

" Truth, that's the gold ! " [12] But don't worry about it !
I, you, or Simpkin [13] can get on without it !
If life's task be work and love's (the soft-lippèd) ease,
Death's be God's glory ? discuss with Euripides !   30

* The numbered notes are given at p. 190.
† Bacon, " Essay on Truth," line 1.
‡ " Childe Roland to the dark Tower came."—BROWNING.

Or, cradle be hardship, and finally coffin, ease,
Love being filth ? let us ask Aristophanes !
Or, heaven's sun bake us, while Earth's bugs and fleas kill us,
Love the God's scourge ?   I refer you to Aeschylus !
(Nay ! that's a slip !   Say we " Earth's grim device, cool
35   loss !—"
Better the old Greek orthography !—Aischulos ! [14])
Or, love be God's champagne's foam ; death in man's
      trough, hock lees,
· Pathos our port's beeswing ? what answers Sophocles ?
Brief, with love's medicine let's draught, bolus, globule us !
40 Wise and succinct bids, I think, Aristobulus.[15]
Whether my Muse be Euterpe or Clio,
Life, Death, and Love are all Batrachomyo [16]—
Machia, what ? ho ! old extinct Alcibiades ?
For me, do ut—God true, be mannikin liar !—des !

45 It's rather hard, isn't it, sir, to make sense of it ?
Mine of so many pounds—pouch even pence of it ? [17]
Try something easier,[18] where the bard seems to me
Seeking that light, which I find come in dreams to me.
Even as he takes two feasts to enlarge upon,
50 So will I do too to launch my old barge upon.
Analyse, get hints from Newton [19] or Faraday,[20]
Use every weapon—love, scorn, reason, parody !
Just where he worships ?   Ah me ! shall his soul,
Far in some glory, take hurt from a mole
55 Grubbing i' th' ground ?   Shall his spirit not see,
Lightning to lightning, the spirit in me ?
Parody ?   Shall not his spirit forgive
Me, who shall love him as long as I live ?
Love's at its height in pure love ?   Nay, but after
60 When the song's light dissolves gently in laughter !
Then and then only the lovers may know
Nothing can part them for ever.   And so,
Muse, hover o'er me ! Apollo, above her !

I, of the Moderns, have let alone Greek.[21]
65 Out of the way Intuition shall shove her.
Spirit and Truth in my darkness I seek.
Little by little they bubble and leak ;
Such as I have to the world I discover.
Words—are they weak ones at best ?   They shall speak !

Apology of poet.
Skeleton of poem. Valuable fact for use of lovers. Invocation.

Imperfect scholastic attainments of author remedied by his great spiritual insight. His intention.

<table>
<tr><td>

His achieve-
ment.
Plan of poem
" Conspuez
Dieu !"

</td><td>

Shields? Be they paper, paint, lath? They shall cover   70
Well as they may, the big heart of a lover !
Swords? Let the lightning of Truth strike the fortress
Frowning of God !   I will sever one more tress
Off the White Beard [22] with his son's blood besprinkled,
Carve one more gash in the forehead [23] hate-wrinkled :—   75
So, using little arms, earn one day better ones ;
Cutting the small chains,[24] learn soon to unfetter one's
Limbs from the large ones, walk forth and be free !—
So much for Browning ! and so much for me !

</td></tr>
<tr><td>

Apology for
manner of
poem.
A chance for
Tibet.

</td><td>

Pray do not ask me where I stand !   80
" Who asks, doth err." [25]   At least demand
No folly such as answer means !
" But if " (you [26] say) " your spirit weans
Itself of milk-and-water pap,
And one religion as another   85
O'erleaps itself and falls on the other ; [27]
You'll tell me why at least, mayhap,
Our Christianity excites
Especially such petty spites
As these you strew throughout your verse."   90
The chance of birth !   I choose to curse
(Writing in English [28]) just the yoke
Of faith that tortures English folk.
I cannot write [29] a poem yet
To please the people in Tibet ;   95
But when I can, Christ shall not lack
Peace, while their Buddha I attack.[30]

</td></tr>
<tr><td>

Hopes. Iden-
tity of poet.
Attention
drawn to my
highly decora-
tive cover.

</td><td>

Yet by-and-by I hope to weave
A song of Anti-Christmas Eve
And First- and Second-Beast-er Day.   100
There's one * [31] who loves me dearly (vrai!)
Who yet believes me sprung from Tophet,
Either the Beast or the False Prophet ;
And by all sorts of monkey tricks
Adds up my name to Six Six Six.   105
Retire, good Gallup ! [32] In such strife her
Superior skill makes *you* a cipher !

</td></tr>
</table>

* Crowley's mother.

Ho ! I adopt the number. Look
At the quaint wrapper of this book ! *
110   I will deserve it if I can :
It is the number of a Man.[33]

So since in England Christ still stands   Necessity of
With iron nails in bloody hands   poem.
.Not pierced, but grasping ! to hoist high
115   Children on cross of agony,
I find him real for English lives.
Up with my pretty pair of fives ![34]
I fight no ghosts.

                    " But why revile "   Mysticism *v.*
120   (You urge me) " in that vicious style   literal interpre-
The very faith whose truths you seem   tation. Former
(Elsewhere) [35] to hold, to hymn supreme   excused.
In your own soul ? " Perhaps you know
How mystic doctrines melt the snow
125   Of any faith : redeem it to
A fountain of reviving dew.
So I with Christ : but few receive
The Qabalistic Balm,[36] believe
Nothing—and choose to know instead.
130   But, to that terror vague and dread,
External worship ; all my life—
War to the knife ! War to the knife !

No ! on the other hand the Buddha   Buddha re-
Says : " I'm surprised at you ! How could a   bukes poet.
135   Person accept my law and still   Detailed
Use hatred, the sole means of ill,   scheme of
In Truth's defence ? In praise of light ? "   modified poem.
Well ! Well ! I guess Brer Buddha's right !
I am no brutal Cain [37] to smash an Abel ;
140   I hear that blasphemy's unfashionable :
So in the quietest way we'll chat about it ;
No need to show teeth, claws of cat about it !
With gentle words—fiat exordium ;
Exeat dolor, intret gaudium !

* It had a design of 666 and Crowley's name in Hebrew (which, like
most names, adds up to that figure) on the reverse.

We'll have the ham to logic's sandwich   145
Of indignation : last bread bland, which
After our scorn of God's lust, terror, hate,
Prometheus-fired, we'll butter, perorate
With oiled indifference, laughter's silver :
" Omne hoc verbum   !et nil, vir " !   150

Aim of poet.
Indignation of
poet.   Poet
defies his uncle.

Let me help Babu Chander Grish up !
As by a posset of Hunyadi [38]
Clear mind ! Was Soudan of the Mahdi
Not cleared by Kitchener ?   Ah, Tchhup !
Such nonsense for sound truth you dish up,   155
Were I magician, no mere cadi,
Not Samuel's ghost you'd make me wish up,
Nor Saul's (the mighty son of Kish) up,
But Ingersoll's or Bradlaugh's, pardie !
By spells and caldron stews that squish up,   160
Or purifying of the Nadi,[39]
Till Stradivarius or Amati
Shriek in my stomach ! Sarasate,
Such strains !   Such music as once Sadi
Made Persia ring with !   I who fish up   165
No such from soul may yet cry : Vade
Retro, Satanas !   Tom Bond Bishop ! [40]

Whip and
spur.   Sport-
ing offer.   The
Times Com-
petition out-
done.

You old screw, Pegasus ! Gee (Swish !) up !
(To any who correctly rhymes [41]
With Bishop more than seven times   170
I hereby offer as emolum-
Ent, a bound copy of this volume.)

Sub-species of
genus Chris-
tian included
in poet's
strictures.

These strictures must include the liar
Copleston,[42] Reverend F. B. Meyer,
(The cock of the Dissenter's midden, he !)   175
And others of the self-same kidney :—
How different from Sir Philip Sidney !
But " cave os, et claude id, ne
Vituperasse inventus sim."
In English let me render him !   180
'Ware mug, and snap potato-trap !
Or elsely it may haply hap

Panel * in libel I bewail me !
(Funny how English seems to fail me !)
185   So, as a surgeon to a man, sir,
Let me excise your Christian cancer
Impersonally, without vanity,
Just in pure love of poor humanity !

Here's just the chance you'd have !   Behold
190   The warm sun tint with early gold
Yon spire : to-day's event provide
My text of wrath—Ascension-tide !
Oh ! 'tis a worthy day to wrest
Hate's diadem from Jesus' Crest !
195   Ascends he ? 'Tis the very test
By which we men may fairly judge,
From the rough roads we mortals trudge
Or God's paths paved with heliotrope,
The morals of the crucified.
200   (Both standpoints join in one, I hope,
In metaphysic's stereoscope !)
But for the moment be denied
A metaphysical inspection—
Bring out the antiseptic soap !—
205   We'll judge the Christ by simple section,
And strictly on the moral side.

But first ; I must insist on taking
The ordinary substantial creed
Your clergy preach from desk and pulpit
210   Each Sunday ; all the Bible, shaking
Its boards with laughter, as you read
Each Sunday. Ibsen [43] to a full pit
May play in the moon. If (lunars they)
They thought themselves to be the play,
215   It's little the applause he'd get.

I met a Christian clergyman, ‡
The nicest man I ever met.
We argued of the Cosmic plan.
I was Lord Roberts, he De Wet.[44]

Ascension Day.
Moral aspect
of Christianity
to be discussed
to prejudice of
the metaphysi-
cal.

Orthodoxy to
be our doxy.†
Gipsies barred.
Henrik Ibsen
and H. G.
Wells

Parson and
poet. Fugitive
nature of
dogma in these
latter days.
The Higher
Criticism.

* Scots legal term for defendant.
† A Romany word for woman.
‡ The Rev. J. Bowley. The conversation described actually occurred
in Mr. Gerald Kelly's studio in Paris.

He tells me when I cite the " Fall "   220
" But those are legends, after all."
He has a hundred hills [46] to lie in,
But finds no final ditch [46] to die in.
" Samuel was man ; the Holy Spook
Did not dictate the Pentateuch."   225
With cunning feint he lures me on
To loose my pompoms on Saint John ;
And, that hill being shelled, doth swear
His forces never had been there.
I got disgusted, called a parley,   230
(Here comes a white-flag treachery !)
Asked : " Is there anything you value,
Will hold to ?"   He laughed, " Chase me, Charlie !"
But seeing in his mind that I
Would not be so converted, " Shall you,"   235
He added, " grope in utter dark ?
The Book of Acts and that of Mark
Are now considered genuine."
I snatch a Testament, begin
Reading at random the first page ;—   240
He stops me with a gesture sage :
" You must not think, because I say
St. Mark is genuine, I would lay
Such stress unjust upon its text,
As base thereon opinion. Next ? "   245
I gave it up. He escaped. Ah me !
But so did Christianity.

Lord George
Sanger * on the
Unknowable.
How the crea-
tures talk.

As for a quiet talk on physics sane ac
Lente, I hear the British Don
Spout sentiments more bovine than a sane yak   250
Ever would ruminate upon,
Half Sabbatarian and half Khakimaniac,
Built up from Paul and John,
With not a little tincture of Leviticus
Gabbled pro formâ, jaldi,† à la Psittacus   255
To aid the appalling hotch-potch ; lyre and lute
Replaced by liar and loot, the harp and flute

* Proprietor of a circus and menagerie.
† Hindustani : quickly.

Are dumb, the drum doth come and make us mute :
The Englishman, half huckster and half brute,
260 Raves through his silk hat of the Absolute.
The British Don, half pedant and half hermit,
Begins : "The Ding an sich *—as Germans term it—"
We stop him short ; he readjusts his glasses,
Turns to his folio—'twill eclipse all precedent,
265 Reveal God's nature, every dent a blessed dent !
The Donkey : written by an ass, for asses.

So, with permission, let us be
Orthodox to our finger-ends ;
What the bulk hold, High Church or Friends,
270 Or Hard-shell Baptists—and we'll see.

Basis of poem
to be that of
the Compro-
mise of 1870.

I will not now invite attack
By proving white a shade of black,
Or Christ (as some [47] have lately tried)
An epileptic maniac,
275 Citing some cases, "where a dose
Of Bromide duly given in time
Drags a distemper so morose
At last to visions less sublime ;
Soft breezes stir the lyre Aeolian,
280 No more the equinoctial gales ;
The patient reefs his mental sails ;
His Panic din that shocked the Tmolian [48]
Admits a softer run of scales—
Seems no more God, but mere Napoleon
285 Or possibly the Prince of Wales " :—
Concluding such a half-cured case
With the remark " where Bromide fails !—
But Bromide people did not know
Those 1900 years ago."
290 I think we may concede to Crowley an
Impartial attitude.

Non-medical
nature of poem.
Crowley J.

And so
I scorn the thousand subtle points
Wherein a man might find a fulcrum
295 (Ex utero Matris ad sepulcrum,

No mention
will be made
of the Figs and
the Pigs.

* *Vide infra*, Science and Buddhism, and the writings of Immanuel Kant
and his successors.

Et præter—such as Huxley tells)
I'll pierce your rotten harness-joints,
Dissolve your diabolic spells,
With the quick truth and nothing else.

So not one word derogatory   300
To your own version of the story !
I take your Christ, your God's creation,
Just at their own sweet valuation.
For by this culminating scene,
Close of that wondrous life of woe   305
Before and after death, we know
How to esteem the Nazarene.
Where's the wet towel ?

                Let us first

Destroy the argument of fools,   310
From Paul right downward to the Schools,
That the Ascension's self rehearsed
Christ's Godhead by its miracle.
Grand !—but the power is mine as well !
In India levitation counts   315
No tithe of the immense amounts
Of powers demanded by the wise
From Chela ere the Chela rise
To Knowledge. Fairy-tales ? Well, first,
Sit down a week and hold your breath   320
As masters teach [49]—until you burst,
Or nearly—in a week, one saith,
A month, perchance a year for you,
Hard practice, and yourself may fly—
Yes ! I have done it ! you may too !   325

Thus, in Ascension, you and I
Stand as Christ's peers and therefore fit
To judge him—" Stay, friend, wait a bit ! "
(You cry) " Your Indian Yogis fall
Back to the planet after all,   330
Never attain to heaven and stand
(Stephen) or sit (Paul) [50] at the hand
Of the Most High !—And that alone,
That question of the Great White Throne,
Is the sole point that we debate."   335
I answer, Here in India wait

Samadhi-Dak,[51] convenient
To travel to Maha Meru,[52]
Or Gaurisankar's [53] keen white wedge
340 Spearing the splendid dome of blue,
Or Chogo's [54] mighty flying edge
Shearing across the firmament,—
But, first, to that exact event
You Christians celebrate to-day.
345 We stand where the disciples stood
And see the Master float away
Into that cloudlet heavenly-hued
Receiving him from mortal sight.
Which of his sayings prove the true,
350 Lightning-bescrawled athwart the blue ?
I say not, Which in hearts aright
Are treasured ? but, What åfter ages
Engrave on history's iron pages ?
This is the one word of " Our Lord " ;
355 " I bring not peace ; I bring a sword."
In this the history of the West [55]
Bears him out well.   How stands the test ?
One-third a century's life of pain—
He lives, he dies, he lives again,
360 And rises to eternal rest
Of bliss with Saints—an endless reign !
Leaving the world to centuries torn
By every agony and scorn,
And every wickedness and shame
365 Taking their refuge in his Name.
No Yogi shot his Chandra [56] *so.*
Will Christ return ?   What ho ?   What ho !
What ?   What ?   " He mediates above
Still with His Sire for mercy, love,—"
370 And other trifles !   Far enough
That Father's purpose from such stuff !

You see, when I was young, they said :
" Whate'er you ponder in your head,
Or make the rest of Scripture mean,
375 You can't evade John iii. 16."

Former compared to Kerubim ; as it is written, Running and Returning.

Shri Parananda applauds Yogi. Gerald jeers at Jeŝus.

John iii. 16.*
Its importance.
Its implied meaning.

---

* " For God so loved the world, that he gave his only begotten Son, that whosoever believeth in him should not perish, but have everlasting life."

Exactly! Grown my mental stature,
I ponder much : but never yet
Can I get over or forget
That bitter text's accursed nature,
The subtle devilish omission,[57]   380
The cruel antithesis implied,
The irony, the curse-fruition,
The calm assumption of Hell's fevers
As fit, as just, for unbelievers—
These are the things that stick beside   385
And hamper my quite serious wish
To harbour kind thoughts of the " Fish." [58]

My own vague
optimism. Im-
possibility of
tracing cause
back or effect
forward to the
ultimate.
Ethics
individual.

Here goes my arrow to the gold !
I'll make no magpies ! Though I hold
Your Christianity a lie,   390
Abortion and iniquity,
The most immoral and absurd
—(A priest's invention, in a word)—
Of all religions, I have hope
In the good Dhamma's [59] wider scope,   395
Nay, certainty ! that all at last,
However came they in the past,
Move, up or down—who knows, my friend ?—
But yet with no uncertain trend
Unto Nibbana in the end.   400
I do not even dare despise
Your doctrines, prayers, and ceremonies !
Far from the word ".you'll go to hell ! "
I dare not say "you do not well ! "
I must obey my own mind's laws,   405
Accept its limits, seek its cause :
My meat may be your poison ! I
Hope to convert you by-and-by ?
Never ! I cannot trace the chain [60]
That brought us here, shall part again   410
Our lives—perchance for aye ! I bring
My hand down on this table-thing,[61]
And that commotion widens thus
And shakes the nerves of Sirius !
To calculate one hour's result   415
I find surpassing difficult ;

One year's effect, one moment's cause ;
What mind could estimate such laws ?
Who then (much more !) may act aright
420 Judged by and in ten centuries' sight ?
(Yet I believe, whate'er we do
Is best for me and best for you
And best for all : I line no brow
With wrinkles, meditating how.)

425 Well, but another way remains.
Shall we expound the cosmic plan
By symbolising God and man
And nature thus ?   As man contains
Cells, nerves, grey matter in his brains,
430 Each cell a life, self-centred, free
Yet self-subordinate to the whole
For its own sake—expand !—so we
Molecules of a central soul,
Time's sons, judged by Eternity.
435 Nature is gone—our joys, our pains,
Our little lives—and God remains.
Were this the truth—why ! worship then
Were not so imbecile for men!
But that's no Christian faith !   For where
440 Enters the dogma of despair ?
Despite his logic's silver flow
I must count Caird [62] a mystic !   No !
You Christians shall not mask me so
The plain words of your sacred books
445 Behind friend Swedenborg his spooks !
Says Huxley [63] in his works (q. v.)
" The microcosmic lives change daily
In state or body "—yet you gaily
Arm a false Hegel cap-à-pie—
450 Your self, his weapons—make him wear
False favours of a ladye fayre,
(The scarlet woman !) bray and blare
A false note on the trumpet, shout :
" A champion ?   Faith's defender !   Out !
455 Sceptic and sinner !   See me !   Quail I ? "
I cite the Little-go.   You stare,
And have no further use for Paley !

Caird's inter-
pretation of
Hegel. His
identification
of it with Chris-
tianity proved
to be mystical.
His interpreta-
tion false.

Mysticism does
not need Christ.
Krishna will
serve, or the
Carpenter.
The Sacred
Walrus.
God, some
Vestments, and
Lady Wim-
borne.

But if you drink your mystic fill
Under the good tree Igdrasil [64]
Where is at all your use for Christ?   460
Hath Krishna not at all sufficed?
I hereby guarantee to pull
A faith as quaint and beautiful
As much attractive to an ass,
And setting reason at defiance,   465
As Zionism, Christian Science,
Or Ladies' League, [65] "Keep off the Grass!"
From "Alice through the Looking-Glass."

Fearful aspect
of John iii. 16.

Hence I account no promise worse,
Fail to conceive a fiercer curse   470
Than John's third chapter (sixteenth verse).

Universalism.
Will God get
the bara* slam?

But now (you say) broad-minded folk
Think that those words the Master spoke
Should save all men at last. But mind!
The text says nothing of the kind!   475
Read the next verses! †

Eternal life.
Divergent
views of its
desirability.
Buddhist idea.

                            Then—one-third
Of all humanity are steady
In a belief in Buddha's word,
Possess eternal life already,   480
And shun delights, laborious days
Of labour living (Milton's phrase)
In strenuous purpose to—? to cease!
"A fig for God's eternal peace!
True peace is to annihilate   485
The chain of causes men call Fate,
So that no Sattva [66] may renew
Once death has run life's shuttle through."
(Their sages put it somewhat thus)
What's fun to them is death to us!   490
That's clear at least.

Dogma of
Belief.

                            But never mind!
Call them idolaters and blind!
We'll talk of Christ. As Shelley sang,
"Shall an eternal issue hang   495

* Great slam—a term of Bridge-Whist.   Bara is Hindustani for great.
† John iii. 18, "He that believeth not is condemned already."

On just belief or unbelief;
And an involuntary act
Make difference infinite in fact
Between the right and left-hand thief?
500   Belief is not an act of will ! "

I think, Sir, that I have you still,   Free will.
Even allowing (much indeed !)   Herbert
That any will at all is freed,   Spencer.
And is not merely the result
505   Of sex, environment, and cult,
Habit and climate, health and mind,
And twenty thousand other things !
So many a metaphysic sings.
(I wish they did indeed : I find
510   Their prose the hardest of hard reading !)

" But if," you cry, " the world's designed   If there is free
As a mere mirage in the mind,   will how can
Up jumps free will." But all I'm pleading   there be pain
     or damnation?
515   Is against pain and hell. Freewill   not-Self being
Then can damn man? No fearful mill,   an illusion.
     Self or not-Self
Grinding catastrophe, is speeding   real? Chute
Outside—some whence, some whither ? And   d'Icare.
I think we easier understand
Where Schelling (to the Buddha leading)
520   Calls real not-self. In any case
There is not, there can never be
A soul, or sword or armour needing,
Incapable in time or space
Or to inflict or suffer. We
525   I think are gradually weeding
The soil of dualism. Pheugh !
Drop to the common Christian's view !

This is my point ; the world lies bleeding :—   I have pity :
(Result of sin ?)—I do not care ;   had Christ
530   I will admit you anywhere !   any? The
     Sheep and the
I take your premisses themselves   Goats.
And, like the droll despiteful elves
They are, they yet outwit your plan.
I will prove Christ a wicked man

(Granting him Godhead) merciless 535
To all the anguish and distress
About him—save to him it clung
And prayed.　Give me omnipotence?
I am no fool that I should fence
That power, demanding every tongue 540
To call me God—I would exert
That power to heal creation's hurt ;
Not to divide my devotees
From those who scorned me to the close :
A worm, a fire, a thirst for these ; 545
A harp-resounding heaven for those !

Will Satan be
saved ?　Who
pardons Judas ?

And though you claim Salvation sure
For all the heathen [68]—there again
New Christians give the lie to plain
Scripture, those words which must endure ! 550
(The Vedas say the same !) and though
His mercy widens ever so,
I never met a man (this shocks,
What I now press) so heterodox,
Anglican, Roman, Methodist, 555
Peculiar Person— all the list !—
I never met a man who called
Himself a Christian, but appalled
Shrank when I dared suggest the hope
God's mercy could expand its scope, 560
Extend, or bend, or spread, or straighten
So far as to encompass Satan
Or even poor Iscariot.

God's fore-
knowledge of
Satan's fall and
eternal misery
makes him re-
sponsible for it.
If he and
Judas are
finally re-
deemed, we
might perhaps
look over the
matter this
once.　Poet
books his seat.
Creator in

Yet God created (did he not ?)
Both these.　Omnisciently, we know ! 565
Benevolently ?　Even so !
Created from Himself distinct
(Note that !—it is not meet for you
To plead me Schelling and his crew)
These souls, foreknowing how were linked 570
The chains in either's Destiny.
" You pose me the eternal Why ? "
Not I ?　Again, " Who asks doth err."
But this one thing I say.　Perchance
There lies a purpose in advance 575

Tending to final bliss—to stir
Some life to better life, this pain
Is needful : that I grant again.
Did they at last in glory live,
Satan and Judas [69] might forgive
The middle time of misery,
Forgive the wrong creation first
Or evolution's iron key
Did them—provided they are passed
Beyond all change and pain at last
Out of this universe accurst.
But otherwise ! I lift my voice,
Deliberately take my choice
Promethean, eager to rejoice,
In the grim protest's joy to revel
Betwixt Iscariot and the Devil,
Throned in their midst ! No pain to feel,
Tossed on some burning bed of steel,
But theirs : My soul of love should swell
And, on those piteous floors they trod,
Feel, and make God feel, out of Hell,
Across the gulf impassable,
That He was damned and I was God !

Ay ! Let him rise and answer me.
That false creative Deity,
Whence came his right to rack the Earth
With pangs of death,[70] disease, and birth :
No joy unmarred by pain and grief :
Insult on injury heaped high
In that quack-doctor infamy
The Panacea of—Belief !
Only the selfish soul of man
Could ever have conceived a plan
Man only of all life to embrace,
One planet of all stars to place
Alone before the Father's face ;
Forgetful of creation's stain,
Forgetful of creation's pain,
Not dumb !—forgetful of the pangs
Whereby each life laments and hangs,
(Now as I speak a lizard [71] lies
In wait for light-bewildered flies)

heaven suffers Hell's pangs, owing to reproaches of bard.

Ethical and eloquent denunciation of Christian Cosmogony.

Each life bound ever to the wheel [72]
Ay, and each being—we may guess
Now that the very crystals feel !—   620
For them no harp-resounding court,
No palm, no crown, but none the less
A cross, be sure !   The worst man's thought
In hell itself, bereft of bliss,
Were less unmerciful than this !   625
No ! for material things, I hear,
Will burn away, and cease to be—
(Nibbana !   Ah !   Thou shoreless Sea !)
Man, man alone, is doomed to fear,
To suffer the eternal woe,   630
Or else, to meet man's subtle foe,
God—and oh ! infamy of terror !
Be like him—like him !   And for ever !
At least I make not such an error:
My soul must utterly dissever   635
Its very silliest thought, belief,
From such a God as possible,
Its vilest from his worship.   Never !
Avaunt, abominable chief
Of Hate's grim legions ; let me well   640
Gird up my loins and make endeavour,
And seek a refuge from my grief,
O never in Heaven—but in Hell !

Death-bed of
poet.   Effect
of body on
mind.

"Oh, very well !" I think you say,
"Wait only till your dying day !   645
See whether then you kiss the rod,
And bow that proud soul down to God !"
I perfectly admit the fact ;
Quite likely that I so shall act !
Here's why Creation jumps at prayer.   650
You Christians quote me in a breath
This, that, the other atheist's death ; [73]
How they sought God !   Of course !   Impair
By just a touch of fever, chill,
My health—where flies my vivid will ?   655
My carcase with quinine is crammed ;
I wish South India were damned ;
I wish I had my mother's nursing,
Find precious little use in cursing,

660 And slide to leaning on another,
God, or the doctor, or my mother.
But dare you quote my fevered word
For better than my health averred ?
The brainish fancies of a man
Hovering on delirium's brink :
666 *Shall these be classed his utmost span ?*
All that he can or ought to think ?
No ! the strong man and self-reliant
Is the true spiritual giant.
670 I blame no weaklings, but decline
To take their maunderings for mine.

You see I do not base my thesis
On your Book's being torn in pieces
By knowledge ; nor invoke the shade
675 Of my own boyhood's agony.
Soul, shudder not ! Advance the blade
Of fearless fact and probe the scar !
You know my first-class memory ?
Well, in my life two years there are
680 Twelve years back—not so very far !
Two years whereof no memory stays.
One ageless anguish filled my days
So that no item, like a star
Sole in the supreme night, above
685 Stands up for hope, or joy, or love.
Nay, not one ignis fatuus glides
Sole in that marsh, one agony
To make the rest look light. Abides
The thick sepulchral changeless shape
690 Shapeless, continuous misery
Whereof no smoke-wreaths might escape
To show me whither lay the end,
Whence the beginning. All is black,
Void of all cause, all aim ; unkenned,
695 As if I had been dead indeed—
All in Christ's name ! And I look back,
And then and long time after lack
Courage or strength to hurl the creed
Down to the heaven it sprang from ! No !
700 Not this inspires the indignant blow

Poem does not
treat of Palæ-
ontology : nor
of poet's youth :
nor of Christian
infamies. Poet
forced to mystic
position.

At the whole fabric—nor the seas
Filled with those innocent agonies
Of Pagan Martyrs that once bled,
Of Christian Martyrs damned and dead
In inter-Christian bickerings,   705
Where hate exults and torture springs,
A lion on anguished flesh and blood,
A vulture on ill-omen wings,
A cannibal [74] on human food.
Nor do I cry the scoffer's cry,   710
That Christians live and look the lie
Their faith has taught them : none of these
Inspire my life, disturb my peace.
I go beneath the outward faith
Find it a devil or a wraith,   715
Just as my mood or temper tends !

Mystical mean-
ing of "Ascen-
sion Day."
Futility of
whole discus-
sion, in view of
facts.

And thus to-day that " Christ ascends,"
I take the symbol, leave the fact,
Decline to make the smallest pact
With your creative Deity,   720
And say : The Christhood-soul in me,
Risen of late, is now quite clear
Even of the smallest taint of Earth.
Supplanting God, the Man has birth
(" New Birth " you'll call the same, I fear,)   725
Transcends the ordinary sphere
And flies in the direction "x."
(There lies the fourth dimension.)   Vex
My soul no more with mistranslations
From Genesis to Revelations,   730
But leave me with the Flaming Star,[75]
Jeheshua (See thou Zohar !) [76]
And thus our formidable Pigeon- [77]
Lamb-and-Old-Gentleman religion
Fizzles in smoke, and I am found   735
Attacking nothing.   Here's the ground,
Pistols, and coffee—three in one,
(Alas, O Rabbi Schimeon !)
But never a duellist—no Son,
No Father, and (to please us most)   740
Decency pleads—no Holy Ghost !
All vanish at the touch of truth,
A cobweb trio--like, in sooth,

That worthy Yankee millionaire,
745 And wealthy nephews, young and fair,
The pleasing Crawfords ! Lost ! Lost ! Lost ! [78]
" The Holy Spirit, friend ! beware ! "

Ah ! ten days yet to Pentecost !   The reader
Come that, I promise you—·but stay !   may hope.
750 At·present 'tis Ascension Day !

At least your faith should be content.   Summary.
I quarrel not with this event.   Reader dis-
The supernatural element ?   missed to
I deny nothing—at the term   chapel.
755 It is just Nothing I affirm.
The fool (with whom is wisdom, deem
The Scriptures—rightly !) in his heart
Saith (silent, to himself, apart)
This secret : " אֵין אֱלֹהִים " [79]
760 See the good Psalm ! And thus, my friend !
My diatribes approach the end
And find us hardly quarrelling.   .
And yet—you seem not satisfied ?
The literal mistranslated thing
765 Must not by sinners be denied.
Go to your Chapel then to pray !
(I promise Mr. Chesterton [80]
Before the Muse and I have done
A grand ap-pre-ci-a-ti-on
770 Of Brixton on Ascension Day.)

He's gone—his belly filled enough !   Future plans of
This Robert-Browning-manqué stuff !   poet. Jesus
'Twill serve—Mercutio's scratch !--to show   dismissed with
Where God and I are disagreed.   a jest.
775 There ! I have let my feelings go
This once. Again ? I deem not so.
Once for my fellow-creature's need !
The rest of life, for self-control,[81]
For liberation of the soul ! [82]
780 This once, the truth ! In future, best
Dismissing Jesus with a jest.

Ah ! Christ ascends ? [83] Ascension day ?   The Jest.
Old wonders bear the bell [84] away ?
Santos-Dumont, though ! Who can say ?

PENTECOST

Poem dissimi-
lar to its pre-
decessor. Will
it lead some-
where this
time?
Reflections on
the weather,
proper to be-
ginning a con-
versation in
English.

TO-DAY thrice halves the lunar week
Since you, indignant, heard me speak
Indignant. Then I seemed to be
So far from Christianity !
Now, other celebrations fit   5
The time, another song shall flit
Reponsive to another tune.
September's shadow falls on June,
But dull November's darkest day
Is lighted by the sun of May.   10

Autobiography
of bard.
Lehrjahre.
Wanderjahre.
"The magician
of Paris."

Here's how I got a better learning.
It's a long lane that has no turning !
Mad as a woman-hunted Urning,
The lie-chased alethephilist : *
Sorcery's maw gulps the beginner :   15
In Pain's mill neophytes are grist :
Disciples ache upon the rack.
Five years I sought : I miss and lack ;
Agony hounds lagoan twist ;
I peak and struggle and grow thinner,   20
And get to hate the sight of dinner.
With sacred thirst, I, soul-hydroptic,[1]
Read Levi[2] and the cryptic Coptic;[3]
With ANET' HER-K UAA EN RA,[4]

How clever I
am !

And ספרא דצניעותא[5]   25
While good MacGregor[5] (who taught freely us)
Bade us investigate Cornelius
Agrippa and the sorceries black
Of grim Honorius and Abramelin ; [6]
While, fertile as the teeming spawn   30
Of pickled lax or stickleback,
Came ancient rituals,[7] whack ! whack !
Of Rosy Cross and Golden Dawn.[8]

* Truth-lover.
164

I lived, Elijah-like, Mt. Carmel in :
35 All gave me nothing. I slid back
To common sense, as reason bids,
And " hence," my friend, " the Pyramids."

At last I met a maniac
With mild eyes full of love, and tresses
40 Blanched in those lonely wildernesses
Where he found wisdom, and long hands
Gentle, pale olive 'gainst the sand's
Amber and gold. At sight, I knew him ;
Swifter than light I flashed, ran to him,
45 And at his holy feet prostrated
My head ; then, all my being sated
With love, cried " Master ! I must know.
Already I can love." E'en so.
The sage saluted me राम । राम । [9]

50 लमबा पड़ाव की बड़ी दाम ।

जानो यह सब से मुशकिल काम

है । वाह शाबाश । तुमहारे नाम

सितारों में सोने से लिखा है ।

हमारे पास आव चेले । हम दवाई

55 चिन्ना के वास्ते देंगे ॥   हों । said I :

" I'm game to work through all eternity,
Your holiness the Guru Swami !" *   Thus
I studied with him till he told me वस ॥ [10]
He taught the A B C of Yoga :
60 I asked किस वास्ते । [11] कया होगा ॥ [12]
In strange and painful attitude, [13]
I sat, while he was very rude. [14]
With eyes well fixed on my proboscis, [15]
I soon absorbed the Yogi Gnosis.
65 He taught me to steer clear of vices,
The giddy waltz, the tuneful aria,
Those fatal foes of Brahma-charya ; [16]
And said, " How very mild and nice is
One's luck to lop out truth in slices,
70 And chance to chop up cosmic crises !"

My Mahatma.
What price
Kut Humi?

? *?* *?* *?* *Oh,
how wise
Grampa must
have been,
Bobbie !*

* The correct form of address from a pupil to his teacher. See Sab-
hapaty Swami's pamphlet on Yoga.

He taught me A, he taught me B,
He stopped my baccy [17] and my tea.
He taught me Y, he taught me Z,
He made strange noises in my head.
He taught me that, he taught me this,   75
He spoke of knowledge, life, and bliss.
He taught me this, he taught me that,
He grew me mangoes in his hat.[18]
I brought him corn : he made good grist of it :—
And here, my Christian friend, 's the gist of it !   80

The philosophical impasse. Practical advice. Advice to poet's fat friend.

First, here's philosophy's despair,
The cynic scorn of self. I think
At times the search is worth no worry,
And hasten earthward in a hurry,
Close spirit's eyes, or bid them blink,   85
Go back to Swinburne's [19] counsel rare,
Kissing the universe its rod,
As thus he sings " For this is God ;
Be man with might, at any rate,
In strength of spirit growing straight   90
And life as light a-living out ! "
So Swinburne doth sublimely state,
And he is right beyond a doubt.
So, I'm a poet or a rhymer ;
A mountaineer or mountain climber.   95
So much for Crowley's vital primer.
The inward life of soul and heart,
That is a thing occult, apart :
But yet his metier or his kismet
As much as these you have of his met.   100
So—you be butcher ; you be baker ;
You, Plymouth Brother, and you, Quaker ;
You, Mountebank, you, corset-maker :—
While for you, my big beauty,[20] (Chicago packs pork)
I'll teach you the trick to be hen-of-the-walk.   105
Shriek a music-hall song with a double ong-tong !
Dance a sprightly can-can at Paree or Bolong !
Or the dance of Algiers—try your stomach at that !
It's quite in your line, and would bring down your fat.
You've a very fine voice—could you only control it !   110
And an emerald ring—and I know where you stole it !
But for goodness sake give up attempting Brünnhilde ;
Try a boarding-house cook, or a coster's Matilda !

Still you're young yet, scarce forty—we'll hope at three
   score
115 You'll be more of a singer, and less of a whore.

Each to his trade ! live out your life !
Fondle your child, and buss your wife !
Trust not, fear not, steer straight and strong !
Don't worry, but just get along.
120 I used to envy all my Balti coolies [21]
In an inverse kind of religious hysteria,
Though every one a perfect fool is,
To judge by philosophic criteria,
My Lord Archbishop. The name of Winchester,
125 Harrow, or Eton [22] makes them not two inches stir.
They know not Trinity, Merton, or Christchurch ;
They worship, but not at your back-pews-high-priced
   Church.
I've seen them at twenty thousand feet
On the ice, in a snow-storm, at night fall, repeat
130 Their prayers [23]—will your Grace do as much for your Three
As they do for their One ? I have seen—may you see !
They sleep and know not what a mat is ;
Seem to enjoy their cold chapaties ; *
Are healthy, strong—and some are old.
135 They do not care a damn [24] for cold,
Behave-like children, trust in Allah ;
(Flies in Mohammed's spider-parlour !)
They may not think : at least they dare
Live out their lives, and little care
140 Worries their souls—worse fools they seem
Than even Christians. Do I dream ?
Probing philosophy to marrow,
What thought darts in its poisoned arrow
But this ? (my wisdom, even to me,
145 Seems folly) may their folly be
True Wisdom ? O esteemed Tahuti ! [25]
You are, you are, you are a beauty !
If after all these years of worship
You hail Ra [26] his bark or Nuit [27] her ship

side note: Live out thy life ! Character of Balti. His religious sincerity. Relations of poet and the Egyptian God of Wisdom. Crowley dismissed with a jest.

* A flat cake of unleavened bread. As a matter of fact they do not enjoy and indeed will not eat them, preferring " dok," a paste of coarse flour and water, wrapped round a hot stone. It cooks gradually, and remains warm all day.

And sail—" the waters wild a-wenting   150
Over your child !   The left lamenting "
(Campbell).[28]   The Ibis head,[29] unsuited
To grin, perhaps, yet does its best
To show its strong appreciation
Of the humour of the situation—   155
In short, dimiss me, jeered and hooted,
Who thought I sported Roland's crest,[30]
With wisdom saddled, spurred, and booted,
(As I my Jesus) with a jest.[31]

Slowness of
Divine Justice.
Poet pockets
Piety Stakes.
National An-
them of Natal.

So here is my tribute —a jolly good strong 'un—   160
To the eunuch, the faddist, the fool, and the wrong 'un !
It's fun when you say " A mysterious way [32]
God moves in to fix up his Maskelyne tricks.
He trots on the tides, on the tempest he rides
(Like Cosmo) ; and as for his pace, we bethought us   165
Achilles could never catch up with that tortoise ! "
No flyer, but very " Who's Griffiths ? " *   No jackpot !
I straddle the blind, age !   At hymns I'm a moral ;
In Sankey, your kettle may call me a black pot.
Here's diamond for coke, and pink pearl for pale coral. 170
Though his mills may grind slowly—what says the old hymn ? [33]
Tune, Limerick !   Author ?   My memory's dim.
The corn said " You sluggard ! "
The mill " You may tug hard," (or lug hard, or plug hard ;
I forget the exact Rhyme ; that's a fact)   175
" If I want to grind slowly I shall,"
A quainter old fable one rarely is able
To drag from its haunt in the—smoke room or stable !
You see (vide supra) I've brought to the test a ton
Of tolerance, broadness.   Approve me, friend Chesterton ! 180

But this talk is
all indigestion.
Now for
health.

So much when philosophy's lacteal river
Turns sour through a trifle of bile on the liver.   s
But now for the sane and the succulent milk
Of truth—may it slip down as smoothly as silk !

Reasons for
undertaking
the task.

" How very hard it is to be " [34]   185
A Yogi !   Let our spirits see
At least what primal need of thought
This end to its career has brought :

* " Who's Griffiths ?   The safe man."   A well-known advertisement,
hence '' Who's Griffiths "=safe.

190 Why, in a word, I seek to gain
A different knowledge. Why retain
The husk of flesh, yet seek to merit
The influx of the Holy Spirit?
And, swift as caddies pat and cap a tee,
Gain the great prize all mortals snap at, he-
195 Roic guerdon of Srotapatti? [35]

With calm and philosophic mind,
No fears, no hopes, devotions blind
To hamper, soberly we'll state
The problem, and investigate
200 In purely scientific mood
The sheer Ananke of the mind,
A temper for our steel to find
Whereby those brazen nails subdued
Against our door-posts may in vain
205 Ring. We'll examine, to be plain,
By logic's intellectual prism
The spiritual Syllogism.

Our logical method. Classical allusion, demonstrating erudition of poet.

We know what fools (only) call
Divine and Supernatural
210 And what they name material
Are really one, not two, the line
By which divide they and define
Being a shadowy sort of test ;
A verbal lusus at the best,
215 At worst a wicked lie devised
To bind men's thoughts ; but we must work
With our own instruments, nor shirk
Discarding what we erstwhile prized ;
Should we perceive it disagree
220 With the first-born necessity.

Whether or not spirit and matter are distinct, let us investigate the fundamental necessities of thought.

I come to tell you why I shun
The sight of men, the life and fun
You know I can enjoy so well,
The Nature that I love as none
225 (I think) before me ever loved.
You know I scorn the fear of Hell,
By worship and all else unmoved.

Impermanence of the soul.

You know for me the soul is nought [36]
Save a mere phantom in the thought,
That thought itself impermanent,   230
Save as a casual element
With such another may combine
To form now water and now wine ;
The element itself may be
Changeless to all eternity,   235
But compounds ever fluctuate
With time or space or various state.
(Ask chemists else !)   So I must claim
Spirit and matter are the same [37]
Or else the prey of putrefaction.   240
This matters to the present action
Little or nothing.   Here's your theories !
Think if you like : I find it wearies !

Recapitulation
of principal cos-
mic theories.

It matters little whether we
With Fichte and the Brahmins preach   245
That Ego-Atman sole must be ;
With Schelling and the Buddha own
Non-Ego-Skandhas are alone ;
With Hegel and—the Christian ? teach
That which completes, includes, absorbs   250
Both mighty unrevolving orbs
In one informing masterless
Master-idea of consciousness—
All differences as these indeed
Are chess play, conjuring.   " Proceed ! "   255
Nay ! I'll go back.   The exposition
Above, has points.   But simple fission
Has reproduced a different bliss,
At last a heterogenesis !

Bard check-
mates himself.
Consciousness
and Christi-
anity.
Dhyana and
Hinduism.
Sammasa-
madhi and
Buddhism.

The metaphysics of these verses   260
Is perfectly absurd.   My curse is
No sooner in an iron word
I formulate my thought than I
Perceive the same to be absurd
(Tannhäuser).   So for this, Sir, why !   265
Your metaphysics in your teeth !
Confer A. Crowley, " Berashith."
But hear !   The Christian is a Dualist ;

Such view our normal consciousness!
270 Tells us. I'll quote you now if you list
From Tennyson. It isn't much ;
(Skip this and 'twill be even less)
He says : " I am not what I see,[38]
And other than the things I touch." *
275 How lucid is our Alfred T. !
The Hindu, an Advaitist,
Crosses off Maya from the list ;
Believes in one—exactly so,
Dhyana-consciousness, you know !
280 May it not be that one step further
" 'Tis lotused Buddha roaring murther ! " ? [39]
Nibbana is the state above you
Christians and them Hindus—Lord love you !--
Where Nothing is perceived as such.

285 This clever thought doth please me much.   Bard is pleased
with himself.

But if das Essen ist das Nichts—   Poetee mani-
Ha ! Hegel's window ! Ancient Lichts !   fests a natural
And two is one and one is two—   irritation.
" Bother this nonsense ! Go on, do ! "
290 My wandering thoughts you well recall !
I focus logic's perfect prism :
Lo ! the informing syllogism !

The premiss major. Life at best   Sabbé pi Duk-
Is but a sorry sort of jest ;   kham ! †
295 At worst, a play of fiends uncouth,
Mocking the soul foredoomed to pain.
In any case, its run must range
Through countless miseries of change.
So far, no farther, gentle youth !
300 The mind can see. So much, no more.
So runs the premiss major plain ;
Identical, the Noble truth
First of the Buddha's Noble Four !

The premiss minor. I deplore   Beyond
305 These limitations of the mind.   thought, is
I strain my eyes until they're blind,   there hope ?
And cannot pierce the awful veil   Maya again.
                                                     Vision of the

---

* *In Memoriam.*   † All is Sorrow.

Visible Image
of the Soul of
Nature, whose
Name is Fat-
ality.

That masks the primal cause of being.
With all respect to Buddha, fleeing
The dreadful problem with the word   310
" Who answers, as who asks, hath erred,"
I must decidedly insist
On asking why these things exist.
My mind refuses to admit
All-Power can be all-Wickedness.   315
—Nay ! but it may ! What shadows flit
Across the awful veil of mist ?
What thoughts invade, insult, impress ?
There comes a lightning of my wit
And sees—nor good nor ill address   320
Itself to task, creation's ill,
But a mere law without a will,[40]
Nothing resolved in something, fit
Phantom of dull stupidity,
And evolution's endless stress   325
All the inanity to knit
Thence : such a dark device I see !
Nor lull my soul in the caress
Of Buddha's " Maya fashioned it." [41]
My mind seems ready to agree ;   330
But still my senses worry me.

Futility of all
investigations
of the Mind
into the First
Cause.

Nor can I see what sort of gain
God finds in this creating pain ;
Nor do the Vedas help me here.
Why should the Paramatma cease [42]   335
From its eternity of peace,
Develop this disgusting drear
System of stars, to gather again
Involving, all the realm of pain,
Time, space, to that eternal calm ?   340
Blavatsky's Himalayan Balm [43]
Aids us no whit—if to improve
Thus the All-light, All-life, All-love,
By evolution's myrrh and gall,
It would not then have been the All.   345

Faith our only
alternative to
Despair ? So
says Mansel.

Thus all conceptions fail and fall.
But see the Cyclopædia-article
On " Metaphysics " ; miss no particle

350 Of thought! How ends the brave B.D.,
Summarising Ontology?
"This talk of 'Real' is a wraith.
Our minds are lost in war of word ;
The whole affair is quite absurd—
Behold! the righteous claims of Faith !"
355 (He does not rhyme you quite so neatly ;
But that's the sense of it, completely.)

I do not feel myself inclined,   *The Advaitist*
In spite of my irreverent mind,   *position.*
So lightly to pass by the schemes
360 Of Fichte, Schelling, Hegel (one,
Small though the apparent unison),
As if they were mere drunken dreams ;
For the first word in India here
From Koromandl to Kashmir
365 Says the same thing these Germans said :
"Ekam Advaita!" [44] one, not two!
Thus East and West from A to Z
Agree—Alas! so do not you?
(It matters nothing—you, I find,
370 Are but a mode of my own mind.)

As far as normal reasoning goes,   *Mind's superior*
I must admit my concepts close   *functions.*
Exactly where my worthy friend,
Great Mansel, says they ought to end.
375 But here's the whole thing in a word :
Olympus in a nutshell! I
Have a superior faculty
To reasoning, which makes absurd,
Unthinkable and wicked too,
380 A great deal that I know is true !
In short, the mind is capable,
Besides mere ratiocination,
Of twenty other things as well,
The first of which is concentration !

385 Here most philosophers agree ;   *Does truth*
Claim that the truth must so intend,   *make itself in-*
Explain at once all agony   *stantly appa-*
Of doubt, make people comprehend   *rent? Not*
                                           reason.

But the results
of concentra-
tion do so.

As by a lightning flash, solve doubt
And turn all Nature inside out :   390
And, if such potency of might
Hath Truth, once state the truth aright,
Whence came the use for all those pages
Millions together—mighty sages
Whom the least obstacle enrages?   395
Condemn the mystic if he prove
Thinking less valuable than love?
Well, let them try their various plans !
Do they resolve that doubt of man's ?
How many are Hegelians?   400
This, though I hold him mostly true.
But, to teach others that same view ?
Surely long years develop reason.[45]
After long years, too, in thy season
Bloom, Concentration's midnight flower !   405
After much practice to this end
I gain at last the long sought power
(Which you believe you have this hour,
But certainly have not, my friend !)
Of keeping close the mind to one   410
Thing at a time — suppose, the Sun.
I gain this (Reverence to Ganesh' !) [46]
And at that instant comprehend
(The past and future tenses vanish)
What Fichte comprehends.   Division,   415
Thought, wisdom, drop away.   I see
The absolute identity
Of the beholder and the vision.

Some poetry.

There is a lake * amid the snows
Wherein five glaciers merge and break.   420
Oh ! the deep brilliance of the lake !
The roar of ice that cracks and goes
Crashing within the water !   Glows
The pale pure water, shakes and slides
The glittering sun through emerald tides,   425
So that faint ripples of young light
Laugh on the green.   Is there a night

* This simile for the mind and its impressions, which must be stilled
before the sun of the soul can be reflected, is common in Hindu literature.
The five glaciers are, of course, the senses.

So still and cold, a frost so chill,
That all the glaciers be still ?
430 Yet in its peace no frost.
                                    Arise !
Over the mountains steady stand,
O sun of glory, in the skies
Alone, above, unmoving ! Brand
435 Thy sigil, thy resistless might,
The abundant imminence of light !
Ah !
        O in the silence, in the dark,
In the intangible, unperfumed,
440 Ingust abyss, abide and mark
The mind's magnificence assumed
In the soul's splendour ! Here is peace ;
Here earnest of assured release.
Here is the formless all-pervading
445 Spirit of the World, rising, fading
Into a glory subtler still.
Here the intense abode of Will
Closes its gates. and in the hall
Is solemn sleep of festival.
450 Peace ! Peace ! Silence of peace !
O visionless abode ! Cease ! Cease !
Through the dark veil press on ! The veil
Is rent asunder, the stars pale,
The suns vanish, the moon drops,
455 The chorus of the spirit stops,
But one note swells. Mightiest souls
Of bard and music maker, rolls
Over your loftiest crowns the wheel
Of that abiding bliss. Life flees
460 Down corridors of centuries
Pillar by pillar, and is lost.
Life after life in wild appeal
Cries to the master ; he remains
And thinks not.
                        The polluting tides
465 Of sense roll shoreward. Arid plains
Of wave-swept sea confront me. Nay !
Looms yet the glory through the grey,
And in the darkest hours of youth
470 I yet perceive the essential truth,

Known as I know my consciousness,
That all division's hosts confess
A master, for I know and see
The absolute identity
Of the beholder and the vision.   475

Fact replacing
folklore, the
Christian snig-
gers. Let him
beware,

How easy to excite derision
In the man's mind !   Why, fool, I think
I am as clever as yourself,
At least as skilled to wake the elf
Of jest and mockery in a wink.   480
I can dismiss with sneers as cheap
As yours this fabric of my own,
One banner of my mind o'erthrown
Just at my will.   How true and deep
Is Carroll [47] when his Alice cries :   485
" It's nothing but a pack of cards !"
There's the true refuge of the wise ;
To overthrow the temple guards,
Deny reality.

For I speak
subtly.

                   And now   490
(I'll quote you Scripture anyhow)
What did the Sage mean when he wrote
(I am the Devil when I quote)
" The mere terrestrial-minded man
Knows not the Things of God, nor can   495
Their subtle meaning understand ?"
A sage, I say, although he mentions
Perhaps the best of his inventions,
God.

Results of prac-
tice. The poet
abandons all to
find Truth.

                   For, at first, this practice leads   500
To holy thoughts (the holy deeds
Precede success) and reverent gaze
Upon the Ancient One of Days,
Beyond which fancy lies the Truth.
To find which I have left my youth,   505
All I held dear, and sit alone
Still meditating, on my throne
Of Kusha-grass,[48] and count my beads,
Murmur my mantra,[49] till recedes
The world of sense and thought—I sink   510

To—what abyss's dizzy brink ?
And fall ! And I have ceased to think !
That is, have conquered and made still
Mind's lower powers by utter Will.

615   It may be that pure Nought will fail   Nothing. The
         Quite to assuage the needs of thought ;   Apotheosis of
         But—who can tell me whether Nought   Realism and
         Untried, will or will not avail ?   Idealism alike.

         Aum ! Let us meditate aright [50]   Gayatri.
620   On that adorable One Light,
         Divine Savitri ! So may She
         Illume our minds ! So mote it be !

         I find some folks think me (for one)   Is " The Soul
         So great a fool that I disclaim   of Osiris " a
625   Indeed Jehovah's hate for shame   Hymn Book ?
                                                       How verse is
         That man to-day should not be weaned   written.
         Of worshipping so foul a fiend   Prayer.
         In presence of the living Sun,
         And yet replace him oiled and cleaned
630   By the Egyptian Pantheon,
         The same thing by another name.
         Thus when of late Egyptian Gods
         Evoked ecstatic periods
         In verse of mine, you thought I praised
635   Or worshipped them—I stand amazed.
         I merely wished to chant in verse
         Some aspects of the Universe,
         Summed up these subtle forces finely,
         And sang of them (I think divinely)
640   In name and form : a fault perhaps—
         Reviewers are such funny chaps !
         I think that ordinary folk,
         Though, understood the things I spoke.
         For Gods, and devils too, I find
645   Are merely modes of my own mind !
         The poet needs enthusiasm !
         Verse-making is a sort of spasm,
         Degeneration of the mind,
         And things of that unpleasant kind.

So to the laws all bards obey   550
I bend, and seek in my own way
By false things to expound the real.
But never think I shall appeal
To Gods.   What folly can compare
With such stupidity as prayer?   555

Marvellous an-
swer to prayer.
Prayer and
averages.

Some years ago I thought to try
Prayer [51]—test its efficacity.
I fished by a Norwegian lake.
" O God," I prayed, " for Jesus' sake
Grant thy poor servant all his wish !   560
For every prayer produce a fish !"
Nine times the prayer went up the spout,
And eight times—what a thumping trout !
(This is the only true fish-story
I ever heard—give God the glory !)   565
The thing seems cruel now, of course.
Still, it's a grand case of God's force !
But, modern Christians, do you dare
With common prudence to compare
The efficacity of prayer?   570
Who will affirm of Christian sages
That prayer can alter averages ?
The individual case allows
Some chance to operate, and thus
Destroys its value quite for us.   575
So that is why I knit my brows
And think—and find no thing to say
Or do, so foolish as to pray.
" So much for this absurd affair [52]
About " validity of prayer.   580
But back !   Let once again address
Our minds to super-consciousness !

Are the results
of meditation
due to auto-
hypnosis ?

You weary me with proof enough
That all this meditation stuff
Is self-hypnosis.   Be it so !   585
Do you suppose I did not know ?
Still, to be accurate, I fear
The symptoms are entirely strange.
If I were hard, I'd make it clear
That criticism must arrange   590

An explanation different
For this particular event.
Though surely I may find it queer
That you should talk of self-hypnosis,
595   When your own faith so very close is
To similar experience ;
Lies, in a word, beneath suspicion
To ordinary common sense
And logic's emery attrition.
600   I take, however, as before
Your own opinions, and demand
Some test by which to understand
Huxley's piano-talk,* and find
If my hypnosis may not score
605   A point against the normal mind.
(As you are pleased to term it, though !
I gather that you do not know ;
Merely infer it.)

            Here's a test !   A test. The
610   What in your whole life is the best   artist's concen-
Of all your memories ?   They say   tration on his
You paint—I think you should one day   work.
Take me to see your Studio—
Tell me, when all your work goes right,
615   Painted to match some inner light,
What of the outer world you know !
Surely, your best work always finds
Itself sole object of the mind's.
In vain you ply the brush, distracted
620   By something you have heard or acted.
Expect some tedious visitor—
Your eye runs furtive to the door ;
Your hand refuses to obey ;
You throw the useless brush away.
625   I think I hear the Word you say !

I practice then, with conscious power   Yogi but a
Watching my mind, each thought controlling,   more ·´
Hurling to nothingness, while rolling   ar`·´
The thunders after lightning's flower,

* See his remarks upon the Rational piano, and the conclusions to whi·
the evidence of its senses would lead it.

Destroying passion, feeling, thought,   630
The very practice you have sought
Unconscious, when you work the best.
I carry on one step firm-pressed
Further than you the path, and you
For all my trouble, comment : " True !   635
" Auto-hypnosis. Very quaint ! " [53]
No one supposes me a Saint—[54]
Some Saints to wrath would be inclined
With such a provocation pecked !
But I remember and reflect   640
That anger makes a person blind,
And my own " Chittam " I'd neglect.
Besides, it's you, and you, I find,
Are but a mode of my own mind.

Objectivity of
universe not
discussed.

But then you argue, and with sense ;   645
" I have this worthy evidence
That things are real, since I cease
The painter's ecstasy of peace,
And find them all unchanged."   To-day
I cannot brush that doubt away ;   650
It leads to tedious argument
Uncertain, in the best event :
Unless, indeed, I should invoke
The fourth dimension, clear the smoke
Psychology still leaves. This question   655
Needs a more adequate digestion.
Yet I may answer that the universe
Of meditation suffers less
From time's insufferable stress
Than that of matter. On, thou puny verse !   660
Weak tide of rhyme !   Another argument
Will block the railway train of blague you meant
To run me over with. This world
Or that ? We'll keep the question furled.

Preferability of
ion-

But, surely, (let me corner you !)
You wish the painter-mood were true!   666
To leave the hateful world, and see
Perish the whole Academy ;
So you remain for ever sated,
On your own picture concentrated !   670

But as for me I have a test
Of better than the very best.
Respice finem! Judge the end ;
The man, and not the child, my friend !
675 First ecstasy of Pentecost,
(You now perceive my sermon's text.)
First leap to Sunward flings you vexed
By glory of its own riposte
Back to your mind. But gathering strength
680 And nerve, you come (ah light !) at length
To dwell awhile in the caress
Of that strange super-consciousness.
After one memory—O abide !
Vivid Savitri lightning-eyed !—
685 Nothing is worth a thought beside.
One hint of Amrita [55] to taste
And all earth's wine may run to waste !
For by this very means Christ gained [56]
His glimpse into that world above
690 Which he denominated "Love."
Indeed I think the man attained
By some such means—I have not strained
Out mind by chance of sense or sex
To find a way less iron-brained
695 Determining direction *x* ; [57]
I know not if these Hindu methods
Be best ('tis no such life and death odds,
Since suffering souls to save or damn
Never existed). So I fall
700 Confessing : Well, perchance I am
Myself a Christian after all !

So far at least. I must concede
Christ did attain in every deed ;
Yet, being an illiterate man,
705 Not his to balance or to scan,
To call God stupid or unjust !
He took the universe on trust ;
He reconciled the world below
With that above ; rolled eloquence
710 Steel-tired [58] o'er reason's "why?" and "whence?"
Discarded all proportion just,
And thundered in our ears "I know,"
And bellowed in our brains "ye must."

Mystic mean-
ing of Pente-
cost.

Such reservations—and I class
Myself a Christian : let us pass   715
Back to the text whose thread we lost,
And see what means this " Pentecost."

Super-con-
sciousness is
the gift of the
Holy Ghost.

This, then, is what I deem occurred
(According to our Saviour's word)
That all the Saints at Pentecost   720
Received the gift—the Holy Ghost ;
Such gift implying, as I guess,
This very super-consciousness.[50]
Miracles follow as a dower ;
But ah ! they used that fatal power   725
And lost the Spirit in the act.
This may be fancy or a fact ;
At least it squares with super-sense
Or "spiritual experience."

Poet not a
materialist.
Mohammed's
ideas.

You do not well to swell the list   730
Of horrid things to me imputed
By calling me "materialist."
At least this thought is better suited
To Western minds than is embalmed
Among the doctrines of Mohammed,   735
The dogma parthenogenetic *
As told me by a fat ascetic.
He said : " Your worthy friends may lack you late,
But learn how Mary was immaculate ! "
I sat in vague expectant bliss.   740

Verbatim re-
port of Moslem
account of the
Annunciation.

The story as it runs is this :
(I quote my Eastern friend [60] verbatim !)
The Virgin, going to the bath,
Found a young fellow in her path,
And turned, prepared to scold and rate him ! 745
" How dare you be on me encroaching ? "
The beautiful young gentleman,
With perfect courtesy approaching,
Bowed deeply, and at once began :
" Fear nothing, Mary !   All is well !   750
I am the angel Gabriel."
She bared her right breast ; (query why ?)
The angel Gabriel let fly

* Concerning conception of a virgin.

755
Out of a silver Tube a Dart
Shooting God's Spirit to her heart—[61]
This beats the orthodox Dove-Suitor !
What explanation could be cuter
Than—Gabriel with a pea-shooter?

In such a conflict I stand neuter.
760
But oh ! mistake not gold for pewter !
The plain fact is : materialise
What spiritual fact you choose,
And all such turn to folly--lose
The subtle splendour, and the wise
765
Love and dear bliss of truth.   Beware
Lest your lewd laughter set a snare
For any !   Thus and only thus
Will I admit a difference
'Twixt spirit and the things of sense.
770
What is the quarrel between us ?
Why do our thoughts so idly clatter ?
I do not care one jot for matter,
One jot for spirit, while you say
One is pure ether, one pure clay.

775
I've talked too long : you're very good—
I only hope you've understood !
Remember that " conversion " lurks
Nowhere behind my words and works.
Go home and think ! my talk refined
780
To the sheer needs of your own mind.
You cannot bring God in the compass
Of human thought ?   Up stick and thump ass !
Let human thought itself expand —
Bright Sun of Knowledge, in me rise !
785
Lead me to those exalted skies
To live and love and understand !
Paying no price, accepting nought—
The Giver and the Gift are one
With the Receiver—O thou Sun
790
Of thought, of bliss transcending thought,
Rise where division dies !   Absorb
In glory of the glowing orb
Self and its shadow !

Degradation of symbols. Essential identity of all forms of existence.

Practical advice.

Now who dares
Call me no Christian? And, who cares?   795
Read ; you will find the Master of Balliol,
Discarding Berkeley, Locke, and Paley, 'll
Resume such thoughts and label clear
" My Christianity lies here !"
With such religion who finds fault ?   800
Stay, it seems foolish to exalt
Religion to such heights as these,
Refine the actual agonies
To nothings, lest the mystic jeer
" So logic bends its line severe   805
Back to my involuted curve !"
These are my thoughts.   I shall not swerve.
Take them, and see what dooms deserve
Their rugged grandeur—heaven or hell?
Mind the dark doorway there ! [62]   Farewell !   810

How tedious I always find
That special manner of my mind !

Aum ! let us meditate aright
On that adorable One Light,
Divine Savitri ! So may She   815
Illume our minds ! So mote it be !

Christian
mystics not
true Christians.
What think ye
of Crowley?
His interlo-
cutor dis-
missed, not
with a jest, but
with a warning.

Poet yawns.

Aum !

NOTES TO ASCENSION DAY AND PENTECOST

> " Blind Chesterton is sure to err,
> And scan my work in vain ;
> I am my own interpreter,
> And I will make it plain. "

NOTE TO INTRODUCTION

[1] WILLIAM SHAKESPEARE.

AN APPRECIATION.

BY ALEISTER CROWLEY.[*]

IT is a lamentable circumstance that so many colossal brains (W. H. Mallock, &c.) have been hitherto thrown away in attacking what is after all a problem of mere academic interest, the authorship of the plays our fathers accepted as those of Shakespeare. To me it seems of immediate and vital importance to do for Shakespeare what Verrall has done so ably for Euripides. The third tabernacle must be filled ; Shaw and " the Human " must have their Superhuman companion. (This is not a scale : pithecanthropoid innuendo is to deprecated.)

Till now—as I write the sun bursts forth suddenly from a cloud, as if heralding the literary somersault of the twentieth century— we have been content to accept Shakespeare as orthodox, with common sense ; moral to a fault, with certain Rabelaisian leanings : a healthy tone (we say) pervades his work. Never believe it ! The sex problem is his Speciality ; a morbid decadence (so-called) is hidden i' th' heart o' th' rose. In other words, the divine William is the morning star to Ibsen's dawn, and Bernard Shaw's effulgence.

The superficial, the cynical, the misanthropic will demand proof of such a statement. Let it be our contemptuous indulgence to afford them what they ask.

May I premise that, mentally obsessed, mono-maniac indeed, as we must now consider Shakespeare to have been on these points, he was yet artful enough to have concealed his

advanced views—an imperative necessity, if we consider the political situation, and the virginal mask under which Queen Bess hid the grotesque and hideous features of a Messaline. Clearly so, since but for this concealment even our Shakespearian scholars would have dis-covered so patent a fact. In some plays, too, of course, the poet deals with less dangerous topics. These are truly conventional, no doubt ; we may pass them by ; they are foreign to our purpose ; but we will take that stupendous example of literary subterfuge—*King Lear.*

Let me digress to the history of my own conversion.

Syllogistically,—All great men (*e.g.* Shaw) are agnostics and subverters of morals. Shake-speare was a great man. Therefore Shakespeare was an agnostic and a subverter of morals.

A priori this is then certain. But—

> Who killed Rousseau ?
> I, said Huxley
> (Like Robinson Crusoe),
> With arguments true,—so
> I killed Rousseau !

Beware of *à priori !* Let us find our facts, guided in the search. by *à priori* methods, no doubt ; but the result will this time justify us.

Where would a man naturally hide his greatest treasure ? In his most perfect treasure-house.

Where shall we look for the truest thought of a great poet ? In his greatest poem.

What is Shakespeare's greatest play ? *King Lear.*

In *King Lear*, then, we may expect the final statement of the poet's mind. The passage that first put me on the track of the amazing discovery for which the world has to thank me is to be found in Act I. Sc. ii. ll. 132-149 :—

" This is the excellent foppery of the world, that, when we are sick in fortune,—often the surfeit of our own behaviour,—we make guilty

[*] The lamented decease of the above gentleman forbids all hope (save through the courtesy of Sir Oliver Lodge) of the appearance of the companion article.—A. C.

185

of our disasters the sun, the moon, and the stars; as if we were villains by necessity, fools by heavenly compulsion, knaves, thieves, and treachers by spherical predominance, drunkards, liars, and adulterers by an enforced obedience of planetary influence; and all that we are evil in, by a divine thrusting on: an admirable evasion of whoremaster man, to lay his goatish disposition to the charge of a star! My father compounded with my mother under the dragon's tail, and my nativity was under *ursa major;* so that it follows I am rough and lecherous. 'Sfoot! I should have been that I am had the maidenliest star in the firmament twinkled on my bastardizing.''

If there is one sound philosophical dictum in the play, it is this. (I am not going to argue with astrologers in the twentieth century.)

It is one we can test. On questions of morality and religion opinions veer; but if Shakespeare was a leader of thought, he saw through the humbug of the star-gazers; if not, he was a credulous fool; not the one man of his time, not a ''debauched genius'' (for Sir R. Burton in this phrase has in a sense anticipated my discovery) but a mere Elizabethan.

This the greatest poet of all time? Then we must believe that Gloucester was right, and that eclipses caused the fall of Lear! Observe that before this Shakespeare has had a sly dig or two at magic. In *King John,* "My lord, they say five moons were seen to-night" —but there is no eyewitness. So in *Macbeth.* In a host of spiritual suggestion there is always the rational sober explanation alongside to discredit the folly of the supernatural.

Shakespeare is like his own Touchstone; he uses his folly as a stalking-horse, and under the presentation of that he shoots his wit.

Here, however, the mask is thrown off for any but the utterly besotted; Edmund's speech stands up in the face of all time as truth; it challenges the acclamation of the centuries.

Edmund is then the hero; more, he is Shakespeare's own portrait of himself; his ways are dark — (and, alas! his tricks are vain!)—for why? For the fear of the conventional world about him.

He is illegitimate: Shakespeare is no true child of that age, but born in defiance of it and its prejudices.

Having taken this important step, let us slew round the rest of the play to fit it. If it fits, the law of probability comes to our aid; every coincidence multiplies the chance of our correctness in ever increasing proportion. We shall see—and you may look up your Proctor —that if the stars are placed just so by chance not law, then also it may be possible that Shakespeare was the wool-combing, knock-kneed, camel-backed, church-going, plaster-

of-Paris, stick-in-the-mud our scholars have always made him.

Edmund being the hero, Regan and Goneril must be the heroines. So nearly equal are their virtues and beauties that our poet cannot make up his mind which shall possess him— besides which, he wishes to drive home his arguments in favour of polygamy.

But the great theme of the play is of course filial duty; on this everything will turn. Here is a test:

Whenever this question is discussed, let us see who speaks the language of sense, and who that of draggle-tailed emotionalism and tepid melodrama.

In the first scene the heroines, who do not care for the old fool their father—as how could any sane women? Remember Shakespeare is here about to show the folly of filial love as such—feel compelled, by an act of gracious generosity to a man they despise, yet pity, to say what they think will please the dotard's vanity. Also no doubt the sound commercial instinct was touched by Lear's promise to make acres vary as words, and they determined to make a final effort to get some parsnips buttered after all.

Shakespeare (it is our English boast) was no long-haired squiggle self-yclept bard; but a business man—see Bishop Blougram's appreciation of him as such.

Shall we suppose him to have deliberately blackguarded in another his own best qualities? Note, too, the simple honesty of the divine sisters! Others, more subtle, would have suspected a trap, arguing that such idiocy as Lear's could not be genuine—Cordelia, the Madame Humbert of the play, does so; her over-cleverness leaves her stranded: yet by a certain sliminess of dissimulation, the oiliness of frankness, the pride that apes humility, she *does* catch the best king going. Yet it avails her little. She is hanged like the foul Vivien she is. [*]

Cordelia's farewell to her sisters shows up the characters of the three in strong relief. Cordelia—without a scrap of evidence to go on —accuses her sisters of hypocrisy and cruelty. (This could not have previously existed, or Lear would not have been deceived.)

Regan gravely rebukes her; recommends, as it were, a course of Six Easy Lessons in Mind-

---

[*] I use the word Vivien provisionally, pending the appearance of an essay to prove that Lord Tennyson was in secret an ardent reformer of our lax modern morals. No doubt, there is room for this. Vivien was perfectly right about the "cycle of strumpets and scoundrels whom Mr. Tennyson has set revolving round the figure of his central wittol," and she was the only one with the courage to say so, and the brains to strip off the barbarous glitter from an idiotic and phantom chivalry.

ing Her Own Business; and surely it was unparalleled insolence on the part of a dismissed girl to lecture her more favoured sister on the very point for which she herself was at that moment being punished. It is the spite of baffled dissimulation against triumphant honesty. Goneril adds a word of positive advice. "You," she says in effect, "who prate of duty thus, see you show it to him unto whom you owe it."

That this advice is wasted is clear from Act V. Sc. iii., where the King of France takes the first trivial opportunity * to be free of the vile creature he had so foolishly married.

Cordelia goes, and the sisters talk together. Theirs is the language of quiet sorrow for an old man's failing mind; yet a most righteous determination not to allow the happiness of the English people to depend upon his whims. Bad women would have rejoiced in the banishment of Kent, whom they already knew to be their enemy; these truly good women regret it. "Such unconstant starts are we like to have from him as this of Kent's banishment" (Act I. Sc. i. ll. 304-5).

In Scene ii. Edmund is shown; he feels himself a man, more than Edgar: a clear-headed, brave, honourable man; but with no maggots. The injustice of his situation strikes him; he determines not to submit.†

This is the attitude of a strong man, and a righteous one. Primogeniture is wrong enough; the other shame, no fault of his, would make the blood of any free man boil.

Gloucester enters, and exhibits himself as a prize fool by shouting in disjointed phrases what everybody knew. Great news it is, of course, and on discovering Edmund, he can think of nothing more sensible than to ask for more! "Kent banished thus! And France in choler parted! And the king gone to-night! subscrib'd his power! Confin'd to exhibition! All this done upon the gad! Edmund, how now! what news?" (Act I. Sc. ii. ll. 23-26).

Edmund "forces a card" by the simple device of a prodigious hurry to hide it. Gloucester gives vent to his astrological futilities, and falls to anxiomania in its crudest form,— "We have seen the best of our time: machinations, hollowness, treachery, and all ruinous disorders, follow us disquietly to our graves" (Sc. ii. ll. 125-127).

Edmund, once rid of him, gives us the

* He leaves her in charge of Marshal Le Fer, whom alone he could trust to be impervious to her wiles, he being devoted to another; for, as an invaluable contemporary MS. has it, "Seccotine colle même Le Fer."

† This may be, but I think should not be, used as an argument to prove the poet an illegitimate son of Queen Elizabeth.

plainest sense we are likely to hear for the rest of our lives; then, with the prettiest humour in the world takes the cue of his father's absurdity, and actually plays it on his enemy. Edgar's leg is not so easily pulled—(" How long have you been a sectary astronomical?" ll. 169, 170)—and the bastard hero, taking alarm, gets right down to business.

In Scene iii. we find Lear's senile dementia taking the peculiarly loathsome forms familiar to alienists—this part of my subject is so unpleasant that I must skim over it; I only mention it to show how anxious Shakespeare is to show his hidden meaning, otherwise his naturally delicate mind would have avoided the depiction of such phenomena.

All this prepares us for Scene iv., in which we get a glimpse of the way Lear's attendants habitually behave. Oswald, who treats Lear throughout with perfect respect, and only shows honest independence in refusing to obey a man who is not his master, is insulted in language worthier of a bargee than a king; and when he remonstrates in dignified and temperate language is set upon by the ruffianly Kent.

Are decent English people to complain when Goneril insists that this sort of thing shall not occur in a royal house? She does so, in language nobly indignant, yet restrained: Lear, in the hideous, impotent rage of senility, calls her —his own daughter—a bastard (no insult to her, but to himself or his wife, mark ye well!). Albany enters—a simple, orderly-minded man; he must not be confused with Cornwall; he is at the last Lear's dog; yet even he in decent measured speech sides with his wife. Is Lear quieted? No! He utters the most horrible curse, not excepting that of Count Cenci, that a father ever pronounced. Incoherent threats succeed to the boilings-over of the hideous malice of a beastly mind; but a hundred knights are a hundred knights, and a threat is a threat. Goneril had not fulfilled her duty to herself, to her people, had she allowed this monster of mania to go on.

I appeal to the medical profession; if one doctor will answer me that a man using Lear's language should be allowed control of a hundred armed ruffians [in the face of Kent's behaviour we know what weight to attach to Lear's defence: "Detested kite! thou liest" (I. iv. l. 286)], should ever be allowed outside a regularly appointed madhouse, I will cede the point, and retire myself into an asylum.

In fact, Lear is going mad; the tottering intellect, at no time strong ("'Tis the infirmity of age; yet he hath ever but slenderly known himself," I. i. ll. 296-7), is utterly cast down by drink and debauchery: he even sees it himself, and with a pointless bestiality from the Fool, fit companion for the—king—and in that word we see all the concentrated loathing of the true Shakespeare for a despotism, massed in one lurid flame, phantasmagoric horror, the grim First Act rolls down.

II.

Act II. Sc. i. adds little new to our thesis, save that in line 80 we see Gloucester (ignorant of his own son's handwriting!) accept the forged letter as genuine, as final proof, with not even the intervention of a Bertillon to excuse so palpable a folly, so egregious a crime. What father of to-day would disinherit, would hunt down to death, a beloved son, on such evidence? Or are we to take it that the eclipse gave proof unshakable of a phenomenon so portentous?

In Scene ii. we have another taste of Kent's gentlemanly demeanour; let our conventionalist interpreters defend this unwarrantable bullying if they dare! Another might be so gross, so cowardly; but not our greatest poet! A good portion of this play, as will be shown later, is devoted to a bitter assault upon the essentially English notion that the pugilist is the supreme device of the Creator for furthering human happiness. (See "Cashel Byron's Profession" for a similar, though more logical and better-worded, attack.) Coarse and violent language continues to disgrace Lear's follower; only Gloucester, the unconscionable ass and villain of Scene i., has a word to say in his defence.

In Scene iii. we have a taste of Edgar's quality. Had this despicable youth the consciousness of innocence, or even common courage, he had surely stood to his trial. Not he! He plays the coward's part — and his disguise is not even decent.

In Scene iv. we are shown the heroic sisters in their painful task of restraining, always with the utmost gentleness of word and demeanour, the headstrong passions of the miserable king. Lear, at first quiet in stating his fancied wrongs "*Reg.* 'I am glad to see your highness.' *Lear.* 'Regan, I think you are; I know what reason I have to think so : if thou shouldst not be glad, I would divorce me from thy mother's tomb, Sepulchring an adult'ress. (*To Kent*). O! are you free? Some other time for that. Beloved Regan, Thy sister's naught : O Regan! she hath tied Sharp-tooth'd unkindness, like a vulture, here : (*Points to his heart*). I can scarce speak to thee ; thou'lt not believe with how deprav'd a quality—O Regan!' *Reg.* 'I pray you, sir, take patience. I have hope'") (ll. 130-139), an excusable speech, at the first hint that he is not to have it all his own way, falls a-cursing again like the veriest drab or scullion Hamlet ever heard.

Here is a man, deprived on just cause of half a useless company of retainers. Is this wrong (even were it a wrong) such as to justify the horrible curses of ll. 164-168, "All the stor'd vengeances of heaven fall On her ingrateful top! Strike her young bones, You taking airs, with lameness! You nimble lightnings, dart your blinding flames Into her scornful eyes!" With this he makes his age contemptible by the drivel-pathos of ll. 156-158, "Dear daughter, I confess that I am old ; Age is unnecessary : on my knees I beg (*Kneeling*) That you'll vouchsafe me raiment, bed, and food," begging what none ever thought to deny him.

Yet such is the patience of Goneril that even when goaded by all this infamous Billingsgate into speech, her rebuke is the temperate and modest ll. 198-200. "Why not by the hand, sir? How have I offended? All's not offence that indiscretion finds And dotage terms so." If we ask a parallel for such meekness under insult, calumny, and foul abuse, we must seek it not in a human story, but a divine.

The heroines see that no half measures will do, and Lear is stripped of all the murderous retinue—what scum they are is shown by the fact that not one of them draws sword for him, or even follows him into the storm—to which his bad heart clings ; yet for him—for him in spite of all his loathsomeness, his hatred, his revengefulness—is Regan's gentle and loving,

"For his particular, I'll receive him gladly."

III.

In Act III. we have another illustration of the morality that passed current with the Tudors, and which only a Shakespeare had the courage to attack. Kent does not stick at treachery—he makes one gulp of treason—straining at the gnat of discipline, he swallows the camel of civil war.

It was then, and is even now, the practice of some—for example, the emigrés of the French Revolution—to invite foreign invasion as a means of securing domestic reaction. The blackguardism implied is beyond language : Shakespeare was perhaps thinking of the proposal, in Mary's reign, to react to Romanism by the aid of Spanish troops. But he will go further than this, will our greatest poet ; it were ill that the life of even one child should atone for mere indignity or discomfort to another, were he the greatest in the realm. To-day we all agree ; we smile or sneer if any one should differ.

"King Lear got caught in the rain—let us go and kill a million men!" is an argument not much understood of Radical Clubs, and even Jingos would pause, did they but take the precaution of indulging in a mild aperient before recording their opinions.

In Scenes iii., vi., and vii., Edmund, disgusted beyond all measure with Gloucester's infamies, honourably and patriotically denounces him.

The other scenes depict the miseries which follow the foolish and the unjust ; and Nemesis falls upon the ill-minded Gloucester. Yet Shakespeare is so appreciative of the virtue of compassion (for Shakespeare was, as I shall hope to prove one day, a Buddhist) that Cornwall, the somewhat cruel instrument of eternal Justice, is killed by his servant. Regan avenges her husband promptly, and I have little doubt that this act of excessive courtesy towards a man she did not love is the moral cause of her unhappy end.

I would note that we should not attempt to draw any opinions as to the author's design from the conversation of the vulgar ; even had we not Coriolanus to show us what he thought.

IV.

Act IV. develops the plot and is little germane to our matter, save that we catch a glimpse of the unspeakably vile Cordelia, with no pity for her father's serious condition (though no doubt he deserved all he got, he was now harmless, and should have inspired compassion), hanging to him in the hope that he would now reverse his banishment and make her (after a bloody victory) sole heiress of great England.

And were any doubt left in our minds as to who really was the hero of the play, the partizanship of France would settle it. Shakespeare has never any word but ridicule for the French ; never aught but praise of England and love for her : are we to suppose that in his best play he is to stultify all his other work and insult the English for the benefit of the ridiculed and hated Frenchman?

Moreover, Cordelia reckons without her host. The British bulldogs make short work of the invaders and rebels, doubtless with the connivance of the King of France, who, with great and praiseworthy acuteness, foresees that Cordelia will be hanged, thus liberating him from his "most filthy bargain": there is but one alarum, and the whole set of scoundrels surrender. Note this well ; it is not by brute force that the battle is won ; for even if we exonerate the King of France, we may easily believe that the moral strength of the sisters cowed the French.

This is the more evident, since in Act V. Shakespeare strikes his final blow at the absurdity of the duel, when Edmund is dishonestly slain by the beast Edgar. Yet the poet's faith is still strong : wound up as his muse is to tragedy, he retains in Edmund the *sublime heroism, the simple honesty,* of the

true Christian ; at the death of his beloved mistresses he cries,

"I was contracted to them both : all three
Now marry in an instant——"

At the moment of death his great nature (self-accusatory, as the finest so often are) asserts itself, and he forgives even the vilest of the human race,—" I pant for life : some good I mean to do Despite of mine own nature.[1] Quickly send, Be brief in it, to the castle ; for my writ Is on the life of Lear and on Cordelia. Nay, send in time " (ll. 245-249).

And in that last supreme hour of agony he claims Regan as his wife, as if by accident ; it is not the passionate assertion of a thing doubtful, but the natural reference to a thing well known and indisputable.

And in the moment of his despair ; confronted with the dead bodies of the splendid sisters, the catafalque of all his hopes, he can exclaim in spiritual triumph over material disaster—the victory of a true man's spirit over Fate—

"Yet Edmund was beloved."

Edgar is left alive with Albany, alone of all that crew ; and if remorse could touch their brutal and callous souls (for the degeneration of the weakling, well-meaning Albany, is a minor tragedy), what hell could be more horrible than the dragging out of a cancerous existence in the bestial world of hate their hideous hearts had made, now, even for better men, for ever dark and gloomy, robbed of the glory of the glowing Goneril, the royal Regan, and only partially redeemed by the absence of the harlot Cordelia and the monster Lear.

V.

It may possibly be objected by the censorious, by the effete parasites of a grim conventionalism, that I have proved too much. Even by conventional standards Edmund, Goneril, and Regan appear angels. Even on the moral point, the sisters, instead of settling down to an enlightened and by no means overcrowded polygamy, prefer to employ poison. This is perhaps true, of Goneril at least ; Regan is, if one may distinguish between star and star, somewhat the finer character.

This criticism is perhaps true in part ; but I will not insult the intelligence of my readers. I will leave it to them to take the obvious step and work backwards to the re-exaltation of Lear, Cordelia, Edgar and company, to the heroic fields of their putty Elysium (putty, not

[1] This may merely mean "despite the fact that I am dying—though I am almost too weak to speak." If so, the one phrase in the play which seems to refute our theory is disposed of. Execution of such criminals would be a matter of routine at the period of the play.

Putney) in their newly-demonstrated capacity as "unnatural" sons, daughters, fathers, and so on. But I leave it. I am content—my work will have been well done—if this trifling essay be accepted as a just instalment towards a saner criticism of our holiest writers, a juster appreciation of the glories of our greatest poet, a possibly jejune yet assuredly historic attempt to place for the first time William Shakespeare on his proper pedestal as an early disciple of Mr. George Bernard Shaw; and by consequence to carve myself a little niche in the same temple : the smallest contributions will be thankfully received.

NOTES TO ASCENSION DAY

1. *I flung out of chapel.*[1]—Browning, *Xmas Eve*, III. last line.

3. *Venus' Bower and Osiris' Tomb.*[2]—Crowley, *Tannhäuser.*

5. *God.*[3]—Hebrew אלהים, Gen. iii. 5.

5. *gods.*[4]—Hebrew אלהים, Gen. iii. 5.
The Revisers, seeing this most awkward juxtaposition, have gone yet one step lower and translated both words by "God." In other passages, however, they have been compelled to disclose their own dishonesty and translate אלהים by "gods."
For evidence of this the reader may look up such passages as Ex. xviii. 11 ; Deut. xxxii. 17 ; Ps. lxxxii. [in particular, where the word occurs twice, as also the word אל. But the revisers twice employ the word "God" and once the word "gods." The A.V. has "mighty" in one case]; Gen. xx. 13, where again the verb is plural ; Sam. xxviii. 13, and so on.
See the Hebrew Dictionary of Gesenius (trans. Tregelles), Bagster, 1859, *s.v.*, for proof that the Author is on the way to the true interpretation of these conflicting facts, as now established—see Huxley, H. Spencer, Kuenen, Reuss, Lippert, and others—and his orthodox translator's infuriated snarls (in brackets) when he suspects this tendency to accept facts as facts.

6. *Soul went down.*[5]—*The Questions of King Milinda*, 40-45, 48, 67, 86-89, 111, 132.

7. *The metaphysical lotus-eyed.*[6]—Gautama Buddha.

10. *Childe Roland.*[7]—Browning, *Dramatic Romances.*

11. *Two hundred thousand Trees.*[8]—Browning wrote about 200,000 lines.

13. *Your Reverence.*[9]—The imaginary Aunt Sally for the poetic cocoanut.*

16. *" God's right use of it."* [10]—" And many an eel, though no adept In God's right reason for it, kept Gnawing his kidneys half a year." —Shelley, *Peter Bell the Third.*

17. *One tree.*[11]—Note the altered value of

* Crowley confuses two common pastoral amusements—throwing wooden balls at cocoanuts and sticks at Aunt Sally.

the metaphor, such elasticity having led Prof. Blümengarten to surmise them to be india-rubber trees.

27. *" Truth, that's the gold."* [12]—*Two Poets of Croisic*, clii. 1, and elsewhere.

28. *" I, you, or Simpkin."* [13]—*Inn Album*, l. 143. "Simpkin" has nothing to do with the foaming grape of Eastern France.

36. *Aischulos.*[14]—See Agamemnon (Browning's translation), Preface.

40. *Aristobulus.*[15]—May be scanned elsehow by pedants. Cf. Swinburne's curious scansion : Arĭstŏphānēs. But the scansion adopted here gives a more creditable rhyme.

42. Βατραχομνομαχια.[16]—Aristophanes Batrachoi.

46. *Mine of so many pounds—pouch even pence of it ?*[17]—This line was suggested to me by a large holder of Westralians.

47. *Something easier.*[18]—*Christmas Eve and Easter Day.*

51. *Newton.*[19]—Mathematician and physicist of repute.

51. *Faraday.*[20]—See Dictionary of National Biography.

64. *I, of the Moderns, have alone Greek.*[21]—As far as they would let me. I know some.

74. *Beard.*[22]—" 150. A Barba Senioris Sanctissimi pendet omnis ornatus omnium : & influentia ; nam omnia appellantur ab illa barba, Influentia.
" 151. Hic est ornatus omnium ornatuum : Influentie superiores & inferiores omnes respiciunt istam Influentiam.
" 152. Ab ista influentia dependet vita omnium.
" 153. Ab hac influentia dependent cœli & terra ; pluviæ beneplaciti ; & alimenta omnium.
" 154. Ab hac influentia venit providentia omnium. Ab hac influentia dependent omnes exercitus superiores & inferiores.
" 155. Tredecim fontes olei magnificentiæ boni, dependent a barba hujus influentiæ gloriosæ ; & omnes emanant in Microprosopum.
" 156. Ne dicas omnes ; sed novem ex iis inveniuntur ad inflectenda judicia.
" 157. Et quando hæc influentia æqualiter pendet usque ad præcordia omnes Sanctitatis Sanctitatum Sanctitatis ab illa dependent.

" 158. In istam influentiam extenditur expansio aporrhœæ supernæ, quæ est caput omnium capitum : quod non cognoscitur nec perficitur, quodque non norunt nec superi, nec inferi : propterea omnia ab ista influentia dependent.

" 159. In hanc barbam tria capita de quibus diximus, expandantur, & omnia consociantur in hac influentia, & inveniuntur in ea.

" 160. Et propterea omnis ornatus ornatuum ab ista influentia dependent.

" 161. Istæ literæ, quæ dependent ab hoc Seniore, omnes pendent in ista barba, & consociantur in ista influentia.

" 162. Et pendent in ea ad stabiliendas literas alteras.

" 163. Nisi enim illæ literæ ascenderent in Seniorem, reliquæ istæ literæ non stabilirentur.

" 164. Et propterea dicit Moses cum opus esset : Tetragrammaton, Tetragrammaton bis : & ita ut accentus distinguat utrumque.

" 165. Certe enim ab influentia omnia dependent.

" 166. Ab ista influentia ad reverentiam adiguntur superna & inferna, & flectuntur coram ea.

" 167. Beatus ille, qui ad hanc usque per tingit.

Idra Suta, seu Synodus minor. Sectio VI.

" 496. *Forehead.*[23]—Frons Cranii est frons ad visitandum : (Al. ad eradicandum) peccatoras.

" 497. Et cum ista frons detegitur tunc excitantur Domini Judiciorum, contra illos qui non erubescunt in operibus suis.

" 498. Hæc frons ruborem habet roseum. Sed illo tempore, cum frons Senioris erga hanc frontem detegitur, hæc apparet alba ut nix.

" 499. Et illa hora vocatur Tempus beneplaciti pro omnibus.

" 500. In libro Dissertationis Scholæ Raf Jebha Senis dicitur : Frons est receptaculum frontis Senioris. Sin minus, litera Cheth inter duas reliquas interponitur, juxta illud : (Num. xxiv. 17) וּמָחַץ et confringet angulos Moab.

" 501. Et alibi diximus, quod etiam vocetur נצח, literis vicinis permutatis : id est, superatio.

" 502. Multæ autem sunt Superationes : ita ut Superatio alia elevata sit in locum alium : & aliæ dentur Superationes quæ extenduntur in totum corpus.

" 503. Die Sabbathi autem tempore precum pomeridianarum, ne excitentur judicia, detegitur frons Senioris Sanctissimi.

" 504. Et omnia judicia subiguntur ; & quamvis extent, tamen non exercentur. (Al. et sedantur.)

" 505. Ab hac fronte dependent viginti quatuor tribunalia, pro omnibus illis, qui protervi sunt in operibus.

" 506. Sicut scriptum est : (Ps. lxxiii. 11.) Et dixerunt : quomodo sit Deus ? Et estne scientia in excelso ?

" 507. At vero viginti saltem sunt. cur adduntur quatuor ? nimirum respectu suppliciorum, tribunalium inferiorum, quæ a supernis dependent.

" 508. Remanent ergo viginti. Et propterea neminem supplicio capitali afficiunt, donec compleverit & ascenderit ad viginti annos; respectu viginti horum tribunalium.

" 509. Sed in thesi nostra arcana docuimus, per ista respici viginti quatuor libros qui continentur in Lege.

Idra Suta, seu Synodus minor. Sectio XIIIv

77. *Chains.*[24]—Sakkâha-di*tth*i, Vi*k*iki*kkh*â, sîlabbata-parâmâsa, kâma, patigha, rûparâga, arûparâga, niâno, uddha*kk*a, avi*gg*â.

81. "*Who asks doth err.*"[25]—Arnold, *Light of Asia.*

83. *You.*[26]—You !

86. "*O'erleaps itself and falls on the other.*"[27] —*Macbeth*, I. vii. 27.

92. *English.*[28] — This poem is written in English.

94. *I cannot write.*[29]—This is not quite true. For instance :

ཨོཾ། བམ་བོང་ རིང་མོ་རང་ ལུང་ པོ།

ལུང་མོ་བོང་

ཁུ་མ་བོང་ ཁུ་ར་པོ་ རང་ཀར་

པོ་ རང་ ཁོང་

ཡི་མ་ནེ་ བག་ སྐོར་ ཆེག་ ཆེག་

བར་ དྷེ་ ཆེས་

ཁར་ པ་ ཡིན་ པོག་ པག་ དྷ་

ཙ་ གྱུ །།

This, the opening stanza of my masterly poem on Ladak, reads :—" The way was long, and the wind was cold : the Lama was infirm and advanced in years ; his prayer-wheel, to revolve which was his only pleasure, was carried by a disciple, an orphan."

There is a reminiscence of some previous incarnation about this : European critics may possibly even identify the passage. But at least the Tibetans should be pleased. *

* They were ; thence the pacific character of the British expedition of 1904.—A. C.

97. *While their Buddha I attack.*—Many Buddhists think I fill the bill with the following remarks on—

PANSIL.[30]

Unwilling as I am to sap the foundations of the Buddhist religion by the introduction of Porphyry's terrible catapult, Allegory, I am yet compelled by the more fearful ballista of Aristotle, Dilemma. This is the two-handed engine spoken of by the prophet Milton ! *
This is the horn of the prophet Zeruiah, and with this am I, though no Syrian, utterly pushed, till I find myself back against the dead wall of Dogma. Only now realising how dead a wall that is, do I turn and try the effect of a hair of the dog that bit me, till the orthodox "literary" † school of Buddhists, as grown at Rangoon, exclaim with Lear : "How sharper than a serpent's tooth it is To have an intellect ! " How is this? Listen, and hear !

I find myself confronted with the crux : that, a Buddhist, convinced intellectually and philosophically of the truth of the teaching of Gotama ; a man to whom Buddhism is the equivalent of scientific methods of Thought ; an expert in dialectic, whose logical faculty is bewildered, whose critical admiration is extorted by the subtle vigour of Buddhist reasoning ; I am yet forced to admit that, this being so, the Five Precepts ‡ are mere nonsense. If the Buddha spoke scientifically, not popularly, not rhetorically, then his precepts are not his. We must reject them or we must interpret them. We must inquire : Are they meant to be obeyed ? Or—and this is my theory—are they sarcastic and biting criticisms on existence, illustrations of the First Noble Truth ; *reasons*, as it were, for the apotheosis of annihilation ? I shall show that this is so. Let me consider them "precept upon precept," if the introduction of the Hebrew visionary is not too strong meat for the Little Mary § of a Buddhist audience.

* *Lycidas*, line 130.
† The school whose Buddhism is derived from the Canon, and who ignore the degradation of the professors of the religion, as seen in practice.
‡ The obvious caveat which logicians will enter against these remarks is that Pansil is the Five Virtues rather than Precepts. Etymologically this is so. However, we may regard this as a clause on my side of the argument, not against it ; for in my view these are virtues, and the impossibility of attaining them is the cancer of existence. Indeed, I support the etymology as against the futile bigotry of certain senile Buddhists of to-day. And, since it is the current interpretation of Buddhistic thought that I attack, I but show myself the better Buddhist in the act.—A. C.
§ A catch word for the stomach, from J. M. Barrie's play "Little Mary."

THE FIRST PRECEPT.

This forbids the taking of life in any form.* What we have to note is the impossibility of performing this ; if we can prove it to be so, either Buddha was a fool, or his command was rhetorical, like those of Yahweh to Job, or of Tannhäuser to himself—

"Go ! seek the stars and count them and explore !
Go ! sift the sands beyond a starless sea ! "

Let us consider what the words can mean. The "Taking of Life" can only mean the reduction of living protoplasm to dead matter : or, in a truer and more psychological sense, the destruction of personality.

Now, in the chemical changes involved in Buddha's speaking this command, living protoplasm was changed into dead matter. Or, on the other horn, the fact (insisted upon most strongly by the Buddha himself, the central and cardinal point of his doctrine, the shrine of that Metaphysic which isolates it absolutely from all other religious metaphysic, which allies it with Agnostic Metaphysic) that the Buddha who had spoken this command was not the same as the Buddha before he had spoken it, lies the proof that the Buddha, by speaking this command, violated it. More, not only did he slay himself ; he breathed in millions of living organisms and slew them. He could nor eat nor drink nor breathe without murder implicit in each act. Huxley cites the "pitiless microscopist" who showed a drop of water to the Brahmin who boasted himself "Ahimsa "—harmless. So among the "rights " of a Bhikkhu is medicine. He who takes quinine does so with the deliberate intention of destroying innumerable living beings ; whether this is done by stimulating the phagocytes, or directly, is morally indifferent.

How such a fiend incarnate, my dear brother Ananda Maitriya, can call him "cruel and cowardly " who only kills a tiger, is a study in the philosophy of the mote and the beam !

Far be it from me to suggest that this is a defence of breathing, eating, and drinking. By no means ; in all these ways we bring suffering and death to others, as to ourselves. But since these are inevitable acts, since suicide would be a still more cruel alternative (especially in case something should subsist below mere Rupa), the command is not to achieve

* Fielding, in "The Soul of a People," has reluctantly to confess that he can find no trace of this idea in Buddha's own work, and calls the superstition the "echo of an older Faith."—A. C.
† The argument that the "animals are our brothers" is merely intended to mislead one who has never been in a Buddhist country. The average Buddhist would, of course, kill his brother for five rupees, or less.—A. C.

the impossible, the already violated in the act of commanding, but a bitter commentary on the foul evil of this aimless, hopeless universe, this compact of misery, meanness, and cruelty. Let us pass on.

THE SECOND PRECEPT.

The Second Precept is directed against theft. Theft is the appropriation to one's own use of that to which another has a right. Let us see therefore whether or no the Buddha was a thief. The answer of course is in the affirmative. For to issue a command is to attempt to deprive another of his most precious possession—the right to do as he will; that is, unless, with the predestinarians, we hold that action is determined absolutely, in which case, of course, a command is as absurd as it is unavoidable. Excluding this folly, therefore, we may conclude that if the command be obeyed—and those of Buddha have gained a far larger share of obedience than those of any other teacher—the Enlightened One was not only a potential but an actual thief. Further, all voluntary action limits in some degree, however minute, the volition of others. If I breathe, I diminish the stock of oxygen available on the planet. In those far distant ages when Earth shall be as dead as the moon is to-day, my breathing now will have robbed some being then living of the dearest necessity of life.

That the theft is minute, incalculably trifling, Is no answer to the moralist, to whom degree is not known; nor to the scientist, who sees the chain of nature miss no link.

If, on the other hand, the store of energy in the universe be indeed constant (whether infinite or no), if personality be indeed delusion, then theft becomes impossible, and to forbid it is absurd. We may argue that even so temporary theft may exist; and that this is so is to my mind no doubt the case. All theft is temporary, since even a millionaire must die; also it is universal, since even a Buddha must breathe.

THE THIRD PRECEPT.

This precept, against adultery, I shall touch but lightly. Not that I consider the subject unpleasant—far from it!—but since the English section of my readers, having unclean minds, will otherwise find a fulcrum therein for their favourite game of slander. Let it suffice if I say that the Buddha—in spite of the ridiculous membrane legend,* one of those foul follies which idiot devotees invent only too freely—was a confirmed and habitual adulterer. It

* Membrum virile illius in membrana inclusum esse aiunt, ne copulare posset.

VOL. II.

would be easy to argue with Hegel-Huxley that he who thinks of an act commits it (cf. Jesus also in this connection, though he only knows the creative value of desire), and that since A and not-A are mutually limiting, therefore interdependent, therefore identical, he who forbids an act commits it; but I feel that this is no place for metaphysical hair-splitting; let us prove what we have to prove in the plainest way.

I would premise in the first place that to commit adultery in the Divorce Court sense is not here in question.

It assumes too much proprietary right of a man over a woman, that root of all abomination!—the whole machinery of inheritance, property, and all the labyrinth of law.

We may more readily suppose that the Buddha was (apparently at least) condemning incontinence.

We know that Buddha had abandoned his home; true, but Nature has to be reckoned with. Volition is no necessary condition of offence. "I didn't mean to" is a poor excuse for an officer failing to obey an order.

Enough of this in any case a minor question; since even on the lowest moral grounds—and we, I trust, soar higher!—the error in question may be resolved into a mixture of murder, theft, and intoxication. (We consider the last under the Fifth Precept.)

THE FOURTH PRECEPT.

Here we come to what in a way is the fundamental joke of these precepts. A command is not a lie, of course; possibly cannot be; yet surely an allegorical order is one in essence, and I have no longer a shadow of a doubt that these so-called "precepts" are a species of savage practical joke.

Apart from this there can hardly be much doubt, when critical exegesis has done its damnedest on the Logia of our Lord, that Buddha did at some time commit himself to some statement. "(Something called) Consciousness exists" is, said Huxley, the irreducible minimum of the pseudo-syllogism, false even for an enthymeme, ".Cogito, ergo sum!" This proposition he bolsters up by stating that whoso should pretend to doubt it, would thereby but confirm it. Yet might it not be said "(Something called) Consciousness appears to itself to exist," since Consciousness is itself the only witness to that confirmation? Not that even now we can deny some kind of existence to consciousness, but that it should be a more real existence than that of a reflection is doubtful, incredible, even inconceivable. If by consciousness we mean the normal consciousness, it is definitely untrue, since the

N

Dhyanic consciousness includes it and denies it. No doubt "something called" acts as a kind of caveat to the would-be sceptic, though the phrase is bad, implying a "calling." But we can guess what Huxley means.

No doubt Buddha's scepticism does not openly go quite as far as mine—it must be remembered that "scepticism" is merely the indication of a possible attitude, not a belief, as so many good fool folk think; but Buddha not only denies "Cogito, ergo sum"; but "Cogito, ergo non sum." See *Sabbasava Sutta*, par. 10.*

At any rate Sakkyaditthi, the delusion of personality, is in the very forefront of his doctrines; and it is this delusion that is constantly and inevitably affirmed in all normal consciousness. That Dhyanic thought avoids it is doubtful; even so, Buddha is here represented as giving precepts to ordinary people. And if personality be delusion, a lie is involved in the command of one to another. In short, we all lie all the time; we are compelled to it by the nature of things themselves — paradoxical as that seems—and the Buddha knew it!

THE FIFTH PRECEPT.

At last we arrive at the end of our weary journey—surely in this weather we may have a drink! East of Suez,† Trombone-Macaulay (as I may surely say, when Browning writes Banjo-Byron ‡) tells us, a man may raise a Thirst. No, shrieks the Blessed One, the Perfected One, the Enlightened One, do not drink! It is like the streets of Paris when they were placarded with rival posters—

> Ne buvez pas de l'Alcool!
> L'Alcool est un poison!

and

> Buvez de l'Alcool!
> L'Alcool est un aliment!

We know now that alcohol is a food up to a certain amount; the precept, good enough for a rough rule as it stands, will not bear close inspection. What Buddha really commands, with that grim humour of his, is: Avoid Intoxication.

But what is intoxication? unless it be the loss of power to use perfectly a truth-telling set of faculties. If I walk unsteadily it is owing to nervous lies—and so for all the phenomena of drunkenness. But a lie involves the assump-

* Quoted below, "Science and Buddhism," note.
† "Ship me somewhere East of Suez, where a man can raise a thirst."—R. KIPLING.
‡ " While as for Quilp Hop o' my Thumb there,
    Banjo-Byron that twangs the strum-strum there."
      —BROWNING, *Pachiarotto* (said of A. Austin).

tion of some true standard, and this can nowhere be found. A doctor would tell you, moreover, that all food intoxicates: all, here as in all the universe, of every subject and in every predicate, is a matter of degree.

Our faculties never tell us true; our eyes say flat when our fingers say round; our tongue sends a set of impressions to our brain which our hearing declares non-existent—and so on.

What is this delusion of personality but a profound and centrally-seated intoxication of the consciousness? I am intoxicated as I address these words; you are drunk—beastly drunk!—as you read them; Buddha was as drunk as a British officer when he uttered his besotted command. There, my dear children, is the conclusion to which we are brought if you insist that he was serious!

I answer No! Alone among men then living, the Buddha was sober, and saw Truth. He, who was freed from the coils of the great serpent Theli coiled round the universe, he knew how deep the slaver of that snake had entered into us, infecting us, rotting our very bones with poisonous drunkenness. And so his cutting irony—drink no intoxicating drinks!

When I go to take Pansil,* it is in no spirit of servile morality; it is with keen sorrow gnawing at my heart. These five causes of sorrow are indeed the heads of the serpent of Desire. Four at least of them snap their fangs on me in and by virtue of my very act of receiving the commands, and of promising to obey them; if there is a little difficulty about the fifth, it is an omission easily rectified—and I think we should all make a point about that; there is great virtue in completeness.

Yes! Do not believe that the Buddha was a fool; that he asked men to perform the impossible or the unwise.† Do not believe that the sorrow of existence is so trivial that easy rules

* To "take Pansil" is to vow obedience to these Precepts.
† I do not propose to dilate on the moral truth which Ibsen has so long laboured to make clear: that no hard and fast rule of life can be universally applicable. Also, as in the famous case of the lady who saved (successively) the lives of her husband, her father, and her brother, the precepts clash. To allow to die is to kill—all this is obvious to the most ordinary thinkers. These precepts are of course excellent general guides for the vulgar and ignorant, but you and I, dear reader, are wise and clever, and know better. Nichtwar?
Excuse my being so buried in "dear Immanuel Kant" (as my friend Miss Br. c. [1] would say) that this biting and pregnant phrase slipped out unaware. As a rule, of course, I hate the introduction of foreign tongues into an English essay.—A. C.

[1] A fast woman who posed as a bluestocking.

easily interpreted (as all Buddhists do interpret the Precepts) can avail against them ; do not mop up the Ganges with a duster ; nor stop the revolution of the stars with a lever of lath.

Awake, awake only! let there be ever remembrance that Existence is sorrow, sorrow by the inherent necessity of the way it is made ; sorrow not by volition, not by malice, not by carelessness, but by nature, by ineradicable tendency, by the incurable disease of Desire, its Creator, is it so, and the way to destroy it is by the uprooting of Desire ; nor is a task so formidable accomplished by any threepenny-bit-in-the-plate-on-Sunday morality, the "deceive others and self-deception will take care of itself" uprightness, but by the severe roads of austere self-mastery, of arduous scientific research, which constitute the Noble Eightfold Path.

101–105. *There's one. . . Six Six Six.*[31]— This opinion has been recently (and most opportunely) confirmed by the Rev. Father Simons, Roman Catholic Missionary (and head of the Corner in Kashmir Stamps), Baramulla, Kashmir.

106. *Gallup.*[32] — For information apply to Mr. Sidney Lee.

111. "*It is the number of a Man.*"[33]—Rev. xiii. 18.

117. *Fives.*[34]—Dukes.

122. (*Elsewhere.*)[35] — See "Songs of the Spirit" and other works.

128. *The Qabalistic Balm.*[36] — May be studied in "The Kabbalah (*sic*) Unveiled" (Redway). It is much to be wished that some one would undertake the preparation of an English translation of Rabbi Jischak Ben Loria's "De Revolutionibus Animarum," and of the book "Beth Elohim."

139. *Cain.*[37]—Gen. iv. 8.

152. *Hunyadi.*[38]—Hunyadi Janos, a Hungarian table water.

161. *Nadi.*[39]—For this difficult subject refer to the late Swami Vivekananda's "Raja Yoga."

167. *Tom Bond Bishop.*[40]—Founder of the "Children's Scripture Union" (an Association for the Dissemination of Lies among Young People) and otherwise known as a philanthropist. His relationship to the author (that of uncle) has procured him this rather disagreeable immortality.

He was, let us hope, no relation to George Archibald Bishop, the remarkable preface to whose dreadfully conventionally psychopathic works is this.

PREFACE.*

In the fevered days and nights under the Empire that perished in the struggle of 1870,

* To a collection of MSS. illustrating the "Psychopathia Sexualis" of von Kraft-Ebing. The names of the parties have been changed.

that whirling tumult of pleasure, scheming, success, and despair, the minds of men had a trying ordeal to pass through. In Zola's "La Curée" we see how such ordinary and natural characters as those of Saccard, Maxime, and the incestuous heroine, were twisted and distorted from their normal sanity, and sent whirling into the jaws of a hell far more affrayant than the mere cheap and nasty brimstone Sheol which is a Shibboleth for the dissenter, and with which all classes of religious humbug; from the Pope to the Salvation ranter, from the Mormon and the Jesuit to that mongrel mixture of the worst features of both, the Plymouth Brother, have scared their illiterate, since hypocrisy was born, with Abel, and spiritual tyranny, with Jehovah! Society, in the long run, is eminently sane and practical ; under the Second Empire it ran mad. If these things are done in the green tree of Society, what shall be done in the dry tree of Bohemianism? Art always has a suspicion to fight against ; always some poor mad Max Nordau is handy to call everything outside the kitchen the asylum. Here, however, there is a substratum of truth. Consider the intolerable long roll of names, all tainted with glorious madness. Baudelaire the diabolist, debauchee of sadism, whose dreams are nightmares, and whose waking hours delirium ; Rollinat the necrophile, the poet of phthisis, the anxiomaniac ; Péladan, the high priest—of nonsense; Mendès, frivolous and scoffing sensualist ; besides a host of others, most alike in this, that, below the cloak of madness and depravity, the true heart of genius burns. No more terrible period than this is to be found in literature ; so many great minds, of which hardly one comes to fruition ; such seeds of genius, such a harvest of—whirlwind ! Even a barren waste of sea is less saddening than one strewn with wreckage.

In England such wild song found few followers of any worth or melody. Swinburne stands on his solitary pedestal above the vulgar crowds of priapistic plagiarists ; he alone caught the fierce frenzy of Baudelaire's brandied shrieks, and his First Series of Poems and Ballads was the legitimate echo of that not fierier note. But English Art as a whole was unmoved, at any rate not stirred to any depth, by this wave of debauchery. The great thinkers maintained the even keel, and the windy waters lay not for their frailer barks to cross. There is one exception of note, till this day unsuspected, in the person of George Archibald Bishop. In a corner of Paris this young poet (for in his nature the flower of poesy did spring, did even take root and give some promise of a brighter bloom, till stricken and blasted in latter years by the lightning of his own sins) was steadily writing day after day, night after night, often working forty hours at a time, work which he destined to entrance the world. All England should ring with his praises; by-and-by the whole world should know his name. Of these works none of the longer and more ambitious remains. How they were lost, and how those fragments we possess were saved, is best told by relating the romantic and almost incredible story of his life.

The known facts of this life are few, vague, and unsatisfactory; the more definite statements lack corroboration, and almost the only source at the disposal of the biographer is the letters of Mathilde Doriac to Mdme. J. S., who has kindly placed her portfolio at my service. A letter dated October 15, 1866, indicates that our author was born on the 23rd of that month. The father and mother of George were, at least on the surface, of an extraordinary religious turn of mind. Mathilde's version of the story, which has its source in our friend himself, agrees almost word for word with a letter of the Rev. Edw. Turle to Mrs. Cope, recommending the child to her care. The substance of the story is as follows.

The parents of George carried their religious ideas to the point of never consummating their marriage! * This arrangement does not seem to have been greatly appreciated by the wife; at least one fine morning she was found to be enceinte. The foolish father never thought of the hypothesis which commends itself most readily to a man of the world, not to say a man of science, and adopted that of a second Messiah! He took the utmost pains to conceal the birth of the child, treated everybody who came to the house as an emissary of Herod, and finally made up his mind to flee into Egypt! Like most religious maniacs, he never had an idea of his own, but distorted the beautiful and edifying events of the Bible into insane and ridiculous ones, which he proceeded to plagiarise.

On the voyage out the virgin mother became enamoured, as was her wont, of the nearest male, in this case a fellow-traveller. He, being well able to support her in the luxury which she desired, easily persuaded her to leave the boat with him by stealth. A small sailing vessel conveyed them to Malta, where they disappeared. The only trace left in the books of earth records that this fascinating character was accused, four years later, in Vienna, of poisoning her paramour, but thanks to the wealth and influence of her newer lover, she escaped.

The legal father, left by himself with a squalling child to amuse, to appease in his tantrums,

* Will it be believed that a clergyman (turned Plymouth Brother and schoolmaster) actually made an identical confession to a boy of ten years old?

and to bring up in the nurture and admonition of the Lord, was not a little perplexed by the sudden disappearance of his wife. At first he supposed that she had been translated, but, finding that she had not left the traditional mantle behind her, he abandoned this supposition in favour of quite a different, and indeed a more plausible one. He now believed her to be the scarlet woman in the Apocalypse, with variations. On arrival in Egypt he hired an old native nurse, and sailed for Odessa. Once in Russia he could find Gog and Magog, and present to them the child as Antichrist. For he was now persuaded that he himself was the First Beast, and would ask the sceptic to count his seven heads and ten horns. The heads, however, rarely totted up accurately!

At this point the accounts of Mr. Turle and Mathilde diverge slightly. The cleric affirms that he was induced by a Tartar lady, of an honourable and ancient profession, to accompany her to Tibet "to be initiated into the mysteries." He was, of course, robbed and murdered with due punctuality, in the town of Kiev. Mathilde's story is that he travelled to Kiev on the original quest, and died of typhoid or cholera. In any case, he died at Kiev in 1839. This fixes the date of the child's birth at 1837. His faithful nurse conveyed him safely to England, where his relatives provided for his maintenance and education.

With the close of this romantic chapter in his early history we lose all reliable traces for some years. One flash alone illumines the darkness of his boyhood; in 1853, after being prepared for confirmation, he cried out in full assembly, instead of kneeling to receive the blessing of the officiating bishop, "I renounce for ever this idolatrous church;" and was quietly removed.

He told Mathilde Doriac that he had been to Eton and Cambridge—neither institution, however, preserves any record of such admission. The imagination of George, indeed, is tremendously fertile with regard to events in his own life. His own story is that he entered Trinity College, Cambridge, in 1856, and was sent down two years later for an article which he had contributed to some University or College Magazine. No confirmation of any sort is to be found anywhere with regard to these or any other statements of our author. There is, however, no doubt that in 1861 he quarrelled with his family; went over to Paris, where he settled down, at first, like every tufthead, somewhere in the Quartier Latin; later, with Mathilde Doriac, the noble woman who became his mistress and held to him through all the terrible tragedy of his moral, mental, and physical life, in the Rue du Faubourg-Poissonnière. At his house there the frightful scene of '68 took place, and it was there too that he was apprehended after the murders which he describes so faithfully in "Abysmos." He had just finished this poem with a shriek of triumph, and had read it through to the appalled Mathilde "avec des yeux de flamme et de gestes incohérentes," when, foaming at the mouth, and "hurlant de blasphèmes indicibles," he fell upon her with extraordinary violence of passion; the door opened, officers appeared, the arrest was effected. He was committed to an asylum, for there could be no longer any doubt of his complete insanity; for three weeks he had been raving with absinthe and satyriasis. He survived his confinement no long time; the burning of the asylum with its inmates was one of the most terrible events of the war of 1870. So died one of the most talented Englishmen of his century, a man who for wide knowledge of men and things was truly to be envied, yet one who sold his birthright for a mess of beastlier pottage than ever Esau guzzled, who sold soul and body to Satan for sheer love of sin, whose mere lust of perversion is so intense that it seems to absorb every other emotion and interest. Never since God woke light from chaos has such a tragedy been unrolled before men, step after step toward the lake of Fire!

At his house all his writings were seized, and, it is believed, destroyed. The single most fortunate exception is that of a superbly jewelled writing-case, now in the possession of the present editor, in which were found the MSS. which are here published. Mathilde, who knew how he treasured its contents, preserved it by saying to the officer, "But, sir, that is mine." On opening this it was found to contain, besides these MSS., his literary will. All MSS. were to be published thirty years after his death, not before. He would gain no spurious popularity as a reflection of the age he lived in. "Tennyson," he says, "will die before sixty years are gone by: if I am to be beloved of men, it shall be because my work is for all times and all men, because it is greater than all the gods of chance and change, because it has the heart of the human race beating in every line."· This is a patch of magenta to mauve, undoubtedly; but — ! The present collection of verses will hardly be popular; if the lost works turn up, of course it may be that there may be found "shelter for songs that recede." Still, even here, one is, on the whole, more attracted than repelled; the author has enormous power, and he never scruples to use it, to drive us half mad with horror, or, as in his earlier most exquisite works, to move us to the noblest thoughts and deeds. True, his debt to contemporary writers is a little obvious here and there; but these are small blemishes on a series of poems whose originality is always striking, and often dreadful, in its broader features.

We cannot leave George Bishop without a word of inquiry as to what became of the heroic figure of Mathilde Doriac. It is a bitter task to have to write in cold blood the dreadful truth about her death. She had the misfortune to contract, in the last few days of her life with him, the same terrible disease which he describes in the last poem of his collection. This shock, coming so soon after, and, as it were, as an unholy perpetual reminder of the madness and sequestration of her lover, no less than of his infidelity, unhinged her mind, and she shot herself on July 5, 1869. Her last letter to Madame J—— S—— is one of the tenderest and most pathetic ever written. She seems to have been really loved by George, in his wild, infidel fashion : "All Night " and "Victory," among others, are obviously inspired by her beauty; and her devotion to him, the abasement of soul, the prostitution of body, she underwent for and with him, is one of the noblest stories life has known. She seems to have dived with him, yet ever trying to raise his soul from the quagmire; if God is just at all, she shall stand more near to His right hand than the vaunted virgins who would soil no hem of vesture to save their brother from the worm that dieth not!

The Works of George Archibald Bishop will speak for themselves; it would be both impertinent and superfluous in me to point out in detail their many and varied excellences, or their obvious faults. The *raison d'être*, though, of their publication, is worthy of especial notice. I refer to their psychological sequence, which agrees with their chronological order. His life-history, as well as his literary remains, gives us an idea of the progression of diabolism as it really is; not as it is painted. Note also, (1) the increase of selfishness in pleasure, (2) the diminution of his sensibility to physical charms. Pure and sane is his early work; then he is carried into the outer current of the great vortex of Sin, and whirls lazily through the sleepy waters of mere sensualism; the pace quickens, he grows fierce in the mysteries of Sapphism and the cult of Venus Aversa with women; later of the same forms of vice with men, all mingled with wild talk of religious dogma and a general exaltation of Priapism at the expense, in particular, of Christianity, in which religion, however, he is undoubtedly a believer till the last (the pious will quote James ii. 19, and the infidel will observe that he died in an asylum); then the full swing of the tide catches him, the mysteries of death become more and more an obsession, and he is flung headlong into Sadism, Necrophilia, all the maddest, fiercest vices that the mind of fiends ever brought up from the pit. But always to the very end his power is unexhausted, immense, terrible. His delirium does not amuse ; it appals ! A man who could conceive as he did must himself have had some glorious chord in his heart vibrating to the eternal principle of Boundless Love. That this love was wrecked is for me, in some sort a relative of his, a real and bitter sorrow. He might have been so great ! He missed Heaven ! Think kindly of him !

169. *Correctly rhymes.*[41]—Such lines, however noble in sentiment, as : " À bas les Anglais ! The Irish up ! " will not be admitted to the competition. Irish is accented on the penultimate—bad cess to the bloody Saxons that made it so !

The same with Tarshish (see Browning, *Pippa Passes*, II., in the long speech of Bluphocks) and many others.

173. *The liar Copleston.*[42] *—Bishop of Cal-

* Copies were sent to any living persons mentioned in the " Sword of Song," accompanied by the following letter :

Letters and Telegrams : BOLESKINE FOYERS is sufficient address.

Bills, Writs, Summonses, etc. : CAMP XI., THE BALTORO GLACIER, BALTISTAN.

O Millionaire !	My lord Marquis,
Mr. Editor !	My lord Viscount,
Dear Mrs. Eddy,	My lord Earl,
Your Holiness the Pope !	My lord,
Your·Imperial Majesty !	My lord Bishop,
Your Majesty !	Reverend sir,
Your Royal Highness !	Sir,
Dear Miss Corelli,	Fellow,
Your Serene Highness !	Dog !
My lord Cardinal,	Mr. Congressman,
My lord Archbishop,	Mr. Senator,
My lord Duke,	Mr. President,

(or the feminine of any of these), as shown by underlining it,
Courtesy demands, in view of the
  (*a*) tribute to your genius
  (*b*) attack on your (1) political
             (2) moral
             (3) social
             (4) mental
             (5) physical character
  (*c*) homage to your grandeur
  (*d*) reference to your conduct
  (*e*) appeal to your better feelings
on page —— of my masterpiece, "The Sword of Song," that I should send you a copy, as I do herewith, to give you an opportunity of defending yourself against my monstrous assertions, thanking me for the advertisement, or——in short, replying as may best seem to you to suit the case.

Your humble, obedient servant,
ALEISTER CROWLEY.

cutta. While holding the see of Ceylon he wrote a book in which " Buddhism " is described as consisting of " devil-dances." Now, when a man, in a position to know the facts, writes a book of the subscription-cadging type, whose value for this purpose depends on the suppression of these facts, I think I am to be commended for my moderation in using the term " liar."

212.—*Ibsen.*[43]—Norwegian dramatist. This and the next sentence have nineteen distinct meanings. As, however, all (with one doubtful exception) are true, and taken together synthetically connote my concept, I have let the passage stand.

219. *I was Lord Roberts, he De Wet.*[44]—*Vide* Sir A. Conan Doyle's masterly fiction, " The Great Boer War."

222. *Hill.*[45]—An archaic phrase signifying kopje.

223. *Ditch.*[46]—Probably an obsolete slang term for spruit.

273. *Some.*[47]—The reader may search modern periodicals for this theory.

282. *The Tmolian.*[48]—Tmolus, who decided the musical contest between Pan and Apollo in favour of the latter.

321. *As masters teach.*[49]—Consult Vivekananda, *op. cit.*, or the *Hathayoga Pradipika.* Unfortunately, I am unable to say where (or even whether) a copy of this latter work exists.

331, 332. *Stand.—(Stephen) or sit (Paul).*[50] Acts vii. 36 ; Heb. xii. 2.

337. *Samadhi-Dak.*[51]— " Ecstasy-of-meditation mail."

338. *Maha-Meru.*[52]—The "mystic mountain" of the Hindus. See Southey's *Curse of Kehama.*

339. *Gaurisankar.*[53]— Called also Chomokankar, Devadhunga, and Everest.

341. *Chogo.*[54]—The Giant. This is the native name of " K²" ; or Mount Godwin-Austen, as Col. Godwin-Austen would call .it. It is the second highest known mountain in the world, as Devadhunga is the first.

356. *The history of the West.*[55]—

De Acosta (José)	Natural and Moral History of the Indies.
Alison, Sir A. .	History of Scotland.
Benzoni . . .	History of the New World.
Buckle. . . .	History of Civilisation.
Burton, J. H . .	History of Scotland.
Carlyle . . .	History of Frederick the Great.
Carlyle . . .	Oliver Cromwell.
Carlyle . . .	Past and Present.
Cheruel, A. . .	Dictionnaire historique de la France.
Christian, P . .	Histoire de la Magie

Clarendon, Ld. History of the Great Rebellion.
De Comines, P . Chronicle.
Edwards, Bryan. History of the British Colonies in the W. Indies.
Elton, C . . . Origins of English History.
Erdmann . . . History of Philosophy. Vol. II.
Froude . . . History of England.
Fyffe, C. A. . . History of Modern Europe.
Gardiner, S. R. . History of the Civil War in England.
Gibbon . . . Decline and Fall of the Roman Empire.
Green, J. R. . . A History of the English People.
Guizot . . . . Histoire de la Civilisation.
Hallam, H. . . State of Europe in the Middle Ages.
Hugo, V. . . Napoléon le Petit.
Innes, Prof. C. . Scotland in the Middle Ages.
Kingscote . . History of the War in the Crimea.
Levi, E. . . . Histoire de la Magie.
Macaulay, Ld. . History of England.
McCarthy, J. . A History of our Own Times.
Maistre, Jos. . Œuvres.
Michelet . . . Histoire des Templiers.
Migne, Abbé . Œuvres.
Montalembert . The Monks of the West.
Morley, J. . . Life of Mr. Gladstone.
Motley . . . History of the Dutch Republic.
Napier , . . History of the Peninsular War.
Prescott . . . History of the Conquest of Mexico.
Prescott . . . History of the Conquest of Peru.
Renan . . . . Vie de Jésus.
Robertson, E. W. Historical Essays.
Rosebery, Ld. . Napoleon.
Shakespeare . . Histories.
Society for the Propagation of Religious Truth . . . Transactions, Vols. I.-DCLXVI.
Stevenson, R. L. A Footnote to History.
Thornton, Ethelred, Rev. . . History of the Jesuits.
Waite, A. E. . The Real History of the Rosicrucians.
Wolseley, Ld. . Marlborough.

The above works and many others of less importance were carefully consulted by the Author before passing these lines for the press. Their substantial accuracy is further guaranteed by the Professors of History at Cambridge, Oxford, Berlin, Harvard, Paris, Moscow, and London.

366. *Shot his Chandra.*[56]—Anglicé, shot the moon.
380. *The subtle devilish omission.*[57]—But what are we to say of Christian dialecticians who quote "All things work together for good" out of its context, and call this verse "Christian optimism?" See Caird's "Hegel." Hegel knew how to defend himself, though. As Goethe wrote of him :

"They thought the master too
Inclined to fuss and finick.
The students' anger grew
To frenzy Paganinic.*
They vowed to make him rue
His work in Jena's clinic.
They came, the unholy crew,
The mystic and the cynic :
He had scoffed at God's battue,
The flood for mortal's sin—Icthyosaurian Waterloo !
They eyed the sage askew ;
They searched him through and through
With violet rays actinic.
They asked him ' Wer bist du ?'
He answered slowly ' Bin ich ?' "

387. *The Fish.*[58]—Because of ἰχθύς, which means Fish, And very aptly symbolises Christ. —*Ring and Book* (The Pope), ll. 89, 90.
395. *Dharma.*[59]—Consult the Tripitaka.
409. *I cannot trace the chain.*[60]—"How vain, indeed, are human calculations !"—*The Autobiography of a Flea*, p. 136.
112. *Table-thing.*[61]—"Ere the stuff grow a ring-thing right to wear,"—*The Ring and the Book*, i. 17.
"This pebble-thing, o' the boy-thing." —CALVERLEY, *The Cock and the Bull.*
442. *Caird.*[62]—See his "Hegel."
446. *Says Huxley.*[63]—See "Ethics and Evolution."
459. *Igdrasil.*[64]—The Otz Chiim of the Scandinavians.
467. *Ladies' League.*[65]—Mrs. J. S. Crowley says : "The Ladies' League Was Formed For The Promotion And Defence Of The Reformed Faith Of The Church Of England." (The capitals are hers.) I think we may accept this statement. She probably knows, and has no obvious reasons for misleading.
487. *Sattva.*[66]—The Buddhists, denying an Atman or Soul (an idea of changeless, eternal, knowledge, being, and bliss) represent the fictitious Ego of a man (or a dog) as a temporary agglomeration of particles. Reincarnation only knocks off, as it were, some of the corners of the mass, so that for several births the Ego is constant within limits; hence the possibility of the "magical memory." The "Sattva" is this agglomeration. See my

* Paganini, a famous violinist.

" Science and Buddhism," *infra*, for a full discussion of this point.

518. *And.*[67]—Note the correct stress upon this word. Previously, Mr. W. S. Gilbert has done this in his superb lines :

" Except the plot of freehold land
That held the cot, and Mary, and—"

But his demonstration is vitiated by the bad iambic "and Ma- " ; unless indeed the juxta-position is intentional, as exposing the sophistries of our official prosodists.

548. *The heathen.*[68]—" The wicked shall be turned into hell, and all the nations that forget God."

580. *Satan and Judas.*[69]—At the moment of passing the final proofs I am informed that the character of Judas has been rehabilitated by Mr. Stead (and rightly : is Mr. Abington * paid with a rope ?) and the defence of Satan undertaken by a young society lady authoress —a Miss Corelli—who represents him as an Angel of Light, *i.e.*, one who has been introduced to the Prince of Wales.

But surely there is some one who is the object of universal reprobation amongst Christians ! Permit me to offer myself as a candidate. Sink, I beseech you, these sectarian differences, and combine to declare me at least Anathema Maranatha.

602. *Pangs of Death.*[70]—Dr. Maudsley demands a panegyric upon death. It is true that evolution may bring us a moral sense of astonishing delicacy and beauty. But we are not there yet. A talented but debauched Irishman has composed the following, which I can deplore, but not refute, for this type of man is probably more prone to reproduce his species than any other. He called it "Summa Spes."

I.

Existence being sorrow,
    The cause of it desire,
A merry tune I borrow
    To light upon the lyre :
If death destroy me quite,
    Then, I cannot lament it ;
I've lived, kept life alight,
    And—damned if I repent it !

        Let me die in a ditch,
            Damnably drunk,
            Or lipping a punk,
        Or in bed with a bitch !
            I was ever a hog ;
            Muck ? I am one with it !
        Let me die like a dog ;
        Die, and be done with it !

* Famous Adelphi villain.

II.

As far as reason goes,
    There's hope for mortals yet :
When nothing is that knows,
    What is there to regret ?
Our consciousness depends
    On matter'in the brain ;
When that rots out, and ends,
    There ends the hour of pain.

III.

If we can trust to this,
    Why, dance and drink and revel !
Great scarlet mouths to kiss,
    And sorrow to the devil !
If pangs ataxic creep,
    Or gout, or stone, annoy us,
Queen Morphia, grant thy sleep !
    Let worms, the dears, enjoy us !

IV.

But since a chance remains
    That "I$_1$" survives the body
(So talk the men whose brains
    Are made of smut and shoddy),
I'll stop it if I can.
    (Ah Jesus, if Thou couldest !)
I'll go to Martaban
    To make myself a Buddhist.

V.

And yet : the bigger chance
    Lies with annihilation.
Follow the lead of France,
    Freedom's enlightened nation !
Off ! sacerdotal stealth
    Of faith and fraud and gnosis !
Come, drink me : Here's thy health,
    Arterio-sclerosis ! *

        Let me die in a ditch,
            Damnably drunk,
            Or lipping a punk,
        Or in bed with a bitch !
            I was ever a hog ;
            Muck ? I am one with it !
        Let me die like a dog ;
        Die, and be done with it !

616. *A lizard.*[71]—A short account of the genesis of these poems seems not out of place here. The design of an elaborate parody on

* The hardening of the arteries, which is the predisposing cause of senile decay ; thus taken as the one positive assurance of death.

Browning to be called "Ascension Day and Pentecost" was conceived (and resolved upon) on Friday, November 15, 1901. On that day I left Ceylon, where I had been for several months, practising Hindu meditations, and exposing the dishonesty of the Missionaries, in the intervals of big game shooting. The following day I wrote "Ascension Day," and "Pentecost" on the Sunday, sitting outside the dak-bangla at Madura. These original drafts were small as compared to the present poems.

Ascension Day consisted of :—

p. 144, I flung·. . . .
p. 146, Pray do . . .
p. 147, "But why . . .
p. 149, Here's just . . .
p. 151, I will . . .
to p. 160 , . . . but in Hell ! . . .
p. 161, You see . . .
to end.

Pentecost consisted of :—

p. 164, To-day . . .
p. 168, How very hard . . .
to p. 170, " Proceed ! " . . .
p. 171, My wandering thoughts . . .
to p. 172, All-wickedness . . .
p. 172, Nor lull my soul . . .
to p. 174, . . . and the vision.
p. 176, How easy . . .
to end.

" Berashith " was written at Delhi, March 20 and 21, 1902. Its original title was " Crowleymas Day." It was issued privately in Paris in January 1903. It and " Science and Buddhism " are added to complete the logical sequence from 1898 till now. All, however, has been repeatedly revised. Wherever there seemed a lacuna in the argument an insertion was made, till all appeared a perfect chrysolite. Most of this was done, while the weary hours of the summer (save the mark !) of 1902 rolled over Camp Misery and Camp Despair on the Chogo Ri Glacier, in those rare intervals when one's preoccupation with lice, tinned food, malaria, insoaking water, general soreness, mental misery, and the everlasting snowstorm gave place to a momentary glimmer of any higher form of intelligence than that ever necessarily concentrated on the actual business of camp life. The rest, and the final revision, occupied a good deal of my time during the winter of 1902-1903. The MS. was accepted by the S. P. R. T. in May of this year, and after a post-final revision, rendered necessary by my Irish descent, went to press.

618. *Each life bound ever to the wheel.*[72]—Cf. Whately, " Revelation of a Future State."

652. *This, that, the other atheist's death.*[73]— Their stories are usually untrue ; but let us follow our plan, and grant them all they ask.

709. *A cannibal.*[74]—This word is inept, as it predicates humanity of Christian-hate-Christian.

J'accuse the English language : *anthropophagous* must always remain a comic word.

731. *The Flaming Star.*[75]—Or Pentagram, mystically referred to Jeheshua.

732. *Zohar.*[76]— "Splendour," the three Central Books of the Dogmatic Qabalah.

733. *Pigeon.*[77]—Says an old writer, whom I translate roughly :

" Thou to thy Lamb and Dove devoutly bow,
But leave me, prithee, yet my Hawk and Cow :
And I approve thy Greybeard dotard's smile,
If thou wilt that of Egypt's crocodile."

746. *Lost ! Lost ! Lost !* [78]—See *The Lay of the Last Minstrel.*

759. *Ain Elohim.*[79]—" There is no God ! " so our Bible. But this is really the most sublime affirmation of the Qabalist. "Ain is God."

For the meaning of Ain, and of this idea, see "Berashith," *infra.* The " fool " is He of the Tarot, to whom the number O is attached, to make the meaning patent to a child.

" I insult your idol," quoth the good missionary; " he is but of dead stone. He does not avenge himself. He does not punish me." " I insult your god," replied the Hindu; " he is invisible. He does not avenge himself, nor punish me."

" My God will punish you when you die ! "

" So, when you die, will my idol punish you ! "

No earnest student of religion or draw poker should fail to commit this anecdote to memory.

767. *Mr. Chesterton.*[80]— I must take this opportunity to protest against the charge brought by Mr. Chesterton against the Englishmen " who write philosophical essays on the splendour of Eastern thought."

If he confines his strictures to the translators of that well-known Eastern work the " Old Testament " I am with him ; any modern Biblical critic will tell him what I mean. It took a long time, too, for the missionaries (and Tommy Atkins) to discover that " Budd " was not a " great Gawd." But then they did not want to, and in any case sympathy and intelligence are not precisely the most salient qualities in either soldiers or missionaries. But nothing is more absurd than to compare men like Sir W. Jones, Sir R. Burton, Von Hammer-Purgstall, Sir E. Arnold, Prof. Max Müller, Me, Prof. Rhys Davids, Lane, and the rest of our illustrious Orientalists to the poor and ignorant Hindus whose letters occasionally delight the readers of the *Sporting Times*, such letters being usually written by public scribes for a few pice in the native bazaar. As to "Babus" (Babu, I may mention, is the equivalent to our "Mister," and not the name of a savage tribe), Mr. Chesterton, from his Brixton Brahmaloka, may look forth and see that the "Babu" cannot understand Western ideas; but a distinguished civil servant in the Madras Presidency, second wrangler in a very good year, assured me that he had met a native whose mathematical knowledge was superior to that of the average senior wrangler, and that he had met several others who approached that standard. His specific attack on Madame Blavatsky is equally unjust, as many natives, not theosophists, have spoken to me of her in the highest terms. "Honest Hindus" cannot be expected to think as Mr. Chesterton deems likely, as he is unfortunately himself a Western, and in the same quagmire of misapprehension as Prof. Max. Müller and the rest. Madame Blavatsky's work was to remind the Hindus of the excellence of their own shastras,* to show that some Westerns held identical ideas, and thus to countermine the dishonest representations of the missionaries. I am sufficiently well known as a bitter opponent of "Theosophy" to risk nothing in making these remarks.

I trust that the sense of public duty which inspires these strictures will not be taken as incompatible with the gratitude I owe to him for his exceedingly sympathetic and dispassionate review of my "Soul of Osiris."

I would counsel him, however, to leave alone the Brixton Chapel, and to "work up from his appreciation of the 'Soul of Osiris' to that loftier and wider work of the human imagination, the appreciation of the *Sporting Times!*"

Mr. Chesterton thinks it funny that I should call upon "Shu." Has he forgotten that the Christian God may be most suitably invoked by the name "Yah"? I should be sorry if God were to mistake his religious enthusiasms for the derisive ribaldry of the London "gamin." Similar remarks apply to "El" and other Hebrai-christian deities.

This note is hardly intelligible without the review referred to. I therefore reprint the

* Sacred Books.

portion thereof which is germane to my matter from the *Daily News*, June 18, 1901 :—

To the side of a mind concerned with idle merriment (*sic!*) there is certainly something a little funny in Mr. Crowley's passionate devotion to deities who bear such names as Mout and Nuit, and Ra and Shu, and Hormakhou. They do not seem to the English mind to lend themselves to pious exhilaration. Mr. Crowley says in the same poem :

The burden is too hard to bear,
    I took too adamant a cross ;
This sackcloth rends my soul to wear,
    My self-denial is as dross.
O, Shu, that holdest up the sky,
    Hold up thy servant, lest he die !

We have all possible respect for Mr. Crowley's religious symbols, and we do not object to his calling upon Shu at any hour of the night. Only it would be unreasonable of him to complain if his religious exercises were generally mistaken for an effort to drive away cats.

Moreover, the poets of Mr. Crowley's school have, among all their merits, some genuine intellectual dangers from this tendency to import religions, this free trade in gods. That all creeds are significant and all gods divine we willingly agree. But this is rather a reason for being content with our own than for attempting to steal other people's. The affectation in many modern mystics of adopting an Oriental civilisation and mode of thought must cause much harmless merriment among the actual Orientals. The notion that a turban and a few vows will make an Englishman a Hindu is quite on a par with the idea that a black hat and an Oxford degree will make a Hindu an Englishman. We wonder whether our Buddhistic philosophers have ever read a florid letter in Baboo English. We suspect that the said type of document is in reality exceedingly like the philosophic essays written by Englishmen about the splendour of Eastern thought. Sometimes European mystics deserve something worse than mere laughter at the hands (*sic!*) of Orientals. If ever was one person whom honest Hindus would have been justified in tearing to pieces it was Madame Blavatsky.

That our world-worn men of art should believe for a moment that moral salvation is possible and supremely important is an unmixed benefit. But to believe for a moment that it is to be found by going to particular places or reading particular books or joining particular societies is to make for the thousandth time the mistake that is at once materialism and superstition. If Mr. Crowley and the new mystics think for one moment that an Egyptian desert is more mystic than an English meadow, that a palm tree is more peetic than a Sussex beech, that a broken temple of Osiris is more supernatural than a Baptist chapel in Brixton, then they are sectarians, and only sectarians of no more value to humanity than those who think that the English soil is the only soil worth defending, and the Baptist chapel the only chapel worthy of worship (*sic*). But Mr. Crowley is a strong and genuine poet, and we have little doubt that he will work up from his appreciation of the Temple of Osiris to that loftier and wider work of the human imagination, the appreciation of the Brixton chapel.

G. K. CHESTERTON.

778, 797. *The rest of life, for self-control,*
         For liberation of the soul.[81]
Who said Rats ? Thanks for your advice, Tony Veller, but it came in vain. As the ex-monk* (that shook the bookstall) wrote in confidence to the publisher :

" Existence is mis'ry.
I' th' month Tisri"

* Joseph McCabe, who became a Rationalist writer. The allusion is to Crowley's marriage and subsequent return to the East.

At th' fu' o' th' moon
I were shot wi' a goon.
[Goon is no Scots,
But Greek, Meester Watts.]
We're awa' tae Burma,
Whaur th' groond be firmer
Tae speer th' Mekong.
Chin Chin ! Sae long.
[Long sald be lang :
She'll no care a whang.]
Ve're Rautional babe,
Aundra McAbe."

Note the curious confusion of personality. This shows Absence of Ego, in Pali Anatta, and will seem to my poor spiritually-minded friends an excuse for a course of action they do not understand, and whose nature is beyond them.

782. *Christ ascends.*[82]—And I tell you frankly that if he does not come back by the time I have finished reading these proofs, I shall give him up.

783. *Bell.*[83]—The folios have " bun."

NOTES TO PENTECOST

22. *With sacred thirst.*[1]—" He, soul-hydroptic with a sacred thirst." A Grammarian's Funeral.

23. *Levi.*[2]—Ceremonial magic is not quite so silly as it sounds. Witness the following masterly elucidation of its inner quintessence :—

THE INITIATED INTERPRETATION
OF CEREMONIAL MAGIC.*

It is loftily amusing to the student of magical literature who is not quite a fool—and rare is such a combination !—to note the criticism directed by the Philistine against the citadel of his science. Truly, since our childhood has ingrained into us not only literal belief in the Bible, but also substantial belief in Alf Laylah wa Laylah,† and only adolescence can cure us, we are only too liable, in the rush and energy of dawning manhood, to overturn roughly and rashly both these classics, to regard them both on the same level, as interesting documents from the standpoint of folk-lore and anthropology, and as nothing more.

Even when we learn that the Bible, by a

* This essay forms the introduction to an edition of the "Goetia" of King Solomon.
† "A Thousand and One Nights," commonly called "Arabian Nights."

profound and minute study of the text, may be forced to yield up Qabalistic arcana of cosmic scope and importance, we are too often slow to apply a similar restorative to the companion volume, even if we are the lucky holders of Burton's veritable edition.

To me, then, it remains to raise the Alf Laylah wa Laylah into its proper place once more.

I am not concerned to deny the objective reality of all "magical" phenomena ; if they are illusions, they are at least as real as many unquestioned facts of daily life; and, if we follow Herbert Spencer, they are at least evidence of *some* cause.*

Now, this fact is our base. What is the cause of my illusion of seeing a spirit in the triangle of Art ?

Every smatterer, every expert in psychology, will answer : " That cause lies in your brain."

English children are taught (*pace* the Education Act) that the Universe lies in infinite Space ; Hindu children, in the Akaśa, which is the same thing.

Those Europeans who go a little deeper learn from Fichte, that the phenomenal Universe is the creation of the Ego ; Hindus, or Europeans studying under Hindu Gurus, are

This, incidentally, is perhaps the greatest argument we possess, pushed to its extreme, against the Advaitist theories.--A. C.

told, that by Akaśa is meant the Chitakaśa. The Chitakasa is situated in the "Third Eye," *i.e.*, in the brain. By assuming higher dimensions of space, we can assimilate this fact to Realism; but we have no need to take so much trouble.

This being true for the ordinary Universe, that all sense-impressions are dependent on changes in the brain,* we must include illusions, which are after all sense-impressions as much as "realities" are, in the class of "phenomena dependent on brain-changes."

Magical phenomena, however, come under a special sub-class, since they are willed, and their cause is the series of "real" phenomena called the operations of ceremonial Magic.

These consist of

(1) Sight.
    The circle, square, triangle, vessels, lamps, robes, implements, etc.
(2) Sound.
    The invocations.
(3) Smell.
    The perfumes.
(4) Taste.
    The Sacraments.
(5) Touch.
    As under (1).
(6) Mind.
    The combination of all these and reflection on their significance.

These unusual impressions (1–5) produce unusual brain-changes; hence their summary (6) is of unusual kind. Its projection back into the apparently phenomenal world is therefore unusual.

Herein then consists the reality of the operations and effects of ceremonial magic,† and I conceive that the apology is ample, so far as the "effects" refer only to those phenomena which appear to the magician himself, the appearance of the spirit, his conversation, possible shocks from imprudence, and so on, even to ecstasy on the one hand, and death or madness on the other.

But can any of the effects described in this our book Goetia be obtained, and if so, can you give a rational explanation of the circumstances? Say you so?

I can, and will.

The spirits of the Goetia are portions of the human brain.

Their seals therefore represent (Mr. Spencer's

* Thought is a secretion of the brain (Weissmann). Consciousness is a function of the brain (Huxley).—A. C.
† Apart from its value in obtaining one-pointedness. On this subject consult בראשית, *infra.*—A. C.

projected cube) methods of stimulating or regulating those particular spots (through the eye).

The names of God are vibrations calculated to establish :

(*a*) General control of the brain. (Establishment of functions relative to the subtle world.)

(*b*) Control over the brain in detail. (Rank or type of the Spirit.)

(*c*) Control of one special portion. (Name of the Spirit.)

The perfumes aid this through smell. Usually the perfume will only tend to control a large area; but there is an attribution of perfumes to letters of the alphabet enabling one, by a Qabalistic formula, to spell out the Spirit's name.

I need not enter into more particular discussion of these points; the intelligent reader can easily fill in what is lacking.

If, then, I say, with Solomon :

"The Spirit Cimieries teaches logic," what I mean is :

"Those portions of my brain which subserve the logical faculty may be stimulated and developed by following out the processes called 'The Invocation of Cimieries.'"

And this is a purely materialistic rational statement; it is independent of any objective hierarchy at all. Philosophy has nothing to say; and Science can only suspend judgment, pending a proper and methodical investigation of the facts alleged.

Unfortunately, we cannot stop there. Solomon promises us that we can (1) obtain information; (2) destroy our enemies; (3) understand the voices of nature; (4) obtain treasure; (5) heal diseases, etc. I have taken these five powers at random; considerations of space forbid me to explain all.

(1) Brings up facts from sub-consciousness.

(2) Here we come to an interesting fact. It is curious to note the contrast between the noble means and the apparently vile ends of magical rituals. The latter are disguises for sublime truths. "To destroy our enemies" is to realise the illusion of duality, to excite compassion.

(Ah! Mr. Waite,* the world of Magic is a mirror, wherein who sees muck is muck.)

(3) A careful naturalist will understand much from the voices of the animals he has studied long. Even a child knows the difference of a cat's miauling and purring. The faculty may be greatly developed.

(4) Business capacity may be stimulated.

(5) Abnormal states of the body may be

* A poet of great ability. He edited a book called "Of Black Magic and of Pacts," in which he vilifies the same.

corrected, and the involved tissues brought back to tone, in obedience to currents started from the brain.

So for all other phenomena. There is no effect which is truly and necessarily miraculous.

Our Ceremonial Magic fines down, then, to a series of minute, though of course empirical, physiological experiments, and whoso will carry them through intelligently need not fear the result.

I have all the health, and treasure, and logic I need; I have no time to waste. "There is a lion in the way." For me these practices are useless; but for the benefit of others less fortunate I give them to the world, together with this explanation of, and apology for, them.

I trust that the explanation will enable many students who have hitherto, by a puerile objectivity in their view of the question, obtained no results, to succeed; that the apology may impress upon our scornful men of science that the study of the bacillus should give place to that of the baculum, the little to the great—how great one only realises when one identifies the wand with the Mahalingam,* up which Brahma flew at the rate of 84,000 yojanas a second for 84,000 mahakalpas, down which Vishnu flew at the rate of 84,000 crores of yojanas a second for 84,000 crores of mahakalpas—yet neither reached an end.

But I reach an end.

23. *The cryptic Coptic.*[3]—Vide the Papyrus of Bruce.

24. *ANET' AER-K, etc.*[4]—Invocation of Ra. From the Papyrus of Harris.

26. *MacGregor.*[5]—The Mage.

29. *Abramelin.*[6]—The Mage.

32. *Ancient rituals.*[7]—From the Papyrus of MRS. Harris.†

33. *Golden Dawn.*[8]—These rituals were later annexed by Madame Horos,‡ that superior Swami. The earnest seeker is liable to some pretty severe shocks. To see one's "Obligation" printed in the *Daily Mail!!!* Luckily, I have no nerves.

49. राम राम || *etc.*[9]—"Thou, as I, art God (*for this is the esoteric meaning of the common Hindu salutation*). A long road and a heavy price! To know is always a difficult work . . . Hullo! Bravo! Thy name (I have seen) is written in the stars. Come with me, pupil! I will give thee medicine for the mind."

* The Phallus of Shiva the Destroyer. It is really identical with the Qabalistic "Middle Pillar" of the "Tree of Life."

† An imaginary lady to whom Sairey Gamp in Dickens' "Martin Chuzzlewit" used to appeal.

‡ *Vide* the daily papers of June–July 1901.

Cf. Macbeth : "Canst thou not minister to a mind diseased?"

58. वस ||.[10]—Enough.

60. किसवासते ||.[11]—Why?

60. कय होग.[1]—What will be?

61. *Strange and painful attitude.*[13] — Siddhasana.

62. *He was very rude.*[14]—The following is a sample :—

"O Devatas! behold this yogi! O Chela! Accursèd abode of Tamas art thou! Eater of Beef, guzzling as an Herd of Swine! Sleeper of a thousand sleeps, as an Harlot heavy with Wine! Void of Will! Sensualist! Enraged Sheep! Blasphemer of the Names of Shiva and of Devi! Christian in disguise! Thou shalt be reborn in the lowest Avitchi! Fast! Walk! Wake! these are the keys of the Kingdom! Peace be with thy Beard! Aum!"

This sort of talk did me good: I hope it may do as much for you.

63. *With eyes well fixed on my proboscis.*[15]—See Bhagavad-Gita, Atmasamyamyog.

67. *Brahma-charya.*[16]—Right conduct, and in particular, chastity in the highest sense.

72. *Baccy.*[17]—A poisonous plant used by nicotomaniacs in their orgies and debauches. "The filthy tobacco habit," says "Elijah the Restorer" of Zion, late of Sydney and Chicago. That colossal genius-donkey, Shaw, is another of them. But see Calverley.

78. *His hat.*[18] It may be objected that Western, but never Eastern, magicians turn their headgear into a cornucopia or Pandora's box. But I must submit that the Hat Question is still *sub judice.* Here's a health to Lord Ronald Gower !

86. *Swinburne.*[19]—

" But this thing is God,
To be man with thy might,
To grow straight in the strength of thy spirit,
and live out thy life as the light."—*Hertha.*

104. *My big beauty.*[20]—Pink on Spot; Player, Green, in Hand. But I have "starred" since I went down in *that* pocket.

120. *My Balti coolies.*[21]—See my "The Higher the Fewer." *

125. *Eton.*[22]—A school, noted for its breed of cads. The battle of Waterloo (1815) was won on its playing-fields.

128-30. *I've seen them.*[23]—Sir J. Maundevill, "Voiage and Travill," ch. xvi., recounts a similar incident, and, Christian as he is, puts a similar poser.

135. *A—What?*[24]—I beg your pardon. It was a slip.

146. *Tahuti.*[25]—In Coptic, Thoth.

* Title of a (forthcoming) collection of papers on mountain exploration, etc.

149. *Ra.*[26]—The Sun-God.

149. *Nuit.*[27]—The Star-Goddess.

152. *Campbell.*[28]—"The waters wild went o'er his child, And he was left lamenting."

152. *The Ibis Head.*[29]—Characteristic of Tahuti.

157. *Roland's crest.*[30]—See "Two Poets of Croisic," xci.

159. *A jest.*[31]—See above : Ascension Day.

126. *A mysterious way.*[32]—
"God moves in a mysterious way
    His wonders to perform ;
He plants His footsteps in the sea,
    And rides upon the storm."
Intentional species?

171. *The old hymn.*[33]—This hymn, quoted I fear with some failure of memory—I have not the documents at hand—is attributed to the late Bishop of Natal, though I doubt this, as the consistent and trustful piety of its sentiment is ill-suited to the author of those disastrous criticisms of the Pentateuch. The hymn is still popular in Durban.

Its extraordinary beauty, for a fragment, is only surpassed by Sappho's matchless :

— ᵕ — ᵕ — ᵕ — ᵕ
— ᵕ — ᵕ — ᵕ — ᵕ
— ᵕ — ᵕ 'εννεα κ' εξε -
κοντα ᵕ — —

185. "*How very hard.*"[34]—
"How very hard it is to be
    A Christian !"—*Easter Day*, I. i. 2.

195. *Srotapatti.*[35]—One who has "entered the stream" of Nirvana.
For the advantages of so doing, see the appended Jataka story, which I have just translated from a Cingalese Palm-leaf MS. See Appendix I.

228. *You know for me, etc.*[36]—See Huxley, Hume, 199, 200.

239. *Spirit and matter are the same.*[37]—See Huxley's reply to Lilly.

273. "*I am not what I see.*"[38]—*In Memoriam.* But see H. Spencer, "Principles of Psychology," General Analysis, ch. vi.

281. "*'Tis lotused Buddha.*"[39]—
"Hark! that sad groan ! Proceed no further ! 'Tis laurelled Martial roaring murther."
            —BURNS, *Epigram.*
But Buddha cannot really roar, since he has passed away by that kind of passing away which leaves nothing whatever behind.

322. *A mere law without a will.*[40]—I must not be supposed to take any absurd view of the meaning of the word "law." This passage denies any knowledge of ultimate causes, not asserts it. But it tends to deny benevolent foresight, and *a fortiori* benevolent omnipotence.
Cf. Zoroaster, *Oracles :* "Look not upon the

visible image of the Soul of Nature, for her name is Fatality."

Ambrosius is very clear on this point. I append his famous MS. complete in its English Translation, as it is so rare. How rare will be appreciated when I say that no copy either of original or translation occurs in the British Museum ; the only known copy, that in the Bodleian, is concealed by the pre-Adamite system of cataloguing in vogue at that hoary but unvenerable institution. For convenience the English has been modernised. See Appendix II.

329. *Maya fashioned it.*[41]—Sir E. Arnold, *Light of Asia.*

335. *Why should the Paramatma cease.*[42]—The Universe is represented by orthodox Hindus as alternating between Evolution and Involution. But apparently, in either state, it is the other which appears desirable, since the change is operated by Will, not by Necessity.

341. *Blavatsky's Himalayan Balm.*[43]—See the corkscrew theories of A. P. Sinnett in that masterpiece of confusion of thought — and nomenclature !—"Esoteric Buddhism." Also see the "Voice of the Silence, or, The Butler's Revenge." Not Bp. Butler.

366. *Ekam Advaita.*[44]—Of course I now reject this utterly. But it is, I believe, a stage of thought necessary for many or most of us. The bulk of these poems was written when I was an Advaitist, incredible as the retrospect now appears. My revision has borne Buddhist fruits, but some of the Advaita blossom is left. Look, for example, at the dreadfully Papistical tendency of my celebrated essay :

AFTER AGNOSTICISM.

Allow me to introduce myself as the original Irishman whose first question on landing at New York was, "Is there a Government in this country?" and on being told "Yes," instantly replied, "Then I'm agin it." For after some years of consistent Agnosticism, being at last asked to contribute to an Agnostic organ, for the life of me I can think of nothing better than to attack my hosts ! Insidious cuckoo! Ungrateful Banyan ! My shame drives me to Semitic analogy, and I sadly reflect that if I had been Balaam, I should not have needed an ass other than myself to tell me to do the precise contrary of what is expected of me.

For this is my position ; while the postulates of Agnosticism are in one sense eternal, I believe that the conclusions of Agnosticism are daily to be pushed back. We know our ignorance ; with that fact we are twitted by those who do not know enough to understand even what we mean when we say so; but the limits of knowledge, slowly receding, yet never so far as to permit us to unveil the awful and impenetrable adytum of consciousness, or that of matter, must one day be suddenly widened by the forging of a new weapon.

Huxley and Tyndall have prophesied this before I was born; sometimes in vague language, once or twice clearly enough; to me it is a source of the utmost concern that their successors should not always see eye to eye with them in this respect.

Professor Ray Lankester, in crushing the unhappy theists of the recent *Times* controversy, does not hesitate to say that Science *can never* throw any light on certain mysteries.

Even the theist is justified in retorting that Science, if this be so, may as well be discarded; for these are problems which must ever intrude upon the human mind—upon the mind of the scientist most of all.

To dismiss them by an act of will is at once heroic and puerile: courage is as necessary to progress as any.quality that we possess; and as courage is in either case required, the courage of ignorance (necessarily sterile, though wanted badly enough while our garden was choked by theological weeds) is less desirable than the courage which embarks on the always desperate philosophical problem.

Time and again, in the history of Science, a period has arrived when, gorged with facts, she has sunk into a lethargy of reflection accompanied by appalling nightmares in the shape of impossible theories. Such a nightmare now rides us; once again philosophy has said its last word, and arrived at a deadlock. Aristotle, in reducing to the fundamental contradictions-in-terms which they involve the figments of the Pythagoreans, the Eleatics, the Platonists, the Pyrrhonists; Kant, in his *reductio ad absurdum* of the Thomists, the Scotists, the Wolffians,—all the warring brood, alike only in the inability to reconcile the ultimate antinomies of a cosmogony only grosser for its pinchbeck spirituality; have, I take it, found their modern parallel in the ghastly laughter of Herbert Spencer, as fleshed upon the corpses of Berkeley and the Idealists from Fichte and Hartmann to Lotze and Trendelenburg he drives the reeking fangs of his imagination into the palpitating vitals of his own grim masterpiece of reconcilement, self-deluded and yet self-conscious of its own delusion.

History affirms that such a deadlock is invariably the prelude to a new enlightenment: by such steps we have advanced, by such we shall advance. The "horror of great darkness" which is scepticism must ever be broken by some heroic master-soul, intolerant of the cosmic agony.

We then await his dawn.

May I go one step further, and lift up my voice and prophesy? I would indicate the direction in which this darkness must break. Evolutionists will remember that nature cannot rest. Nor can society. Still less the brain of man.

" Audax omnia perpeti
Gens humana ruit per vetitum nefas." *

We have destroyed the meaning of vetitum nefas and are in no fear of an imaginary cohort of ills and terrors. Having perfected one weapon, reason, and found it destructive to all falsehood, we have been (some of us) a little apt to go out to fight with no other weapon. "FitzJames's blade was sword and shield," † and that served him against the murderous bludgeon-sword of the ruffianly Highlander he happened to meet; but he would have fared ill had he called a Western Sheriff a liar, or gone off Boer-sticking on Spion Kop.

Reason has done its utmost; theory has glutted us, and the motion of the ship is a little trying; mixed metaphor—excellent in a short essay like this—is no panacea for all mental infirmities; we must seek another guide. All the facts science has so busily collected, varied as they seem to be, are in reality all of the same kind. If we are to have one salient fact, a fact for a real advance, it must be a fact of a different *order*.

Have we such a fact to hand? We have.

First, what do we mean by a fact of a different order? Let me take an example; the most impossible being the best for our purpose. The Spiritualists, let us suppose, go mad and begin to talk sense. (I can only imagine that such would be the result.) All their "facts" are proved. We prove a world of spirits, the existence of God, the immortality of the soul, etc. But, with all that, we are not really one step advanced into the heart of the inquiry which lies at the heart of philosophy, "What *is* anything?"

I see a cat.

Dr. Johnson says it is a cat.

Berkeley says it is a group of sensations.

Cankaracharya says it is an illusion, an incarnation, or God, according to the hat he has got on, and is talking through.

Spencer says it is a mode of the Unknowable.

But none of them seriously doubt the fact that I exist; that a cat exists; that one sees the other. All—bar Johnson—hint—but oh! how dimly!—at what I now know to be—*true?*—no, not necessarily true, but *nearer the truth.* Huxley goes deeper in his demolition of Descartes. With him, "I see a cat," proves "some-

* Horace, *Odes*, I. 3.
† Scott, *The Lady of the Lake.*

thing called consciousness exists." He denies the assertion of duality ; he has no datum to assert the denial of duality. I have.

Consciousness, as we know it, has one essential quality : the opposition of subject and object. Reason has attacked this and secured that complete and barren victory of convincing without producing conviction.* It has one quality apparently not essential, that of exceeding impermanence. If we examine what we call steady thought, we shall find that its rate of change is in reality inconceivably swift. To consider it, to watch it, is bewildering, and to some people becomes intensely terrifying. It is as if the solid earth were suddenly swept away from under one, and there were some dread awakening in outer space amid the rush of incessant meteors—lost in the void.

All this is old knowledge ; but who has taken steps to alter it? The answer is forbidding : truth compels me to say, the mystics of all lands.

Their endeavour has been to slow the rate of change ; their methods perfect quietude of body and mind, produced in varied and too often vicious ways. Regularisation of the breathing is the best known formula. Their results are contemptible, we must admit ; but only so because empirical. An unwarranted reverence has overlaid the watchfulness which science would have enjoined, and the result is muck and misery, the wreck of a noble study.

But what is the one fact on which all agree? The one fact whose knowledge has been since religion began the all-sufficient passport to their doubtfully-desirable company ?

This : that " I see a cat" is not only an unwarrantable assumption but a lie ; that the duality of consciousness ceases suddenly, once the rate of change has been sufficiently slowed down, so that, even for a few seconds, the relation of subject and object remains impregnable.

It is a circumstance of little interest to the present essayist that this annihilation of duality is associated with intense and passionless peace and delight ; the fact has been a bribe to the unwary, a bait for the charlatan, a hindrance to the philosopher ; let us discard it.†

* Hume, and Kant in the " Prolegomena," discuss this phenomenon unsatisfactorily.—A. C.

† It is this rapture which has ever been the bond between mystics of all shades ; and the obstacle to any accurate observation of the phenomenon, its true causes, and so on. This must always be a stumbling-block to more impressionable minds ; but there is no doubt as to the fact—it *is* a fact—and its present isolation is to be utterly deplored. May I entreat men ,of Science to conquer the prejudices natural to them when the justly despised ideas of mysticism are mentioned, and to attack the problem *ab initio* on the severely critical and austerely arduous lines which have distinguished their labours in other fields? —A. C.

More, though the establishment of this new estate of consciousness seems to open the door to a new world, a world where the axioms of Euclid may be absurd, and the propositions of Keynes * untenable, let us not fall into the error of the mystics, by supposing that in this world is necessarily a final truth, or even a certain and definite gain of knowledge.

But that a field for research is opened up no sane man may doubt. Nor may one question that the very first fact is of a nature disruptive of difficulty philosophical and reasonable ; since the phenomenon does not invoke the assent of the reasoning faculty. The arguments which reason may bring to bear against it are self-destructive ; reason has given consciousness the lie, but consciousness survives and smiles. Reason is a part of consciousness and can never be greater than its whole ; this Spencer sees ; but reason is not even any part of this new consciousness (which I, and many others, have too rarely achieved) and therefore can never touch it : this I see, and this will I hope be patent to those ardent and spiritually-minded agnostics of whom Huxley and Tyndall are for all history-time the prototypes. Know or doubt ! is the alternative of highwayman Huxley ; " Believe" is not to be admitted ; this is fundamental ; in this agnosticism can never change ; this must ever command our moral as our intellectual assent.

But I assert my strong conviction that ere long we shall have done enough of what is after all the schoolmaster work of correcting the inky and ill-spelt exercises of the theological dunces in that great class-room, the world ; and found a little peace—while they play—in the intimate solitude of the laboratory and the passionless rapture of research—research into those very mysteries which our dunces have solved by rule of thumb ; determining the nature of a bee by stamping on it, and shouting " bee"; while we patiently set to work with microscopes, and say nothing till we know, nor more than need be when we do.

But I am myself found guilty of this rôle of schoolmaster : I will now therefore shut the doors and retire again into the laboratory where my true life lies.

403, 405. *Reason and concentration.*[45]—The results of reasoning are always assailable : those of concentration are vivid and certain, since they are directly presented to consciousness. And they are more certain than consciousness itself, since one who has experienced them may, with consciousness, doubt consciousness, but can in no state doubt them.

412. *Ganesh.*[46]—The elephant-headed God, son of Shiva and Bhavani. He presides over obstacles.

* Author of a text-book on " Formal Logic."

The prosodist will note the "false quantity" of this word. But this is as it should be, for Ganesha pertains to Shiva, and with Shiva all quantity is false, since, as Parameshvara, he is without quantity or quality.

485. *Carroll.*[47]—See "Alice in Wonderland," Cap. Ult.

508. *Kusha-grass.*[48]—The sacred grass of the Hindus.

509. *Mantra.*[49]—A sacred verse, suitable for constant repetition, with a view to quieting the thought. Any one can see how simple and effective a means this is.

519. *Gayatri.*[50]—This is the translation of the most holy verse of the Hindus. The gender of Savitri has been the subject of much discussion, and I believe grammatically it is masculine. But for mystical reasons I have made it otherwise. Fool!

557. *Prayer.*[51]—This fish-story is literally true. The condition was that the Almighty should have the odds of an unusually long line,—the place was really a swift stream, just debouching into a lake—and of an unusual slowness of drawing in the cast.

But what does any miracle prove? If the Affaire Cana were proved to me, I should merely record the facts: Water may under certain unknown conditions become wine. It is a pity that the owner of the secret remains silent, and entirely lamentable that he should attempt to deduce from his scientific knowledge cosmic theories which have nothing whatever to do with it.

Suppose Edison, having perfected the phonograph, had said, "I alone can make dumb things speak; argal, I am God." What would the world have said if telegraphy had been exploited for miracle-mongering purposes? Are these miracles less or greater than those of the Gospels?

Before we accept Mrs. Piper,* we want to know most exactly the conditions of the experiment, and to have some guarantee of the reliability of the witnesses.

At Cana of Galilee the conditions of the transformation are not stated—save that they give loopholes innumerable for chicanery—and the witnesses are all drunk! (thou hast kept the good wine *till now: i.e.* till men have well drunk—Greek, μεθυσθωσι, *are* well drunk).

And I am to believe this, and a glaring *non sequitur* as to Christ's deity, on the evidence, not even of the inebriated eye-witnesses, but of MSS. of doubtful authorship and date, bearing all the ear-marks of dishonesty. For we must not forget that the absurdities of to-day were most cunning proofs for the poor folk of seventeen centuries ago.

Talking of fish-stories, read John xxi. 1-6,

* A twentieth century medium.

or Luke V. 1-7 (comparisons are odious). But once I met a man by a lake and told him that I had toiled all the morning and had caught nothing, and he advised me to try the other side of the lake; and I caught many fish. But I knew not that it was the Lord.

In Australia they were praying for rain in the churches. The *Sydney Bulletin* very sensibly pointed out how much more reverent and practical it would be, if, instead of constantly worrying the Almighty about trifles, they would pray once and for all for a big range of mountains in Central Australia, which would of course supply rain automatically. No new act of creation would be necessary; faith, we are expressly told, can remove mountains, and there is ice and snow and especially moraine on and about the Baltoro Glacier to build a very fine range; we could well have spared it this last summer.

579. *So much for this absurd affair.*[52]—"About Lieutenant-Colonel Flare."—Gilbert, *Bab Ballads.*

636. *Auto-hypnosis.*[53]—The scientific adversary has more sense than to talk of auto-hypnosis. He bases his objection upon the general danger of the practice, considered as a habit of long standing. In fact,

Lyre and Lancet.
  Recipe for Curried Eggs.

The physiologist reproaches
Poor Mr. Crowley. "This encroaches
Upon your frail cerebral cortex,
And turns its fairway to a vortex.
Your cerebellum with cockroaches
Is crammed; your lobes that thought they caught "X"
Are like mere eggs a person poaches.
But soon from yoga, business worries,
And (frankly I suspect the rubble
Is riddled by specific trouble!)
Will grow like eggs a person curries."
This line, no doubt, requires an answer.

The Last Ditch.

First.   "Here's a johnny with a cancer;
An operation may be useless,
May even harm his constitution,
Or cause his instant dissolution:
Let the worm die, 'tis but a goose less!"
Not you! You up and take by storm him.
You tie him down and chloroform him.
You do not pray to Thoth or Horus,
But make one dash for his pylorus:—
And if ten years elapse, and he
Complains, "O doctor, pity me!
Your cruel 'ands, for goodness sakes
Gave me such 'orrid stomach-aches.

You write him, with a face of flint,
An order for some soda-mint.
So Yoga.   Life's a carcinoma,
Its cause uncertain, not to check.
In vain you cry to Isis : "O ma!
I've got it fairly in the neck."
The surgeon Crowley, with his trocar,
Says you a poor but silly bloke are,
Advises concentration's knife
Quick to the horny growth called life.
"Yoga?   There's danger in the biz !
But, it's the only chance there is!"
(For life, if left alone, is sorrow,
And only fools hope God's to-morrow.)

Up, Guards, and at 'em !

Second, your facts are neatly put ;
—Stay !   In that mouth there lurks a foot !
One surgeon saw so many claps
He thought : "One-third per cent., perhaps,
Of mortals 'scape its woes that knock us,
And bilk the wily gonococcus."
So he is but a simple cynic
Who takes the world to match his clinic ;
And he assuredly may err
Who, keeping cats, thinks birds have fur.
You   say :   "There's   Berridge,   Felkin,
         Mathers,
Hysterics, epileptoids, blathers,
Guttersnipe, psychopath, and mattoid,
With ceremonial magic that toyed."
Granted.   Astronomy's no myth,
But it produced Piazzi Smyth.
What crazes actors ? Why do surgeons
Go mad and cut up men like sturgeons?
(These questions are the late Chas. Spur-
         geon's.)
Of yogi I could quote you hundreds
In science, law, art, commerce noted.
They fear no lunacy : their one dread's
Not for their noddles doom-devoted.
They are not like black bulls (that shunned
         reds
In vain) that madly charge the goathead
Of rural Pan, because some gay puss
Had smeared with blood his stone Priapus.
They are as sane as politicians
And people who subscribe to missions.
This says but little ; a long way are
Yogi more sane than such as they are.
You have conceived your dreadful bogey,
From seeing many a raving Yogi.
These haunt your clinic ; but the sound
Lurk in an unsuspected ground,
Dine with you, lecture in your schools,
Share your intolerance of fools,
And, while the Yogi you condemn,
Listen, say nothing, barely smile.
O if you but suspected them
Your silence would match theirs awhile !

*A Classical Research. [Protectionists may serve
if the supply of Hottentots gives out.]*

I took three Hottentots alive.
Their scale was one, two, three, four, five,
Infinity. To think of men so
I could not bear : a new Colenso
I bought them to assuage their plight,
Also a book by Hall and Knight
On Algebra. . I hired wise men
To teach them six, seven, eight, nine, ten.
One of the Hottentots succeeded.
Few schoolboys know as much as he did !
The others sank beneath the strain :
It broke, not fortified, the brain.

The Bard a Brainy Beggar.

Now (higher on the Human Ladder)
Lodge is called mad, and Crowley madder.
(The shafts of Science who may dodge ?
I've not a word to say for Lodge.)
Yet may not Crowley be the one
Who safely does what most should shun ?

Alpine Analogy.

Take Oscar Eckenstein—he climbs
Alone, unroped, a thousand times.
He scales his peak, he makes his pass ;
He does not fall in a crevasse !
But if the Alpine Club should seek
To follow him on pass or peak—
(Their cowardice, their mental rot,
Are balanced nicely—they will not.)
—I see the Alpine Journal's border
Of black grow broader, broader, broader,
Until the Editor himself
Falls from some broad and easy shelf,
And in his death the Journal dies.
Ah ! bombast, footle, simple lies !
Where would you then appear in type ?

*The Poet "retires up." His attitude undig-
nified, his pleasure momentary, the after
results quite disproportionate. He contem-
plates his end.*

Therefore poor Crowley lights his pipe,
Maintains : "The small-shot kills the snipe,
But spares the tiger ; " goes on joking,
And goes on smirking, on invoking,
On climbing, meditating,—failing to think
         of a suitable rhyme at a critical juncture,
Ah !—goes on working, goes on smoking,
Until he goes right on to Woking.

637. *No one supposes me a Saint.*[54]—On inquiry, however, I find that some do.
686. *Amrita.*[55]—The Elixir of Life : the Dew
of Immortality.

688. *Christ.*[56]—See Shri Parananda, ''Commentaries on Matthew and John.''

695. *Direction x.*[57]—*Vide supra,* '' Ascension Day.''

710. *Steel-tired.*[58]—
For Dunlop people did not know
Those nineteen hundred years ago.

723. *Super-consciousness.*[59]—The Christians also claim an ecstasy. But they all admit, and indeed boast, that it is the result of long periods of worry and anxiety about the safety of their precious souls : therefore their ecstasy is clearly a diseased process. The Yogic ecstasy requires absolute calm and health of mind and body. It is useless and dangerous under other conditions even to begin the most elementary practices.

742. *My Eastern friend.*[60]—Abdul Hamid, of the Fort, Colombo, on whom be peace.

755. *Heart.*[61]—
Heart is a trifling misquotation :
This poem is for publication.

810. *Mind the dark doorway there !*[62]—This, like so many other (perhaps all) lines in these poems, is pregnant with a host of hidden meanings. Not only is it physical, of saying good-bye to a friend : but mental, of the darkness of metaphysics ; occult, of the mystical darkness of the Threshold of Initiation : and physiological, containing allusions to a whole group of phenomena, which those who have begun meditation will recognise.

Similarly, a single word may be a mnemonic key to an entire line of philosophical argument.

If the reader chooses, in short, he will find the entire mass of Initiated Wisdom between the covers of this unpretending volume.

AMBROSII MAGI HORTUS ROSARUM *

Translated into English by Christeos Luciftias. Printed by W. Black, at the Wheatsheaf in Newgate, and sold at the Three Keys in Nags-Head Court, Gracechurch St.

Opus.

IT is fitting that I, Ambrose, called I. A. O., should set down the life of our great Father (who now is not, yet whose name must never be spoken among men), in order that the Brethren may know what journeys he undertook in pursuit of that Knowledge whose attainment is their constant study.

Prima Materia.
A. O.

It was at his 119th year,[1] the Star Suaconch [2] being in the sign of the Lion, that our Father set out from his Castle of Ug [3] to attain the Quint-essence or Philosophical Tincture. The way being dark and the Golden Dawn at hand, he did call forth four servants to keep him in the midst of the way, and the Lion roared before him to bid the opposers beware of his coming. On the Bull he rode, and on his left hand and his right marched the Eagle and the Man. But his back was uncovered, seeing that he would not turn.

Custodes.[4]

Sapiens dom-inabitur astris.

And the Spirit of the Path met him. It was a young girl of two and twenty years, and she warned him fairly that without the Serpent [5] his ways were but as wool cast into the dyer's vat. Two-and-twenty scales had the Serpent, and every scale was a path, and every path was alike an enemy and a friend. So he set out, and the darkness grew upon him. Yet could he well perceive a young maiden [6] having a necklace of two-and-seventy

S. S. D. D.

---

* It would require many pages to give even a sketch of this remarkable document. The Qabalistic Knowledge is as authentic as it is profound, but there are also allusions to contemporary occult students, and a certain very small amount of mere absence of meaning. The main satire is of course on the "Chymical Marriage of Christian Rosencreutz." A few only of the serious problems are elucidated in footnotes.

---

[1] *I.e.* when 118 = change, a ferment, strength. Also = before he was 120, the mystic age of a Rosicrucian.
[2] Her-shell = Herschell, or Uranus, the planet which was ascending (in Leo) at Crowley's birth.
[3] Vau and Gimel, the Hierophant and High-Priestess in the Tarot. Hence "from his Castle of Ug" means "from his initiation." We cannot in future do more than indicate the allusions.
[4] The Kerubim.
[5] See Table of Correspondences.
[6] The 22nd Key of the Tarot. The other Tarot symbols can be traced by any one who possesses, and to some degree understands, a pack of the cards. The occult views of the nature of these symbols are in some cases Crowley's own.

pearls, big and round like the breasts of a sea-nymph ; and they gleamed round her like moons. She held in leash the four Beasts, but he strode boldly to her, and kissed her full on her full lips. Wherefore she sighed and fell back a space, and he pressed on. Now at the end of the darkness a fire glowed : she would have hindered him : clung she to his neck and wept. But the fire grew and the light dazzled her ; so that with a shriek she fell. But the beasts flung themselves against the burning gateway of iron, and it gave way. Our Father passed into the fire. Some say that it consumed him utterly and that he died ; howbeit, it is certain that he rose from a sarcophagus, and in the skies stood an angel with a trumpet, and on that trumpet he blew so mighty a blast that the dead rose all from their tombs, and our Father among them. "Now away !" he cried. "I would look upon the sun !" And with that the fire hissed like a myriad of serpents and went out suddenly. It was a green sward golden with buttercups ; and in his way lay a high wall. Before it were two children, and with obscene gestures they embraced, and laughed aloud, with filthy words and acts unspeakable. Over all of which stood the sun calm and radiant, and was glad to be. Now, think ye well, was our Father perplexed ; and he knew not what he would do. For the children left their foulness and came soliciting with shameless words his acquiescence in their sport ; and he, knowing the law of courtesy and of pity, rebuked them not. But master ever of himself he abode alone, about and above. So saw he his virginity deflowered, and his thoughts were otherwhere. Now loosed they his body ; he bade it leap the wall. The giant flower of ocean bloomed above him ! He had fallen headlong into the great deep. As the green and crimson gloom disparted somewhat before his eyes, he was aware of a Beetle that steadily and earnestly moved across the floor of that Sea unutterable. Him he followed ; "for I wit well," thought the Adept, "that he goeth not back to the gross sun of earth. And if the sun hath become a beetle, may the beetle transform into a bird." Wherewith he came to land. Night shone by lamp of waning moon upon a misty landscape. Two paths led him to two towers ; and jackals howled on either. Now the jackal he knew ; and the tower he knew not yet. Not two would he conquer—that were easy : to victory over one did he aspire. Made he therefore toward the moon. Rough was the hillside and the shadows deep and treacherous ; as he advanced the towers seemed to approach one another closer and closer yet. He drew his sword : with a crash they came together ; and he fell with wrath upon a single fortress. Three windows had the tower ; and against it ten cannons thundered. Eleven bricks had fallen dislodged by lightnings : it was no house wherein our Father might abide. But there he must abide. "To destroy it I am come," he said. And though he passed out therewithal, yet 'twas his home until he had attained. So he came to a river, and sailing to its source he found a fair woman all naked, and she filled the river from two vessels of pure water. "She-devil," he cried, "have I gone back one step?" For the Star Venus burned above. And with his sword he clave her from the head to the feet, that she fell clean asunder. Cried the echo : "Ah ! thou hast slain hope now !" Our Father gladdened at

Intellectus.

Deus.

H. et S. V. A.

Luna

Quid Umbratur In Mari.

Deo Duce Comite Ferro.

Vestigia Nulla Retrorsum.

Adest Rosa
Secreta Eros.

that word, and wiping his blade he kissed it and went on, knowing
that his luck should now be ill. And ill it was, for a temple was set up in
his way, and there he saw the grisly Goat enthroned. But he knew
better than to judge a goat from a goat s head and hoofs. And he abode
in that temple awhile therefore, and worshipped ten weeks. And the first
week he sacrificed to that goat [1] a crown every day. The second a phallus.
The third a silver vase of blood. The fourth a royal sceptre. The fifth
a sword. The sixth a heart. The seventh a garland of flowers. The
eighth a grass-snake. The ninth a sickle. And the tenth week did he
daily offer up his own body. Said the goat : "Though I be not an ox,
yet am I a sword." "Masked, O God !" cried the Adept. "Verily, an
thou hadst not sacrificed— " There was silence. And under the Goat's
throne was a rainbow [2] of seven colours : our Father fitted himself as an
arrow to the string (and the string was waxed well, dipped in a leaden pot
wherein boiled amber and wine) and shot through stormy heavens. And
they that saw him saw a woman wondrous fair [3] robed in flames of hair,
moon-sandalled, sun-belted, with torch and vase of fire and water. And
he trailed comet-clouds of glory upward.

Hemaphrodi-
tus.

Thus came our Father (Blessed be his name !) to Death,[4] who stood,
scythe in hand, opposed. And ever and anon he swept round, and men
fell before him. "Look," said Death, "my sickle hath a cross-handle.
See how they grow like flowers !" "Give me salt !" quoth our Father.
And with sulphur (that the Goat had given him) and with salt did he
bestrew the ground. "I see we shall have ado together," says Death.
"Aye !" and with that he lops off Death's cross-handle. Now Death
was wroth indeed, for he saw that our Father had wit of his designs (and
they were right foul !), but he bade him pass forthwith from his dominion.
And our Father could not at that time stay him : though for himself had
he cut off the grip, yet for others—well, let each man take his sword !
The way went through a forest. Now between two trees hung a man by
one heel (Love was that tree).[5] Crossed were his legs, and his arms
behind his head, that hung ever downwards, the fingers locked. "Who
art thou?" quoth our Father. "He that came before thee." "Who
am I ?" "He that cometh after me." With that worshipped our Father,
and took a present of a great jewel from him, and went his ways. And
he was bitterly a-cold, for that was the great Water he had passed. But
our Father's paps glittered with cold, black light, and likewise his navel.

Mors Janua
Vitae.

Adeptus.

Terrae Ultor
Anima Terrae.

Wherefore he was comforted. Now came the sudden twittering of heart
lest the firmament beneath him were not stable, and lo ! he danceth up
and down as a very cork on waters of wailing. "Woman," he bade
sternly, "be still. Cleave that with thy sword : or that must I well
work ?" But she cleft the cords, bitter-faced, smiling goddess as she was ;

---

[1] The sacrifices are the ten Sephiroth.
[2] See Table.
[3] Ancient form of the Key of ‫ﬢ‬.
[4] Considered as the agent of resurrection.
[5] In the true Key of ‫ﬢ‬ the tree is shaped like the letter ‫ﬠ‬ = Venus or love.
The figure of the man forms a cross above a triangle, with apex upwards,
the sign of redemption.

and he went on. "Leave thine ox-goad,"[1] quoth he, "till I come back an ox!" And she laughed and let him pass. Now is our Father come to the Unstable Lands, 'Od wot, for the Wheel whereon he poised was ever turning. Sworded was the Sphinx, but he out-dared her in riddling: deeper pierced his sword: he cut her into twain: her place was his. But that would he not, my Brethren; to the centre he clomb ever: and having won thither, he vanished. As a hermit ever he travelled and the lamp and wand were his. In his path a lion roared, but to it ran a maiden, strong as a young elephant, and held its cruel jaws. By force he ran to her: he freed the lion—one buffet of his hand dashed her back six paces! —and with another blow smote its head from its body. And he ran to her and by force embraced her. Struggled she and fought him: savagely she bit, but it was of no avail: she lay ravished and exhausted on the Lybian plain. Across the mouth he smote her for a kiss, while she cried: "O! thou hast begotten on me twins. And mine also is the Serpent, and thou shalt conquer it and it shall serve thee: and they, they also for a guide!" She ceased; and he, having come to the world's end, prepared his chariot. Foursquare he builded it, and that double: he harnessed the two sphinxes that he had made from one, and sailed, crab-fashion, backwards, through the amber skies of even. Wherefore he attained to see his children. Lovers they were and lovely, those twins of rape. One was above them, joining their hands. "That is well," said our Father, and for seven nights he slept in seven starry palaces, and a sword to guard him. Note well also that these children, and those others, are two, being four. And on the sixth day (for the seven days were past) he rose and came into his ancient temple, a temple of our Holy Order, O my Brethren, wherein sat that Hierophant who had initiated him of old. Now read he well the riddle of the Goat (Blessed be his name among us for ever! Nay, not for ever!), and therewith the Teacher made him a Master of the Sixfold Chamber, and an ardent Sufferer toward the Blazing Star. For the Sword, said the Teacher, is but the Star unfurled.[2] And our Father being cunning to place Aleph over Tau read this reverse, and so beheld Eden, even now and in the flesh.

Whence he sojourned far, and came to a great Emperor, by whom he was well received, and from whom he gat great gifts. And the Emperor (who is Solomon) told him of Sheba's Land and of one fairest of women there enthroned. So he journeyed thither, and for four years and seven months abode with her as paramour and light-of-love, for she was gracious to him and showed him those things that the Emperor had hidden; even the cubical stone and the cross beneath the triangle that were his and un-revealed. And on the third day he left her and came to Her who had initiated him before he was initiated; and with her he abode eight days and twenty days:[3] and she gave him gifts.

Marginal notes:

Sapientiae Lux Viris Baculum.

Femina Rapta Inspirat Gaudium.

Pleiades.

Dignitates.

Amicitia.

Amor.

Sophia.

---

[1] Lamed means ox-goad; Aleph, an ox. Lamed Aleph means No, the denial of Aleph Lamed, El, God.
[2] Read reverse, the Star [=the Will and the Great Work] is to fold up the Sephiroth; *i.e.* to attain Nirvana.
[3] The houses of the Moon. All the gifts are lunar symbols.

The first day, a camel ;
The second day, a kiss ;
The third day, a star-glass ;
The fourth day, a beetle's wing ;
The fifth day, a crab ;
The sixth day, a bow ;
The seventh day, a quiver ;
The eighth day, a stag ;
The ninth day, an horn ;
The tenth day, a sandal of silver ;

Dona Virginis.

The eleventh day, a silver box of white sandal wood ;
The twelfth day, a whisper ;
The thirteenth day, a black cat ;
The fourteenth day, a phial of white gold ;
The fifteenth day, an egg-shell cut in two ;
The sixteenth day, a glance ;
The seventeenth day, an honeycomb ;
The eighteenth day, a dream ;
The nineteenth day, a nightmare ;
The twentieth day, a wolf, black-muzzled ;
The twenty-first day, a sorrow ;
The twenty-second day, a bundle of herbs ;
The twenty-third day, a piece of camphor ;
The twenty-fourth day, a moonstone ;
The twenty-fifth day, a sigh ;
The twenty-sixth day, a refusal ;

Puella Urget Sophiam Sodalibus.

The twenty-seventh day, a consent ; and the last night she gave him all herself, so that the moon was eclipsed and earth was utterly darkened.   And the marriage of that virgin was on this wise : She had three arrows, yet but two flanks, and the wise men said that who knew two was three,[1] should know three was eight,[2] if the circle were but squared ; and this also one day shall ye know, my Brethren !   And she gave him the great and perfect gift of Magic, so that he fared forth right comely and well-provided.   Now

The Sophic Suggler.

at that great wedding was a Suggler,[3] a riddler : for he said, " Thou hast beasts : I will give thee weapons one for one."   For the Lion did our Father win a little fiery wand like a flame, and for his Eagle a cup of ever flowing water : for his Man the Suggler gave him a golden-hilted dagger (yet this was the worst of all his bargains, for it could not strike other, but himself only), while for a curious coin he bartered his good Bull.   Alas for our Father !   Now the Suggler mocks him and cries : " Four fool's bargains hast thou made, and thou art fit to go forth and meet a fool[4] for thy mate." But our Father counted thrice seven and cried : " One for the fool," seeing

---

[1] 3, the number of ℈.   2, the number of the card ℈.
[2] The equality of three and eight is attributed to Binah, a high grade of Theurgic attainment.
[3] Scil. Juggler, the 1st Key.   The magical weapons correspond to the Kerubim.
[4] The Key marked O and applied to Aleph, 1.

the Serpent should be his at last. " None for the fool," they laughed
back—nay, even his maiden queen. For she would not any should know
thereof. Yet were all right, both he and they. But truth ran quickly
about ; for that was the House of Truth ; and Mercury stood far from the   Hammer of
Sun. Yet the Suggler was ever in the Sign of Sorrow, and the Fig Tree   Thor.
was not far. So went our Father to the Fool's Paradise of Air. But it is
not lawful that I should write to you, brethren, of what there came to him
at that place and time ; nor indeed is it true, if it were written. For alway
doth this Arcanum differ from itself on this wise, that the Not and the   Arcanum.
Amen,[1] passing, are void either on the one side or the other, and Who shall
tell their ways ?

So our Father, having won the Serpent Crown, the Uraeus of Antient
Khem, did bind it upon his head, and rejoiced in that Kingdom for the
space of two hundred and thirty and one days [2] and nights, and turned him
toward the Flaming Sword.[3] Now the Sword governeth ten mighty King-
doms, and evil, and above them is the ninefold lotus, and a virgin came
forth unto him in the hour of his rejoicing and propounded her riddle.

The first riddle : [4]   Griphus I.
The maiden is blind.
Our Father : She shall be what she doth not.
And a second virgin came forth to him and said :
The second riddle : Detegitur Yod.   Griphus II.
Quoth our Father : The moon is full.
So also a third virgin the third riddle :   Griphus III.
Man and woman : O fountain of the balance !
To whom our Father answered with a swift flash of his sword, so swift
she saw it not.
Came out a fourth virgin, having a fourth riddle :   Griphus IV.
What egg hath no shell ?
And our Father pondered a while and then said :
On a wave of the sea : on a shell of the wave : blessed be her name !
The fifth virgin issued suddenly and said :   Griphus V.
I have four arms and six sides : red am I, and gold. To whom our Father :
Eli, Eli, lama sabachthani !
(For wit ye well, there be two Arcana therein.)
Then said the sixth virgin openly :   Griphus VI.
Power lieth in the river of fire.
And our Father laughed aloud and answered : I am come from the
waterfall.
So at that the seventh virgin came forth : and her countenance was   Griphus VII.
troubled.
The seventh riddle :
The oldest said to the most beautiful : What doest thou here ?

---

[1] This is obscure.   [2] $0+1+2+ \ldots +21=231$.   [3] The Seplinoth.
[4] The maiden (Malkuth) is blind (unredeemed). Answer : She shall be
what she doth not, *i.e.* see. She shall be the sea, *i.e.* "exalted to the throne
of Binah " (the great sea), the Qabalistic phrase to express her redemption.
We leave it to the reader's ingenuity to solve the rest. . Each refers to the
Sephira indicated by the number, but going upward.

Our Father :
And she answered him : I am in the place of the bridge.   Go thou
up higher : go thou where these are not.

Griphus VIII.   Thereat was commotion and bitter wailing, and the eighth virgin came
forth with rent attire and cried the eighth riddle :
The sea hath conceived.
Our Father raised his head, and there was a great darkness.

Griphus IX.   The ninth virgin, sobbing at his feet, the ninth riddle :
By wisdom.
Then our Father touched his crown and they all rejoiced : but laughing
he put them aside and he said : Nay ! By six hundred and twenty [1] do
ye exceed !

Griphus X.   Whereat they wept, and the tenth virgin came forth, bearing a royal
crown having twelve jewels : and she had but one eye, and from that
the eyelid had been torn.   A prodigious beard had she, and all of white :
and they wist he would have smitten her with his sword.   But he would
not, and she propounded unto him the tenth riddle :
Countenance beheld not countenance.
So thereto he answered : Our Father, blessed be thou !—
Countenance ?
Then they brought him the Sword and bade him smite withal : but
he said :

Culpa Urbium   If countenance behold not countenance, then let the ten be five.   And
Nota Terrae.   they wist that he but mocked them ; for he did bend the sword fivefold
and fashioned therefrom a Star, and they all vanished in that light ; yet
the lotus abode nine-petalled and he cried, "Before the wheel, the axle."
So he chained the Sun,[2] and slew the Bull, and exhausted the Air,
breathing it deep into his lungs : then he broke down the ancient tower,
that which he had made his home, will he nill he, for so long, and he
slew the other Bull, and he broke the arrow in twain ; after that he was
silent, for they grew again in sixfold order, so that this latter work was
double : but unto the first three he laid not his hand, neither for the first
time, nor for the second time, nor for the third time.   So to them he
added [3] that spiritual flame (for they were one, and ten, and fifty, thrice,
and again) and that was the Beast, the Living One that is Lifan.   Let
us be silent, therefore, my brethren, worshipping the holy sixfold Ox [4]
that was our Father in his peace that he had won into, and that so
hardly.   For of this shall no man speak.
Now therefore let it be spoken of our Father's journeyings in the land
of Vo [5] and of his suffering therein, and of the founding of our holy and
illustrious Order.

Nechesh.   Our Father, Brethren, having attained the mature age of three hundred

1 Kether adds up to 620.
2 These are the letters of Ain Soph Aur, the last two of which he destroys,
so as to leave only Ain, Not, or Nothing.
3 To $(1 + 10 + 50)$ 3×2 he adds 300, Shin, the flame of the Spirit=666.
4 $666 = 6 \times 111$. $111 =$ Aleph, the Ox.
5 His journeys as Initiator.

and fifty and eight years,[1] set forth upon a journey into the Mystic Mountain of the Caves. He took with him his Son,[2] a Lamb, Life, and   Abiegnus.
Strength, for these four were the Keys of that Mountain. So by ten
days and fifty days and two hundred days and yet ten days he went forth.
After ten days fell a thunderbolt, whirling through black clouds of rain :
after sixty the road split in two, but he travelled on both at once : after   Mysterium
two hundred and sixty, the sun drove away the rain, and the Star shone   I.N.R.I.
in the day-time, making it night. After the last day came his Mother,
his Redeemer, and Himself; and joining together they were even as I
am who write unto you. Seventeen they were, the three Fathers : with
the three Mothers they were thirty-two, and sixfold therein, being as
countenance and countenance. Yet, being seventeen, they were but
one, and that one none, as before hath been showed. And this enumera-
tion is a great Mysterium of our art. Whence a light hidden in a Cross.   Mysterium
Now therefore having brooded upon the ocean, and smitten with the   LVX.
Sword, and the Pyramid being builded in its just proportion, was that
Light fixed even in the Vault of the Caverns. With one stroke he rent
asunder the Veil ; with one stroke he closed the same. And entering
the Sarcophagus of that Royal Tomb he laid him down to sleep. Four   Pastos.
guarded him, and One in the four ; Seven enwalled him, and One in
the seven, yet were the seven ten, and One in the ten. Now therefore
his disciples came unto the Vault of that Mystic Mountain, and with the
Keys they opened the Portal and came to him and woke him. But
during his long sleep the roses had grown over him, crimson and flaming
with interior fire, so that he could not escape. Yet they withered at his
glance ; withat he knew what fearful task was before him. But slaying
his disciples with long Nails, he interred them there, so that they were
right sorrowful in their hearts. May all we die so ! And what further
befell him ye shall also know, but not at this time.

Going forth of that Mountain he met also the Fool. Then the discourse
of that Fool, my Brethren ; it shall repay your pains. They think they   Trinitas.
are a triangle,[3] he said, they think as the Picture-Folk. Base they are,
and little infinitely.

Ain Elohim.

They think, being many, they are one.[4] They think as the Rhine-Folk
think. Many and none.   Unitas.

Ain Elohim.

They think the erect[5] is the twined, and the twined is the coiled, and
the coiled is the twin, and the twins are the stoopers. They think as the   Serpentes.
Big-Nose-Folk. Save us, O Lord !

[1] Nechesh the Serpent and Messiach the Redeemer.
[2] Abigenos, Abiagnus, Bigenos, Abiegnus, metatheses of the name of the
Mystic Mountain of Initiation. The next paragraph has been explained in
the Appendix to Vol. I.
[3] The belief in a Trinity—ignorance of Daath.
[4] Belief in Monism, or rather Advaitism. Crowley was a Monist only in
the modern scientific sense of that word.
[5] Confusion of the various mystic serpents. The Big-Nose-Folk=the Jews.
We leave the rest to the insight of the reader.

Ain Elohim.

Abracadabra. The Chariot. Four hundred and eighteen. Five are one, and six are diverse, five in the midst and three on each side. The Word of Power, double in the Voice of the Master.

Ain Elohim.

Amethsh. Four sounds of four forces. O the Snake hath a long tail! Amen

Ain Elohim.

Sudden death : thick darkness : ho! the ox!

Ye Fylfat †. One, and one, and one : Creator, Preserver, Destroyer, ho! the Redeemer! Thunder-stone : whirlpool : lotus-flower : ho! for the gold of the sages!

Ain Elohim.

And he was silent for a great while, and so departed our Father from Him.

Mysterium Matris.[1] Forth he went along the dusty desert and met an antient woman bearing a bright crown of gold, studded with gems, one on each knee. Dressed in rags she was, and squatted clumsily on the sand. A horn grew from her forehead; and she spat black foam and froth. Foul was the hag and evil, yet our Father bowed down flat on his face to the earth. "Holy Virgin of God," said he, "what dost thou here? What wilt thou with thy servant?" At that she stank so that the air gasped about her, like a fish brought out of the sea. So she told him she was gathering simples for **Evocatio.** her daughter that had died to bury her withal. Now no simples grew in the desert. Therefore our Father drew with his sword lines of power in the sand, so that a black and terrible demon appeared squeezing up in thin flat plates of flesh along the sword-lines. So our Father cried : "Simples, O Axcaxrabortharax, for my mother!" Then the demon was wroth and shrieked : "Thy mother to black hell! She is mine!" So the old hag confessed straight that she had given her body for love to that fiend of the pit. But our Father paid no heed thereto and bade the demon **Lucus.** to do his will, so that he brought him herbs many, and good, with which our Father planted a great grove that grew about him (for the sun was now waxen bitter hot) wherein he worshipped, offering in vessels of clay these seven offerings :[2]

The first offering, dust ;
The second offering, ashes ;
The third offering, sand ;
The fourth offering, bay-leaves ;
The fifth offering, gold ;
The sixth offering, dung ;
The seventh offering, poison.

With the dust he gave also a sickle to gather the harvest of that dust.
With the ashes he gave a sceptre, that one might rule them aright.
With the sand he gave a sword, to cut that sand withal.
With the bay-leaves he gave a sun, to wither them.
With the gold he gave also a garland of sores, and that was for luck.
With the dung he gave a Rod of Life to quicken it.

---

[1] This is all obscure.   [2] Refer to the planets.

With the poison he gave also in offering a stag and a maiden.

But about the noon came one shining unto our Father and gave him to drink from a dull and heavy bowl. And this was a liquor potent and heavy, by'r lady ! So that our Father sank into deep sleep and dreamed a dream, and in that mirific dream it seemed unto him that the walls of all things slid into and across each other, so that he feared greatly, for the stability of the universe is the great enemy ; the unstable being the ever-lasting, saith Adhou Bin Aram, the Arab. O Elmen Zata, our Sophic Pilaster ! Further in the dream there was let down from heaven a mighty tessaract, bounded by eight cubes, whereon sat a mighty dolphin having eight senses. Further, he beheld a cavern full of most ancient bones of men, and therein a lion with a voice of a dog. Then came a voice: "Thirteen [1] are they, who are one. Once is a oneness: twice is the Name: thrice let us say not: by four is the Son: by five is the Sword: by six is the Holy Oil of the most Excellent Beard, and the leaves of the Book are by six : by seven is that great Amen." Then our Father saw one hundred and four horses that drove an ivory car over a sea of pearl, and they received him therein and bade him be comforted. With that he awoke and saw that he would have all his desire. In the morning therefore he arose and went his way into the desert. There he clomb an high rock and called forth the eagles, that their shadow floating over the desert should be as a book that men might read it. The shadows wrote and the sun recorded ; and on this wise cometh it to pass, O my Brethren, that by darkness and by sunlight ye will still learn ever these the Arcana of our Science. Lo ! who learneth by moonlight, he is the lucky one ! So our Father, having thus founded the Order, and our sacred Book being opened, rested awhile and beheld many wonders, the like of which were never yet told. But ever chiefly his study was to reduce unto eight things his many.

And thus, O Brethren of our Venerable Order, he at last succeeded. Those who know not will learn little herein: yet that they may be shamed all shall be put forth at this time clearly before them all, with no obscurity nor obfuscation in the exposition thereof.

Writing this, saith our Father to me, the humblest and oldest of all his disciples, write as the story of my Quintessential Quest, my Spagyric Wandering, my Philosophical Going. Write plainly unto the Brethren, quoth he, for many be little and weak ; and thy hard words and much learning may confound them.

Therefore I write thus plainly to you. Mark well that ye read me aright !

Our Father (blessed be his name !) entered the Path on this wise. He cut off three from ten : [2] thus he left seven. He cut and left three : he cut and left one: he cut and became. Thus fourfold. Eightfold. [3] He opened his eyes: he cleansed his heart : he chained his tongue : he fixed

Somnium Auri Potabilis.

Tredecim Voces.

Ordinis Inceptio.

Vitae.

Viae.

---

[1] Achad, unity, adds to thirteen. There follow attributions of the "thirteen times table."

[2] These are the Buddhist "paths of enlightenment."

[3] The eightfold path. The rest is very obscure.

his flesh : he turned to his trade : he put forth his strength : he drew all to a point : he delighted.

Therefore he is not, having become that which he was not.   Mark ye all : it is declared.   Now of the last adventure of our Father and of his going into the land of Apes, that is, England, and of what he did there, it is not fitting that I, the poor old fool who loved him, shall now discourse.   But it is most necessary that I should speak of his holy death and of his funeral and of the bruit thereof, for that is gone into divers lands as a false and lying report, whereby much harm and ill-luck come to the Brethren.   In this place, therefore, will I set down the exact truth of all that happened.

In the year of the Great Passing Over were signs and wonders seen of all men, O my Brethren, as it is written, and well known unto this day.

And the first sign was of dancing : for every woman that was under the moon began to dance and was mad, so that headlong and hot-mouthed she flung herself down, desirous.   Whence the second sign, that of

musical inventions ; for in that year, and of Rosewomen, came A and U and M,[1] the mighty musicians !   And the third sign likewise, namely, of

animals : for in that year every sheep had lambs thirteen, and every cart [2] was delivered of a wheel !   And other wonders innumerable : they are

well known, insomuch that that year is yet held notable.

Now our Father, being very old, came unto the venerable Grove of our August Fraternity and abode there.   And so old was he and feeble that he could scarce lift his hands in benediction upon us.   And all we waited about him, both by day and night ; lest one word should fall, and we not hear the same.   But he spake never unto us, though his lips moved and his eyes sought ever that which we could not see.   At last, on the day of D., the mother of P.,[3] he straightened himself up and spake.   This his final discourse was written down then by the dying lions in their own blood, traced willingly on the desert sands about the Grove of the Illustrious. Also here set down : but who will confirm the same, let him seek it on the sands.

Children of my Will, said our Father, from whose grey eyes fell gentlest tears, it is about the hour.   The chariot (Ch.)[4] is not, and the chariot (H.) is at hand.   Yet I, who have been car-borne through the blue air by sphinxes, shall never be carried away, not by the whitest horses of the world.   To you I have no word to say.   All is written in the sacred Book.   To that look ye well !

Ambrose, old friend, he said, turning to me—and I wept ever sore— do thou write for the little ones, the children of my children, for them that understand not easily our high Mysteries ; for in thy pen is, as it were, a river of clear water ; without vagueness, without ambiguity,

---

[1] Aum !   The sacred word.

[2] Qy. ⊓ (the car) becomes O (a wheel).   The commentators who have suspected the horrid blasphemy implied by the explanation " becomes ⊃, the Wheel of Fortune," are certainly in error.

[3] Demeter and Persephone.

[4] Ch = ⊓ ; H = Hades.   See the Tarot cards, and classical mythology, for the symbols.

without show of learning, without needless darkening of counsel and word,
dost thou ever reveal the sacred Heights of our Mystic Mountain. For,
as for him that understandeth not thy writing, and that easily and well,
he ye well assured all that he is a vile man and a losel of little worth or
worship; a dog, an unclean swine, a worm of filth, a festering sore in
the vitals of earth : such an one is liar and murderer, debauched, drunken,
sexless, and spatulate ; an ape-dropping, a lousy, flat-backed knave : from
such an one keep ye well away ! Use hath he little : ornament maketh
he nothing : let him be cast out on the dunghills beyond Jordan ; let   Sedes Profunda
him pass into the S. P. P., and that utterly !   Paimonis.

With that our Father sighed deep and laid back his reverend head,
and was silent. But from his heart came a subtle voice of tenderest farewell, so that we knew him well dead. But for seventy days and seventy   Oculi Nox
nights we touched him not, but abode ever about him : and the smile   Secreta.
changed not on his face, and the whole grove was filled with sweet and
subtle perfumes. Now on the 71st day arose there a great dispute about   Portae Silen-
his body ; for the angels and spirits and demons did contend about it,   tium.
hat they might possess it. But our eldest brother V. N. bade all be still ;   Partitio.
nd thus he apportioned the sacred relics of our Father.

To the Angel Agbagal, the fore part of the skull ;
To the demon Ozoz, the back left part of the skull;
To the demon Olcot,[1] the back right part of the skull ;
To ten thousand myriads of spirits of fire, each one hair ;
To ten thousand myriads of spirits of water, each one hair ;
To ten thousand myriads of spirits of earth, each one hair;
To ten thousand myriads of spirits of air, each one hair ;
To the archangel Zazelazel, the brain ;
To the angel Usbusolat, the medulla ;
To the demon Ululomis, the right nostril ;
To the angel Opael, the left nostril ;
To the spirit Kuiphiah, the membrane of the nose ;
To the spirit Pugrah, the bridge of the nose ;
To eleven thousand spirits of spirit, the hairs of the nose, one each ;
To the archangel Tuphtuphtuphal,[2] the right eye ;
To the archdevil Upsusph, the left eye ;

The parts thereof in trust to be divided among their servitors ; as the
right cornea, to Aphlek ; the left, to Urnbal;—mighty spirits are they,
and bold !

To the archdevil Rama,[3] the right ear and its parts ;
To the archangel Umumatis, the left ear and its parts ;

The teeth to two-and-thirty letters of the sixfold Name : one to the air,
and fifteen to the rain and the ram, and ten to the virgin, and six to
the Bull ;

The mouth to the archangels Alalal and Bikarak, lip and lip;
The tongue to that devil of all devils Yehowou.[4] Ho, devil ! canst thou
speak ?

---

[1] Col. Olcott, the theosophist.   [2] ? the spirit of motor-cars.
[3] Vishnu, the preserver.   [4] Jehovah.

The pharynx to Mahabonisbash, the great angel ;

To seven-and-thirty myriads of legions of planetary spirits the hairs of the moustache, to each one ;

To ninety and one myriads of the Elohim, the hairs of the beard ; to each thirteen, and the oil to ease the world ;

To Shalach, the archdevil, the chin.

So also with the lesser relics ; of which are notable only : to the Order, the heart of our Father : to the Book of the Law, his venerable lung-space to serve as a shrine thereunto : to the devil Aot, the liver, to be divided : to the angel Exarp and his followers, the great intestine : to Bitom the devil and his crew, the little intestine : to Aub, Aud, and Aur, the venerable Phallus of our Father : to Ash the little bone of the same : to our children K., C., B., C., G., T., N., H., I., and M., his illustrious finger-nails, and the toe-nails to be in trust for their children after them : and so for all the rest ; is it not written in our archives ? As to his magical weapons, all vanished utterly at the moment of that Passing Over. Therefore they carried away our Father's body piece by piece and that with reverence and in order, so that there was not left of all one hair, nor one nerve, nor one little pore of the skin. Thus was there no funeral pomp ; they that say other are liars and blasphemers against a fame untarnished. May the red plague rot their vitals !

Amen.

Thus, O my Brethren, thus and not otherwise was the Passing Over of that Great and Wonderful Magician, our Father and Founder. May the dew of his admirable memory moisten the grass of our minds, that we may bring forth tender shoots of energy in the Great Work of Works. So mote it be !

BENEDICTVS DOMINVS DEVS
NOSTER QVI NOBIS DEDIT
SIGNVM
R. C.

THE THREE CHARACTERISTICS

"LISTEN to the Jataka !" said the Buddha. And all they gave ear. "Long ago, when King Brahmadatta reigned in Benares,[1] it came to pass that there lived under his admirable government a weaver named Suraj Ju[2] and his wife Chandi.[3] And in the fulness of her time did she give birth to a man child, and they called him Perdu' R Abu.[4] Now the child grew, and the tears of the mother fell, and the wrath of the father waxed : for by no means would the boy strive in his trade of weaving. The loom went merrily, but to the rhythm of a mantra ; and the silk slipped through his fingers, but as if one told his beads. Wherefore the work was marred, and the hearts of the parents were woe because of him. But it is written that misfortune knoweth not the hour to cease, and that the seed of sorrow is as the seed of the Banyan Tree. It groweth and is of stature as a mountain, and, ay me ! it shooteth down fresh roots into the aching earth. For the boy grew and became a man ; and his eyes kindled with the lust of life and love ; and the desire stirred him to see the round world and its many marvels. Wherefore he went forth, taking his father's store of gold, laid up for him against that bitter day, and he took fair maidens, and was their servant. And he builded a fine house and dwelt therein. And he took no thought. But he said : Here is a change indeed !

"Now it came to pass that after many years he looked upon his lover, the bride of his heart, the rose of his garden, the jewel of his rosary ; and behold, the olive loveliness of smooth skin was darkened, and the flesh lay loose, and the firm breasts drooped, and the eyes had lost alike the gleam of joy and the sparkle of laughter and the soft glow of love. And he was mindful of his word, and said in sorrow, 'Here is then a change indeed !' And he turned his thought to himself, and saw that in his heart was also a change : so that he cried, 'Who then am I ?' And he saw that all this was sorrow. And he turned his thought without and saw that all things were alike in this ; that nought might escape the threefold misery. 'The soul,' he said, 'the soul, the I, is as all these ; it is impermanent as the ephemeral flower of beauty in the water that is born and shines and dies ere sun be risen and set again.'

"And he humiliated his heart and sang the following verse :

Brahma, and Vishnu, and great Shiva ! Truly
I see the Trinity in all things dwell,
Some rightly tinged of Heaven, others duly
Pitched down the steep and precipice of Hell.
Nay, not your glory ye from fable borrow !
These three I see in spirit and in sense,
These three, O miserable seer ! Sorrow,
Absence of ego, and impermanence !

And at the rhythm he swooned, for his old mantra surged up in the long-sealed vessels of sub-conscious memory, and he fell into the calm ocean of a great Meditation.

[1] The common formula for beginning a "Jataka," or story of a previous incarnation of Buddha. Brahmadatta reigned 120,000 years.
[2] The Sun.
[3] The Moon.
[4] Perdurabo..Crowley's motto.

II.

" Jehjaour [1] was a mighty magician ; his soul was dark and evil ; and his lust was of life and power and of the wreaking of hatred upon the innocent. And it came to pass that he gazed upon a ball of crystal wherein were shown him all the fears of the time unborn as yet on earth. And by his art he saw Perdu' R Abu, who had been his friend : for do what he would, the crystal showed always that sensual and frivolous youth as a Fear to him : even to him the Mighty One ! But the selfish and evil are cowards ; they fear shadows, and Jehjaour scorned not his art. ' Roll on in time, thou ball ! ' he cried. ' Move down the stream of years, timeless and hideous servant of my will ! Taph ! Tath ! Arath ! ' [2] He sounded the triple summons, the mysterious syllables that bound the spirit to the stone. " Then suddenly the crystal grew a blank ; and thereby the foiled wizard knew that which threatened his power, his very life, was so high and holy that the evil spirit could perceive it not. ' Avaunt ! ' he shrieked, ' false soul of darkness ! ' And the crystal flashed up red, the swarthy red of hate in a man's cheek, and darkened utterly.

" Foaming at the mouth the wretched Jehjaour clutched at air and fell prone.

III.

" To what God should he appeal ? His own, Hanuman, was silent. Sacrifice, prayer, all were in vain. So Jehjaour gnashed his teeth, and his whole force went out in a mighty current of hate towards his former friend.

[1] Allan MacGregor Bennett (whose motto in the " Hermetic Order of the Golden Dawn," was Iehi Aour, *i.e.* " Let there be light "), now Ananda Metteya, to whom the volume in which this story was issued is inscribed.

[2] Taphtatharath, the spirit of Mercury.

" " Now hate hath power, though not the power of love. So it came about that in his despair he fell into a trance ; and in the trance Mara [1] appeared to him. Never before had his spells availed to call so fearful a potency from the abyss of matter. ' Son,' cried the Accursèd One, ' seven days of hate unmarred by passion milder, seven days without one thought of pity, these avail to call me forth.' ' Slay me my enemy ! ' howled the wretch. But Mara trembled. ' Enquire of Ganesha concerning him ! ' faltered at last the fiend.

" Jehjaour awoke.

IV.

" ' Yes ! ' said Ganesha gloomily, ' the young man has given me up altogether. He tells me I am as mortal as he is, and he doesn't mean to worry about me any more.' ' Alas ! ' sighed the deceitful Jehjaour, who cared no more for Ganesha and any indignities that might be offered him than his enemy did. ' One of my best devotees too ! ' muttered, or rather trumpeted, the elephantine anachronism. ' You see,' said the wily wizard, ' I saw Perdu' R Abu the other day, and he said he had become Srotapatti. Now that's pretty serious. In seven births only, if he but pursue the path, will he cease to be reborn. So you have only that time in which to win him back to your worship.' The cunning sorcerer did not mention that within that time also must his own ruin be accomplished. ' What do you advise ? ' asked the irritated and powerful, but unintelligent deity. ' Time is our friend,' said the enchanter. ' Let your influence be used in the Halls of Birth that each birth may be as long as possible. Now the elephant is the longest lived of all beasts—' ' Done with you ! ' sa d Ganesha in great glee, for the idea struck him as ingenious. And he lumbered off to clinch the affair at once.

" And Perdu' R Abu died.

[1] The archdevil of the Buddhists.

V.

"Now the great elephant strode with lordly footsteps in the forest, and Jehjaour shut himself up with his caldrons and things and felt quite happy, for he knew his danger was not near till the approaching of Perdu' R Abu's Arahatship. But in spite of the young gently-ambling cows which Ganesha took care to throw in his way, in spite of the tender shoots of green and the soft cocoanuts, this elephant was not as other elephants. The seasons spoke to him of change—the forest is ever full of sorrow— and nobody need preach to him the absence of an ego, for the brutes have had more sense than ever to imagine there was one. So the tusker was usually to be found, still as a rock, in some secluded place, meditating on the Three Characteristics. And when Ganesha appeared in all his glory, he found him to his disgust quite free from elephanto-morphism. In fact, he quietly asked the God to leave him alone.

"Now he was still quite a young elephant when there came into the jungle, tripping merrily along, with a light-hearted song in its nucleolus, no less than a Bacillus.

"And the elephant died. He was only seventeen years old.

VI.

"A brief consultation ; and the Srotapatti was reincarnated as a parrot. For the parrot, said the wicked Jehjaour, may live 500 years and never feel it.

"So a grey wonder of wings flitted into the jungle. So joyous a bird, thought the God, could not but be influenced by the ordinary passions and yield to such majesty as his own.

"But one day there came into the jungle a strange wild figure. He was a man dressed in the weird Tibetan fashion. He had red robes and hat, and thought dark things. He whirled a prayer-wheel in his hands; and ever as he went he muttered the mystic words 'Aum Mani Padme Hum.'[1] The parrot, who had never heard human speech, tried to mimic the old Lama, and was amazed at his success. Pride first seized the bird, but it was not long before the words had their own effect, and it was in meditation upon the conditions of existence that he eternally re-peated the formula.

* *

"A home at distant Inglistan. An old lady, and a grey parrot in a cage. The parrot was still muttering inaudibly the sacred mantra. Now, now, the moment of Destiny was at hand ! The Four Noble Truths shone out in that parrot's mind ; the Three Char-acteristics appeared luminous, like three spectres on a murderer's grave : unable to contain himself he recited aloud the mysterious sentence.

"The old lady, whatever may have been her faults, could act promptly. She rang the bell. 'Sarah !' said she, 'take away that dreadful creature ! Its language is positively awful.' 'What shall I do with it, mum ?' asked the 'general.' 'Aum Mani Padme Hum,' said the parrot. The old lady stopped her ears. 'Wring its neck !' she said.

"The parrot was only eight years old.

VII.

"'You're a muddler and an idiot !' said the infuriated God. 'Why not make him a spiritual thing ? A Nat[2] lives 10,000 years.' 'Make him a Nat then !' said the magician, already beginning to fear that fate would be too strong for him, in spite of all his cunning. 'There's some one working against us on the physical plane. We must transcend it.' No sooner said than done :

[1] "O the Jewel in the Lotus ! Aum !" The most famous of the Buddhist formularies.

[2] The Burmese name for an elemental spirit.

a family of Nats in a big tree at Anuradhapura had a little stranger, very welcome to Mamma and Papa Nat.

"Blessed indeed was the family. Five-and-forty feet[1] away stood a most ancient and holy dagoba : and the children of light would gather round it in the cool of the evening, or in the misty glamour of dawn, and turn forth in love and pity towards all mankind—nay, to the smallest grain of dust tossed on the utmost storms of the Sahara !

"Blessed and more blessed ! For one day came a holy Bhikkhu from the land of the Peacock,[2] and would take up his abode in the hollow of their very tree. And little Perdu' R Abu used to keep the mosquitoes away with the gossamer of his wings, so that the good man might be at peace.

"Now the British Government abode in that land, and when it heard that there was a Bhikkhu living in a tree, and that the village folk brought him rice and onions and gramophones, it saw that it must not be.

"And little Perdu' R Abu heard them talk ; and learnt the great secret of Impermanence, and of Sorrow, and the mystery of Unsubstantiality.

"And the Government evicted the Bhikkhu ; and set guard, quite like the end of Genesis iii., and cut down the tree, and all the Nats perished.

"Jehjaour heard and trembled. Perdu' R Abu was only three years old.

VIII.

"It really seemed as if fate was against him. Poor Jehjaour ! In despair he cried to his partner, 'O Ganesha, in the world of Gods only shall we be safe. Let him be born as a flute-girl before Indra's throne !' 'Difficult is the task,' replied the alarmed deity, ' but I will use all my influence. I

[1] The Government, in the interests of Buddhists themselves, reserves all ground within 50 feet of a dagoba. The incident described in this section actually occurred in 1901.
[2] Siam.

know a thing or two about Indra, for example——'

"It was done. Beautiful was the young girl's face as she sprang mature from the womb of Matter, on her life-journey of an hundred thousand years. Of all Indra's flute-girls she played and sang the sweetest. Yet ever some remembrance, dim as a pallid ghost that fleets down the long avenues of deodar and moonlight, stole in her brain ; and her song was ever of love and death and music from beyond.

"And one day as she sang thus the deep truth stole into being and she knew the Noble Truths. So she turned her flute to the new song, when—horror !—there was a mosquito in the flute. 'Tootle ! Tootle !' she began. 'Buzz ! Buzz !' went the mosquito from the very vitals of her delicate tube.

"Indra was not unprovided with a disc.[1] Alas ! Jehjaour, art thou already in the toils ? She had only lived eight months.

IX.

"'How you bungle !' growled Ganesha. 'Fortunately we are better off this time. Indra has been guillotined for his dastardly murder ; so his place is vacant.' 'Eurekas !' yelled the magus, 'his very virtue will save him from his predecessor's fate.'

"Behold Perdu' R Abu then as Indra ! But oh, dear me ! what a memory he was getting ! ' It seems to me,' he mused, 'that I've been changing about a lot lately. Well, I am virtuous—and I read in Crowley's new translation of the Dhammapada[2] that virtue is the thing to keep one steady. So I think I may look forward to a tenure of my mahakalpa in almost Arcadian simplicity. Lady Bhavani, did you say, boy ? Yes, I am at home. Bring the betel !' ' Jeldi !' he added, with some dim recollection of the

[1] A whirling disc is Indra's symbolic weapon.
[2] He abandoned this. A few fragments are reprinted, *supra*.

British Government, when he was a baby Nat.

"The Queen of Heaven and the Lord of the Gods chewed betel for quite a long time, conversed of the weather, the crops, the affaire Humbert, and the law in relation to motor-cars, with ease and affability. But far was it from Indra's pious mind to flirt with his distinguished guest! Rather, he thought of the hollow nature of the Safe, the change of money and of position; the sorrow of the too confiding bankers, and above all the absence of an Ego in the Brothers Crawford.

"While he was thus musing, Bhavani got fairly mad at him. The Spretae Injuria Formae gnawed her vitals with pangs unassuageable: so, shaking him quite roughly by the arm, she Put It To Him Straight. 'O Madam!' said Indra.

"This part of the story has been told before—about Joseph; but Bhavani simply lolled her tongue out, opened her mouth, and gulped him down at a swallow.

"Jehjaour simply wallowed.   Indra had passed in seven days.

X.

"'There is only one more birth,' he groaned. 'This time we must win or die.' 'Goetia[1] expects every God to do his duty,' he excitedly lunographed to Swarga.[2] But Ganesha was already on his way.

"The elephant-headed God was in great spirits. 'Never say die!' he cried genially, on beholding the downcast appearance of his fellow-conspirator. 'This'll break the slate. There is no change in the Arupa-Brahma-Loka!'[3] 'Rupe me no rupes!' howled the necromancer. 'Get up, fool!' roared the God. 'I have got Perdu' R Abu elected Maha Brahma.' 'Oh Lord, have you really?' said the wizard, looking a little

[1] The world of black magic.
[2] Heaven.
[3] The highest heaven of the Hindu. "Formless place of Brahma" is its name.

less glum. 'Ay!' cried Ganesha impressively, 'let Aeon follow Aeon down the vaulted and echoing corridors of Eternity: pile Mahakalpa upon Mahakalpa until an Asankhya[1] of Crores[2] have passed away: and Maha Brahma will still sit lone and meditate upon his lotus throne.' 'Good, good!' said the magus, 'though there seems a reminiscence of the Bhagavad-Gita and the Light of Asia somewhere. Surely you don't read Edwin Arnold?' 'I do,' said the God disconsolately, 'we Hindu Gods have to. It's the only way we can get any clear idea of who we really are.'

"Well, here was Perdu' R Abu, after his latest fiasco, installed as a Worthy, Respectable, Perfect, Ancient and Accepted, Just, Regular Mahabrahma. His only business was to meditate, for as long as he did this, the worlds—the whole system of 10,000 worlds—would go on peaceably. Nobody had better read the lesson of the Bible—the horrible results to mankind of ill-timed, though possibly well-intentioned, interference on the part of a deity.

"Well, he curled himself up, which was rather clever for a formless abstraction, and began. There was a grave difficulty in his mind—an obstacle right away from the word 'Jump!' Of course there was really a good deal: he didn't know where the four elements ceased, for example:[3] but his own identity was the real worry. The other questions he could have stilled; but this was too near his pet Chakra.[4] 'Here I am,' he meditated, 'above all change; and yet an hour ago I was Indra; and before that his flute-girl; and then a Nat; and then a parrot; and then a Hathi—"Oh, the Hathis pilin' teak in the sludgy, squdgy creek!" sang Parameshvara. Why, it goes

[1] "Innumerable," the highest unit of the fantastic Hindu arithmetic.
[2] 10,000.
[3] See the witty legend in the Questions of King Milinda.
[4] Meditation may be performed on any of seven "Chakra" (wheels or centres) in the body.

back and back, like a biograph out of order, and there's no sort of connection between one and the other. Hullo, what's that? Why, there's a holy man near that Bo-Tree. He'll tell me what it all means.' Poor silly old Lord of the Universe! Had he carried his ·memory back one more step he'd have known all about Jehjaour and the conspiracy, and that he was a Srotapatti and had only one more birth; and might well have put in the 311,040,000,000,000 myriads of aeons which would elapse before lunch in rejoicing over his imminent annihilation.

"'Venerable Sir!' said Mahabrahma, who had assumed the guise of a cowherd, 'I kiss your worshipful Trilbies :[1] I prostrate myself before your estimable respectability.' 'Sir,' said the holy man, none other than Our Lord Himself! 'thou seekest illumination!' Mahabrahma smirked and admitted it. 'From negative to positive,' explained the Thrice-Honoured One, 'though Potential Existence eternally vibrates the Divine Absolute of the Hidden Unity of processional form masked in the Eternal Abyss of the Unknowable, the synthetical hieroglyph of an illimitable, pastless, futureless PRESENT.

"'To the uttermost bounds of space rushes the voice of Ages unheard of save in the concentrated unity of the thought-formulated Abstract; and eternally that voice formulates a word which is glyphed in the vast ocean of limitless life.[2] Do I make myself clear?' 'Perfectly. Who would have thought it was all so simple?' The God cleared his throat, and rather diffidently, even shamefacedly, went on:

"'But what I really wished to know was about my incarnation. How is it I have so suddenly risen from change and death to the unchangeable?'

"'Child!' answered Gautama, 'your facts are wrong—you can hardly expect to make

[1] Feet.
[2] This astonishing piece of bombastic drivel is verbatim from a note by S. L. Mathers to the "Kabbalah Unveiled."

correct deductions.' 'Yes, you can, if only your logical methods are unsound. That's the Christian way of getting truth.' 'True!' replied the sage, 'but precious little they get. Learn, O Mahabrahma (for I penetrate this disguise), that all existing things, even from thee unto this grain of sand, possess Three Characteristics. These are Mutability, Sorrow, and Unsubstantiality.'

"'All right for the sand, but how about Me? Why, they *define* me as unchangeable.' 'You can define a quirk as being a two-sided triangle,' retorted the Saviour, 'but that does not prove the actual existence of any such oxymoron.[1] The truth is that you're a very spiritual sort of being and a prey to longevity. Men's lives are so short that yours seems eternal in comparison. But —why, *you're* a nice one to talk! You'll be dead in a week from now.'

"'I quite appreciate the force of your remarks!' said the seeming cowherd; 'that about the Characteristics is very clever; and curiously enough, my perception of this has always just preceded my death for the last six goes.'

"'Well, so long, old chap,' said Gautama, 'I must really be off. I have an appointment with Brother Mara at the Bo-Tree. He has promised to introduce his charming daughters——'

"'Good-bye, and don't do anything rash!'

"'Rejoice! our Lord wended unto the Tree![2] As blank verse this scans but ill, but it clearly shows what happened.

XI.

"The 'Nineteenth Mahakalpa' brought out its April Number. There was a paper by Huxlananda Swami.

"Mahabrahma had never been much more than an idea. He had only lived six days.

[1] A contradiction in terms.
[2] Arnold, "Light of Asia."

XII.

"At the hour of the great Initiation," continued the Buddha, in the midst of the Five Hundred Thousand Arahats, "the wicked Jehjaour had joined himself with Mara to prevent the discovery of the truth. And in Mara's fall he fell. At that moment all the currents of his continued and concentrated Hate recoiled upon him and he fell into the Abyss of Being. And in the Halls of Birth he was cast out into the Lowest Hell—he became a clergyman of the Church of England, further than he had ever been before from Truth and Light and Peace and Love ; deeper and deeper enmeshed in the net of Circumstance, bogged in the mire of Tanha [1] and Avigga [2] and all things base and vile. False Vichi-Kichi [3] had caught him at last !

XIII.

"Aye ! The hour was at hand. Perdu' R Abu was reincarnated as a child of Western parents, ignorant of all his wonderful past. But a strange fate has brought him to this village." The Buddha paused, probably for effect.

A young man there, sole among all them not yet an Arahat, turned pale. He alone was of Western birth in all that multitude.

"Brother Abhavananda,[4] little friend," said the Buddha, " what can we predicate of all existing things ? "   " Lord ! " replied the neophyte, "they are unstable, everything is sorrow, in them is no inward Principle, as some pretend, that can avoid, that can hold itself aloof from, the forces of decay."

"And how do you know that, little Brother ? " smiled the Thrice-Honoured One.

"Lord, I perceive this Truth whenever

[1] Thirst : *i.e.* desire in its evil sense.
[2] Ignorance.
[3] Doubt.
[4] " Bliss-of-non-existence." One of Crowley's eastern names.

I consider the Universe. More, its consciousness seems ingrained in my very nature, perhaps through my having known this for many incarnations. I have never thought otherwise."

" Rise, Sir Abhavananda, I dub thee Arahat ! " cried the Buddha, striking the neophyte gently on the back with the flat of his ear.[1]

And he perceived.

When the applause and praise and glory had a little faded, the Buddha, in that golden delight of sunset, explained these marvellous events. " Thou, Abhavananda," he said, " art the Perdu' R Abu of my lengthy tale. The wicked Jehjaour has got something lingering with boiling oil in it, while waiting for his clerical clothes : while, as for me, I myself was the Bacillus in the forest of Lanka : I was the old Lady : I was (he shuddered) the British Government : I was the mosquito that buzzed in the girl's flute : I was Bhavani : I was Huxlananda Swami ; and at the last, at this blessed hour, I am— that I am."

" But, Lord," said the Five Hundred Thousand and One Arahats in a breath, " thou art then guilty of six violent deaths ! Nay, thou hast hounded one soul from death to death through all these incarnations ! What of this First Precept [2] of yours ? "

" Children," answered the Glorious One, " do not be so foolish as to think that death is necessarily an evil. I have not come to found a Hundred Years Club, and to include mosquitoes in the membership. In this case to have kept Perdu' R Abu alive was to have played into the hands of his enemies. My First Precept is merely a general rule.[3]   In

[1] The Buddha had such long ears that he could cover the whole of his face with them. Ears are referred to Spirit in Hindu symbolism, so that the legend means that he could conceal the lower elements and dwell in this alone.
[2] Here is the little rift within the lute which alienated Crowley from active work on Buddhist lines ; the orthodox failing to see his attitude.
[3] A more likely idea than the brilliantly logical nonsense of Pansil, *supra.*

the bulk of cases one should certainly abstain from destroying life, that is, wantonly and wilfully : but I cannot drink a glass of water without killing countless myriads of living beings. If you knew as I do, the conditions of existence : struggle deadly and inevitable, every form of life the inherent and immitigable foe of every other form, with few, few exceptions, you would not only cease to talk of the wickedness of causing death, but you would perceive the First Noble Truth, that no existence can be free from sorrow ; the second, that the desire for existence only leads to sorrow ; that the ceasing from existence is the ceasing of sorrow (the third) ; and you would seek in the fourth the Way, the Noble Eightfold Path.

" I know, O Arahats, that you do not need this instruction : but my words will not stay here : they will go forth and illuminate the whole system of ten thousand worlds, where Arahats do not grow on every tree. Little brothers, the night is fallen : it were well to sleep."

1902

בראשית

AN ESSAY IN ONTOLOGY

WITH SOME REMARKS ON CEREMONIAL MAGIC

בראשית

O Man, of a daring nature, thou subtle production !
Thou wilt not comprehend it, as when understanding some common thing.
ORACLES OF ZOROASTER.

IN presenting this theory of the Universe to
the world, I have but one hope of making
any profound impression, viz.—that my theory
has the merit of explaining the divergences
between three great forms of religion now
existing in the world—Buddhism, Hinduism,
and Christianity, and of adapting them
to ontological science by conclusions not
mystical but mathematical. Of Mohamme-
danism I shall not now treat, as, in whatever
light we may decide to regard it (and its
esoteric schools are often orthodox), in any
case it must fall under one of the three
heads of Nihilism, Advaitism, and Dvaitism.

Taking the ordinary hypothesis of the
universe, that of its infinity, or at any rate
that of the infinity of God, or of the infinity
of some substance or idea actually existing,
we first come to the question of the possibility of the co-existence of God and man.

The Christians, in the category of the existent, enumerate among other things, whose
consideration we may discard for the purposes of this argument, God, an infinite
being ; man ; Satan and his angels ; man
certainly, Satan presumably, finite beings.
These are not aspects of one being, but
separate and even antagonistic existences.
All are equally real : we cannot accept

mystics of the type of Caird as being orthodox
exponents of the religion of Christ.

The Hindus enumerate Brahm, infinite in
all dimensions and directions—indistinguishable from the Pleroma of the Gnostics—and
Maya, illusion. This is in a sense the ante-
thesis of noumenon and phenomenon, noumenon being negated of all predicates until
it becomes almost extinguished in the Nichts
under the title of the Alles. (Cf. Max Müller
on the metaphysical Nirvana, in his Dhammapada, Introductory Essay.) The Buddhists express no opinion.

Let us consider the force-quality in the
existences conceived of by these two religions
respectively, remembering that the God of
the Christian is infinite, and yet discussing
the alternative if we could suppose him to
be a finite God. In any equilibrated system
of forces, we may sum and represent them as
a triangle or series of triangles which again
resolve into one. In any moving system, if
the resultant motion be applied in a contrary
direction, the equilibrium can also thus be
represented. And if any one of the original
forces in such a system may be considered,
that one is equal to the resultant of the re-
mainder. Let x, the purpose of the universe
be the resultant of the forces G, S, and M
(God, Satan, and Man). Then M is also the
resultant of G, S, and $-x$. So that we can
regard either of our forces as the supreme,
and there is no reason for worshipping one
rather than another. All are finite. This
argument the Christians clearly see : hence
the development of God from the petty

joss of Genesis to the intangible, but self-contradictory spectre of to-day. But if *G* be infinite, the other forces can have no possible effect on it. As Whewell says, in the strange accident by which he anticipates the metre of *In Memoriam :* " No force on earth, however great, can stretch a cord, however fine, into a horizontal line that shall be absolutely straight."

The definition of God as infinite therefore denies man implicitly ; while if he be finite, there is an end of the usual Christian reasons for worship, though I daresay I could myself discover some reasonably good ones. [I hardly expect to be asked, somehow.]

The resulting equilibrium of God and man, destructive of worship, is of course absurd. We must reject it, unless we want to fall into Positivism, Materialism, or something of the sort. But if, then, we call God infinite, how are we to regard man, and Satan ? (the latter, at the very least, surely no integral part of him). The fallacy lies not in my demonstration (which is also that of orthodoxy) that a finite God is absurd, but in the. assumption that man has any real force.[1]

In our mechanical system (as I have hinted above), if one of the forces be infinite, the others, however great, are both relatively and absolutely nothing.

In any category, infinity excludes finity, unless that finity be an identical part of that infinity.

In the category of existing things, space being infinite, for on that hypothesis we are still working, either matter fills or does not fill it. If the former, matter is infinitely great ; if the latter, infinitely small. Whether the matter-universe be 10^{10000} light-years in diameter or half a mile makes no difference ; it is infinitely small—in effect, Nothing. The unmathematical illusion that it does exist is what the Hindus call Maya.

If, on the other hand, the matter-universe is infinite, Brahm and God are crowded out, and the possibility of religion is equally excluded.

[1] Lully, Descartes, Spinoza, Schelling. See their works.

We may now shift our objective. The Hindus cannot account intelligibly, though they try hard, for Maya, the cause of all suffering. Their position is radically weak, but at least we may say for them that they have tried to square their religion with their common sense. The Christians, on the other hand, though they saw whither the Manichean Heresy [1] must lead, and crushed it, have not officially admitted the precisely similar conclusion with regard to man, and denied the existence of the human soul as distinct from the divine soul.

Trismegistus, Iamblichus, Porphyry, Boehme, and the mystics generally have of course substantially done so, though occasionally with rather inexplicable reservations, similar to those made in some cases by the Vedantists themselves.

Man then being disproved, God the Person disappears for ever, and becomes Atman, Pleroma, Ain Soph, what name you will, infinite in all directions and in all categories —to deny one is to destroy the entire argument and throw us back on to our old Dvaitistic bases.

I entirely sympathise with my unhappy friend Rev. Mansel, B.D.,[2] in his piteous and pitiful plaints against the logical results of the Advaitist School. But on his basal hypothesis of an infinite God, infinite space, time, and so on, no other conclusion is possible. Dean Mansel is found in the impossible position of one who will neither give up his premises nor dispute the validity of his logical processes, but who shrinks in horror from the inevitable conclusion ; he supposes there must be something wrong somewhere, and concludes that the sole use of reason is to discover its own inferiority to faith. As Deussen [3] well points out, faith in the Christian sense merely amounts to

[1] The conception of Satan as a positive evil force ; the lower triangle of the Hexagram.
[2] *Encyclopedia Britannica,* Art. Metaphysics.
[3] "The Principles of Metaphysics." Macmillan.

being convinced on insufficient grounds.[1] This is surely the last refuge of incompetence.

But though, always on the original hypothesis of the infinity of space, &c., the Advaitist position of the Vedantists and the great Germans is unassailable, yet on practical grounds the Dvaitists have all the advantage. Fichte and the others exhaust themselves trying to turn the simple and obvious position that : " If the Ego alone exists, where is any place, not only for morals and religion, which we can very well do without, but for the most essential and continuous acts of life? Why should an infinite Ego fill a non-existent body with imaginary food cooked in thought only over an illusionary fire by a cook who is not there? Why should infinite power use such finite means, and very often fail even then?"

What is the sum total of the Vedantist position? "'I' am an illusion, externally. In reality, the true 'I' am the Infinite, and if the illusionary 'I' could only realise Who 'I' really am, how very happy we should all be!" And here we have Karma, rebirth, all the mighty laws of nature operating nowhere in nothing!

There is no room for worship or for morality in the Advaitist system. All the specious pleas of the Bhagavad-Gita, and the ethical works of Western Advaitist philosophers, are more or less consciously confusion of thought. But no subtlety can turn the practical argument ; the grinning mouths of the Dvaitist guns keep the fort of Ethics, and warn metaphysics to keep off the rather green grass of religion.

That its apologists should have devoted so much time, thought, scholarship, and ingenuity to this question is the best proof of the fatuity of the Advaita position.

There is then a flaw somewhere. I boldly take up the glove against all previous wisdom,

revert to the most elementary ideas of cannibal savages, challenge all the most vital premisses and axiomata that have passed current coin with philosophy for centuries, and present my theory.

I clearly foresee the one difficulty, and will discuss it in advance. If my conclusions on this point are not accepted, we may at once get back to our previous irritable agnosticism, and look for our Messiah elsewhere. But if we can see together on this one point, I think things will go fairly smoothly afterwards.

Consider[1] Darkness ! Can we philosophically or actually regard as different the darkness produced by interference of light and that existing in the mere absence of light?

Is Unity really identical with .9 recurring?

Do we not mean different things when we speak respectively of $2 \sin 60°$ and of $\sqrt{3}$?

Charcoal and diamond are obviously different in the categories of colour, crystallisation, hardness, and so on ; but are they not really so even in that of existence?

The third example is to my mind the best. $2 \sin 60°$ and $\sqrt{3}$ are unreal and therefore never conceivable, at least to the present constitution of our human intelligences. Worked out, neither has meaning; unworked, both have meaning, and that a different meaning in one case and the other.

We have thus two terms, both unreal, both inconceivable, yet both representing intelligible and diverse ideas to our minds (and this is the point!) though identical in reality and convertible by a process of reason which simulates or replaces that apprehension which we can never (one may suppose) attain to.

Let us apply this idea to the Beginning of all things, about which the Christians lie frankly, the Hindus prevaricate, and the

---

[1] Or as the Sunday-school boy said : " Faith is the power of believing what we know to be untrue." I quote Deussen with the more pleasure, because it is about the only sentence in all his writings with which I am in accord. —A. C.

[1] Ratiocination may perhaps not take us far. But a continuous and attentive study of these quaint points of distinction may give us an intuition, or direct mind-apperception of what we want, one way or the other.—A. C.

Buddhists are discreetly silent, while not contradicting even the gross and ridiculous accounts of the more fantastic Hindu visionaries.

The Qabalists explain the " First Cause "[1] by the phrase : " From 0 to 1, as the circle opening out into the line." The Christian dogma is really identical, for both conceive of a previous and eternally existing God, though the Qabalists hedge by describing this latent Deity as " Not." Later commentators, notably the illustrious[2] Mac-Gregor-Mathers, have explained this Not as "negatively-existing." Profound as is my respect for the intellectual and spiritual attainments of him whom I am proud to have been permitted to call my master,[2] I am bound to express my view that when the Qabalists said Not, they meant Not, and nothing else. In fact, I really claim to have re-discovered the long-lost and central Arcanum of those divine philosophers.

I have no serious objection to a finite god, or gods, distinct from men and things. In fact, personally, I believe in them all, and admit them to possess inconceivable though not infinite power.

The Buddhists admit the existence of Maha-Brahma, but his power and knowledge are limited ; and his agelong day must end. I find evidence everywhere, even in our garbled and mutilated version of the Hebrew Scriptures, that Jehovah's power was limited in all sorts of ways. At the Fall, for instance, Tetragrammaton Elohim has to summon his angels hastily to guard the Tree of Life, lest he should be proved a liar. For had it occurred to Adam to eat of that Tree before their transgression was discovered, or had the Serpent been aware of its properties, Adam would indeed have lived and not died. So that a mere accident saved the remnants of the already besmirched reputation of the Hebrew tribal Fetich.

[1] An expression they carefully avoid using.— A. C.
[2] I retain this sly joke from the first edition.

When Buddha was asked how things came to be, he took refuge in silence, which his disciples very conveniently interpreted as meaning that the question tended not to edification.

I take it that the Buddha (ignorant, doubtless, of algebra) had sufficiently studied philosophy and possessed enough worldly wisdom to be well aware that any system he might promulgate would be instantly attacked and annihilated by the acumen of his numerous and versatile opponents.

Such teaching as he gave on the point may be summed up as follows. " Whence whither, why, we know not ; but we do know that we are here, that we dislike being here, that there is a way out of the whole loathsome affair—let us make haste and take it ! "

I am not so retiring in disposition ;· I persist in my inquiries, and at last the appalling question is answered, and the past ceases to intrude its problems upon my mind.

Here you are ! Three shies a penny ! Change all bad arguments.

I ASSERT THE ABSOLUTENESS OF THE QABALISTIC ZERO.

When we say that the Cosmos sprang from 0, what kind of 0 do we mean ? By 0 in the ordinary sense of the term we mean " absence of extension in any of the categories."

When I say "No cat has two tails," I do not mean, as the old fallacy runs, that "Absence-of-cat possesses two tails "; but that " In the category of two-tailed things, there is no extension pf cat."

Nothingness is that about which no positive proposition is valid. We cannot truly affirm : " Nothingness is green, or heavy, or sweet."

Let us call time, space, being, heaviness, hunger, the categories.[1] If a man be heavy

[1] I cannot here discuss the propriety of representing the categories as dimensions. It will be obvious to any student of the integral calculus, or to any one who· appreciates the geometrical significance of the term x^4.—A. C.

and hungry, he is extended in all these, besides, of course, many more. But let us suppose that these five are all. Call the man X; his formula is then $X^{t+s+b+h+\hbar}$. If he now eat, he will cease to be extended in hunger; if he be cut off from time and gravitation as well, he will now be represented by the formula X^{s+b}. Should he cease to occupy space and to exist, his formula would then be X^0. This expression is equal to 1; whatever X may represent, if it be raised to the power of 0 (this meaning mathematically "if it be extended in no dimension or category"), the result is Unity, and the unknown factor X is eliminated.

This is the Advaitist idea of the future of man; his personality, bereft of all its qualities, disappears and is lost, while in its place arises the impersonal Unity, The Pleroma, Parabrahma, or the Allah of the Unity-adoring followers of Mohammed. (To the Musulman fakir, Allah is by no means a personal God.)

Unity is thus unaffected, whether or no it be extended in any of the categories. But we have already agreed to look to 0 for the Uncaused.

Now if there was in truth 0 "before the beginning of years," THAT 0 WAS EXTENDED IN NONE OF THE CATEGORIES, FOR THERE COULD HAVE BEEN NO CATEGORIES IN WHICH IT COULD EXTEND! If our 0 was the ordinary 0 of mathematics, there was not truly absolute 0, for 0 is, as I have shown, dependent on the idea of categories. If these existed, then the whole question is merely thrown back; we must reach a state in which the 0 is absolute. Not only must we get rid of all subjects, but of all predicates. By 0 (in mathematics) we really mean 0^n, where n is the final term of a natural scale of dimensions, categories, or predicates. Our Cosmic Egg, then, from which the present universe arose, was Nothingness, extended in no categories, or, graphically, 0^0. This expression is in its present form meaningless. Let us dis-

cover its value by a simple mathematical process!

$$0^0 = 0^{1-1} = \frac{0^1}{0^1} \left[\text{Multiply by } 1 = \frac{n}{n} \right]$$

$$\text{Then } \frac{0^1}{n} \times \frac{n}{0^1} = 0 \times \infty.$$

Now the multiplying of the infinitely great by the infinitely small results in SOME UNKNOWN FINITE NUMBER EXTENDED IN AN UNKNOWN NUMBER OF CATEGORIES. It happened, when this our Great Inversion took place, from the essence of all nothingness to finity extended in innumerable categories, that an incalculably vast system was produced. Merely by chance, chance in the truest sense of the term, we are found with gods, men, stars, planets, devils, colours, forces, and all the materials of the Cosmos: and with time, space, and causality, the conditions limiting and involving them all.[1]

Remember that it is not true to say that our 0^0 existed; nor that it did not exist. The idea of existence was just as much unformulated as that of toasted cheese.

But 0^0 is a finite expression, or has a finite phase, and our universe is a finite universe; its categories are themselves finite, and the expression "infinite space" is a contradiction in terms. The idea of an absolute and of an infinite [2] God is relegated to the limbo of all similar idle and pernicious perversions of truth. Infinity remains, but only as a mathematical conception as impossible in nature as the square root of -1. Against all this mathematical, or semi-mathematical, reasoning, it may doubtless be objected that our

[1] Compare and contrast this doctrine with that of Herbert Spencer ("First Principles," Pt. I.), and see my "Science and Buddhism" for a full discussion of the difference involved. —A. C.

[2] If by "infinitely great" we only mean "indefinitely great," as a mathematician would perhaps tell us, we of course begin at the very point I am aiming at, viz., Ecrasez l'Infini. – A. C.

whole system of numbers, and of manipulating them, is merely a series of conventions When I say that the square root of three is unreal, I know quite well that it is only so in relation to the series 1, **2**, 3, &c., and that this series is equally unreal if I make $\sqrt{3}$, π, $\sqrt[3]{50}$ the members of a ternary scale. But this, theoretically true, is practically absurd. If I mean "the number of a, b, and c," it does not matter if I write 3 or $\sqrt[3]{50}$; the idea is a definite one ; and it is the funda-mental ideas of consciousness of which we are treating, and to which we are compelled to refer everything, whether proximately or ultimately.

So also my equation, fantastic as it may seem, has a perfect and absolute parallel in logic. Thus : let us convert twice the pro-position "some books are on the table." By negativing both terms we get "Absence-of-book is not on the table," which is precisely my equation backwards, and a thinkable thing. To reverse the process, what do I mean when I say "some pigs, but not the black pig, are not in the sty"? I imply that the black pig is in the sty. All I have done is to represent the con-version as a change, rather than as merely another way of expressing the same thing. And "change" is really not my meaning either ; for change, to our minds, involves the idea of time. But the whole thing is inconceivable—to ratiocination, though not to thought. Note well too that if I say "Absence-of-books is not on the table," I cannot convert it into "All books are on the table" but only to "some books are on the table." The proposition is an " I " and not an " A " proposition. It is the Advaita blunder to make it so; and many a schoolboy has fed off the mantelpiece for less.

There is yet another proof—the proof by exclusion. I have shown, and meta-physicians practically admit, the falsity alike of Dvaitism and Advaitism. The third, the only remaining theory, *this* theory, must, however antecedently impro-

bable, however difficult to assimilate, be true.[1]

"My friend, my young friend," I think I hear some Christian cleric say, with an air of profound wisdom, not untinged with pity, condescending to pose beardles and brainless impertinence : " where is the *Cause* for this truly remarkable change?"

That is exactly where the theory rears to heaven its stoutest bastion ! There is not, and could not be, any cause. Had 0^0 been extended in causality, no change could have taken place.[2]

Here, then, are we, finite beings in a finite universe, time, space, and causality them-selves finite (inconceivable as it may seem) with our individuality, and all the "illu-sions" of the Advaitists, just as real as they practically are to our normal consciousness.

As Schopenhauer, following Buddha, points out, suffering is a necessary condition of this existence.[3] The war of the contend-ing forces as they grind themselves down to the final resultant must cause endless agony. We may one day be able to transform the categories of emotion as certainly and easily as we now transform the categories of force, so that in a few years Chicago may be im-porting suffering in the raw state and turning it into tinned salmon : but at present the reverse process is alone practicable.

How, then, shall we escape? Can we expect the entire universe to resolve itself back into the phase of 0^0? Surely not. In the first place, there is no reason why the whole should do so ; $\frac{x}{y}$ is just as con-vertible as x. But worse, the category of causality has been formed, and its inertia is

---

[1] I may remark that the distinction between this theory and the normal one of the Imma-nence of the Universe, is trivial, perhaps even verbal only. Its advantage, however, is that, by hypostatising nothing, we avoid the neces-sity of any explanation. How did nothing come to be? is a question which requires no answer.

[2] See the Questions of King Milinda, vol. ii. p. 103.

[3] See also Huxley, " Evolution and Ethics."

sufficient to oppose a most serious stumbling-block to so gigantic a process.

The task before us is consequently of a terrible nature. It is easy to let things slide, to grin and bear it in fact, until everything is merged in the ultimate unity, which may or may not be decently tolerable. But while we wait ? There now arises the question of freewill. Causality is probably not fully extended in its own category,[1] a circumstance which gives room for a fractional amount of freewill. If this be not so, it matters little ; for if I find myself in a good state, that merely proves that my destiny took me there. We are, as Herbert Spencer observes, self-deluded with the idea of freewill ; but if this be so, nothing matters at all. If, however, Herbert Spencer is mistaken (unlikely as it must appear), then our reason is valid, and we should seek out the right path and pursue it. The question therefore need not trouble us at all.

Here then we see the use of morals and of religion, and all the rest of the bag of tricks. All these are methods, bad or good, for extricating ourselves from the universe.

Closely connected with this question is that of the will of God. People argue that an Infinite intelligence must have been at work on this cosmos. I reply No ! There is no intelligence at work worthy of the name. The Laws of Nature may be generalised in one—the Law of Inertia. Everything moves in the direction determined by the path of least resistance ; species arise, develop, and die as their collective inertia determines ; to this Law there is no exception but the doubtful one of Free-will ; the Law of Destiny itself is formally and really identical with it.[2]

[1] Causality is itself a secondary, and in its limitation as applied to volition, an inconceivable idea. H. Spencer, *op. cit.* This consideration alone should add great weight to the agnostic, and *à fortiori* to the Buddhist, position.

[2] See H. Spencer, "First Principles," "The Knowable," for a fair summary of the facts underlying this generalisation ; which indeed he comes within an ace of making in so many words. It may be observed that this law is nearly if not quite axiomatic, its contrary being enormously difficult if not impossible to formulate mentally.

As to an *infinite* intelligence, all philosophers of any standing are agreed that all-love and all-power are incompatible. The existence of the universe is a standing proof of this.

The Deist needs the Optimist to keep him company ; over their firesides all goes well, but it is a sad shipwreck they suffer on emerging into the cold world.

This is why those who seek to buttress up religion are so anxious to prove that the universe has no real existence, or only a temporary and relatively unimportant one ; the result is of course the usual self-destructive Advaitist muddle.

The precepts of morality and religion are thus of use, of vital use to us, in restraining the more violent forces alike of nature and of man. For unless law and order prevail, we have not the necessary quiet and resources for investigating, and learning to bring under our control, all the divergent phenomena of our prison, a work which we undertake that at last we may be able to break down the walls, and find that freedom which an inconsiderate Inversion has denied.

The mystical precepts of pseudo-Zoroaster, Buddha, Çankaracharya, pseudo-Christ and the rest, are for advanced students only, for direct attack on the problem. Our servants, the soldiers, lawyers, all forms of government, make this our nobler work possible, and it is the gravest possible mistake to sneer at these humble but faithful followers of the great minds of the world.

What, then, are the best, easiest, directest methods to attain our result ? And how shall we, in mortal language, convey to the minds of others the nature of a result so beyond language, baffling even imagination eagle-pinioned ? It may help us if we endeavour to outline the distinction between the Hindu and Buddhist methods and aims of the Great Work.

The Hindu method is really mystical in the truest sense ; for, as I have shown, the Atman is not infinite and eternal : one day it must sink down with the other forces. But by creating in thought an infinite Impersonal Personality, by *defining* it as such, all religions except the Buddhist and, as I believe, the Qabalistic, have sought to annihilate their own personality. The Buddhist aims directly at extinction ; the Hindu denies and abolishes his own finity by the creation of an absolute.

As this cannot be done in reality, the process is illusory ; yet it is useful in the early stages—as far, at any rate, as the fourth stage of Dhyana, where the Buddha places it, though the Yogis claim to attain to Nirvikalpa-Samadhi, and that Moksha is identical with Nirvana ; the former claim I see no reason to deny them ; the latter statement I must decline at present to accept.

The task of the Buddhist recluse is roughly as follows. He must plunge every particle of his being into one idea : right views, aspirations, word, deed, life, will-power, meditation, rapture, such are the stages of his liberation, which resolves itself into a struggle against the law of causality. He cannot prevent past causes taking effect, but he can prevent present causes from having any future results. The exoteric Christian and Hindu rather rely on another person to do this for them, and are further blinded by the thirst for life and individual existence, the most formidable obstacle of all, in fact a negation of the very object of all religion. Schopenhauer shows that life is assured to the will-to-live, and unless Christ (or Krishna, as the case may be) destroys these folk by superior power—a task from which almightiness might well recoil baffled !—I much fear that eternal life, and consequently eternal suffering, joy, and change of all kinds, will be their melancholy fate. Such persons are in truth their own real enemies. Many of them, however, believing erroneously that they are being " unselfish," do fill their hearts with devotion for the beloved Saviour, and this process is, in its ultimation, so similar to the earlier stages of the Great

Work itself, that some confusion has, stupidly enough, arisen ; but for all that the practice has been the means of bringing some devotees on to the true Path of the Wise, unpromising as such material must sound to intelligent ears.

The esoteric Christian or Hindu adopts a middle path. Having projected the Absolute from his mind, he endeavours to unite his consciousness with that of his Absolute, and of course his personality is destroyed in the process. Yet it is to be feared that such an adept too often starts on the path with the hideous idea of aggrandising his own personality to the utmost. But this tendency is soon corrected, as it were automatically.

(The mathematical analogue of this process is to procure for yourself the realisation of the nothingness of yourself by keeping the fourth dimension ever present to your mind.)

The illusory nature of this idea of an infinite Atman is well shown by the very proof which that most distinguished Vedantist, the late Swami Vivekananda (no connection with the firm of a similar name[1] across the street), gives of the existence of the infinite. " Think of a circle ! " says he. "You will in a moment become conscious of an infinite circle around your original small one." The fallacy is obvious. The big circle is not infinite at all, but is itself limited by the little one. But to take away the little circle, that is the method of the esoteric Christian or the mystic. But the process is never perfect, because however small the little circle becomes, its relation with the big circle is still finite. But even allowing for a moment that the Absolute is really attainable, is the nothingness of the finity related to it really identical with that attained directly by the Buddhist Arahat ? This, consistently with

[1] The Swami Vive Ananda, Madame Horos, for whose history consult the Criminal Law Reports.

my former attitude, I feel constrained to deny. The consciousness of the Absolute-wala[1] is really extended infinitely rather than diminished infinitely, as he will himself assure you. True, Hegel says : "Pure being is pure nothing!" and it is true that the infinite heat and cold, joy and sorrow, light and darkness, and all the other pairs of opposites,[2] cancel one another out : yet I feel rather afraid of this Absolute! Maybe its joy and sorrow are represented in phases, just as 0^0 and finity are phases of an identical expression, and I have an even chance only of being on the right side of the fence! The Buddhist leaves no chances of this kind; in all his categories he is infinitely un-extended ; though the categories themselves exist; he is in fact $0^{A+B+C+D+E+..+N}$ and capable of no conceivable change, unless we imagine Nirvana to be incomprehensibly divided by Nirvana, which would (supposing the two Nirvanas to possess identical categories) result in the production of the original 0^0. But a further change would be necessary even then before serious mischief could result. In short, I think we may dismiss from our minds any alarm in respect of this contingency.

On mature consideration, therefore, I confidently and deliberately take my refuge in the Triple Gem. Namo Tasso Bhagavato Arahato Sammasambuddhasa![3]

Let there be hereafter no discussion of the classical problems of philosophy and religion! In the light of this exposition the

antitheses of noumenon and phenomenon, unity and multiplicity, and their kind, are all reconciled, and the only question that remains is that of finding the most satisfactory means of attaining Nirvana—extinction of all that exists, knows, or feels ; extinction final and complete, utter and absolute extinction. For by these words only can we indicate Nirvana : a state which transcends thought cannot be described in thought's language. But from the point of view of thought extinction is complete : we have no data for discussing that which is unthinkable, and must decline to do so. This is the answer to those who accuse the Buddha of hurling his Arahats (and himself) from Samma Samadhi to annihilation.

Pray observe in the first place that my solution of the Great Problem permits the co-existence of an indefinite number of means : they need not even be compatible ; Karma, rebirth, Providence, prayer, sacrifice, baptism, there is room for all. On the old and, I hope, now finally discredited hypothesis of an infinite being, the supporters of these various ideas, while explicitly affirming them, implicitly denied. Similarly, note that the Qabalistic idea of a supreme God (and innumerable hierarchies) is quite compatible with this theory, provided that the supreme God is not infinite.

Now as to our weapons. The more advanced Yogis of the East, like the Nonconformists at home, have practically abandoned ceremonial as idle. I have yet to learn, however, by what dissenters have replaced it! I take this to be an error, except in the case of the very advanced Yogi. For there exists a true magical ceremonial, vital and direct, whose purpose has, however, at any rate of recent times, been hopelessly misunderstood.

Nobody any longer supposes that any means but that of meditation is of avail to grasp the immediate causes of our being ; if some person retort that he prefers to rely on a Glorified Redeemer, I simply answer

[1] Wala, one whose business is connected with anything. *E.g.* Jangli-wala, one who lives in, or has business with, a jungle, *i.e.* a wild man, or a Forest Conservator.
[2] The Hindus see this as well as any one, and call Atman *Sat-chit-ananda*, these being above the pairs of opposites, rather on the Hegelian lines of the reconciliation (rather than the identity) of opposites in a master-idea. We have dismissed infinity as the figment of a morbid mathematic : but in any case the same disproof applies to it as to God.—A. C.
[3] Hail unto Thee, the Blessed One, the Perfect One, the Enlightened One!

that he is the very nobody to whom I now refer.

Meditation is then the means ; but only the supreme means. The agony column of the *Times* is the supreme means of meeting with the gentleman in the brown billycock and frock coat, wearing a green tie and chewing a straw, who was at the soirée of the Carlton Club last Monday night ; no doubt ! but this means is seldom or never used in the similar contingency of a cow-elephant desiring her bull in the jungles of Ceylon.

Meditation is not within the reach of every one ; not all possess the ability ; very few indeed (in the West at least) have the opportunity.

In any case what the Easterns call "one-pointedness" is an essential preliminary to even early stages of true meditation. And iron will-power is a still earlier qualification.

By meditation I do not mean merely "thinking about" anything, however profoundly, but the absolute restraint of the mind to the contemplation of a single object, whether gross, fine, or altogether spiritual.

Now true magical ceremonial is entirely directed to attain this end, and forms a magnificent gymnasium for those who are not already finished mental athletes. By act, word, and thought, both in quantity and quality, the one object of the ceremony is being constantly indicated. Every fumigation, purification, banishing, invocation, evocation, is chiefly a reminder of the single purpose, until the supreme moment arrives, and every fibre of the body, every force-channel of the mind, is strained out in one overwhelming rush of the Will in the direction desired. Such is the real purport of all the apparently fantastic directions of Solomon, Abramelin, and other sages of repute. When a man has evoked and mastered such forces as Taphtatharath, Belial, Amaimon, and the great powers of the elements, then he may safely be permitted to begin to try to stop thinking.

For, needless to say, the universe, including the thinker, exists only by virtue of the thinker's thought.[1]

In yet one other way is magic a capital training ground for the Arahat. True symbols do really awake those macrocosmic forces of which they are the eidola, and it is possible in this manner very largely to increase the magical "potential," to borrow a term from electrical science.

Of course, there are bad and invalid processes, which tend rather to disperse or to excite the mind-stuff than to control it ; these we must discard. But there is a true magical ceremonial, the central Arcanum alike of Eastern and Western practical transcendentalism. Needless to observe, if I knew it, I should not disclose it.

I therefore definitely affirm the validity of the Qabalistic tradition in its practical part as well as in those exalted regions of thought through which we have so recently, and so hardly, travelled.

Eight are the limbs of Yoga : morality and virtue, control of body, thought, and force, leading to concentration, meditation, and rapture.

Only when the last of these has been attained, and itself refined upon by removing the gross and even the fine objects of its

---

[1] See Berkeley and his expounders, for the Western shape of this Eastern commonplace. Huxley, however, curiously enough, states the fact almost in these words.—A. C.

[2] A possible mystic transfiguration of the Vedanta system has been suggested to me on the lines of the Syllogism—

God   = Being (Patanjali).
Being = Nothing (Hegel).
God   = Nothing (Buddhism).

Or, in the language of religion :

Every one may admit that monotheism, exalted by the introduction of the ∞ symbol, is equivalent to pantheism. Pantheism and atheism are really identical, as the opponents of both are the first to admit.

If this be really taught, I must tender my apologies, for the reconcilement is of course complete.—A. C.

sphere, can the causes, subtle and coarse, the unborn causes whose seed is hardly sown, of continued existence be grasped and annihilated, so that the Arahat is sure of being abolished in the utter extinction of Nirvana, while even in this world of pain, where he must remain until the ancient causes, those which have already germinated, àre utterly worked out (for even the Buddha himself could not swing back the Wheel of the Law), his certain anticipation of the approach of Nirvana is so intense as to bathe him constantly in the unfathomable ocean of the apprehension of immediate bliss.

AUM MANI PADME HOUM.

1903

SCIENCE AND BUDDHISM

(*Inscribed to the revered Memory of Thomas Henry Huxley*)

I.

THE purpose of this essay is to draw a strict comparison between the modern scientific conceptions of Phenomena and their explanation, where such exists, and the ancient ideas of the Buddhists; to show that Buddhism, alike in theory and practice, is a scientific religion; a logical superstructure on a basis of experimentally verifiable truth; and that its method is identical with that of science. We must resolutely exclude the accidental features of both, especially of Buddhism; and unfortunately in both cases we have to deal with dishonest and shameless attempts to foist on either opinions for which neither is willing to stand sponsor. Professor Huxley has dealt with the one in his "Pseudo-Scientific Realism"; Professor Rhys Davids has demolished the other in that one biting comment on "Esoteric Buddhism" that it was "not Esoteric and certainly not Buddhism." But some of the Theosophic mud still sticks to the Buddhist chariot; and there are still people who believe that sane science has at least a friendly greeting for Atheism and Materialism in their grosser and more militant forms.

Let it be understood then, from the outset, that if in Science I include metaphysics, and in Buddhism meditation-practices, I lend myself neither to the whittlers or "reconcilers" on the one hand, nor to the Animistic jugglers on the other. Apart from the Theosophic rubbish, we find Sir Edwin Arnold writing:

"Whoever saith Nirvana is to cease,
Say unto such they lie."

Lie is a strong word and should read "translate correctly." [1]

I suppose it would not scan, nor rhyme: but Sir Edwin is the last person to be deterred by a little thing like that. Dr. Paul Carus, too, in the "Gospel of Buddha," is pleased to represent Nirvana as a parallel for the Heaven of the Christian It is sufficient if I reiterate the unanimous opinion of competent scholars, that there is no fragment of evidence in any canonical book sufficient to establish such interpretations in the teeth of Buddhist tradition and practice; and that any person who persists in tuning Buddhism to his own Jew's harp in this way is risking his reputation, either for scholarship or good faith. Scientific men are common enough in the West, if Buddhists are not; and I may safely leave in their hands the task of castigating the sneak-thieves of the Physical area.

II.

The essential features of Buddhism have been summed up by the Buddha himself. To me, of course, what the Buddha said or did not say is immaterial; a thing is true or not true, whoever said it. We believe Mr. Savage Landor when he affirms that Lhassa is an important town in Tibet. Where only probabilities are concerned we are of course influenced by the moral char-

[1] See Childers, Pali Dictionary, *s. v.* Nibbana.

acter and mental attainments of the speaker; but here I have nothing to do with the uncertain.[1]

There is an excellent test for the value of any passage in a Buddhist book. We are, I think, justified in discarding stories which are clearly Oriental fiction, just as modern criticism, however secretly Theistic, discards the Story of Hasisadra or of Noah. In justice to Buddhism, let us not charge its Scripture with the Sisyphean task of seriously upholding the literal interpretation of obviously fantastic passages.[2] May our Buddhist zealots be warned by the fate of old-fashioned English orthodoxy! But when Buddhism condescends to be vulgarly scientific; to observe, to classify, to *think;* I conceive we may take the matter seriously, and accord a reasonable investigation to its assertions. Examples of such succinctness and clarity may be found in The Four Noble Truths; The Three Characteristics; The Ten Fetters; and there is clearly a definite theory in the idea of Karma. Such ideas are basic, and are as a thread on which

---

[1] See Huxley's classical example of the horse, zebra, and centaur.

[2] Similarly, where Buddhist parables are of a mystical nature, where a complicated symbolism of numbers (for example) is intended to shadow a truth, we must discard them. My experience of mysticism is somewhat large; its final dictum is that the parable *x* may be equated to *a, b, c, d* . . . *z* by six-and-twenty different persons, or by one person in six-and-twenty different moods. Even had we a strong traditional explanation I should maintain my position. The weapons of the Higher Criticism, supplemented by Common Sense, are perfectly valid and inevitably destructive against any such structure. But I am surely in danger of becoming ridiculous in writing thus to the scientific world. What I really wish to show is that one need not look for all the Buddhist fancy dishes to be served at the scientific table to the peril of the scientific digestion. And by a backhanded stroke I wish to impress as deeply as possible upon my Buddhist friends that too much zeal for the accidentals of our religion will surely result in the overwhelming of its essentials in the tide of justly scornful or justly casuistic criticism.—A. C.

the beads of Arabian-Night-Entertainment are strung.[1]

I propose therefore to deal with these and some other minor points of the Buddhist metaphysic, and trace out their scientific analogies, or, as I hope to show, more often identities.

First then let us examine that great Summary of the Buddhist Faith, the Four Noble Truths.

III.

THE FOUR NOBLE TRUTHS.

(1) SORROW.—Existence is Sorrow. This means that "no known form of Existence is separable from Sorrow." This truth is stated by Huxley, almost in so many words, in Evolution and Ethics. "It was no less plain to some of these antique philosophers than to the fathers of modern philosophy that suffering is the badge of all the tribe of sentient things; that it is no accidental accompaniment, but an essential constituent of the Cosmic Process." And in the same essay, though he is disposed to deny more than the rudiments of consciousness to the lower forms of life, he is quite clear that pain varies directly (to put it loosely) with the degree of consciousness. Cf. also "Animal Automatism," pp. 236-237.

(2) SORROW'S CAUSE.—The cause of sorrow is desire. I take desire here to include such a phenomenon as the tendency of two molecules of hydrogen and chlorine to combine under certain conditions. If death be painful to me, it is presumably so to a molecule; if we represent one operation as pleasant, the converse is presumably painful. Though I am not conscious of the individual pain of the countless deaths involved in this my act of writing, it may be there. And what I call "fatigue" may be the echo in my central consciousness of the

---

[1] See Prof. Rhys Davids on the "Jataka."

shriek of a peripheral anguish. Here we leave the domain of fact ; but at least as far our knowledge extends, all or nearly all the operations of Nature are vanity and vexation of spirit. Consider food, the desire for which periodically arises in all conscious beings.[1]

The existence of these desires, or rather necessities, which I realise to be mine, is unpleasant. It is this desire inherent in me for continued consciousness that is responsible for it all, and this leads us to the Third Noble Truth.

(3) SORROW'S CEASING.—The cessation of desire is the cessation of sorrow. This is a simple logical inference from the second Truth, and needs no comment.

(4) THE NOBLE EIGHTFOLD PATH.— There is a way, to be considered later, of realising the Third Truth. But we must, before we can perceive its possibility on the one hand, or its necessity on the other, form a clear idea of what are the Buddhist tenets with regard to the Cosmos ; and, in particular, to man.[2]

IV.

THE THREE CHARACTERISTICS.

The Three Characteristics (which we may predicate of all known existing things):

(a) Change. Anikka.
(b) Sorrow. Dukkha.
(c) Absence of an Ego. Anatta.

[1] Change is the great enemy, the immediate cause of pain. Unable to arrest it, I slow the process, and render it temporarily painless, by eating. This is a concession to weakness, no doubt, in one sense. Do I eat really in order to check change, or to maintain my ego-consciousness? Change I desire, for my present condition is sorrow. I really desire the impossible ; completely to retain my present egoity with all its conditions reversed.—A. C.
[2] For an able and luminous exposition of " The Four Noble Truths " I refer the reader to the pamphlet bearing that title by my old friend Bhikkhu Ananda Maitriya, published by the Buddhasasana Samagama, 1 Pagoda Road, Rangoon.—A. C.

This is the Buddhist Assertion. What does Science say ?

(a) Huxley, " Evolution and Ethics " :

" As no man fording a swift stream can dip his foot twice into the same water, so no man can, with exactness, affirm of anything in the sensible world that it is. As he utters the words, nay, as he thinks them, the predicate ceases to be applicable; the present has become the past ; the ' is ' should be ' was.' And the more we learn of the nature of things the more evident is it that what we call rest is only unperceived activity; that seeming peace is silent but strenuous battle. In every part, at every moment, the state of the cosmos is the expression of a transitory adjustment of contending forces, a scene of strife, in which all the combatants fall in turn. What is true of each part is true of the whole. Natural knowledge tends more and more to the conclusion that " all the choir of heaven and furniture of the earth " are the transitory forms of parcels of cosmic substance wending along the road of evolution, from nebulous potentiality, through endless growths of sun and planet and satellite, through all varieties of matter ; through infinite diversities of life and thought, possibly, through modes of being of which we neither have a conception, nor are competent to form any, back to the indefinable latency from which they arose. Thus the most obvious attribute of the cosmos is its impermanence. It assumes the aspect not so much of a permanent entity as of a changeful process, in which naught endures save the flow of energy and the rational order which pervades it."

This is an admirable summary of the Buddhist doctrine.

(b) See above on the First Noble Truth.

(c) This is the grand position which Buddha carried against the Hindu philosophers. In our own country it is the argument of Hume, following Berkeley to a place where Berkeley certainly never meant to go—a curious parallel fulfilment of Christ's curse against Peter (John xxi.). The Bishop demolishes the idea of a substratum of matter, and

Hume follows by applying an identical process of reasoning to the phenomena of mind.[1]

Let us consider the Hindu theory. They classify the phenomena (whether well or ill matters nothing), but represent them all as pictured in, but not affecting, a certain changeless, omniscient, blissful existence called Atman. Holding to Theism, the existence of evil forces them to the Fichtean position that "the Ego posits the Non-Ego," and we learn that nothing really exists after all but Brahm. They then distinguish between Jivatma, the soul-conditioned; and Paramatma, the soul free; the former being the base of our normal consciousness; the latter of the Nirvikalpa-Samadhi conscious-

---

[1] The Buddhist position *may* be interpreted as agnostic in this matter, these arguments being directed against, and destructive of, the unwarranted assumptions of the Hindus; but no more. See Sabbasava Sutta, 10.

"In him, thus unwisely considering, there springs up one or other of the six (absurd) notions.

"As something real and true he gets the notion, ' I have a self.'

"As something real and true he gets the notion, ' I have not a self.'

"As something real and true he gets the notion, ' By my self, I am conscious of my self.'

"As something real and true he gets the notion, ' By my self, I am conscious of my non-self.'

"Or again, he gets the notion, ' This soul of mine can be perceived, it has experienced the result of good or evil actions committed here and there; now this soul of mine is permanent, lasting, eternal, has the inherent quality of never changing, and will continue for ever and ever ! '

"This, brethren, is called the walking in delusion, the jungle of delusion, the wilderness of delusion, the puppet-show of delusion, the writhing of delusion, the fetter of delusion."

There are, it may be noted, only five (not six) notions mentioned, unless we take the last as double. Or we may consider the sixth as the contrary of the fifth, and correct. The whole passage is highly technical, perhaps untrustworthy; in any case, this is not the place to discuss it. The sun of Agnosticism breaking through the cloud of Anatta is the phenomenon to which I wished to call attention.—A. C.

---

ness; this being the sole condition on which morals, religion, and fees to priests can continue. For the Deist has only to advance his fundamental idea to be forced round in a vicious circle of absurdities.[1]

The Buddhist makes a clean sweep of all this sort of nonsense. He analyses the phenomena of mind, adopting Berkeley's paradox that "matter is immaterial," in a sane and orderly way. The "common-sense Philosopher," whom I leave to chew the bitter leaves of Professor Huxley's Essay "On Sensation and the Unity of the Structure of Sensiferous Organs," observes, on lifting his arm, "I lift my arm." The Buddhist examines this proposition closely, and begins :

"There is a lifting of an arm."

By this terminology he avoids Teutonic discussions concerning the Ego and Non-ego.[2] But how does he know this proposition to be true? By sensation. The fact is therefore :

"There is a sensation of the lifting of an arm."

But how does he know that? By perception. Therefore he says :

"There is a perception of a sensation, &c."

And why this perception? From the inherent tendency.

(Note carefully the determinist standpoint involved in the enunciation of this Fourth Skandha ; and that it comes lower than Viññanam.)

"There is a tendency to perceive the sensation, &c."

And how does he know there is a tendency? By consciousness. The final analysis reads :

"There is a consciousness of a tendency to perceive the sensation of a lifting of an arm."

He does not, for he cannot, go further back. He will not suppose, on no sort of evidence, the substratum of Atman uniting

---

[1] As Bishop Butler so conclusively showed.

[2] I may incidentally remark that a very few hours' practice (see Section VIII.) cause "I lift my arm " to be intuitively denied.—A. C.

consciousness to consciousness by its eternity, while it fixes a great gulf between them by its changelessness. He states the knowable, states it accurately, and leaves it there. But there is a practical application of this analysis which I will treat of later. (See VIII. Mahasatipa*tth*ana.)

We are told that the memory is a proof of some real "I." But how treacherous is this ground! Did a past event in my life not happen because I have forgotten it? O the analogy of the river water given above is most valid! I who write this am not I who read it over and correct it. Do I desire to play with lead soldiers? Am I the doddering old cripple who must be wheeled about and fed on whisky and bread and milk? And is my difference from them so conspicuously less than from the body lying dead of which those who see it will say, "This was Aleister Crowley"?

What rubbish is it to suppose that an eternal substance, sentient or not, omniscient or not, depends for its information on so absurd a series of bodies as are grouped under that "Crowley"!

Yet the Buddhist meets all arguments of the spiritual order with a simple statement which, if not certain, is at least not improbable. There is, he will tell you, a "spiritual" world, or to avoid any (most unjustifiable) misunderstandings, let us say a world of subtler matter than the visible and tangible, which has its own laws (analogous to, if not identical with, those laws of matter with which we are acquainted) and whose inhabitants change, and die, and are re-born very much as ordinary mortal beings. But as they are of subtler matter, their cycle is less rapid.[1]

As a nominalist, I hope not to be misunderstood when I compare this to the relative mutability of the individual and the species.[2] We have enough examples free

[1] Cf. Huxley, cited *supra*, "possibly, through modes of being of which we neither have a conception, nor are competent to form any. . . ."

[2] Cf. "Evolution and Ethics," note 1.

from such possibility of misinterpretation in our own bodies. Compare the longevity of a bone with that of a corpuscle. But it is this "Substratum" universe, which must not be confounded with the substratum, the arguments for whose existence Berkeley so utterly shattered,[1] which may conserve memory for a period greatly exceeding that of one of its particular avatars. Hence the "Jataka." But the doctrine is not very essential; its chief value is to show what serious difficulties confront us, and to supply a reason for the struggle to some better state. For if nothing

[1] Without an elaborate analysis of the ideas involved in the Ding an sich of Kant, and of H. Spencer's definition of all things as Modes of the Unknowable, I may point out in passing that these hypotheses are as sterile as the "vital principle" in biology, or "phlogiston" in chemistry. They lead literally nowhere. That the phenomenal world is an illusion is all very well; one girds up one's loins to seek reality: but to prove reality unknowable is to shut all avenues to the truth-loving man, to open all to the sensualist. And, if we accept either of the above philosophies, it does not matter. That we feel it does matter is sufficient refutation, for we must obey the sentence awarded on our own testimony, whether we like it or not.

I am aware that this is a somewhat cowardly way of dealing with the question; I prefer to insist that if we once admit that the unknowable (by reason) to consciousness may be known (by concentration) to super-consciousness, the difficulty vanishes.

I think Huxley goes too far in speaking of a man "self-hypnotised into cataleptic trances" without medical evidence of a large number of cases. Edward Carpenter, who has met Yogis, and talked long and learnedly with them, tells a different story.

Even had we a large body of evidence from Anglo-Indian medical men, the proof would still be lacking. They might not be the real men. The Indian native would take intense delight in bringing round the village idiot to be inspected in the character of a holy man by the "Doctor Sahib."

The Anglo-Indian is a fool; a minimum medical education is in most cases insufficient to abate the symptoms to nil, though perhaps it must always diminish them. The Hindu is the Sphinx of civilisation; nearly all that has been written on him is worthless; those who know him best know this fact best.—A. C.

survives death, what does it matter to us?
Why are we to be so altruistic as to avoid
the reincarnation of a being in all points
different from ourselves? As the small boy
said, "What has posterity done for me?"
But something does persist ; something
changing, though less slowly. What evidence have we after all that an animal does
not remember his man-incarnation? Or, as
Levi says, "In the suns they remember,
and in the planets they forget." I think it
unlikely (may be), but in the total absence of
all evidence for or against—at least with
regard to the latter hypothesis !—I suspend
my judgment, leave the question alone, and
proceed to more practical points than are
offered by these interesting but not over-
useful metaphysical speculations.

V.

KARMA.

The law of causation is formally identical
with this. Karma means "that which is
made," and I think it should be considered
with strict etymological accuracy. If I place
a stone on the roof of a house, it is sure to
fall sooner or later ; i.e., as soon as the conditions permit. Also, in its ultimation, the
doctrine of Karma is identical with deter-
minism. On this subject much wisdom, with
an infinite amount of rubbish, has been
written. I therefore dismiss it in these few
words, confident that the established identity
can never be shaken.

VI.

THE TEN FETTERS OR SANYOGANAS.

1. Sakkaya-ditthi.   Belief in a "soul."
2. Vikikikkha.   Doubt.
3. Silabbata-parâ-   Reliance on the effi-
     mâsa.   cacy of rites and
                         ceremonies.
4. Kama.   Bodily Desires.

5. Patigha.   Hatred.
6. Ruparaga.   Desire for bodily immor-
                         tality.
7. Aruparaga.   Desire for spiritual im-
                         mortality.
8. Mano.   Pride.
9. Udhakka.   Self-righteousness.
10. Avigga.   Ignorance.

(1) For this is a *petitio principii.*

(2) This, to a scientist, is apparently
anathema. But it only means, I think, that
if we are not settled in our minds we cannot
work. And this is unquestionable. Suppose
a chemist to set to work to determine the
boiling-point of a new organic substance.
Does he stop in the midst, struck by the
fear that his thermometer is inaccurate?
No ! he has, unless he is a fool, tested it
previously. We must have our principia
fixed before we can do research work.

(3) A scientist hardly requires conviction
on this point !

(4) Do you think to combine Newton
and Caligula? The passions, allowed to
dominate, interfere with the concentration
of the mind.

(5) Does brooding on your dislikes help
you to accurate observation? I admit that
a controversy may stir you up to perform
prodigies of work, but while you are actually
working you do not suffer the concentration
of your mind to be interfered with.

(6 & 7) This Fetter and the next are con-
tingent on your having perceived the suffering of all forms of conscious existence.

(8) Needs no comment. Pride, like
humility, is a form of delusion.

(9) Is like unto it, but on the moral
plane.

(10) The great enemy. Theists alone
have found the infamous audacity to extol
the merits of this badge of servitude.

We see, then, that in this classification
a scientist will concur. We need not discuss
the question whether or no he would find
others to add. Buddhism may not be complete, but, as far as it goes, it is accurate.

VII.

THE RELATIVE REALITY OF CERTAIN STATES OF CONSCIOUSNESS.

Whether we adopt Herbert Spencer's dictum that the primary testimony of consciousness is to the existence of externality, or no ;[1] whether or no we fly to the extreme idealistic position ; there is no question that, to our normal consciousness, things as they present themselves — apart from obvious illusion, if even we dare to except this—are undisprovable to the immediate apprehension. Whatever our reason may tell us, we act precisely as though Berkeley had never lived, and the herculean Kant had been strangled while yet in his cradle by the twin serpents of his own perversity and terminology.

What criterion shall we apply to the relative realities of normal and dream consciousness ? Why do I confidently assert that the dream state is transitory and unreal ?

In that state I am equally confident that my normal consciousness is invalid. But as my dreams occupy a relatively small portion of my time, and as the law of causation seems suspended, and as their vividness is less than that of normal consciousness, and above all, as in the great majority of cases I can show a cause, dating from my waking hours, for the dream, I have four strong reasons (the first explanatory to some extent of my reasons for accepting the others) for concluding that the dream is fictitious.

But what of the " dreamless " state ? To the dreamer his normal faculties and memories arise at times, and are regarded as fragmentary and absurd, even as the remembrance of a dream is to the waking man. Can we not conceive then of a " dreamless " life, of

[1] Mahasatipatthana (Sec. VIII.) does admit this perhaps. Yet its very object is to correct consciousness on the lines indicated by reason.

which our dreams are the vague and disturbed transition to normal consciousness ?

The physiological evidence goes literally for nothing. Even were it proved that the recipio-motor apparatus of a " dreamless " sleeper was relatively quiescent, would that supply any valid argument against the theory I have suggested ? Suggested, for I admit that our present position is completely agnostic in respect to it, since we have no evidence which throws light on the matter ; and study of the subject would appear to be mere waste of time.

But the suggestion is valuable as affording us a possibly rational explanation, conformable to the waking man, which the dreamer would indignantly reject.

Suppose, however, a dream so vivid that the whole waking man is abased before its memory, that his consciousness of it appears a thousand times more real than that of the things about him ; suppose that his whole life is moulded to fit the new facts thus revealed to him ; that he would cheerfully renounce years of normal life to obtain minutes of that dream-life ; that his time sense is uprooted as never before, and that these influences are permanent. Then, you will say, delirium tremens (and the intoxication of hashish, in respect more particularly of the time sense) afford us a parallel. But the phenomena of delirium tremens do not occur in the healthy. As for the suggestion of auto-hypnosis, the memory of the " dream " is a sufficient reply. However this may be, the simple fact of the superior apparent reality—a conviction unshakable, *inépuisable* (for the English has no word), is a sufficient test. And if we condescend to argue, it is for pleasure, and aside from the vital fact ; a skirmish, and not a pitched battle.

The " dream " I have thus described is the state called Dhyana by the Hindus and Buddhists. The method of attaining it is sane, healthy, and scientific. I would not take the pains to describe that method, had not illiterate, and too often mystical advocates of the practice obscured the simple grandeur of our edifice by jimcrack pinnacles of stucco — as who should hang the Taj Mahal with fairy lamps and chintz.

It is simple. The mind is compelled to fix its attention on a single thought ; while the controlling power is exercised and a profound watchfulness kept up lest the thought should for a moment stray.[1] The latter portion is, to my mind, the essential one. The work is comparable to that of an electrician who should sit for hours with his finger on a delicately adjusted resistance-box and his eye on the spot of light of a galvanometer, charged with the duty of keeping the spot still, at least that it should never move beyond a certain number of degrees, and of recording the more important details of his experiment. Our work is identical in design, though worked with subtler—if less complex—means. For the finger on the resistance - box we substitute the Will; and its control extends but to the Mind; for the eye we substitute the Introspective Faculty with its keen observation of the most minute disturbance, while the spot of light is the Consciousness itself, the central point of the galvanometer scale the predetermined object, and the other figures on the scale, other objects, connected with the primary by order and degree, sometimes obviously, sometimes obscurely, perhaps even untraceably, so that we have no real right to predicate their connection.[2]

[1] Huxley, Essays, V., 136.
[2] This last sentence will be best understood by those who have practised up to a certain point. At first it is easy to trace back by a connected chain of thoughts from the thought which awakes us to the fact that we are wandering to the original thought. Later, and notably as we improve, this becomes first difficult, then impossible. At first sight this fact suggests that we are injuring our brains by the practice, but the explanation is as follows : Suppose we figure the central consciousness as the Sun, intent on seeing that nothing falls into him. First the near planets are carefully arranged, so that no collision can occur; afterwards Jupiter and Saturn, until his whole system is safe. If then any body fall upon the Sun, he knows that it is

How any sane person can describe this process as delusive and unhealthy passes my comprehension ; that any scientist should do so implies an ignorance on his part of the facts.

I may add that the most rigid necessity exists for perfect health of body and mind before this practice can begin; asceticism is as sternly discouraged as indulgence. How would the electrician do his work after a Guildhall Banquet? The strain of watching would be too much, and he would go off to sleep. So with the meditator. If, on the other hand, he had been without food for twenty-four hours, he might—indeed it has been done often—perform prodigies of work for the necessary period ; but a reaction must follow of proportionate severity. Nobody will pretend that the best work is done starving.[1]

Now to such an observer certain phenomena present themselves sooner or later which have the qualities above predicated of our imaginary "dream" preceded by a transition-state very like total loss of consciousness. Are these fatigue phenomena? Is it that this practice for some as yet unknown reason stimulates some special nerve-centre? Perhaps; the subject requires investigation ; I am not a physiologist. Whatever physiology may say, it is at least clear that if this state is accompanied with an intense and passionless bliss beyond anything that the normal man can conceive of, and unaccompanied with the slightest prejudice to the mental and physical health, it is most highly desirable. And to the scientist it presents a magnificent field of research.

not from any of those planets with which he is familiar, and, lord of his own system, cannot trace the course or divine the cause of the accident which has disturbed him. And he will accept this ignorance as a proof of how well his own system is going, since he no longer receives shocks from it.—A. C.

[1] Hallucination especially is to be feared. Light-headedness from want of food is quite sufficient explanation for many "Mystic raptures." I do not care to invoke hysteria and epilepsy without positive evidence.—A. C.

Of the metaphysical and religious theories which have been built upon the facts here stated, I have nothing to say in this place. The facts are not at the disposition of all; from the nature of the subject each man must be his own witness. I was once twitted by some shallow-pated person with the fact that my position cannot be demonstrated in the laboratory, and that therefore (save the mark!) I must be a mystic, an occultist, a theosophist, a mystery-monger, and what not. I am none of these. The above criticism applies to every psychologist that ever wrote, and to the man who makes the criticism by the fact of his making it. I can only say: "You have your own laboratory and apparatus, your mind; and if the room is dirty and the apparatus ill put together, you have certainly not me to blame for it."

The facts being of individual importance, then, there is little use if I detail the results of my own experience. And the reason for this reticence—for I plead guilty to reticence—that to explain would damage the very apparatus whose use I am advocating. For did I say that such and such a practice leads one to see a blue pig, the suggestion is sufficient to cause one class of people to see a blue pig where none existed, and another to deny or suspect the blue pig when it really appeared, though the latter alternative is unlikely. The consciousness phenomenon, and the bliss, is of so stupendous and well-defined a nature that I cannot imagine any preconceived idea powerful enough to diminish it appreciably. But for the sake of the former class I hold my tongue.[1]

I trust it is now perfectly clear, if my statements are accepted—and I can only

[1] On the advisability of so doing I am open to conviction. The scientific mind, I might argue, will not readily fall into that error; and for the others, they will be useless as a research phalanx, and may as well see blue pigs and be happy as not. In the past, no doubt, research has been choked by the multitude of pseudo-blue-pig-people, from the "T. S." to the "G. D." We must distinguish by methods, not by results.—A. C.

most seriously assure you that honest laborious experiment will be found to verify them in every particular—that whatever arguments are brought forward destructive of the reality of Dhyana, apply with far more force to the normal state, and it is evident that to deny the latter seriously is *ipso facto* to become unserious. Whether the normal testimony may be attacked from above, by insisting on the superior reality of Dhyana—and *à fortiori* of Samadhi, which I have not experienced, and consequently do not treat of, being content to accept the highly probable statements of those who profess to know, and who have so far not deceived me (*i.e.* as to Dhyana), is a question which it is not pertinent to the present argument to discuss.[1] I shall, however, suggest certain ideas in the following section, in which I propose to discuss the most famous of the Buddhist meditations (Mahasatipatthana), its method, object, and results.

VIII.

MAHASATIPATTHANA.

This meditation differs fundamentally from the usual Hindu methods by the fact that the mind is not restrained to the contemplation of a single object, and there is no interference with the natural functions of the body as there is, e.g., in Pranayama. It is essentially an observation-practice, which later assumes an analytic aspect in regard to the question, "What is it that is really observed?"

The Ego-idea is resolutely excluded from the start, and so far Mr. Herbert Spencer will have nothing to object ("Principles of

[1] The gravest doubts assail me on further examination of this point. I am now (1906) convinced that the experiences to which I refer constitute Samadhi. The accursed pedantry of the pundits has led to the introduction of a thousand useless subtleties in philosophical terminology, the despair alike of the translator and the investigator, until he realises that it is pedantry, and as worthless as the rest of oriental literature in all matters of exactitude. —A. C.

Psychology," ii. 404). The breathing, motions of walking, &c., are merely observed and recorded ; for instance, one may sit down quietly and say : " There is an indrawing of the breath." " There is an expiration," &c. Or, walking, " There is a raising of the right foot," and so on, just as it happens. The thought is of course not quick enough to note all the movements or their subtle causes. For example, we cannot describe the complicated muscular contractions, &c. ; but this is not necessary. Concentrate on some series of simple movements.

When this through habit becomes intuitive so that the thought is *really* " There is a raising," as opposed to " I raise " (the latter being in reality a complex and adult idea, as philosophers have often shown, ever since Descartes fell into the trap), one may begin to analyse, as explained above, and the second stage is " There is a sensation (Vedana) of a raising, &c." Sensations are further classed as pleasant or unpleasant.

When this is the true intuitive instantaneous testimony of consciousness (so that " There is a raising, &c." is rejected as a palpable lie),[1] we proceed to Sañña, perception.

" There is a perception of a (pleasant or unpleasant) sensation of a raising, &c."

When this has become intuitive—why ! here's a strange result ! The emotions of pain and pleasure have vanished. They are subincluded in the lesser skandha of Vedana, and Sañña is free from them. And to him who can live in this third stage, and live so for ever, there is no more pain ; only an intense interest similar to that which has enabled men of science to watch and note the progress of their own death-agony. Un-

[1] " Why should you expect Vedana to make Rupa appear illusory ?" asked a friend of mine, on reading through the MS. of this essay. The reason of my omission to explain is that to me it seemed obvious. The fact had been assimilated. To meditate on anything is to perceive its unreal nature. Notably this is so in concentrating on parts of the body, such as the nose. On this phenomenon the Hindus have based their famous aphorism, " That which can be thought is not true."—A. C.

fortunately the living in such a state is conditional on sound mental health, and terminable by disease or death at any moment. Were it not so, the First Noble Truth would be a lie.

The two further stages Sankhara and Viññanam pursue the analysis to its ultimation, " There is a consciousness of a tendency to perceive the (pleasant or unpleasant) sensation of a raising of a right foot " being the final form. And I suppose no psychologist of any standing will quarrel with this.[1] Reasoning in fact leads us to this analysis ; the Buddhist goes further only so far as he may be said to knock down the scaffolding of reasoning processes, and to assimilate the actual truth of the matter.

It is the difference between the schoolboy who painfully construes " Balbus murum ædificavit," and the Roman who announces that historic fact without a thought of his grammar.

I have called this meditation the most famous of the Buddhist meditations, because it is stated by the Buddha himself that if one practises it honestly and intelligently a result is certain. And he says this of no other.

I have personally not found time to devote myself seriously to this Mahasatipatthana, and the statements here made are those derived from reason and not from experience. But I can say that the unreality of the grosser (rupa) relatively to the subtler Vedana and still more subtle Sañña becomes rapidly apparent, and I can only conclude that with time and trouble the process would continue.

What will occur when one reaches the final stage of Viññanam, and finds no Atman behind it ? Surely the Viññanam stage will soon seem as unreal as the former have become. It is idle to speculate ; but if I may escape the imputation of explaining the obscure by the more obscure, I may hint that such a person must be very near the state called Nirvana, whatever may be meant by

[1] I deal with Mr. Spencer and " Transfigured Realism " in a note at the end of this section. —A. C.

this term. And I am convinced in my own mind that the Ananda (bliss) of Dhyana will surely arise long before one has passed even up to Sankhara.

And for the reality, 'twill be a brave jest, my masters, to fling back on the materialists that·terrible gibe of Voltaire's at the mystery-mongers of his day: "Ils nient ce qui est, et expliquent ce qui n'est pas."

NOTE TO SECTION VIII.
Transfigured Realism.

I will not waste my own time and that of my readers by any lengthy discussion of Mr. Herbert Spencer's "Transfigured Realism." I will not point out in greater detail how he proposes, by a chain of reasoning, to over-throw the conclusions he admits as being those of reason.

But his statement that Idealism is but verbally intelligible is for my purpose the most admirable thing he could have said.

He is wrong in saying that the idealists are bewildered by their own terminology; the fact is that idealist conclusions are pre-sented directly to consciousness, when that consciousness is Dhyanic. (Cf. Section XI.)

Nothing is clearer to my mind than that the great difficulty habitually experienced by the normal mind in the assimilation of meta-physics is due to the actual lack of experi-ence in the mind of the reader of the phenomena discussed. I will go so far as to say that perhaps Mr. Spencer himself is so bitter because he himself has actual ex-perience of "Transfigured Realism" as a directly presented phenomenon; for if he supposes that the normal healthy mind can perceive what he perceives, Berkeley's argu-ments must seem to him mere wanton stupidity.

I class the Hindu philosophy with the Idealist; the Buddhistic with that of Mr. Herbert Spencer; the great difference be-tween the two being that the Buddhists re-cognise clearly these (or similar) conclusions as phenomena, Mr. Spencer, inconsistently

enough, only as truths verified by a higher and more correct reasoning than that of his opponents.

We recognise, with Berkeley, that reason teaches us that the testimony of conscious-ness is untrue; it is absurd, with Spencer, to refute reason; instead we take means to bring consciousness to a sense of its impro-bity. Now our (empiric) diagnosis is that it is the dissipation of mind that is chiefly re-sponsible for its untruthfulness. We seek (also by empiric means, alas!) to control it, to con-centrate it, to observe more accurately—has this source of possible error been sufficiently recognised?—what its testimony really is.

Experience has taught me, so far as I have been able to go, that Reason and Conscious-ness have met together; Apprehension and Analysis have kissed one another. The re-conciliation (in fact, remember, and not in words) is at least so nearly perfect that I can confidently predict that a further pursuit of the (empirically-indicated) path will surely lead to a still further and higher unity.

The realisation of the hopes held out by the hypothesis is then of clear evidential value in support of that hypothesis, empiric as it was, and is. But with the growth and gathering-together, classifying, criticism of our facts, we are well on the way to erect a surer structure on a broader basis.

IX.
AGNOSTICISM.

It should be clearly understood, and well remembered, that throughout all these medi-tations and ideas, there is no necessary way to any orthodox ontology whatever. As to the way of salvation, we are not to rely on the Buddha; the vicious lie of vicarious atonement finds no place here. The Buddha himself does not escape the law of causation; if this be metaphysics, so far Buddhism is metaphysical, but no further. While deny-ing obvious lies, it does not set up dogmas; all its statements are susceptible of proof—a child can assent to all the more important.

And this is Agnosticism. We have a scientific religion. How far would Newton have got if he had stuck to Tycho Brahe as the One Guide? How far the Buddha had he reverenced the Vedas with blind faith? Or how far can we proceed even from partial truth, unless a perfectly open mind be kept regarding it, aware that some new phenomenon may possibly overthrow our most fundamental hypotheses! Give me a reasonable proof of some (intelligent) existence which is not liable to sorrow, and I will throw the First Noble Truth to the dogs without a pang. And, knowing this, how splendid is it to read the grand words uttered more than two thousand years ago: "Therefore, O Ananda, be ye lamps unto yourselves. Be ye a refuge to yourselves. Betake yourselves to no external refuge. Hold fast to the truth as a lamp. Hold fast as a refuge to the truth. Look not for refuge to any one besides yourselves." (Mahaparanibbana Sutta, ii. 33.) And to such seekers only does the Buddha promise "the very topmost Height" —if only they are "anxious to learn." This is the corner-stone of Buddhism ; can scientific men deny their assent to these words when they look back on the history of Thought in the West ; the torture of Bruno, the shame of Galileo, the obscurantism of the Schoolmen, the "mystery" of the hardpressed priests, the weapons carnal and spiritual of stake and rack, the labyrinths of lying and vile intrigue by which Science, the child, was deformed, distorted, stunted, in the interest of the contrary proposition?

If you ask me why you should be Buddhists and not indifferentists, as you are now, I tell you that I come, however unworthy, to take up the sword that Huxley wielded; I tell you that the Oppressor of Science in her girlhood is already at work to ravish her virginity ; that a moment's hesitation, idleness, security may force us back from the positions so hardly won. Are we never to go forward, moreover? Are our children still to be taught as facts the stupid and indecent fables of the Old Testament, fables

that the Archbishop of Canterbury himself would indignantly repudiate? Are minds to be warped early, the scientific method and imagination checked, the logical faculty thwarted—thousands of workers lost each year to Science?

And the way to do this is not only through the negative common-sense of indifference ; organise, organise, organise ! For a flag we offer you the stainless lotus-banner of the Buddha, in defence of which no drop of blood has ever been, nor ever will be shed, a banner under which you will join forces with five hundred million of your fellow-men. And you will not be privates in the army ; for you the highest place, the place of leaders, waits ; as far as the triumphs of the intellect are concerned, it is to Western Science that we look. Your achievements have shattered the battle-array of dogma and despotism ; your columns roll in triumphant power through the breaches of false metaphysic and baseless logic ; you have fought that battle, and the laurels are on your brows. The battle was fought by us more than two thousand years ago ; the authority of the Vedas, the restrictions of caste, were shattered by the invulnerable sword of truth in Buddha's hand ; we are your brothers. But in the race of intellect we have fallen behind a little ; will you take no interest in us, who have been your comrades? To Science Buddhism cries: Lead us, reform us, give us clear ideas of Nature and her laws; give us that basis of irrefragable logic and wide knowledge that we need, and march with us into the Unknown !

The Buddhist faith is not a blind faith ; its truths are obvious to all who are not blinded by the spectacles of bibliolatry and deafened by the clamour of priests, presbyters, ministers : whatever name they choose for themselves, we can at least put them aside in one great class, the Thought-stiflers ; and these truths are those which we have long accepted and to which you have recently and hardly won.

It is to men of your stamp, men of independent thought, of keen ecstasy of love of knowledge, of practical training, that the Buddhasanana Samagama[1] appeals; it is time that Buddhism reformed itself from within; though its truths be held untarnished (and even this is not everywhere the case), its methods, its organisation, are sadly in need of repair; research must be done, men must be perfected, error must be fought. And if, in the West a great Buddhist society is built up of men of intellect, of the men in whose hands the future lies, there is then an awakening, a true redemption, of the weary and forgetful Empires of the East.

X.

THE NOBLE EIGHTFOLD PATH.

To return from our little digression to the original plan of our essay. It is time to note the "Noble Eightfold Path," referred to, and its consideration deferred, in Section III.

In this Fourth Noble Truth we approach the true *direction* of Buddhism; progress is but another word for change; is it possible to move in a direction whose goal is the changeless? The answer is Yea and Amen! and it is detailed in the Noble Eightfold Path, of which I propose to give a short resumé. First, however, of the goal. It may be readily syllogised:

All existing things are (by nature, inevitably) subject to change.

In Nirvana is no change.

∴ No existing thing is or can be in Nirvana.

Now here is the great difficulty; for this syllogism is perfectly sound, and yet we speak of attaining Nirvana, tasting Nirvana, &c.

[We must distinguish the Hindu Nirvana, which means Cessation of Existence in certain Lokas; never absolute Cessation, as the

[1] Or International Buddhist Society, founded in Rangoon in 1903.

Buddhist tradition, the etymology, and the logical value alike require for the word as applied to the Buddhist goal. See Childers, Pali Dictionary, *sub voce* Nibbana.]

The explanation is really as follows: only by this term Nirvana can we foreshadow to you the reality; for as even the Dawn of Dhyana is indescribable in language, *à fortiori* Nirvana is so. To give an example, for that something of the sort is necessary I freely admit, to defend so apparently mystical a statement, I may give the following from my own experience.

In a certain meditation one day I recorded:

"I was (a) conscious of external things seen behind after my nose had vanished. (b) Conscious that I was *not* conscious of these things. These (a) and (b) were simultaneous."

I subsequently discovered this peculiar state of consciousness classified in the Abhidhamma. That it is a contradiction in terms I am perfectly aware; to assign any meaning to it is frankly beyond me; but I am as certain that such a state once existed in me as I am of anything.

Similarly with Nirvana and its definition. The Arahat knows what it is, and describes it by its accidentals, such as bliss. I must raise, very reluctantly, a protest against the idea of Professor Rhys Davids (if I have understood him aright) that Nirvana is the mental state resulting from the continuous practice of all the virtues and methods of thought characteristie of Buddhism. No; Nirvana is a state belonging to a different plane, to a higher dimension than anything we can at present conceive of. It has perhaps its analogies and correspondences on the normal planes, and so shall we find of the steps as well as of the Goal. Even the simple first step, which every true Buddhist has taken, Sammaditthi, is a very different thing from the point of view of an Arahat. The Buddha stated expressly that none but an Arahat could really comprehend the Dhamma.

And so for all the Eight Stages; as regards their obvious meaning on the moral plane, I can do no better than quote my friend Bhikkhu Ananda Maitriya, in his "Four Noble Truths."

"He who has attained, by force of pure understanding, to the realisation of the Four Noble Truths, who has realised the fact that depends from that understanding, namely that all the constituents of being are by nature endowed with the Three Characteristics of Sorrow, Transitoriness, and Absence of any immortal principle or Atma—such a one is said to be Sammaditthi, to hold right views, and the term has come to mean one of the Buddhist Faith. We may not have taken the other and higher steps on the Noble Eightfold Path; but must have realised those Four Truths and their sequential three Characteristics. He who has attained Sammaditthi has at least entered upon the Holy Way, and, if he but try, there will come to him the power to overcome the other fetters that restrict his progress. But first of all he must abandon all those false hopes and beliefs; and one who has done this is called a Buddhist. And this holding of Right Views, in Pali Sammaditthi, is the first step upon the Noble Eightfold Path.

The second stage is Right Aspiration—Sammasankappo. Having realised the woe and transitoriness and soullessness of all life, there rises in the mind this Right Aspiration. When all things suffer, we at least will not increase their burden, so we aspire to become pitiful and loving, to cherish ill-will toward none, to retire from those pleasures of sense which are the fruitful cause of woe. The will, we all know, is ever readier than the mind, and so, though we aspire to renounce the pleasures of sense, to love and pity all that lives, yet perhaps we often fail in the accomplishment of our aspiration. But if the desire to become pitiful and pure be but honest and earnest, we have gained the Second Step upon the Path—Sammasankappo, Right Aspiration.

He whose motives are pure has no need

to conceal the Truth—he who truly loves and who has a malice towards none, will ever speak only fair and soft words. By a man's speech do we learn his nature, and that one whose Right Aspirations are bearing fruit attains to the Third Step, Right Speech, Sammaváca. Speaking only the Truth in all things, never speaking harshly or unkindly, in his speech realising the love and pity that is in his heart—that man has attained to Stage the Third.

And because of the great power of a man's thoughts and words to change his being, because by thinking of the pitiful our acts grow full of mercy, therefore is Stage the Fourth called Right Conduct. To him who has gained this Fourth Stage, his intense aspiration, his right understanding, his carefully guarded speech—perhaps for many years of self-control—have at last borne outward fruit, till all his acts are loving, and pure, and done without hope of gain, he has attained the Fourth Step, called Sammakammanto.

And when, growing yet holier, that habit of Right Action grows firm and inalienable, when his whole life is lived for the Faith that is in him, when every act of his daily life, yea, of his sleep also, is set to a holy purpose, when not one thought or deed that is cruel or unpitiful can stain his being—when, not even as a duty, will he inflict pain by deed, word, or thought—then he has gained the Fifth High Path, the Living of the Life that's Right — Sammá ajivo. Abstaining from all that can cause pain, he has become blameless, and can live only by such occupations as can bring no sorrow in their train.[1]

To him who has lived so, say the Holy Books, there comes a power which is unknown to ordinary men. Long training and restraint have given him conquest of his mind, he can

[1] From my point of view, this is of course impossible. See Sec. III. If wilful infliction of pain only is meant, our state becomes moral, or even worse!—mystical. I should prefer to cancel this sentence. Cf. Appendix I., supra.—A. C.

now bring all his powers with tremendous force to bear upon any one object he may have in view, and this ability to so use the energies of his being to put forth a constant and tremendous effort of the will, marks the attainment of the Sixth Stage, Sammávayamo, usually translated Right Effort, but perhaps Right Will-power would come nearer to the meaning, or Right Energy, for effort has been made even to attain to Sammaditthi.[1] And this power being gained by its use he is enabled to concentrate all his thoughts and hold them always upon one object—waking or sleeping, he remembers who he is and what his high aim in life—and this constant recollection and keeping in mind of holy things, is the Seventh Stage, Sammasati. And by the power of this transcendent faculty, rising through the Eight High Trances to the very threshold of Nirvana, he at last, in the Trance called Nirodha Samapatti, attains, even in this life, to the Deathless Shore of Nirvana, by the power of Sammasamadhi, Right Concentration. Such a one has finished the Path—he has destroyed the cause of all his chain of lives, and has become Arahan, a Saint, a Buddha himself."

But none knows better than the venerable Bhikkhu himself, as indeed he makes clear with regard to the steps Sammávayamo and above, that these interpretations are but reflections of those upon a higher plane—the scientific plane. They are (I have little doubt) for those who have attained to them mnemonic keys to whole classes of phenomena of the order anciently denominated magical, phenomena which, since the human mind has had its present constitution, have been translated into language, classified, sought after, always above language, but not beyond a sane and scientific classification, a rigid and satisfactory method, as I most firmly believe. It is to establish such a method ; to record in the language, not of the temple but of the laboratory, its results,

[1] It is of course a specific kind of effort, not mere struggle.

that I make this appeal ; that I seek to enlist genuine, not pseudo-scientific men in the Research ; so that our children may be as far in advance of us in the study of the supernormal phenomena of mind as we are in advance of our fathers in the sciences of the physical world.[1]

Note carefully this practical sense of my intention. I care nothing for the academic meanings of the steps in the Path ; what they meant to the Arahats of old is indifferent to me. " Let the dead past bury its dead ! " What I require is an advance in the Knowledge of the Great Problem, derived no longer from hearsay revelation, from exalted fanaticism, from hysteria and intoxication ; but from method and research.

Shut the temple ; open the laboratory !

XI.

THE TWILIGHT OF THE GERMANS.[2]

It is a commonplace of scientific men that metaphysics is mostly moonshine ; that it is largely argument in a circle cannot easily be disputed ; that the advance since Aristotle is principally verbal none may doubt ; that no parallel advance to that of science has been made in the last fifty years is certain.

The reason is obvious.

Philosophy has had two legitimate weapons —introspection and reason ; and introspection is not experiment.

[1] A few weeks after writing these words I came upon the following passage in Tyndall's "Scientific Materialism," which I had not previously read : " Two-thirds of the rays emitted by the sun fail to arouse the sense of vision. The rays exist, but the visual organ requisite for their translation into light does not exist. And so, from this region of darkness and mystery which now surrounds us, rays may now be darting, which require but the development of the proper intellectual organs to translate them into knowledge as far surpassing ours as ours surpasses that of the wallowing reptiles which once held possession of this planet."—A. C.

[2] A Note showing the necessity and scope of the Work in question.

The mind is a machine that reasons : here are its results. Very good ; can it do anything else ? This is the question not only of the Buddhist ; but of the Hindu, of the Mohammedan, of the Mystic. All try their various methods ; all attain results of sorts ; none have had the genuine training which would have enabled them to record those results in an intelligible, orderly form. Others deliberately set their face against such an attempt. I am not of them ; humanity has grown up ; if the knowledge be dangerous in unsuspected ways, what of bacteriology ? I have obtained one result ; a result striking 'at the very condition of consciousness ; which I may formulate as follows :

" If a single state of consciousness persist unchanged for a period exceeding a very few seconds, its duality is annihilated ; its nature is violently overthrown ; this phenomenon is accompanied by an indescribable sensation of bliss."

Very well ! but I want this formula verified a hundred times, a thousand times, by independent investigators. I want it better stated ; its conditions modified, defined exactly. I want it to leave its humble station as my observation, and put into the class of regular phenomena.

But I am verging back towards Hindu philosophy, and it is a reminder well needed at this moment. For this experience of the destruction of duality, this first phenomenon in the series, has, in all its illusory beauty, been seized upon, generalised from, by philosophers, and it is to this basis of partial and therefore deceptive fact that we owe the systems of Vedanta and Idealism, with their grotesque assumptions and muddle-headed " reconcilements " all complete.

One fact, O Sri Çankaracharya, does not make a theory ; let us remember your fate, and avoid generalising on insufficient evidence. With this word of warning, I leave the metaphysician to wallow in his mire, and look toward better times for the great problems of philosophy. Remember that

when the solution is attained it is not the solution of one learned man for his fellows, but one realised and assimilated by every man in his own consciousness.

And what the solution may be none of us can foreshadow. To hoist the problem on to the horns of a dilemma will avail nothing when $A = A$ may be no longer true ; and this by no Hegelian word-juggle ; but by direct apperception as clear as the sun at noon.

Therefore ; no word more, but—to the work !

XII.

THE THREE REFUGES.

Buddham Saranangachami.
Dhammam Saranangachami.
Sangham Saranangachami.
I take my refuge in the Buddha.
I take my refuge in the Dhamma.
I take my refuge in the Sangha.

This formula of adhesion to Buddhism is daily repeated by countless millions of humanity ; what does it mean ? It is no vain profession of reliance on others ; no cowardly shirking of burdens—burdens which cannot be shirked. It is a plain estimate of our auxiliaries in the battle ; the cosmic facts on which we may rely, just as a scientist " relies " on the conservation of energy in making an experiment.

Were that principle of uncertain application, the simplest quantitative experiment would break hopelessly down.

So for the Buddhist.

I take my refuge in the Buddha. That there was once a man who found the Way is my encouragement.

I take my refuge in the Dhamma. The Law underlying phenomena and its unchanging certainty ; the Law given by the Buddha to show us the Way, the inevitable tendency to Persistence in Motion or Rest—and Persistence, even in Motion, negates change in consciousness—these observed orders of fact are our bases.

I take my refuge in the Sangha.

These are not isolated efforts on my part ; although in one sense isolation is eternally perfect and can never be overcome,[1] in another sense associates are possible and desirable. One third of humanity are Buddhists ; add men of Science and we form an absolute majority ; among Buddhists a very large proportion have deliberately gone out from social life of any kind to tread these paths of Research. Is the Way very hard ? Is the brain tired ? The results slow to come ? Others are working, failing, struggling, crowned here and there with rare garlands of success. Success for ourselves, success for others ; is it not *Compassion* that binds us closer than all earthlier ties ? Ay, in joy and in sorrow, in weakness and in strength, do I take my refuge in the Sangha.

XIII.

CONCLUSION.

Let me give a rapid resumé of what we have gone through.

(*a*) We have stripped Science and Buddhism of their accidental garments, and administered a rebuke to those who so swathe them.

(*b*) We have shown the identity of Science and Buddhism in respect of :

(1) Their fact.
(2) Their theory.
(3) Their method.
(4) Their enemies.

(*c*) While thus admitting Buddhism to be merely a branch of Science, we have shown it to be a most important branch, since its promise is to break down the wall at which all Science stops.

When Professor Ray Lankester has to write, " The whole order of nature, including living and lifeless matter—man, animal, and

gas—is a network of mechanism, the main features and many details of which have been made more or less obvious to the wondering intelligence of mankind by the labour and ingenuity of scientific investigators. But no sane man has ever pretended, since science became a definite body of doctrine, that we know or ever can hope to know or conceive of the possibility of knowing, whence this mechanism has come, why it is there, whither it is going, and what there may or may not be beyond and beside it which our senses are incapable of appreciating. These things are not ' explained ' by science, and never can be," he gives a curious example of that quaint scientific pride which knows the limits of its powers, and refuses to entertain the hope of transcending them. Unfortunately, he is as one who, a hundred years ago, should have declared any knowledge of the chemistry of the fixed stars impossible. To invent new methods, and to revolutionise the functions of the senses by training or otherwise is the routine work of to-morrow.[1] But, alas ! he goes even further.

"Similarly we seek by the study of cerebral disease to trace the genesis of the phenomena which are supposed by some physicists who have strayed into biological fields to justify them in announcing the ' discovery ' of ' Telepathy ' and a belief in ghosts."

To talk of cerebral disease as the characteristic of one who merely differs from you (and that because he has more knowledge than yourself) is itself a symptom familiar to alienists. (I may say I hold no brief for Professor Lodge, here attacked. I am not even interested in any of his results, as such of them as I am acquainted with deal with objective and trivial phenomena.)

Of course, as long as what Darwin called variation is called disease by Professor Ray Lankester, we shall (if we accept his views,

---

[1] *i.e.* on normal planes.

[1] See note p. 258.

and it will go hard with us if we do not !) regard all progress in any direction as morbid. So (as with Lombroso) "disease" will become a mere word, like its predecessor "infidelity," and cease to convey any obloquy.

If Science is never to go beyond its present limits; if the barriers which metaphysical speculation shows to exist are never to be transcended, then indeed we are thrown back on faith, and all the rest of the nauseous mess of mediæval superstition, and we may just as well have vital principle and creative power as not, for Science cannot help us. True, if we do not use all the methods at our disposal ! But we go beyond. We admit that all mental methods known are singularly liable to illusion and inaccuracy of every sort. So were the early determinations of specific heat. Even biologists have erred. But to the true scientist every failure is a stepping-stone to success ; every mistake is the key to a new truth

And the history of our Science is the history of all Science. If you choose to ape Christendom and put the pioneers of rational investigation into the nature of consciousness on the rack (*i.e.* into lunatic asylums) I doubt not we shall find our Bruno. But it will add an additional pang that persecution should come from the house of our friends.

Let us, however, turn away from the aspect of criticism which an accidental controversy has thus caused me to notice, and so to anticipate the obvious line of attack which the more frivolous type of critic will employ, and return to our proper business, the summary of our own position with regard to Buddhism.

Buddhism is a logical development of observed facts ; whoso is with me so far is *Sammaditthi*, and has taken the first step on the Noble Eightfold Path.

Let him aspire to knowledge, and the Second Step is under his feet.

The rest lies with Research.

Aum ! I take my refuge holy in the Light and Peace of Buddh.
Aum ! I take my refuge, slowly working out His Law of Good.
Aum ! I take my refuge lowly in His Pitying Brotherhood.

THE EXCLUDED MIDDLE ; OR, THE SCEPTIC REFUTED

A DIALOGUE BETWEEN A BRITISH MAN OF SCIENCE AND A CONVERTED HINDU

[This absurdity is a parody upon the serious essay which follows. It is an exceedingly characteristic trait that Crowley himself should have insisted upon this order, and a severe strain upon the devoted band who try to force themselves to study him. The notes are, of course, Crowley's throughout. To elucidate the allusions would require a note to nearly every phrase. The fact seems to be that any one with universal knowledge at the tips of his fingers can read and enjoy Crowley ; but few others.]

THE EXCLUDED (OR DIVIDED) MIDDLE

M. Well,[1] Scepticus,[2] are[3] you[4] restored[5] to[6] health[7]? Our[8] conflict[9] of[11] yesterday[12] was[13] severe.[14]

[1] Plato, *Critias*, 214 ; Schopenhauer, *Die Welt als Wille und Vorstellung*, xxxii. 76 ; Haeckel, *Anthropogenie*, II. viii. 24 ; Aeschylus, *Prom. Vinct.*, 873–6 ; Hegel, *Logik*, lvi. 3 ; Robertson, *Pagan Christs*, cvii. 29 ; Mark ii. 8, iv. 16, x. 21 ; Tertullian, *Contra Marcionem*, cxv. 33; Cicero, *Pro Varrone*, iv. ; *De Amicitia*, xii. ; Goethe, *Faust*, I. iv. 18 ; Crowley, *Opera*, i. 216 ; R. Ischak ben Loria, *De Revolutionibus Animarum*, cci. 14 (see under קלפות, *et seq.*, *q.v.* p. iii) ; O. Wilde, *Lord Arthur Savile's Crime*, ed. princ., p. 4 ; Lev. xvii. Further historical authority may be found in Gibbon and others.

[2] *Punch*, vols. viii., lxvi. *Cf.* Art. " Burnand " in *Dict. Nat. Biog.*, *scil.* Viz. *a-u-c*, xlvii., S. P. Q. R.

[3] From *Encyc. Brit.*, Art. " Existence," and " Buddha," Mahaparinibbana Sutta, to whom the author wishes to express his acknowledgments.

[4] This joke is the old one. Jones asks Smith, " Why are you so late?" Smith wittily answers : " Absurd ! I must always come before tea ; you can never come till after tea." Here "you" only comes after the " tea" in Scepticus, which shows that Scepticus was a tea-totaller. Mysticus is therefore the drinker ; which proves (what Burton and all Eastern scholars affirm) that Omar Khayyam means spiritual wine and not common alcoholic beverages. *Cf.* Burton, *Kasidah : Love and Safety*, ed. princ., p. 45, &c., &c. This word needs little or no explanation.

[6] Ontogeny can only be misunderstood by thorough study of phylogeny. Crepitation of the bivalves is a concurrent phenomenon. Take away the number you first thought of, and we see that the exostoses of the melanotic pyemata by the river's brim are exostoses and nothing more.

[7] An unpleasant subject—a great comfort to think of—*vide* Wilde, *op. cit.*, and *A Woman of no Importance*. Also Krafft-Ebing, *Psychopathia Sexualis*, xx. ; *The Family Doctor ;* Quain, *Anatomy of Grey Matter*, cxlv. 24.

[8] The 24th part of a (solar) day.

[9] From French *con ;* and Ang. Sax. *flican*, to tickle : hence, a friendly conflict.[10]

[10] See 9, above.

[11] *Vies imaginaires* (Cratès) ; also *Eaux-de-Vie réelles* (Martel). There is a fine model at the Louvre (Room Z, west wall), and any number of the most agreeable disposition at Julien's or Delacluze's.

[12] Distinguish from to-day and to-morrow, except in the case of Egyptian gods ; from to-day and for ever, except in the case of Jesus Christ ; from to-day, but not from to-morrow, in the case of the Hindustani word "kal," which may mean either—not either itself, but " to-morrow " or " yesterday," according to the context. Note the comma.

[13] From to be, verb intrans. auxil. mood indic. tense imperf. pers. 3rd.

[14] From French sevère ; from Lat. severus-a-um ; from Greek σαυρος, a crocodile ; from Sanskrit Sar, a king. *Cf.* Persian Sar, a king ; also W. African and Kentucky, " sar," master ; Lat. Caesar, Germ. Kaiser, Russ. Tsar. *Cf.* Sanskrit Siva, the destroyer, or severe one.

S. Cogitavi,[1] ergo fui. To my breezy nature such a controversy as this of ours on "Tessaracts" was as the ozone-laden discharge from a Brush machine.

M. I was not aware that the termination -ozoon was connected with the allotropic form of oxygen.

S. Little boys should be seen, but not obscene.

M. Seen, no doubt for the Arabic form of Samech ; in Yetzirah Sagittarius, or Temperance in the Tarot of your ridiculous Rosicrucians.

S. No more so than your Semitic Romeike.

M. Semitic?

S. Ike for Isaac, non est dubium—

M. Quin—

S. God save His Majesty![2] but is this Midsummer Night, and are we dreaming ?

M. "There are wetter dreams !"[3] Let us discuss the Divided Middle !

S. Beware of the Water Jump !

M. Hurrah for Taliganj ! I can improve on John Peel's Map of Asia and that ere dawn. I will map you the lucubrations of the (converted) Hindu intellect upon this vital part of the Hegelian logic.   Aum Shivaya vashi ![4]

S. Dulce ridentem Mysticum amabo, Dulce loquentem.

M. Will you not elide the 'um'?

S. Then I were left with a bee in my breeches — worse than Plato's in his bonnet.

M. A Scottish sceptic !

S. A Wee Free, Mysticus. A gaelic-speaking Calvinist with three thousand million bawbees in my sporran and a brace of bed-ridden cattle-thieves in my kirk. So I withdraw breeks.

M. And you rely not on Plato ?

S. Verily and Amen. As the French lady exclaimed, O mon Plate !—she would not say Platon, having already got one rhyme in ' mon '—and the Italian took her up that omoplat was indeed good to support the head, wherein are ideas. But to our divided middle !

M. As I should have said before I became a Christian :[1] "O Bhavani ! be pleased graciously to bow down to thy servants : be pleased to construe our prattlings as Japas our prayers as Tapas, our mantras as Rudradarshana, our bead-tellings as Devas ! be pleased moreover to accept our Badli for Sach-bat, our Yupi for Lalitasarira, our subject—O bless our divided middle !—for thine own venerable Yoni.   Aum !"

S. I am touched by your eloquence ; but Science has not said its last word on Sabapaty Swami and his application of Pranayama to the aberrations of the evolutionary retrocessions—flexomotor in type, yet sensorial in function—of the Sahasrara-Chakra, as you urged yesterday.

M. I will not press it. But in the so-affected ambulatory vibrations (as I must insist, and you practically agreed) of the lower chakras may yet be found to lie the solution of our primordial dilemma. What is the divided middle ? lest enthymeme ruin our exegesis ere it be fairly started.

S. I will answer you without further circumlocution. The laws of Thought are reducible to three : that of identity, *A* is *A ;* that of contradiction, *A* is not *not-A ;* and

---

[1] See Descartes, *Discours de la Méthode,* i. 1; Huxley, *Des Cartes;* and Mucksley, *Night Carts,* published San. Auth., Bombay 1902. (At this point the damned don who was writing these notes was mercifully struck by lightning. He had intended to annotate every word in this manner in order (as he supposed) to attain a reputation like that of Max Müller *et hoc genus omne.*)

[2] Auberon Quin, King of England, in a novelette called "The Napoleon of Notting Hill."

[3] Wells, "There are better dreams"; but it turns out to mean that the young man is drowned, and at Folkestone too.

[4] *Cf.* Prof. Rice. "The waters of the Hoang-Ho rushing by intoned the Kung."

[1] This is the invariable invocation used by the pious Hindu before any meditation or holy conference.

that of Excluded Middle,[1] A and $not\text{-}A$ taken together constitute the Universe.

M. That is a proposition easy to criticise. What of the line of demarcation between A and $not\text{-}A$? To A it is $not\text{-}A$, I suppose ; to $not\text{-}A$ it is A.

S. As in defining the boundaries of nations— Gallia est divisa in partes tres — we may suppose that half the line is of A, and half of $not\text{-}A$.

M. No ; for a line cannot be longitudinally split, or bifurcated in a sense parallel with itself. As Patanjali hints in his Kama Linga Sharira—that most delicate of Eastern psychologico - physiologico - philosophical satires—" Bare Sahib ne khansamahko bahut rupaiya diya hai."

S. The Ethic Dative ! But your contention is true, unless we argue with Aristotle ὡκεες στρουθοι περι γας μελαινας and so on.

M. I was sure you would not seriously defend so untenable a position.

S. The eleemosynary functions of the— Jigar, I fancy the Vedas have it—

M. Yes—

S. Forbid.

M. Then do you accept the conclusions of the Hegelian logic ?

S. My logic begins with the Stagyrite and ends with a manual kunt. I shall not surrender without a struggle. I am not an Achilles to be wounded in the heel.

M. Then the wound is healed ? Forgive me if I trespass on the preserves of Max Beerbohm,[a] and your other ripping cosmopolitan wits !

---

[1] Sir W. Hamilton's proposed quantification of the predicate would serve in this instance. We have to combine the propositions :
All A is all A.
All A is not all $not\text{-}A$.
No A is not no $not\text{-}A$.
Fantastic as it seems, this is the simplest of the eighty-four primary ways of expressing these three laws in a single proposition.
No $not\text{-}A$ is not no some not $not\text{-}A$.
[a] A distinguished author on philosophical and kindred subjects. See his " works." John Lane,[b] 1894.
[b] Lane—a long one, with neither variable-

S. No, for I say that the line is, like the Equator, imaginary.

ness nor shadow of turning. Christian name John.[c]
[c] Not to be confused with John, the beloved disciple, who wrote " Caliban [d] on Patmos." [h]
[d] A dwarfish miscreate, celebrated in the works of Browning and Shakespeare (W.).[e]
[e] Dramatic author, flourished A.D. 1600 *circa ;* wrote *The Tempest*[f], *Susannah ; or, The Two Gentlemen of Veronica's Garden, The Manxman,* and other plays.
[f] A garbled version of this was misbegotten in A.D. 1904 on a London stage ; the worst actor of a dreadful crew, in spite of his natural aptitude for the part of Caliban (*q.v. supra, note d*), being one Beerbohm Tree.[g]
[g] Tree, because such a stick. Beerbohm— *vide supra, note a.* I take this opportunity to introduce my system of continuous footnotes, on the analogy of continuous fractions. In this case they are recurring—a great art in itself, though an error in so far that they fail to subserve the great object of all footnotes, viz. to distract the attention of the reader.
[h] Text appended :—

CALIBAN ON PATMOS.
Being the Last Adventure of the Beloved Disciple.

[COME, kids, lambs, doves, cubs, cuddle !
  Hear ye John
Pronounce on the primordial protoplast
Palingenetic, palæontologic,
And beat that beggar's bleeding ראשית
With truth veracious, aletheiac, true !
John ye hear.   Cuddle, cubs, doves, lambs,
  kids, come !]

First, God made heav'n, earth : Earth gauche,
  void ; deep, dark.
God's Ghost stirred sea.   God said ' Light ! '
  'Twas.   'Saw light,
Good, split off dark, call'd light ' day,' dark
  ' night.'   Eve,
Morn, day I.   'Said, " 'Twixt wets be air,
  split wets ! "
'Made air, split wets 'neath air, wets top air ; so.
Call'd air ' heav'n.'   Eve, morn, day II.   'Said,
  " Low wets,
Cling close, show earth."   So.   'Call'd dry
  ' earth,' wet ' sea.'
Rubbed hands, smacked lips, said ' good.'
  [Here John was seized
By order of Augustus.   He maintained,
In spite of the imperial holograph,
" My seizer must be Caesar," with a smile :
And for persisting in his paradox
Was disembowelled : so Genesis got square.]

M. But is not imagination to be classed as either *A* or *not-A* ?

S. Vae victis ! as Livy says.   I admit it.

M. And its products ?

S. Me miserum !   I cannot deny it.

M. Such as lines ?   Namo Shivaya namaha Aum—to quote our holiest philosopher.

S. I am done.   But no !   I can still argue :

(a) There is no line of demarcation.

(b) There is a line, but it does not exist.

(c) There is more than one line—since it is not straight and so cannot enclose a space—and *more than one thing* cannot form part of a universe, since unus implies a whole.

M. I should reply :

(a) It is true that there is no line of demarcation, but that that non-existing line is after all just as much a part of the (non-existing) universe as any other non-existing thing.

We divide the universe into

(1) Existing things.

(2) Non-existing things.

If *A* exists, the line must be *not-A :* and vice versa.

Which we know to be false.

(b) It is true that there is a line, and that it does not exist, but—

S. Let us settle (a) first, and return at leisure. You fail utterly to make the important distinction between mere absence of line and presence of a non-existing line, which is as gross a fallacy as to argue that a man who has gone out to lunch has been annihilated.

M. But he *has* been annihilated, from the point of view of the emptiness of his bungalow.

S. No ! for the traces of his presence remain and will do so for ever.

M. Then a mehta's broom may be as mortal as a femme-de-ménage !

S. A trois : πατηρ—υιος, the λογος—and πνευμα άγιον.

M. Then you surrender ? The tripartite anatomy of Tat Sat is granted me ? Hegel is God, and Zoroaster his prophet ? " The mind of the Father said ' Into 3 !' and immediately all things w e r e so divided ! " ?

S. Arrahmanu arrahimu al maliku al qadusu as salamu—Vete cabron ! Chinga su madre !   I give in on that issue.

M. Alhamdolillah !   For there are four letters in Allah الله.   A for Ab—Father, L for Logos—double, for he is both God and man, and H for Holy Ghost.

S. The language of your Notariqon is tripartite too !   On point (1) though, 'twas but by a slip.   I fell : I was not pushed. Can you controvert my second defence ?

M. It is not a defence at all.   It is a trick to lure me away from the question.   I admit that there is such a line, and that it does not exist—but might it not *negatively subsist,* in the Ain, as it were ?   Further, whether it is or is not a concept, a noumenon, a psychosis, an idea — anything ! does not matter.   For since it is a subject with or without predicates and the possibility of predicates, they are themselves predicates [1] which copulate with it even the impossibility of assigning predicates to it, with the exception—you are bound to urge!—of itself.   But this would violate your law of identity, that a predicate should exclude itself from its own category, even were it non-existent, inconceivable, bum.   Consequently, thinkable or unthinkable, our creation of it subjectively has fixed it eternally in the immeasurable void.

S. Your argument is as convincing as it is lucid.   But to my third fortress !

M. Dorje Vajra Samvritti !   As to your third line of defence, I must admit that my difficulties are considerable.   Yet, Bhavani my aid, I will essay them. You said, I think—

S. There is more than one line, since the line is not straight (otherwise it could not enclose a space).

M. I do not see this !

S. A curved line is not truly a line, since

---

[1] *Litera scripta manet.* Do not steal it, or *tertia poena manet.*

a line must have length without breadth, and a curved line may certainly have breadth, for it need not lie in one plane.[1]

M. True.

S. Hence we may conclude that the line of demarcation between *A* and *not-A* is many and not one. Now an universe is that which turns to one,[2] when truly considered. Our line does the reverse of this, for it appeared one at first, and split up on examination.

M. Exactly ; but that is where I have you in a corner.

S. Dollar wheat ! Dollar wheat ! Dollar wheat !

M. It is the ' reverse ' which does you.[3] If you turn a man fourth-dimensionally round, his hemispherical ganglia will prove interchangeable ?

S. No doubt, for they are symmetrical.

M. His polygonal fissures are identical with themselves ?

S. I admit it, for they are ambidextrous.

M. His hypertrophied constrictor Cunni will feel nothing ?

S. No ; it is medial.

M. Then how is he changed ?

[1] The mathematical proof of this is simple. A surface is composed of an infinite number of parallel straight lines touching each other. Now for parallel straight lines place a single convoluted chortoid with a parabolic direction of $\pi^{n-\theta} + n^{\theta-\pi}$. At all the foci will be ellipses of the form $\dfrac{(n-1)(n+m+1)\sqrt{-1}}{(p+v) \pm \sin^{\theta-1}\cos a}$. Now since $p+v$ is in this case unity and $m=n$, we have—

$$\left\{ \frac{c[\tan\theta - O\cos(\pi+a)\sqrt{-\pi}]c\sin\theta\,\epsilon^{\,i\theta} - \epsilon\,\theta^{\pi} + K}{[c\cos\theta + u\sin\theta][u\tan\theta + t\sec\theta]} \right\}^{-1}$$

If the chortoid lie in one plane this expression=O ; but if not, it $= \sin\theta^{-1}\cos\theta^{-2}$, θ being the angle subtended by the common arc of the original curve, by Halley's theorem, or $\sin\dfrac{\theta}{\pi}$, in which case the expression is unreal, and may be neglected.

[2] Two or more things cannot form part of any one thing, in so far as they remain two. Considered in relation to that of which they form part, they become fractions.

[3] *Cf.* A. B. Douglas, *Reminiscences.*

S. Fourth-dimensionally ; no more.

M. Yet his right optic nerve will see through his left eye ?

S. Of course.

M. Then of an event, an argument, a dialectic euhemerism, protoplasmic or blastodermic ?

S. I see what you mean. You would say that duality irresolvable into unity has no parallel in the regions of pure intelligence, seeks no corollary from the intuitive organic reactions of the hyperbolic cells ?[1]

M. I would.

S. The devil you would !

M. I would. Our line becomes single ?

S. In the higher sense.

M. So that the Mind of the Father riding on the subtle guiders got it right after all ?

S. Pretty right.

M. And all things are divisible into Three, not into Two ?

S. Into *A*, *not-A*, and the dividing line.

M. Though the Reason of Man has boggled often enough at this, the intuition of Woman has always perceived it.

S. But she has gone too far, placing the importance of that dividing middle above all other things in earth or heaven. We hold the balance fair and firm.

M. (*glad*). How blessed is this day, Scepticus !

S. (*Conceding the point, and catching the glow*). Let us make a night of it !

M. (*Enjoying his triumph*). We will. Do not forget twilight !

S. (*In holy rapture*). Into Three, Mysticus, into Three !

M. (*Ditto, only more so*). Glory be to the Father, and to the Son, and to the Holy Ghost.

S. (*In the trance called Nerodha-Samapatti*). As it was in the beginning, is now, and ever shall be, world without end.

M. (*Ditto, after an exhilarating switchback ride through the Eight High Trances*). Amen.

[1] Both colloid, caudate, and epicycloid, of course.

TIME *

A DIALOGUE BETWEEN A BRITISH SCEPTIC AND AN INDIAN MYSTIC

"He (Shelley) used to say that he had lived three times as long as the calendar gave out, which he would prove between jest and earnest by some remarks on Time—
'That would have puzzled that stout Stagyrite.'"

—Prefix to the "Wandering Jew" in "Fraser's Magazine."

[The philosophical premisses of this and the other essays in this volume should be studied in

Keynes. Formal Logic.
Erdmann. History of Philosophy.
Berkeley. Three Dialogues κ.τ.λ.
Hume. Works.
Kant. Prolegomena : Critique of Pure Reason.
Locke. Human Understanding.
Huxley. Essays (Philosophical).

Patanjali. Aphorisms.
Bhikkhu Ananda Metteya. Essays (principally in the quarterly "Buddhism").
The Tao Teh King and the Writings of Kwang Tze.
The Sufis, to whom chiefly Crowley is indebted for the foundations of his system of sceptical mysticism.]

TIME.

A DIALOGUE BETWEEN A BRITISH SCEPTIC AND AN INDIAN MYSTIC.

Scepticus. Well, my dear Babu, I trust you have slept well after our fatiguing talk of yesterday.

Mysticus. Ah, dear Mister, if you will forgive my adopting what is evidently your idiom, I found it, on the contrary, invigorating. What is it the Psalmist says? That the conversation of the wise is like unto good wine, which intoxicates with delight, while it hurts not the drinker? The balm of your illustrious words, borne like spice upon the zephyr——

Scept. Shall we not rather renew our inquiries into the nature of things, than, in unfertile compliment, waste the few hours we snatch awhile from death?

Myst. Willingly. But lately you were the "sahib" asking questions concerning Indian Philosophy as a great prince who should condescend to study the habits of horses or dogs —yesterday we changed all that.

Scept. I have but one apology to offer— that of Dr. Johnson.[1]

Myst. Pray forbear ! Yet it may be for a moment instructive to notice the consideration which led you to assume a happier attitude ; viz., that such identities of thought (implying such fine parallelisms of brain structure) were discovered, that, in short, you admitted the Indian (as you have been compelled to admit the Gibbon)[2] to classification in your own genus.

Scept. You are hard upon my insolence.

Myst. Only to make the opportunity of remarking a further parallelism : that the said insolence is matched, maybe surpassed, by my own. A witty Irishman, indeed, observed of the natives of the Tongue of Asia that "the Hindu, with all his faults, was civilised, like the Frenchman : the Musul-

[1] Taunted with having described a horse's "pastern" as his "knee," the great lexicographer pleaded "Ignorance, Madam, pure ignorance."
[2] See Huxley, "Man's Place in Nature," and elsewhere.

* It must not be supposed that the author of this dialogue *necessarily* concurs in the views of either disputant, even where they are agreed.—A. C.

man, with all his virtues, was, like the Englishman, a savage."

And indeed we are too apt to think of you only as red-faced, drunken, beef-eating boors and ruffians, with no soul and less sense, as if you were all soldiers ; or as prim, conceited, supercilious, opinionated prigs, as if you were all civilians ; or as unspeakable stupidity incarnate in greedy oiliness, as if you were all missionaries. Your highest placed women make virtuous our courtezans by a comparison of costume and manners ; if our advices be true, the morality test is still in favour of our light ones. Your law wisely forbids your own venal women to set foot on Indian soil ; a rumour is even got about that you have no such women : but political economy is to be thanked, if it be so.[1] Now, though you know that I am aware that India is simply the refuse-heap for your vilest characters and your dullest brains, I see that you so little appreciate the compliment I am trying to pay you, that your foot is already itching to assault my person, and to cause me to remember that your cook never forgets to spit into your honour's soup, were it not that we may find a refuge from difference of caste and race, custom and language, in the supreme unity, that of the ultimate force of which this universe is the expression.

Scept. I have listened with patience to what is after all (you must admit) a rather spiteful tirade——

Myst. Forgive me if I interrupt. Do me the honour to remember that it was said in self-blame. I tried to give your honour "the giftie" (as one of your worst poets has said) "to see yoursel as ithers see you," the "ithers" in this case being average Hindus, as ignorant of your real character as you confess your untravelled folk to be of ours.

Scept. Pray spare me Burns ! We are— that is, you and I—on a better understanding now. Let us return, if you will, to the sub-

[1] *Cf.* Crowley, *Epigrams* (1550 A.D.)—

" The bawds of the stews be turnèd al out ;
But some think they inhabit al England
    throughout."—A. C.

ject we too lightly touched on yesterday ; that of TIME, and the real signification of that mysterious word, which is in the mouths of children, and which to affect not to understand is to stamp oneself, in the opinion of the so-called intellectual classes, as a fantastic.

Myst. Yet who of us does understand it ? I, at least, am at one with you in declaring its mystery.

Scept. You are of the few. Even Huxley, the most luminous of modern philosophers, evidently misunderstands Kant's true though partial dictum that it is subjective, or, in the pre-Kantian jargon, a form of the intellect.

Myst. Lest we involve ourselves in controversy, Homeric body-snatchers of Patroclus Kant, let us hastily turn to the question at issue itself. The scholastic method of discussing a point by quotation of Brown's position against Smith may do for the weevily brain of a University don, but is well known to bring one no nearer to solution, satisfactory or otherwise, of the original problem.

Scept. I heartily agree with you so far. We will therefore attack the question *ab initio* : I await you.

Myst. As exordium, therefore, may I ask you to recall what we agreed on yesterday with regard to *Tat Sat*, the existent, or real ?

Scept. That it was one, unknowable, absolute.

Myst. Objective ?

Scept. Without doubt.

Myst. Did I not, however, observe that, however that might be, all intuitions, if knowable, were subjective ; if objective, unknown ?

Scept. You did : to which I pointed out that Spencer had well shown how subjectivity, real or no, was a mere proof of objectivity.

Myst. And *vice versâ.*[1] Ah ! my friend, we shall be tossed about, as the world this 2500 years, if we once enter this vortex. Let us remain where all is smooth in the certainty that the Unknowable is Unreal !

Scept. We agreed it to be real !

[1] This is not an *ignoratio elenchi*, but a criticism, too extended in scope to introduce here.—A. C.

Myst. Oh never! The word "real" implies to us subjectivity; a thing is only real *to us* so far as it is known by us; even its Unknowability is a species of knowledge of it: and, by Savitri! when I say real *to us*, I say real absolutely, since all things lie to me in the radius of my sensorium. "To others" is a vain phrase,——

Scept. True; for those "others" only exist for you inasmuch as, and in so far as, they are modifications of your own thought-stuff.[1]

Myst. Agreed, then; instead of looking through the glasses of the metaphysician, we will content ourselves with the simpler task of measuring our thoughts by the only standard which is unquestionably valid, *i.e.*, consciousness.

Scept. But if that consciousness deceive us?

Myst. We are the more deceived! But it is after all indifferent; for it is we who are deceived. Idle to pretend that any other standard can ever be of any use to us, since all others are referred to it!

Scept. Ah! this is equally a branch of the former argument.

Myst. That is so. However, we may defer consideration of this problem, though I suspect that it will sooner or later force itself upon our notice.

Scept. No doubt. This is very possibly the ultimate unknown and infinite quantity, which lurks unsuspected in all equations, and vitiates our most seeming-certain results.

Myst. But, for Heaven's sake, let us postpone it as long as possible, eh?

Scept. Indeed, it is the devil of a subject. But we wander far—By the way, how old are you? You appear young, but you know much.

Myst. You are too polite. I am but an ultimate truth, six world-truths, fourteen grand generalisations, eighty generalisations, sixty-two dilemmas, and the usual odd million impressions.

Scept. What is all this? You are surely—

Myst. No, most noble Festus. Put me

[1] The physical basis of thought, as distinguished from its physical mechanism. A Hindu conception. Sanskrit, Chittam.

to the test, and I the matter will reword: which madness would gambol from.[1] How old may your honour be?

Scept. Forty-five years.

Myst. Excuse the ignorance of a "Babu," but as Mr. Chesterton[2] well knows, we do

[1] I am not mad, most noble Festus. Acts xxvi. 25. The rest is from *Hamlet*. There are many other such apt or perverted quotations in the essay.

[2] MR. CROWLEY AND THE CREEDS

AND

THE CREED OF MR. CHESTERTON

WITH A POSTSCRIPT ENTITLED

A CHILD OF EPHRAIM *

CHESTERTON'S COLOSSAL COLLAPSE

———

MR. CROWLEY AND THE CREEDS

BY G. K. CHESTERTON

Mr. Aleister Crowley publishes a work, "The Sword of Song: Called by Christians 'The Book of the Beast,'" and called, I am ashamed to say, "Ye Sword of Song" on the cover, by some singularly uneducated man. Mr. Aleister Crowley has always been, in my opinion, a good poet; his "Soul of Osiris," written during an Egyptian mood, was better poetry than this Browningesque rhapsody in a Buddhist mood; but this also, though very affected, is very interesting. But the main fact about it is that it is the expression of a man who has really found Buddhism more satisfactory than Christianity.

Mr. Crowley begins his poem, I believe, with an earnest intention to explain the beauty of the Buddhist philosophy; he knows a great deal about it; he believes in it. But as he went on writing one thing became stronger and stronger in his soul — the living hatred of Christianity. Before he has finished he has descended to the babyish "difficulties" of the Hall of Science — things about "the plain words of your sacred books," things about "the panacea of belief"—things, in short, at which any philosophical Hindoo would roll about with laughter. Does Mr. Crowley suppose that Buddhists do not feel the poetical nature of the books of a religion? Does he suppose that they do not realise the immense

* The children of Ephraim, being armed, and carrying bows, turned them back in the day of battle.

not easily grasp Western ideas. What is a "year"?

Scept. Hm! Well, ah, the earth moves round ——

importance of believing the truth? But Mr. Crowley has got something into his soul stronger even than the beautiful passion of the man who believes in Buddhism; he has the passion of the man who does not believe in Christianity. He adds one more testimony to the endless series of testimonies to the fascination and vitality of the faith. For some mysterious reason no man can contrive to be agnostic about Christianity. He always tries to prove something about it—that it is unphilosophical or immoral or disastrous—which is not true. He can never say simply that it does not convince him—which is true.

A casual carpenter wandered about a string of villages and suddenly a horde of rich men and sceptics and Sadducees and respectable persons rushed at him and nailed him up like vermin; then people saw that he was a god. He had proved that he was not a common man, for he was murdered. And ever since his creed has proved that it is not a common hypothesis, for it is hated.

Next week I hope to make a fuller study of Mr. Crowley's interpretation of Buddhism, for I have not room for it in this column to-day. Suffice it for the moment to say that if this be indeed a true interpretation of the creed, as it is certainly a capable one, I need go no further than its pages for examples of how a change of abstract belief might break a civilisation to pieces. Under the influence of this book earnest modern philosophers may, I think, begin to perceive the outlines of two vast and mystical philosophies, which if they were subtly and slowly worked out in two continents through many centuries, might possibly, under special circumstances, make the East and West almost as different as they really are.

THE CREED OF MR. CHESTERTON

By Aleister Crowley

When a battle is all but lost and won, the victor is sometimes aware of a brilliancy and dash in the last forlorn hope which was lacking in those initial manœuvres which decided the fortune of the day.

Hence comes it that Our Reviewer's apology for Christianity compares so favourably with the methods of ponderous blunder on which people like Paley and Gladstone have relied. But alas! the very vivacity of the attack may leave the column without that support which might enable it, if checked, to retire in good order; and it is with true pity for a gallant

Myst. How long have you been a sectary astronomical?

Scept. Er—what?

Myst. You are then an astronomer?

opponent—who would be wiser to surrender—that I find myself compelled to despatch half a squadron (no more!) to take him in flank.

Our Author's main argument for the Christian religion is that it is hated. To bring me as a witness to this colossal enthymeme, he has the sublime courage to state that my "Sword of Song" begins with an effort to expound Buddhism, but that my hatred of Christianity overcame me as I went on, and that I end up literally raving. My book is possibly difficult in many ways, but only Mr. Chesterton would have tried to understand it by reading it backward.

Repartee apart, it is surely an ascertainable fact that while the first 29 pages * are almost exclusively occupied with an attack on Christianity as bitter and violent as I can make it, the remaining 161 are composed of (*a*) an attack on materialism, (*b*) an essay in metaphysics opposing advaitism, (*c*) an attempt to demonstrate the close analogy between the canonical Buddhist doctrine and that of modern Agnostics. None of these † deal with Christianity at all, save for a chance and casual word.

I look forward with pleasure to a new History of England, in which it will be pointed out how the warlike enthusiasm aroused by the Tibetan expedition led to the disastrous plunge into the Boer War; disastrous because the separation of the Transvaal which resulted therefrom left us so weak that we fell an easy prey to William the Conqueror. Our Novelist should really make a strong effort to materialise his creation in "The Napoleon of Notting Hill" of the gentlemen weeping by the graves of their descendants.

Any sound philosophy must be first destructive of previous error, then constructive by harmonising truths into Truth.

Nor can the human mind rest content with negation; I honour him rather whose early emotion is hatred of Christianity, bred of compulsion to it, but who subdues that negative passion, and forces his way to a positive creed, were it but the cult of Kali or Priapus.

Here, indeed, modern Agnostics are at fault. They sensibly enough reject error; but they are over-proud of their lofty attitude, and, letting slip the real problems of life, busy themselves with side-issues, or try to satisfy the spiritual part of the brain (which needs food like any other part) with the husks of hate.

* Pp. 144-163 in this volume.
† Pp. 164-184, 233-243, and 244-261 respectively, in this volume.

Scept. I? Goodness gracious bless my soul, no!

Myst. Then how do you know all this about the earth?

How few among us can reach the supreme sanity of Dr. Henry Maudsley in such a book as " Life in Mind and Conduct "!

Hence I regard Agnosticism as little more than a basis of new research into spiritual facts, to be conducted by the methods won for us by men of science. I would define myself as an agnostic with a future.

But to the enthymeme itself. A word is enough to expose it.

Other things have been hated before and since Christ lived—if he lived. Slavery was hated. A million men * died about it, and it was cast out of everywhere but the hearts of men.† Euripides hated Greek religion, and he killed the form thereof. Does Our Logician argue from these facts the vitality of slavery or Delphi? Yes, perhaps, when Simon Legree and the Pythoness were actually making money, but to argue their eternal truth, or even their value at that time, is a further and a false step. Does the fact that a cobra is alive prove it to be innocuous?

With the reported murder of Jesus of Nazareth I am not concerned ; but Vespasian's " Ut puto Deus fio " is commonly thought to have been meant as a jest.

Our Romanticist's unique and magnificent dramatisation of the war between the sceptic or lover of truth, and the religious man or lover of life, may be well quoted against me. Though Vespasian did jest, though Christ's " It is finished " were subjectively but the cry of his physical weakness, like Burton's " I am a dead man," it is no less true that millions have regarded it as indeed a cry of triumph. That is so, subjectively for them, but no more, and the one fact does not alter the other.

Surely Our Fid. Def. will find little support in this claim on behalf of death. We all die ; it was the Resurrection and Ascension which stamped Christ as God. Our Philosopher will, I think, fight shy of these events. The two thieves were "nailed up like vermin " on either side of Christ by precisely the same people ; are they also gods? To found a religion on the fact of death, murder though it were, is hardly more than African fetichism. Does death prove more than life? Will Mr. Chesterton never be happy until he is hanged?

These then are the rear-guard actions of his retiring and beaten army.

---

* In the American Civil War, 1861-64. But they were not men, only Americans.

† This is mere rhetoric. Crowley was perfectly familiar with the conditions of "free" wage labour.

Scept. Astronomers are paid, insufficiently paid, it is true, but still paid, to calculate the movements of the various heavenly bodies. These, being regular, or regularly irregular,

The army itself is pretty well out of sight. There is a puff of artillery from afar to the effect that " no man can contrive to be agnostic about Christianity." This is very blank cartridge. Who is agnostic about the shape of the earth? Who prides himself upon a profound reserve about the colour of a blue pig, or hesitates to maintain that grass is green? Unless under the reservation that both subject and predicate are Unknowable in their essence, and that the copula of identity is but a convention—a form of Agnosticism which after all means nothing in this connection, for the terms of the criticism require the same reservation.

Our Tamburlaine's * subsequent remark that the poor infidel (failing in his desperate attempt to be agnostic) " tries to prove something untrue" is a *petitio principii* which would be a blunder in a schoolboy ; but in a man of Our Dialectician's intelligence can only be impudence.

The main army, as I said, is out of sight. There is, however, a cloud of dust on the horizon which may mark its position. " Does Mr. Crowley suppose that the Buddhists do not feel the poetical nature of the books of religion?" I take this to mean : " You have no business to take the Bible literally !"

I have dealt with this contention at some length in the " Sword of Song " itself (Ascension Day, lines 216-247): but here I will simply observe that a poem which authorises the Archbishop of Canterbury to convey Dr. Clifford's pet trowels, and makes possible the Gilbertian (in the old sense of pertaining to W. S. Gilbert) position of the Free Kirk to-day, is a poem which had better be burnt, as the most sensible man of his time proposed to do with Homer, or at least left to the collector, as I believe is the case with the publications of the late Isidore Liseux. Immoral is indeed no word for it. It is as criminal as the riddle in " Pericles."

That Our Pantosympatheticist is himself an Agnostic does not excuse him. True, if every one thought as he does there would be no formal religion in the world, but only that individual communion of the consciousness with its self-consciousness which constitutes genuine religion, and should never inflame passion or inspire intolerance, since the non-Ego lies beyond its province.

But he knows as well as I do that there are thousands in this country who would gladly

---

* Not to confuse with Tambourine or alter into Tamburlesque.

which comes to the same thing, serve us as standards of time.

Myst. A strange measure! What is the comparison in one of your poets between "Fifty years of Europe" and "a cycle of Cathay"?

Scept. You know our poets well.

* *Myst.* Among my loose tags of thought are several thousand useless quotations. I would give much to have my memory swept and garnished.

Scept. Seven other devils wait at the door. But you were saying?

Myst. That an astronomer might perhaps justly compute the time during which his eye was actually at the telescope by the motion of the planets, or by the clockwork of his reflector, but that you should do so is absurd.

Scept. Yet all men do so and have ever done so.

see him writhing in eternal torture—that physiological impossibility—for his word "a casual carpenter," albeit he wrote it in reverence. That is the kind of Christian I would hang. The Christian who can write as Our Champion of Christendom does about his faith is innocuous and pleasant, though in my heart I am compelled to class him with the bloodless desperadoes of the "Order of the White Rose" and the "moutons enragés" that preach revolution in Hyde Park.

When he says that he will trace "the outlines of two vast and mystical philosophies, which if they were subtly and slowly worked out, &c., &c.," he is simply thrown away on Nonconformity; and I trust I do not go too far, as the humblest member of the Rationalist Press Association, when I suggest that that diabolical body would be delighted to bring out a sixpenny edition of his book. I am not fighting pious opinions. But there are perfectly definite acts which encroach upon the freedom of the individual: indefensible in themselves, they seek apology in the Bible, which is now to be smuggled through as a "poem." If I may borrow my adversary's favourite missile, a poem in this sense is "unhistorical nonsense."

We should, perhaps, fail to appreciate the beauty of the Tantras if the Government (on their authority) enforced the practices of hook-swinging and Sati, and the fact that the cited passages were of doubtful authority, and ambiguous at that, would be small comfort to our grilled widows and lacerated backs.

Yet this is the political condition of England

Myst. And all are absurd in doing so, if they really do so, which I doubt. Even the lowest dimly, or perhaps automatically, perceive the folly thereof——

Scept. As?

Myst. A man will say "Since the Derby was run" more intelligibly than "since May such-and-such a day"; for his memory is of the race, not of a particular item in the ever changing space-relation of the heavens, a relation which he can never know, and of which he can never perceive the significance: nay, which he can never recognise, even by landmarks of catastrophic importance.

Scept. One might be humorous on this subject by the hour. Picture to yourself a lawyer cross-examining a farm hand as to the time of an occurrence: "Now, Mr. Noakes, I must warn you to be very careful. Had Herschell occulted α Centauri before you left Farmer Stubbs' field?" while the instructed swain should not blush to reply at this hour. You invoke a "casual camel-driver" to serve your political ends and prevent me having eighteen wives as against four: I prove him an impostor, and you call my attention to the artistic beauty of Ya Sin. I point out that Ya Sin says nothing about four wives, and you say that all moral codes limit the number. I ask you why all this fuss about Mohammed, in that case, and you write all my sentences—and your own—Qabalistically backwards, and it comes out: "Praise be to Allah for the Apostle of Allah, and for the Faith of Islam. And the favour of Allah upon him, and the peace!"

War, I think, if those be the terms.

POSTSCRIPT

War under certain conditions becomes a question of pace, and I really cannot give my cavalry so much work as Our Brer Rabbit would require. On the appearance of the first part of his article "Mr. Crowley and the Creeds" I signified my intention to reply. It aborted his attack on me, and he has not since been heard of.

In the midst of the words he was trying to say,
In the midst of his laughter and glee,
He has softly and suddenly vanished away—

I suppose I always was a bit of a Boojum!

that Halley's Comet, being the sole measure of time in use on his farm, was 133° S., entering Capricorn, at the very moment of the blow being struck.

Myst. I am glad you join me in ridicule of the scheme ; but do you quite grasp how serious the situation has become ?

Scept. I confess I do not see whither you would lead me. Your own computation strikes one as fantastic in the extreme.

Myst. Who knows ? Think, yourself, of certain abnormal and pathological phenomena, whose consideration might lay down the bases for a possible argument.

Scept. There are several things that spring instantly into the mind. First and foremost is the wonderfully suggestive work, misnamed fiction, of our greatest novelist, H. G. Wells. This man, the John Bunyan of modern scientific thought, has repeatedly attacked the problem, or at least indicated the lines on which a successful research might be prosecuted, in many of his wonderful tales. He has (I say it not to rob you of the honour of your discoveries, but in compliment, and I can imagine none higher) put his finger on the very spot whence all research must begin : the illusionary nature of the time-idea. But I will leave you to study his books at your leisure, and try to give a more direct answer to your question. We have cases of brain disorder, where grave local mischief survives the disappearance of general symptoms. One man may forget a year of his life ; another the whole of it ; while yet another may have odd patches effaced here and there, while the main current flows undisturbed.

Myst. He is so much the poorer for such losses ?

Scept. Certainly.

Myst. Did the stars efface their tracks to correspond ?

Scept. Joshua is dead.

Myst. Yama [1] be praised !

Scept. Amen.

Myst. You have also, I make no doubt,

cases where the brain, from infancy, never develops.

Scept. True : so that a man of thirty thinks and acts like a child : often like a stupid child. Our social system is indeed devised to provide for these cases ; so common are they : the Army, the Cabinet, are reserved for such : in the case of women thus afflicted they are called "advanced " or "intellectual " : the advantages of these situations and titles is intended to compensate them for Nature's neglect. Even sadder is it when young men of great parts and talent, flourishing up to a certain age, have their brains gradually spoiled by the preposterous system of education in vogue throughout the more miasmal parts of the country, till they are fit for nothing but "chairs" and "fellowships" at "universities." The schools of philosophy are full of these Pliocene anachronisms, as the responsible government departments are of the congenitally afflicted : in both cases thinking men are disposed to deny (arguing from the absence of human reason and wit, though some of the creatures have a curious faculty resembling the former, shorn of all light-quality) to these unfortunates any conscious life worthy of the name, or the capacity to increase with years in the wisdom or happiness of their more favoured fellow-creatures.

Myst. Yet the stars have a regular rate of progression ?

Scept. I see what you would be at. You would say that of two men born on a day, dying on a day, one may be young, the other old.

Myst. Ay ! But I would say this to vitiate the standard you somewhat incautiously set up.

Scept. Abrogate it then ! But where are we ?

Myst. Here, that we may determine this most vital point ; how so to act that we may obtain the most from life ; or, if existence, the word of which intuitions are the letters, be, as the Buddhists pretend, misery, how to obtain the least from it.

Scept. Let us not speak ill of a noble

[1] The Hindu Pluto.

religion, though we lament the paradoxical follies of its best modern professors !

Myst. A truce to all controversy, then. How shall we obtain the best from life? It is this form of the question that should give you a clue to my goal.

Scept. It is so difficult to determine whether Sherlock Holmes[1] is dead or no that I will take no risks. But the answer to your query is obvious. *He lives the longest who remembers most.*

Myst. Insufficient. There are lives full of the dreariest incident, like a farmyard novel, or a window in Thrums, or the autobiography of the Master of a College,[2] who lives ninety years and begets sons and daughters, and there is an end of him by-and-by, and the world is nor richer nor poorer, scarce for an anecdote ! Add to your "number of impressions remembered" (and therefore not expunged) the vividness of each impression !

Scept. As a coefficient rather. Let us construct a scale of vividness from a to n, and we can erect a formula to express all that a Man is. For example he might be :

$$10a + 33125b + 890c + 800112658e + 992f + \ldots\ldots + \ldots\ldots + \ldots\ldots + n,$$

and, if we can find the ratio of $a : b : c : d : e : f : \ldots\ldots : n$, we can resolve the equation into a single term, and compare man and man.

Myst. I catch the idea. Fanciful as it of course is in practice, the theory is sound to the core. You delight me !

Scept. Not at all, not at all. Further, I see that since the memory is a storehouse of limited capacity, it follows that he who can remember most is he who can group and generalise most. How easy is it to conjugate your Hindustani verbs ! Because one rule covers a thousand cases. How impossible is it to learn German genders ! Because the gender of each word must be committed arbitrarily to memory.

[1] A detective in sensational fiction of the period.
[2] The gibe is at Butler, Master of Trinity during Crowley's residence.

Myst. He then is the longest-lived, and the wisest, and the worthiest of respect, who can sum up all in one great generalisation?

Scept. So Spencer defines philosophy : as the art of doing this.

Myst. But you leave out this "vividness." He is greater who generalised the data of evolution than he who did the same thing for heraldry : not only because of the number of facts covered, but because of the greater intrinsic value and interest of each fact. Not only, moreover, is the philosopher who can sum up the observations "All men are mortal," "All horses are mortal," "All trees are mortal," and their like, into the one word Anicca, as did Buddha, a wise and great man ; but Aeschylus is also wise and great, who from this universal, but therefore commonplace generalisation, selects and emphasises the particular "Oedipus is mortal."

Scept. Your Greek is perhaps hardly equal to your English ; but you are perfectly right, and I do wrong to smile. Since we agree to abandon the mechanical device of the astronomer, all states of consciousness are single units, or time-marks, by which we measure intervals. That some, no longer than others, are more notable, just as the striking of a clock emphasises the hours, though the escapement maintains its rate, is the essential fact in counting.

Myst. And what is the test of vividness?

Scept. I should say the durability of the memory thereof.

Myst. No doubt ; it is then of importance to class these states of "high potential" —— may I borrow the term?

Scept. It is a suggestive one, though I must say I am opposed to the practice of Petticoat Lane in philosophical literature. The broad-minded Huxley's aversion to "polarity" is not his least bequest to psychologists. Of course, to begin our classification, all states of normal waking consciousness stand in a class above any other——

Myst. I have known dreams——

Scept. Wells says : "There are better

dreams !"—and a damned good way to look at death, by heaven !

Myst. Yes! But I meant that some dreams are more vivid than some waking states, even adult states hours long. You remember the "Flying dream," though I daresay you have not experienced it since childhood : it is part of your identity, a shape or defining idea of your mind : but you have forgotten the picnic at—where you will.

Scept. There is something to be thankful for in that. Then, there are incidents of sport——

Myst. Mysteries of initiation——

Scept. Narrow escapes——

Myst. The presence of death ——

Scept. Shocks——

Myst. Some incidents of earliest childhood——

Scept. Memories which can be classed, and therefore fall under great headings ; intellectual victories——

Myst. Religious emotions——

Scept. Ah ! this minute too, for I group them ! All these are intuitions which come near, which touch, which threaten, which alarm, the Ego itself !

Myst. Yet in those great ecstasies of love, poetry, and their like ; the Ego is altogether abased, absorbed in the belovèd : the phenomenon is utterly objective.

Scept. To be abased is to be exalted. But we are again at metaphysics. The Ego and the Non-Ego are convertible terms. We are agreed that one of the two is a myth ; but we might argue for months and aeons as to which of the two it is.

Myst. Here Hindu practice bears out Western speculation, whether we take the shadowy idealism of Berkeley, or the self-refuted [1] Monism of Haeckel. All these men got our results, and interpreted them in the partial light of their varied intellect, their diverse surrounding and education. But the result is the same physiological pheno-

[1] Haeckel, postulating a unity, is compelled to ascribe to it a tendency to dividuality, thus stultifying his postulate. See the "Riddle of the Universe."

menon, from Plato and Christ to Spinoza and Çankaracharya,[1] from Augustine and Abelard, Boehme and Weigel in their Christian communities to Trismegistus and Porphyry, Mohammed and Paracelsus in their mystic palaces of Wisdom, the doctrine is essentially one : and its essence is that existence is one. But to my experience it is certain that in Dhyana the Ego is rejected.

Scept. Before inquiring further of you : What is this Dhyana ? let me say, in view of what you have just urged : How do you know that the Ego is rejected ?

Myst. Peccavi. My leanings are Buddhistic, I will confess : indeed, the great majority of Eastern philosophers, arguing *à priori* from the indestructibility of the Ego— a dogma, say I, and no more !—have asserted that in the Dhyanic state the Object is lost in the Ego rather than *vice versâ*, and they support this conclusion by the fact of the glorification of the object.

Scept. But this is all *à priori*. For be it supposed that Dhyana is merely a state of more correct perception of the nature of the object than that afforded by normal inspection —and this is a reasonable view !—the argument simply goes to prove that matter, as the Ego, is divine. And this is our old vicious circle !

Myst. Also, since the object may be the Infinite. All Dhyana proves is that "things are not what they seem."

Scept. Not content with our poets, you seem to have wandered into Longfellow.

Myst. Also Tennyson.

Scept. I can sympathise : there is a blot on my own scutcheon. You are just, though, in your statement that the glorification of one of two factors——

Myst. At the moment of the disappearance of their dividuality——

Scept. So ?

Myst. Surely. They also themselves disappear, just as carbon, the black solid, and

[1] Hindu reformer (about 1000 A.D.), who raised the cult of Shiva from that of a local phallic deity to that of an universal God. The Tamil Isaiah.

chlorine, the green gas, combine to form a limpid and colourless liquid. So it might be absurd to assert either that Subject or Object disappears in Dhyana to the advantage of the other.

Scept. But at least this glorification of the consciousness is a proof that reality (as shown in Dhyana) is more glorious than illusion (as shown in consciousness).

Myst. Or, that illusion——

Scept. Of course ! We are then no further than before.

Myst. Indeed we are. Glory, real or false, is desirable. Indeed we are too bold in saying " real or false," by virtue of our previous agreement that the Subjective is the Knowable, and that deeper inquiry is foredoomed futile.

Scept. Unless, admitting Physiology,[1] such glory is phantom, poisonous, and your Dhyana a debauch.

Myst. You will at least admit, as a basis for the consideration of this and other points that Dhyana is more vivid than any of the normal dualistic states.

Scept. I must. I have myself experienced, as I believe, this or a similar condition, and I find it to be so ; intensely so.

Myst. I suspected as much.

Scept. But pray, lest we talk at cross purposes, define me this Dhyana.

Myst. The method is to concentrate the attention on any object (though in Hindu estimation some objects may be far more suitable than others, I believe Science would say any object) ——

Scept. That was my method.

Myst. Suddenly the object disappears: in its stead arises a great glory, characterised by a feeling of calm, yet of intense, of unimaginable bliss.

Scept. That was my result. But, more remarkable still, the change was not from the consciousness " I behold a blue pig"—the object I have ever affected—to " I behold

a glory," but to " There is a glory," or " Glory is."

Myst. Glory be ! Exactly. That is the test of Dhyana. I am glad to have met you.

Scept. Same here. Be good enough to proceed with your exposition !

Myst. In a moment. There are other Westerns who study these matters ?

Scept. To follow up the line of thought you gave me but just now, we have a great number of philosophers in the West who have enunciated ideas which to the dull minds of the common run of men seem wild and absurd.

Myst. You refer to Idealism.

Scept. To more ; to nearly all philosophy, save only that self-styled " of common sense," which is merely stupidity glossing ignorance. But Berkeley——

Myst. The devout, the angelic——

Scept. Hegel——

Myst. The splendid recluse ! The lonely and virtuous student who would stand motionless for hours gazing into space, so that his pupils thought him idle or insane——[1]

Scept. Spencer——

Myst. The noble, ascetic, retired spirit ; the single-hearted, the courageous, the holy——

Scept. Yes : all these and many others. But what mean your comments ?

Myst. That extreme virtue is a necessary condition for one who is desirous of attaining this state of bliss.

Scept. There, my friend, you generalise from three. Let me stand fourth (like Ananias) and tell you that after many vain attempts while virtuous, I achieved my first great result only a week after a serious lapse from the condition of a Brahmacharyi.[2]

Myst. You ?

Scept. The result of despair.

Myst. This may serve you as excuse before Shiva.

[1] As represented by Huxley, who, I fancy, spoke from imperfect knowledge of the facts. But *vide infra.*—A. C.

[1] *Cf.* Plato, *Symposium :* Diotima's description of the Vision of absolute Beauty, identical with Hindu doctrine ; and Alcibiades' anecdote of Socrates at Potidæa.—A. C.

[2] Chastity is probably referred to, though Brahmacharya involves many other virtues.

Scept. Quit not the scientific ground we walk on !

Myst. I regret ; but my astonishment annulled me. On the main point, however, there is no doubt. These Westerns did, more or less, pursue our methods. Why doubt that they attained our results ?

Scept. I never did doubt it. Certain of our philosophers have even imagined that "self-consciousness," as they style it, is the very purpose of the Universe.

Myst. They were so enamoured of the Ananda—the bliss——

Scept. Presumably. Far be it from me to set myself up against them ; but I may more modestly take the position that "self-consciousness" is a mere phenomenon ; a bye-product, and no more, in the laboratory of life.

Myst. Alas ! I can think no better of you for your modesty : whoso would make bricks without straw may as well plan pyramids as hovels.

Scept. Your stricture is but too just. Teleology [1] is a science which will make no progress until the most wicked and stupid of men are philosophers, since like is comprehended by like : unless, indeed, we excuse the Creator by saying that, the Universe being a mere mechanism, that it should suffer pain (an emotion He does not feel) is as unintelligible to Him as that a machine should do so is to the engineer. Strain and fatigue are observed by the latter, but not associated by him with the idea of pain : much more so, then, God.

Myst. You are bold enough now ! Our philosophers think it not fitting that man should discuss the ways of the inscrutable, the eternal God.

Scept. I have you tripping fairly at last ! What do you mean by "eternal"? You who have uprooted my ideas of time, answer me that ?

Myst. A woodcock to mine own springe, indeed. I am justly caught with mine own metaphysic.

[1] The science of the Purpose of Things.

Scept. Throw metaphysic to the dogs ! I'll none of it. I will resolve it to you, then, on your own principles. The term, so constantly in use, or rather abuse, by your devotees as by ours, is meaningless. All they can mean is a state of consciousness which is never changed—that is, one unit of time, since time is no more than a succession of states of consciousness, and we have no means of measuring the length of one against another : indeed, a "state of consciousness" is atomic, and to measure is really to furnish the means for dissolution of a molecule, and no more. Thus in the New Jerusalem the song must be either a single note, or a phenomenon in time. Length without change is equivalent to an increase in the vividness, as we said before. And after all the Ego can never be happy, for happiness is impersonal, is distinct from the contemplation of happiness. This quite unchanging, this single vivid state, is as near "Eternity" as we can ever get—it is a foolish word.

Myst. That state is then impersonal ?

Scept. Ah !—Yes, I have described Dhyana.

Myst. The heaven of the Christian is then identical with the daily relaxation of the Hindu ?

Scept. If we analyse their phrase, yes. But Christians mean "eternal time," a recurring cycle of pleasant states, as when a child wishes that the pantomime "could go on for ever."

Myst. Why, do they ever mean anything ? . . . But how does this eternal time differ from ordinary time ? Our guarantee against cessation is the fact that the tendency to change is inherent in all component things.

Scept. Our guarantee indeed ! Rather the seal upon the tomb of our hopes ! But to sing, even out of tune, as the Christian does, that "time shall be no more," is, indeed, to cease to mean anything. The dogma of the Trinity itself is not less inane, the only thing that saves it from being blasphemous.

Myst. To be intelligible is to be misunderstood.

Scept. To be unintelligible is to be found out.

Myst. To be secretive is to be blatant.

Scept. To be frank is to be mysterious.

Myst. I wish your poet-martyr[1] (I do not refer to Chatterton) could hear us.

Scept. To return, I would have you note the paradox that unconsciousness must be reckoned as a form of consciousness, since otherwise the last state of consciousness of a dying person is for him eternity. That this is not so is shown by the phenomena of anæsthesia.

Myst. Is it, though? Is the analogy so certain? Is there nothing in the attempt of all religions to secure that a man's last thoughts should be of triumph, peace, joy, and their like?

Scept. I have been reading that somewhat mawkish book "The Soul of a People." Disgusted as I was by its ooze of sentimentality, I was yet not unobservant of its cognisance of this fact, and I was even pleased—though this is by the way—to see that the author recognises in the ridiculous First Precept of the Buddhist Faith, or rather in the orthodox travesty of Buddha's meaning, a mere survival of some fetichistic theophagy.

Myst. Doesn't it say somewhere that "Long words butter no parsnips"?

Scept. It ought to. But pray proceed with your defence of religion—for I presume it is intended as such.

Myst. I was saying that if unconsciousness be not reckoned as consciousness, the death-thought is eternal heaven or hell, as it chances to be pleasant or painful. But, on the other hand, if it be so reckoned, if that and that alone has in death no awakening, no change, then is it not certain that there is the Great Peace? Disprove immortality, reincarnation, all survival or revival of the identical——

Scept. Identical? Hm!

Myst.—of the consciousness which the man calls "I"——

Scept. Which Haeckel has pretty effectively done.

Myst. And Nirvana is ours for the price of

[1] The reference, presumably ironical, is to the late Oscar Wilde.

a packet of arsenic, and a glass of Dutch courage.

Scept. In a poem called "Summa Spes,"[1] a gifted but debauched Irishman has grossly, yet effectively, stated this view. "Let us eat and drink, for to-morrow we die!" is the Hebrew for it. But if we survive or revive—

Myst. The problem is merely postponed. If "death is a sleep": why, we know what happens after sleep.

Scept. The question resolves itself, therefore, into the other which we both of us anticipated and feared: What is this "identical consciousness" which is the cause of so much confusion of thought. We have in the phenomena of mind (*a*) a set of simple impressions; (*b*)[2] a machinery for grasping and interpreting these; of sifting, grouping, organizing, co-ordinating, integrating them; and (*c*) a "central" consciousness, more or less persistent, that is to say, united to a long series of similar states by the close bond of the emphatic idea, I, which "central" consciousness takes notice of the results presented to it by (*b*). A state which can be summoned at will——

Myst. What then is "will"?

Scept. You know what I mean. God knows I am bothered enough already without being caught up on a word! Which can be summoned at will: which in a succession of simple, though highly abstract states, observes the results (forgive the repetition!) presented to it by (*b*). But if we turn the consciousness upon itself, if we add a sixth sense to the futile five?

Myst. It is resolved after all into a simple impression, indistinguishable, so far as I can see, from any other. That is, logically.

Scept. An impression, moreover, on what? It is not the (*c*) that is really examined; for (*c*) is the examiner: and you have merely formulated a (*d*) expressible by the ratio

[1] See p. 200.

[2] This (*b*) may be divided and subdivided into certain groups; some, perhaps all of them, liable, in the event of the suppression of (*a*), to become (automatically?) active, and prevent (*c*) from becoming quiet.—A. C.

$d : c :: c : a$—an infinite process. The final factor is always unknowable—yet it is the one thing known.

Myst. And because it is always present, therefore it is unkenned.

Scept. We are now nearer Spencer than appeared. For the fact that it must be there, unchanging in function, while consciousness persists, gives the idea of a definite substratum to subserve that function.

Myst. I cannot but agree ; and I would further observe that when, in Dhyana, it ceases to examine, and apperceives, the " relative eternity," *i.e.*, the intense vividness of the phenomenon gives us a further argument in favour of its permanence.

Scept. But that it should persist after death is a question which we should leave physiology to answer, as much as the obvious question whether sight and taste persist. And the answer is unhesitatingly " No."

Myst. Yet the mystic may still reply that the association of consciousness with matter is as incredible as the contrary conception. Cause and effect, he will say, are if anything less likely (*à priori*) than concomitance or casuality. Even occasionalism is no more improbable than that the material should have a manifestly immaterial function.

Scept. Yet it is so !

Myst. Ah ! would it serve to reply that it is so ! But no ! the materialistic position, fully allowed, is an admission of spirit.[1] They must conceive spirit and matter both as unknowable, as irresolvable, like x and y in a single equation (whose counterpart we seek in Dhyana), so that we may eternally evolve

---

[1] Maudsley, " Physiology of Mind," asks why it should be more unlikely that consciousness should be a function of matter than that pain should be of nervous tissue.
True. So also Huxley extended the meaning of "nature" to include the "supernatural" in order to deny the supernatural.
So also I (maintaining that darkness only exists) meet the cavil of the people who insist on the separate existence of light by showing that light is, after all, merely a sub-section of one kind of darkness.—A. C. This note is of course ironical.

values for either, but always in terms of the other.

Scept. Just so we agreed lately about subject and object.

Myst. It is another form of the same Protean problem.

Scept. Haeckel even insists upon this in his arrogant way.

Myst. Huxley, at once the most and the least sceptical of philosophers, urges it. There is only one method of investigating this matter. Reason is bankrupt ; not only Mansel the Christian but Hume the Agnostic has seen it.

Scept. We all see it. The Bank being broken, we do not put what little we have saved into the wildcat stock Faith, as Mansel counsels us ; but add little to little, and hoard it in the old stocking of Science.

Myst. Well if no holes !

Scept. We expect little, even if we hope for much. We are pretty safe ; 'tis the plodding ass that is Science, and the fat priest rides us still.

Myst. We offer you a Bank, where your intellectual coin will breed a thousandfold.

Scept. What security do you offer ? Once bit, twice shy ; especially as your business is known to be patronised by some very shady customers.

Myst. Do you offer to stop my mouth with security ? We give you all you can wish. Let Science keep the books ! I say it in our own interest ; the slovenly system that has prevailed hitherto has resulted in serious losses to the shareholders. One of our best cashiers, Christ, went off and left mere verbal messages, and those only too vague, as to the business that passed through his hands. Too many of our most brilliant research staff keep their processes secret, and so not only incur the suspicion of quackery, but leave the world no wiser for their work. Others abuse their position as directors to further the ends of other companies not even allied to the parent firm : as when Mohammed, the illuminated of Allah, lent his spiritual force to bolster up the literal sense of the Bible, thus degrading a sublime text-book of mystic lore into the merest nursery, or too often bawdy-house, twaddle and filth. You will alter all this, my friends! Let Science keep the books!

Scept. For a cross between a plodding ass and an old stocking, she will do well! And what dividends do you promise?

Myst. In the first year. Dhyana; in the second, Samadhi; and in the third, Nirvana.

Scept. It is not the first year yet. Is this coin current?

Myst. Ah! I remember now your phrase "Dhyana a debauch." You are of course familiar with the name of Maudsley, perhaps the greatest living authority on the brain?

Scept. None greater.

Myst. By rare good fortune, at the very moment when this aspect of the question was confronting me, and I was (so any one would have imagined) many thousand miles from expert opinion, I had the opportunity of putting the matter before him. Our conversation was pretty much as follows: "What is the cause of the phenomenon I have described?" (I had given just such a sketch as we have drawn above, and added that it was the most cherished possession of all Eastern races. The state was familiar to him.) "Excessive activity of one portion of the brain: relative lethargy of the rest." "Of which portion?" "It is unknown." "Is the phenomenon of pathological significance?" "I cannot say so much: it would be a dangerous habit to acquire: but since recovery is spontaneous, and is apparently complete, it is to be classed as physiological." I obtained the idea, however, that the danger was very serious, perhaps more so than the actual words used would imply. A further inquiry as to whether he could suggest any medical, surgical, or other means, by which this state might be produced at will, led to no result.

Scept. This is most interesting: for the very doubts which I did entertain as to the safety of mental methods directed to attaining this result, are dispelled by what is a cautious, if not altogether unfavourable, view

from a naturally-inclined-to-be-unfavourable Western mind. (My mother was of German extraction.) How so? Because my teacher, himself a Western scientific man of no mean attainments, thought no trouble too great, no language too violent (though he is ordinarily a man of unusual mildness and suavity of manner) to be used, to impress upon me the extreme danger of too vigorous attempts to reach the state of concentration. "If you feel the least tired in the course of your daily practice," he never wearied of repeating, "you have done too much, and must absolutely rest for four-and-twenty hours. However fresh you feel, however keen you are to pursue the work, rest you must, or you will but damage the apparatus you are endeavouring to perfect. Rest for longer if you like, never for less." This adjuration recurs with great force to my mind at the present moment. Our Western "Adepts"— if you were a Western I would ask you to forgive the word—know, as the great brain specialist knows, the dangers of the practice; the dangers of the training, the dangers of success.

Myst. Blavatsky's mysteriously - phrased threats were to this effect. Maybe she knew.

Scept. Maybe she did. Well, what I wished to point out was that, had you pressed Dr. Maudsley, he might possibly have admitted that scientific precaution, under trained guidance and watching, might diminish the danger greatly, and permit the student to follow out this line of research without incurring the stigma—if it be a stigma—of risking his sanity, or at least his general mental welfare? [1]

[1] Dr. Maudsley, to whom I submitted the MS. of this portion of the dialogue, was good enough to say that it represented very much what he had said, and to add that "the 'ecstasy,' if attained, signifies such a 'standing-out,' ἐκ-στασις, quasi-spasmodic, of a special tract of the brain as, if persisted in, involves the risk of a permanent loss of power, almost in the end a paralysis of the other tracts.—Like other bad habits, it grows by what it feeds on, and may put the fine and complex co-ordinated machinery quite out of gear. The

Myst. It may be; in any case I follow knowledge; if my methods be absurd or pernicious, I am but one of millions in the like strait. Nor do I perceive that any other line of action offers even a remote chance of success.

Scept. The problem is perennial. It must be attacked on scientific lines, and if the pioneers fall,—well, who expects more from a forlorn hope? Time will show.

Myst. We have wandered far from this question of time.

Scept. Even from that of consciousness; itself a digression, though a necessary one.

Myst. An elusive fellow, this consciousness! Is he continuous, you, who declare him permanent?

Scept. Do I, indeed? I gave a possible reason for thinking so; but my adhesion does not follow. The lower consciousnesses, which I called (*a*), are of course rhythmic. The biograph is a sufficient proof of this.

---

ecstatic attains an illumination (so-called) at the expense of sober reason and solid judgment."

Mysticus would not, I think, wish to contest this view, but rather would argue that if this be the case, it is at least a choice between two evils. Sober reason and solid judgment offer no prize more desirable than death after a number of years, less or greater, while ecstasy can, if the facts stated in this dialogue are accepted, give the joys of all these years in a moment.

But for the sake of argument he would say that there are certainly many men who have practised with success from boyhood, and who still enjoy health and a responsible and difficult position in the world of thinking men. This would suggest the idea that there may be men with special aptitude for, and immunity in greater or less degree against the dangers of, the practice. He would cheerfully admit that the common mystic is an insufferable fool, and that his habits possibly assist the degenerative process. But he would submit that in such cases the brain, such as it is, is not worth protecting. At the same time, it is true, the truest type of Hindu mystic regards the ecstasy as an obstacle, since its occurrence stops his meditation; and as a temptation, since he is liable to mistake the obstacle for the goal.—A. C. (See note 53, p. 209.)

Myst. Were one needed. Spencer's generalisation covers this point?

Scept. À priori. That the higher (*c*) are also rhythmic — for we will have no *à priori* here!—is evident, since the (*a*)s are presented by (*b*) no faster than they come. Even if (*a*), being fivefold, comes always so fast as to overlap, no multitude of impacts can compose a continuity.

Myst. But those reasons for permanence were very strong.

Scept. Strong, but overcome. Is it not absurd to represent anything as permanent whose function is rhythmic?

Myst. Not necessarily. It is surely possible for a continuous pat of butter to be struck rhythmically, for example. That it is inert in the intervals is unproved; but if it were, it might still be continuous. That a higher consciousness exists is certain; that it is unknowable is certain, as shown just now, unless, indeed, we can truly unite (*c*) with itself: *i.e.*, without thereby formulating a (*d*).

Scept. But how is that to be done?

Myst. Only, if at all, by cutting off (*c*) from (*a*): *i.e.*, by suspending the mechanism (*b*). Prevent sense-impressions from reaching the sensorium, and there will at least be a better chance of examining the interior. You cannot easily investigate a watch while it is going: nor does the reflection of the sun appear in a lake whose surface is constantly ruffled by wind and rain, by hail and thunderbolt, by the diving of birds and the falling of rocks. To do this, thus shown to be essential to even the beginning of the true settlement of the time problem, and the solution of the paradoxes it affords——

Scept. How to do this is then a question not to be settled offhand by our irresponsible selves, but one of method and research.

Myst. And as such the matter of years.

Scept. I have long recognised this. That it should be started on a firm basis by responsible scientific men; that it should be placed on equal terms in all respects with other research : such is the object of my life.

Myst. But of mine the research itself.

Scept. I applaud you. You are the happy one. I am the martyr. I shall sow, but not reap ; my eyes shall hardly see the first-fruits of my labour ; yet something I shall see. Also, to construct one must clear the ground : to harvest, the plough and harrow are required. First we must rid us of false phrase and lying assumption, of knavery and ignorance, of bigotry and shirking. Let us pull down the church and the Free Library ;[1] with each stone torn thence let us build the humble and practical homes of the true " holy men " of our age, the

[1] The sarcasm is perhaps against the popularity of the worthless novel, as shown in Free Library statistics ; or against the uselessness of any form of reading to a man not otherwise educated.

austere and single-minded labourers in the fields of Physics and Physiology.

Myst. Here, moreover, is the foundation of race harmony ; here the possible basis for a genuine brotherhood of man ! ˙ He will never be permanently solidarised—excuse the neologism !—by grandiose phrase and transitory emotion ; but in the Freemasonry of the Adepts of Dhyana what temple may not yet be builded ?

Scept. Not made with hands — ἐν τοις οὐρανοις αἰωνιος.

Myst. Has not this mystical bond brought you and me together, us diverse, even repugnant in all other ways, yet utterly at one in this great fact ?

Scept. We have talked too lightly, friend. Silence is best.

Myst. Let us meditate upon the adorable light of that divine Savitri !

Scept. May she enlighten our minds !

EPILOGUE

When the chill of earth black-breasted is
uplifted at the glance
Of the red sun million-crested, and the forest
blossoms dance
With the light that stirs and lustres of the
dawn, and with the bloom
Of the wind's cheek as it clusters from the
hidden valley's gloom :
Then I walk in woodland spaces, musing on
the solemn ways
Of the immemorial places shut behind the
starry rays ;
Of the East and all its splendour, of the
West and all its peace ;
And the stubborn lights grow tender, and
the hard sounds hush and cease.
In the wheel of heaven revolving, mysteries
of death and birth,
In the womb of time dissolving, shape anew
a heaven and earth
Ever changing, ever growing, ever dwind-
ling, ever dear,
Ever worth the passion glowing to distil a
doubtful tear.
These are with me, these are of me, these
approve me, these obey,
Choose me, move me, fear me, love me,
master of the night and day.
These are real, these illusion : I am of them,
false or frail,
True or lasting, all is fusion in the spirit's
shadow-veil,
Till the Knowledge-Lotus flowering hides
the world beneath its stem ;

Neither I, nor God life-showering, find a
counterpart in them.
As a spirit in a vision shows a countenance
of fear,
Laughs the looker to derision, only comes
to disappear,
Gods and mortals, mind and matter, in the
glowing bud dissever :
Vein from vein they rend and shatter, and
are nothingness for ever.
In the blessed, the enlightened, perfect eyes
these visions pass,
Pass and cease, poor shadows frightened,
leave no stain upon the glass.
One last stroke, O heart-free master, one
last certain calm of will,
And the maker of Disaster shall be stricken
and grow still.
Burn thou to the core of matter, to the
spirit's utmost flame,
Consciousness and sense to shatter, ruin
sight and form and name !
Shatter, lake-reflected spectre ; lake, rise up
in mist to sun ;
Sun, dissolve in showers of nectar, and the
Master's work is done.
Nectar perfume gently stealing, masterful and
sweet and strong,
Cleanse the world with light of healing in
the ancient House of Wrong !
Free a million million mortals on the wheel
of being tossed !
Open wide the mystic portals, and be
altogether lost !

END OF VOL. II.

Milton Keynes UK
Ingram Content Group UK Ltd.
UKHW021621030823
426219UK00001B/5